In *Freudian Repression*, Michael Billig presents an original reformulation of Freud's concept of repression, showing that in his theory of the unconscious he fails to examine *how* people actually repress shameful thoughts. Drawing on recent insights from discursive psychology, Billig suggests that in learning to speak we also learn what not to say: language is thus both expressive and repressive. He applies this perspective to some of Freud's classic case histories such as 'Dora' and the 'Rat Man' and the great psychologist's own life to show the importance of small words in speech. By focusing on previously overlooked exchanges, even Freud himself can be seen to be repressing. *Freudian Repression* also offers new insights on the current debate about recovered memories and the ideological background to psychoanalysis which will guarantee its interdisciplinary appeal to psychologists, language theorists, discourse analysts, students of psychoanalysis, literary studies and sociologists.

MICHAEL BILLIG is Professor of Social Sciences at Loughborough University. He has published extensively. His most recent book *Banal Nationalism* (1995) was awarded the Myers Centre Award for 'outstanding work on intolerance'.

Freudian Repression

Conversation Creating the Unconscious

Michael Billig

CAMBRIDGE UNIVERSITY PRESS

PUBLISHED BY THE PRESS SYNDICATE OF THE UNIVERSITY OF CAMBRIDGE
The Pitt Building, Trumpington Street, Cambridge, United Kingdom

CAMBRIDGE UNIVERSITY PRESS
The Edinburgh Building, Cambridge CB2 2RU, United Kingdom
http://www.cup.cam.ac.uk
40 West 20th Street, New York, NY 10011–4211, USA   http://www.cup.org
10 Stamford Road, Oakleigh, Melbourne 3166, Australia

First published 1999

Printed in the United Kingdom at the University Press, Cambridge

Typeset in 10/12pt Plantin [CE]

A catalogue record for this book is available from the British Library

Library of Congress cataloguing in publication data

Billig, Michael.
Freudian repression: conversation creating the unconscious/ Michael Billig.
     p.   cm.
Includes bibliographical references and index.
ISBN 0 521 65052 6 (hardback). – ISBN 0 521 65956 6 (paperback)
1. Repression (Psychology)   2. Psychoanalysis.
3. Freud, Sigmund, 1856–1939.   I. Title.
BF175.5R44B55   1999
154.2'4–dc21   99–12788   CIP

ISBN 0 521 65052 6 hardback
ISBN 0 521 65956 6 paperback

Contents

Acknowledgements

When academics gather together these days, you can frequently hear them complaining – about their colleagues, their departments, their 'line managers'. I feel smugly out of things. At Loughborough, in the Department of Social Sciences and in the Discourse and Rhetoric Group, I am privileged to work among talented, generous colleagues. In Peter Golding, I have a head of department who bravely and selflessly ensures that academic values prevail and that we can still enjoy ideas for their own sake.

This book has benefited greatly from discussions with members of the Discourse and Rhetoric Group, who have shown again and again how intellectual disagreement can be enjoyed in a spirit of humour and understanding. For their particular comments, I would like to thank Charles Antaki, Malcolm Ashmore, Derek Edwards, Celia Kitzinger, Katie Macmillan, Dave Middleton, Jonathan Potter and Claudia Puchta. But all the members of the group have contributed to providing an intellectual environment, in which the present manuscript could rebelliously develop.

I am grateful to my other department colleagues, who have also taken time to read chapters or discuss particular points, allowing me to raid their own expertise shamelessly. I am particularly grateful to Mike Gane, Angela McRobbie, Graham Murdock, Mike Pickering and Alan Radley. But, in truth, I should thank all my colleagues for ensuring that the Department is more than two corridors of separate offices. It is a genuine intellectual home.

I am fortunate, also, in there being people outside my department who in various ways have given support and help. In this regard, I would particularly like to thank: Halla Beloff, Becky Billig, Erica Burman, Susan Condor, Ken Gergen, Mary Gergen, Helen Haste, Bruce Mazlish, Ian Parker, Tom Scheff, Teun van Dijk, Ida Waksberg and Margaret Wetherell. As always, I would like to acknowledge the translatlantic friendship and warm support of John Shotter and Herb Simons.

Parts of chapter 5 were published in *Culture and Psychology* and parts of chapter 8 in *Theory, Culture and Society*. I am grateful to the editors of those journals, and to Sage their publisher, for allowing extracts to be used again.

As I look back on the acknowledgements in my previous books, I am aware that someone has always been omitted. There could be few excuses for continuing this omission in a book about Freud. So, as I thank once more Sheila and our children for so much, I must not, this time, forget my mother. Thanks to you all.

1   Introduction

'Freudian repression' – the very phrase is ambiguous. At first glance, it indicates quite simply Freud's theory of repression. Freud believed that people repress, or drive from their conscious minds, shameful thoughts that, then, become unconscious. This was his key idea. As he wrote, repression was the 'centre' to which all the other elements of psycho-analytic thinking were related.[1] More obliquely, the phrase 'Freudian repression' suggests something else: maybe Freud, himself, was engaging in a bit of repression, forgetting things that were inconveniently embarrassing. The ambiguity is deliberate, for both meanings are intended. Freud's idea of repression remains vital for understanding human behaviour. Yet, right at the centre of Freud's central idea is a gap: Freud does not say exactly how repression takes place. It is as if Freudian theory, which promises to reveal what has been hidden, itself has hidden secrets. However, if we want to understand repression, we must try to see what Freud was leaving unsaid.

The present book aims to reformulate the idea of repression in order to fill the central gap. Repression is not a mysterious inner process, regulated by an internal structure such as the 'ego'. It is much more straightforward. Repression depends on the skills of language. To become proficient speakers, we need to repress. The business of everyday conversation provides the skills for repressing, while, at the same time, it demands that we practise those skills. In this respect, language is inherently expressive and repressive.

To sustain the argument, it is necessary to treat repression as a psychological concept. That might seem obvious. After all, Freud was building a psychological theory. In the last few years, there has been an enormous amount written about Freud and his theories. However, practically none of this interest has come from authors with any background in academic psychology. One only has to look at the books published about Freud and note the university departments to which

---

[1] 'An autobiographical study', *PFL* 15, pp. 214–15.

the authors belong. One will find plenty of scholars from departments of literary studies, history, philosophy and even sociology. Of course, psychoanalysts still write about Freud, but they tend not to belong to university departments. Amongst the Freud-writers, there will be hardly a psychologist.

Today, a student in literary studies will have a better chance of learning about Freud than does a student of psychology. This is unfortunate. Psychology students are being denied the opportunity of learning about the greatest writer of their discipline. They are being encouraged to cram their notebooks with the latest studies that mostly will be forgotten by the time it comes to teach the next generation of students. Freud's enduring works will be ignored. Sometimes, students start their courses, expecting to learn about Freud. They will be rapidly disabused. Freud will be dismissed as an infantile pleasure, like thumb-sucking or cuddling soft toys. The mature, properly educated psychologist should grow out of such childishness.[2]

On the other side of the campus, students of English are likely to find Freud on their reading lists. But, in the hands of literary experts, Freud has ceased to be a psychologist. One cannot assess the continuing value of Freud's ideas – especially those relating to repression – without some understanding of their psychological basis. Some recent studies, especially those written by specialists in literary studies, give the impression that knowledge of psychological issues is irrelevant. What matters, it appears, is how to 'read' Freud. It is as if Freud has been reduced to being a text. Sometimes, literary theorists will use psychological terminology taken largely from the French psychoanalyst Lacan (of whom more shortly). The rest of psychology is conspicuous only by its absence. This is no way to judge Freudian ideas. Literary scholars would no doubt be up in arms were someone to evaluate a notable poet, having only read one other poet (of dubious literary talent) and possessing absolutely no familiarity with literary criticism.

In consequence, a dual task needs to be performed. The Freudian idea of repression should be reformulated in a way suitable for today's psychologists. On the other hand, this psychology should not be so off-putting that it drives away Freudian specialists from other disciplines. It must be admitted there are many reasons why literary theorists should find much of current psychology methodologically restrictive and intellectually narrow. Here, the new critical psychologies, developed in opposition to mainstream experimentalism, are crucial. They draw attention to the details of language and to the social nature of talk, in

[2] Parker (1998a and 1998b) has claimed that psychoanalysis is psychology's 'repressed other'.

ways that should interest those from the humanities and the social sciences. And, it will be argued, these new approaches can breath fresh life into Freud.

Enjoying the little words

In the present intellectual climate someone, with a background in psychology, needs to justify writing a book about Freud. Within psychology, it's not the done thing to take psychoanalysis seriously. As Freud taught, and as his own life illustrated, in psychoanalytic matters the theoretical is bound up with the personal. What in other fields would be dismissed as gossip is, as John Forrester has pointed out, legitimate evidence in the field of psychoanalysis.[3] Therefore, the justification can be both personal and intellectual.

I have never been able to grow out of the pleasures of reading Freud. Time and again, especially when I have found myself in-between more 'serious' projects, I regress to those pleasures. I have long drifted away from mainstream experimental psychology. Recently, with colleagues at Loughborough University, I have been concerned to develop a form of 'discursive psychology', which concentrates on the study of language, particularly the analysis of conversation. Discursive psychologists argue that standard psychology looks in the wrong place for an understanding of human conduct. Instead of hypothesizing what goes on in the mind, we should be analysing the details of conversation, paying careful attention to the micro-features of talk. This discursive psychology, like the psychology it has rebelled against, has little place for Freud or notions of the unconscious.

As I finished a book on nationalism, I found myself again with time to turn back to Freud. I took advantage of a remaining privilege of academic life – being paid to read works of outstanding quality. Once again, I found myself entranced by the beauty of Freud's writing and the movement of his intellect. But I am not a 'silent', passive reader: I wanted to argue back.

As I read Freud this time, concentrating on the case studies, with which I was less familiar, I was struck by two things. First, just at the crucial moment, when repression takes place, Freud seems to go silent, or to substitute a bit of jargon for clear description. Second, my background in discursive psychology kept drawing me to seemingly unimportant phrases in Freud's texts. Here was a clue. Discursive psychologists stress that little words are crucial to the smooth running of

---

[3] Forrester (1990).

dialogue. Freud and his followers typically overlooked the little words in conversation's banal routines. So often, the attention is drawn to the unusual or to the 'big' symbolism. Perhaps, it was these little words that held the key to repression. Through their use, speakers can switch the topics of talk almost imperceptibly. Maybe these same little words allow us to change the topics of our internal thoughts, thereby driving away uncomfortable desires.

And so the present book emerged. There was no conscious decision to move from reader to writer. I was intellectually seduced. But it seemed to me that a wealth of new conversational detail would be revealed, if the insights of discursive psychology could be applied to the cases that Freud reported. In the case of Little Hans, we do not just hear a young boy's growing fascination with sexuality. In addition, we hear parents guiding his attention, teaching him morality and projecting their own insecurities. A much richer, more sociological, picture emerges, with repression occurring in the details of everyday life.

In consequence, the message to Freudian scholars is to take seriously the details of talk. However, the good news cannot be simply brought from discursive psychology to Freudian studies. In the course of the journey, the news is changed. A return journey is required to inform the discursive psychologists how their message was altered in the transmission. By and large, conversation analysts take a strict position, that opposes the depth psychology of Freud. The new psychologists do not want to speculate about the inner processes of the mind, and certainly not about unconsciousness. However, if repression is seen to occur through conversation, then the notion of a 'dialogic unconscious' becomes reasonable. The return message to the new psychologists is that they should lighten up theoretically, by 'darkening' their image of human psychology. They should admit that we repress shameful desires and that not all human life is outwardly expressed in conversation. In short, Freudian scholars are asked to read a bit of psychology – and discursive psychologists to accept a revised Freud.

Concentrating on Freud?

The present book, therefore, homes in on the idea of repression. Inevitably, it differs in style and intent from those few books on Freud that have been written by psychologists and that claim to assess Freudian ideas according to the current state of current psychological knowledge. Such books tend to chop Freud's theories into discrete hypotheses, and then collect the relevant experimental evidence. At first sight, such a strategy might seem eminently sensible as a definitive means of sorting the psychologically useful from the disproved. However, the results are inconclusive as the writers disagree among themselves. Some claim that, after the empirical evidence has been gathered, virtually nothing of Freud's theories remains.[4] Other psychologists, assembling much the same evidence, argue that the main elements of Freudian theory have been confirmed.[5] The disagreements are not surprising. The authors of such compendia tend to be partisan. Defenders dismiss negative findings, on the grounds that the subtle processes which Freud described cannot be reproduced artificially in the laboratory. Prosecutors take the opposite line, displaying the negative findings as the ultimate trophies of war.

There is another difficulty with this strategy: it tacitly accepts the conventional experimental ways of doing psychology. Freud's ideas are evaluated in terms of psychological approaches that have historically dismissed his work. At best, several Freudian hypotheses might pass the stringent tests of experimentation. Even if they do, the end results will be disappointing. The 'Freudian findings' are absorbed into a much larger framework, where they will be tolerated because they are vastly outnumbered by other methods and findings. By being isolated and then assimilated into alien territory, the hypotheses lose their indigenous character, which, in Freud's hands, constitutes a wide-ranging view of the human condition.

Still another question remains: why Freud? Surely there have been psychoanalytic developments since Freud – why not discuss Klein or Jung or Lacan or Winnicott or a dozen other well-known psychoanalytic names? A respectable outward justification could be given for concentrating on Freud, but it would be a pretext for, or development of, personal inclinations.

The outward justification is simple. Freud is the dominating presence in the history of psychoanalysis. Subsequent writings are either an argument with him or a self-conscious tidying up of loose ends. To understand neo- or post-Freudians, one must always go back to Freud; he is the background against which the later figures appear either 'neo' or 'post'. Psychoanalytic thought would not stand as a distinct interpretation of the world without Freud, any more than Marxism could exist without Marx or Islam without Mohammed. If the aim is to analyse the

---

[4] See, for instance, Erwin (1996), Eysenck (1986), Grünbaum (1989 and 1993) and Macmillan (1997). Both Erwin and Grünbaum, who count among Freud's most tenacious critics today, are themselves philosophers, although they criticize Freud also in terms of the empirical evidence.

[5] For example, Fisher and Greenberg (1976 and 1996); Kline (1972 and 1981).

'primal' concept of psychoanalysis, then one must search out the primal figure.

Personal reasons must also be admitted. I have gained more intellectual pleasure from reading Freud than from reading any other psychologist. Only William James comes near to matching Freud's style, but, compared with the founder of psychoanalysis, James is theoretically a plodder, not a dasher. Literary theorists should take note of Freud's deceptively simple prose, his eye for the telling metaphor and his choice of quotation. He is a writer who demonstrates how learning can be combined with the pleasure principle. Personally, I have not engaged with later psychoanalytic writers in the same way. For political reasons I cannot allow myself to read Jung with pleasure. Melanie Klein's style of writing affords few joys. And as for Lacan . . .

Literary style is more than mere adornment. It is a way of relating to the reader and, thus, it is a moral, as well as aesthetic, matter. Freud speaks directly to the reader. He clarifies, he teaches, he shares his own excitement. Of course, he uses rhetorical tricks, primarily to prevent the reader from closing the page. The reader invariably controls the situation: how easy it is to put the book down, remove the reading-glasses, doze off, and so on. In one thing, above all, Freud sets an example. He demonstrates that profundity of thought does not require a tangle of jargon. As Peter Gay has pointed out, Freud valued precision in writers, seeing clear writing as a sign that authors were at one with themselves.[6]

This raises the issue of Lacan. It has been said of Lacan that his efforts made 'psychoanalysis the dominant theory in France'.[7] A theory dominant in France soon becomes, or so it seems, dominant in Anglophone social theory. Anyone coming from a background in cultural studies is likely to assume that a book, which self-consciously attempts to link the unconscious with language, would be (or should be) sprinkled with quotes from Lacan and would follow that thinker's peculiar style of writing. This book does neither. It is non-Lacanian – perhaps even anti-Lacanian in its intention. However, I did not want the book to develop into a running battle with Lacan. Only occasionally do I point the finger to say 'this is all very different from what a Lacanian would do'.

This is not the place to detail how the present approach differs from Lacan's.[8] But a few quick words can be offered. In the first place, Lacan's treatment of language is very different. Chapter 4 discusses the importance of examining the details of spoken utterances (and, by implication, written texts). Language is treated as a form of social

[6] Gay (1978), pp. 53–4.
[7] Borch-Jacobsen (1997).   [8] See Billig (1997c) for details.

action: it is not considered as a complete entity with its own internal structure. In this respect, the present position follows the traditions of Bakhtin and Wittgenstein, who unlike Lacan, recommend that we pay close attention to what people actually say.

In my view, Lacan shows a wanton disregard for other psychologies. This has become disastrous when Lacanian ideas have been taken up by cultural or literary theorists who themselves know no other psychology. Just because Lacan refers to a 'mirror-stage', it does not mean that children actually go through such a developmental stage. In fact, the evidence from child psychology suggests that the learning of language occurs in a very different way than Lacan imagined. Lacan ignores such research and his followers make little effort to make good the deficiency. As will be seen, research, which studies the details of children's talk, helps to understand what was going on in the Little Hans case and, more generally, how children learn to repress.

One of Lacan's former pupils has described the Lacanian school as 'one of the last bastions of arrogance'.[9] Lacan's prose style does nothing to dispel the impression of intellectual arrogance. His writings, to put it mildly, are convoluted. If his project was a 'return to Freud', it certainly was not to be achieved by his means of expression. Whereas Freud set himself the moral duty of persuading the reader through clear argument and telling example, Lacan is too haughty to explain what he means. His patients are insufficiently important to be introduced as characters in his books. So page after page, the lowly reader is tacitly bullied. Occasionally, Lacan openly announced that his thoughts were above the understanding of his readers.[10] But difficulty is not to be confused with depth.

So, to return to the personal justification, I have never enjoyed reading Lacan. As a reader, I do not appreciate the ritual humiliation that he inflicts. I do not want my students to believe that it is clever to write in obscure ways – nor to be impressed by incomprehensibility. I do not want them to show contempt for such mundane matters as evidence. They should be reassured that Lévi-Strauss and Merleau-Ponty also found Lacan incomprehensible.[11] By contrast, I want students to read Freud, so that they can enjoy intellectual writing at its finest. Also, I would like them to pick up the habits of clarity – to appreciate its difficulty and its morality.

Beware tales of self-justification, for they are also tales of self-presentation, concealing more than they reveal. In today's academic climate,

---

[9] Bougnoux (1997), p. 93.
[10] Todd Dufresne (1997) had said, Lacan did his best to say very difficult things, p. 3.
[11] Roudinesco (1997), p. 211.

the pleasure principle is not a sufficient motive for action. We have been taught that there has to be a pay-off. Reading must be justified by 'output' – by writing, by publication. So the current book is also a 'pay-off' – the written product that I, like other academics today, habitually accept as the outcome of reading. Pleasure is co-opted in the name of duty, as the pay-off repays debts. But some intellectual debts, and this includes the debt to Freud, are way beyond the reach of the conventional pay-off.

Structure of the argument

The dual nature of the present book is reflected in its attitude towards Freud. To claim that Freud left a gap right at the centre of his theory is to take a critical stance. Orthodox psychoanalysts, who come only to praise the legacy of their founder, might not take kindly to the suggestion that his original theory of repression is insufficient. Even if they concede that the theory must be recast, they may not want to take the further step of acknowledging that Freud was doing a bit of repressing. Hero-worshippers do not always like to see the object of their devotions as possessing all too human qualities. However, if Freud had been a faultless super-hero, it is hard to see how he could have managed such profound insights into human frailty. He would have been unable to draw upon the benefits of self-insight.

The specific criticisms, however, are contained within a much wider appreciation. The idea of repression is so important that it cannot be left to decay, for want of an inner core. Here, the Freud-bashers will not be best pleased. Those scholars, who come to Freud only in the hope of a burial, will not want to stay to praise the central idea of psychoanalysis's great founding figure. Certainly, they will not want to see Freudian repression being reformulated so that it might offer new theoretical possibilities and, thereby, keep alive the intellectual legacy of its originator.

This duality – critically analysing Freud and his case studies, as his key concept is reformulated – is developed in the subsequent chapters. Chapter 2 sets up the basic problem: namely that repression is the central concept of psychoanalysis and that Freud failed to say how we go about the business of repressing. The remedy is not to develop Freud's metapsychological theory of the mind, with its descriptions of 'id', 'ego' and 'superego'. It is to return to a plainer language, which concentrates on the actions of people. Chapter 3 suggests how language might be used to repress thoughts. Language is not an abstract system of grammar or a dictionary of defined words. Language is something that is used in the practice of dialogue. In conversation speakers regularly push aside, or repress, topics from their talk. These skills can be applied to our own internal dialogues. They can be heard in the thoughts of Freud's patient, the so-called 'Rat Man'.

In chapter 4 the point is widened to suggest that, in order to become mature conversationalists, we must repress disturbing desires. In particular, conversation depends on the smooth, routine practice of politeness. The desire to be rude must be habitually repressed. Thus, the very practice of talk provides the model for repression. Freud's own routines of life, both at home and in the consulting-room, represent vivid examples of this.

All the while, the theoretical issues are illustrated by examples from Freud's case histories and also from incidents in Freud's own life. Regarding the case histories, often the aspects, to which Freud seemed to have attached little importance, are highlighted. Chapter 5 considers the case of Little Hans. If repression is contained in the practice of talk, then children will learn to repress as they learn to talk. They will learn their lessons from older speakers, most notably parents. The conversations reported by Little Hans's father illustrate this dramatically. The analysis turns the psychological tables. Instead of the child being the source of primal Oedipal desires, we find Oedipal parents, through their talk, projecting their own desires onto the child.

Chapter 6 develops these points, by exploring the relations between repressing, remembering and forgetting. Some ideas about memory and forgetfulness need to be reversed. It is argued that children cannot remember explicitly until they have language. Moreover, forgetting is part of remembering, so that the child cannot properly forget, nor repress, until it has acquired the linguistic skills to remember. Inevitably, this discussion of repression in childhood involves considering the current debates about child sexual abuse. Freud himself switched from believing that neuroses were caused by the 'seduction' (or abuse) of infants to formulating his Oedipal theory, which claimed that infants desired to have sexual relations with their parents. Here, Freud will be found wanting: he looked too early in the life of the child for signs of repression.

Chapter 7 discusses the seemingly difficult issue of repressing an emotion. How was it possible for some of Freud's patients, such as Elisabeth von R., to be unaware of shameful feelings of love? The answer, it will be suggested, lies in recognizing that ordinary conscious emotions, such as those of love, are not pure inner states. If we understand the discursive aspects of conscious emotions, then unconscious ones cease to look so strange. There are interesting parallels between

Freud's patients and his own private life. All, including Freud himself, were responding to the demands of the times. As such emotions are not so much internal, individual states of feelings, but they are bound up in social, cultural and ideological relations.

Chapter 8 develops this theme, by looking in detail at the case of Dora. Here the psychoanalytic account, as well as the conversation between Freud and Dora, are seen to be hiding something. The Jewish dimension, so central to Freud's own conditions of life, is pushed aside. Freud and Dora found it easier to talk of the supposedly taboo topics of sex, than they did of their own precarious circumstances as Jews in anti-semitic Vienna. Surprisingly, the discursive repressions of Freud and Dora are being repeated to this day, even by ostensibly radical writers. Again, this goes to show the repressive aspects of language. Even analyses, which claim to reveal, may themselves be repressing.

In general, the present approach can be said to look at repression as something that is socially, rather than biologically, constituted. One might say it is ideologically constituted, for ideologies concern what people in a particular historical epoch do not talk of. The notion of repression points out that there are topics, of which we could speak, but which, nevertheless, we tend to avoid collectively. The final chapter will discuss some of the ideological implications of seeing language as inherently repressive.

Freud's texts

Lastly, I should comment on the edition of Freud, from which most of the references are taken. It is the convention for Freud scholars, when writing in English, to quote from the Standard Edition of the Complete Psychological Works of Sigmund Freud – conventionally known by the abbreviation 'SE'. But I have used, for the most part, the Penguin Freud Library (PFL), although, because of its incompleteness, I have also had to refer to the SE. The days are well gone when an academic, with a family to support, could afford to buy a complete set of the Standard Edition. Even university libraries cannot guarantee to have all twenty-four volumes, let alone reserve a complete set for the benefit of an individual academic.

Penguin, nevertheless, has put most of Freud's major writings within the range of academic pockets. I am grateful to be able to possess my paperback copies, and to be able to consult them at will. I cannot be bothered with the charade of re-checking all quotations to find the page references in the Standard Edition, so that I can present myself as the sort of serious academic who uses nothing but the SE. Why should I pretend?

Again, personal preference, or convenience, can be dressed up with a wider moral justification. I would like to encourage readers back to Freud. Perhaps those readers from literary studies might be tempted to read Freud's psychological writings with a psychological eye. Psychologists might realize that an attachment to Freud is not an infantile pleasure. Maybe they, too, might return to the works of the greatest writer of their subject. To possess the ideas, sometimes you have to possess the books – to have them ready to hand. Owning the cheap, mass circulation edition is not second best. It respects an author, who wished to communicate his ideas to as wide an audience as possible and, in so doing, produced the most luminous prose ever written under the heading of 'psychology'.

2   The importance of repression

Freud, as is well known, produced a multi-layered view of the human mind. He called psychoanalysis a 'depth psychology' because it examined 'those processes in mental life which are withdrawn from consciousness'.[1] Behind the thoughts and wishes, of which we are aware, lurks a shadowed hinterland of secret desire. It is this sense of depth that distinguishes psychoanalytic views from most other psychologies. Behaviourism posits no hidden secrets, merely chains of association and responses to outward stimuli, thereby according the human psyche all the depth of a pigeon. Cognitive psychologists envisage the human mind as an extraordinary machine, processing, storing and combining information. The average human mind is seen to be many mega-bytes more powerful than the most sophisticated computer. At worst in this model, the human information-processor is to be criticized for taking lazy short-cuts in its computation of information.[2] At best, there is a self-admiration, because the wonders of Microsoft still paddle way behind the software of our human brains. Complexity, however, is very different from depth. The computer has no sense of shame, only multiple programs and parallel processes.

The element of depth in the Freudian vision comes from the notion that we have secrets, which we keep from ourselves.[3] Freud put the matter simply in 'The Question of Lay Analysis', a short work intended for a wide audience. Freud was at pains to make the idea of unconscious ideas seem reasonable. He claimed that 'everyone is aware that there are some things in himself that he would be very unwilling to tell other

---

[1] 'Two encyclopaedia articles', *PFL* 15, p. 150.

[2] For a discussion of the way that cognitive social psychology assumes the person to be a lazy information-processor, see Fiske and Taylor (1984). For criticisms of this bureaucratic model of the mind, see Billig (1985 and 1991).

[3] Fingarette (1983) has argued that at root psychoanalysis is a theory of self-deception. He writes that Freudian theory constitutes 'the most elaborately worked out, most extensively applied contemporary doctrine touching (on) self-deception' (p. 213).

people'.[4] Similarly, everyone has thoughts 'that one likes to keep from oneself'.[5] We deceive ourselves, believing that we are righteous and without blemish, in just the same way as we might deceive others. If we accept this possibility, Freud went on, then 'a very remarkable psychological problem begins to appear in this situation – of a thought of his own being kept secret from his own self'.[6]

The idea of self-deceit, or willed forgetting, forms the basis for the Freudian concept of repression. If we have secrets from ourselves, then not only must we forget the secrets, but we must also forget that we have forgotten them. To use Freudian terminology, the secrets must be repressed: and the fact that we are repressing them must also be repressed. Just how such self-deceit or repression occurs is not easy to say. One might think that one of the major tasks of Freudian theory would be to detail the workings of repression. But, as will be seen, that is not so.

This chapter will examine the central importance of repression in Freud's depth psychology. It will also show that Freud leaves a rather surprising gap in his account, as he glosses over how people might repress or keep secrets from themselves. Freud strongly believed that theoretical concepts are only of value if they illuminate the particularities of human behaviour.[7] His theories, therefore, should be checked against the details of the case histories. The arguments in this chapter will be illustrated by the case of Elisabeth von R., who came to see Freud as a patient in 1892. This case is particularly fitting as an illustration of repression, which, to adopt familiar Freudian phraseology, could be called the 'primal concept' of psychoanalysis. The case of Elisabeth appears, along with four other cases, in Freud's first major work *Studies on Hysteria*, which was written with his early mentor Josef Breuer and which was first published in 1895. One distinguished Freudian scholar has called *Studies* the 'primal book' of psychoanalysis, for it contains many of the basic elements of Freudian theory.[8] Moreover, the case of Elisabeth has a special place in Freud's

---

[4] 'The question of lay analysis', *PFL* 15, p. 288, emphasis in original. Here and elsewhere in his writing, Freud followed the customs of his times by using masculine pronouns to stand for all humanity. In quoting from Freud, no adjustments will be made to the masculine biases of his grammar. Many authors today, when quoting other sources, insert, after each instance of grammatical sexism, the eyebrow raising 'sic!' It will be assumed here that readers are capable of detecting the solecisms and raising their own eyebrows.

[5] Ibid.   [6] Ibid.

[7] See, for instance, the opening comments of 'Instincts and their vicissitudes', *PFL* 11, pp. 113f.

[8] Grubrich-Simitis (1997).

intellectual history. As he wrote in *Studies*, it was his 'first full-length analysis of a hysteria'.[9]

This 'primal' case well illustrates Freud's views on repression, but it also reveals something more. The report, so full of detail and keen observation, shows how Freud avoided specifying exactly what his patient was doing in order to repress the hidden thoughts that supposedly lay at the root of her neurosis. As such, this primal case provides a good start for tracing the primal concept and the primal gap in psychoanalytic theorizing.

The big discovery

In the popular imagination, Freud is often hailed as the discoverer of the unconscious, as if he were a psychological equivalent of an Amundsen or a Livingstone. Instead of planting his flag of discovery on polar ices, or by the banks of the Limpopo, Freud was the first to discover the hitherto uncharted regions of the unconscious mind. Psychoanalysts have encouraged this picture of Freud. The distinguished British psychoanalyst, Edward Glover, wrote in *The Times* many years ago that 'Freud's discovery of the unconscious was in every sense momentous'.[10] The title of Glover's article conveyed the image of the geographical explorer: 'Journey in the Unconscious'. Similarly, the authors of the classic exposition of psychoanalytic terminology, published by the Institute of Psycho-Analysis, assert that 'if Freud's discovery had to be summed up in a single word, that word would without doubt have to be "unconscious"'.[11] Freud's critics also claim that, if the founder of psychoanalysis has any claim to originality, it must rest on his discovery of the unconscious. The critics, then, downplay the 'discovery', by saying that others had got there first, and, anyway, the unconscious is so wrong-headed an idea that it hardly amounts to much of a discovery.[12]

The surprise is that Freud did not present himself as the discoverer of the unconscious. This was no false modesty, for he did not disavow being a discoverer: it was just that the unconscious was not his real discovery. In 1924, when he was sixty-eight, Freud was asked to contribute an autobiographical essay to an edited book about the lives of eminent physicians. Freud described his own role in the founding of

[9] 'Studies on hysteria', *PFL* 3, p. 206. The case of Elisabeth has not attracted the attention given to the first case study reported in 'Studies' – namely that of Anna O. On Anna O, see, for instance, Borch-Jacobsen (1996); Forrester (1990), chapter 1; Rosenbaum and Muroff (1984); Ellenberger (1972).

[10] Glover (1956).

[11] Laplanche and Pontalis (1983), p. 474.

[12] See, for example, Ellenberger (1970) and Borch-Jacobsen (1995).

psychoanalysis, as well as the major discovery of this new 'science'. He declared that psychoanalysis had uncovered the process by which impulses are debarred 'from access to consciousness'. Freud wrote: 'I named this process *repression*; it was a novelty, and nothing like it had ever before been recognized in mental life.' This discovery, he continued, lay at the heart of psychoanalytic ideas and 'the theory of repression became the corner-stone of our understanding of the neuroses'.[13] This was not an aberrant claim. Ten years earlier, Freud, writing a history of the psychoanalytic movement, claimed that 'the theory of repression is the corner-stone on which the whole structure of psychoanalysis rests'.[14]

But why should Freud have claimed that repression, rather than the unconscious, was his big discovery, upon which his claim to enduring fame deserved to rest? It is not a verbal quibble whether the one or other is hailed as psychoanalysis's central discovery. What is at stake is the core, irreducible element of psychoanalytic theory – or, to use Freud's phrase, the corner-stone on which the whole theoretical structure rests.

The German word, which Freud generally, but not invariably, used to describe repression was *Verdrängung*, which literally means 'pushing away' or 'thrust aside'. A repressed idea is one that has been pushed aside, or driven from conscious awareness. Freud had good theoretical reasons for giving pride of place to psychoanalysis's claim to have unearthed this driving away. He knew that it was insufficient to say that a thought was being kept secret just because it was unconscious. Something other than merely being unconscious was necessary to turn thoughts into shameful secrets.

According to Freud, there were two sorts of unconscious thought, only one of which could psychoanalysis possibly have claimed to have discovered. First, there were ordinarily unconscious thoughts, which from Freud's point of view were not particularly interesting. These are thoughts which happen not to be occupying one's attention at any given moment. The philosopher, John Searle discusses this type of thought in his book *The Rediscovery of the Human Mind*. He gives the example of his belief that the Eiffel Tower is in France. While he is thinking of other matters, this belief is 'nonconscious' or 'unconscious'. When his attention turns to Eiffel-related matters, then the belief becomes relevant and conscious.[15] Since we can only think of one thing at a time, and since we have thousands of other thoughts, then the greater part of our mental life must be unconscious. Freud expressed this idea when he wrote that

[13] 'An autobiographical study', *PFL* 15, p. 213.
[14] 'On the history of the psychoanalytic movement', *PFL* 15, p. 73.
[15] Searle (1992), pp. 154–5.

'at any given moment' we are only aware of just a fraction of our thoughts, 'so that the greater part of what we call conscious knowledge must be for very considerable periods of time in a state of latency, that is to say, of being psychically unconscious'.[16] This was so obvious, according to Freud, that it was 'totally incomprehensible how the existence of the unconscious can be denied'.[17]

In writing thus, Freud was employing an argument which he often used in order to make his supposedly shocking psychology seem entirely reasonable. However, the rhetorical move comes with a theoretical cost. We might have many unconscious thoughts, which are uncontroversial and undeniable, but these are not the thoughts, which the depth psychology studies. There must, therefore, be two sorts of unconscious thoughts – 'ordinary' unconscious thoughts, like Searle's belief that the Eiffel Tower is in France, and 'hidden' thoughts that we keep secret from ourselves.

The difference between these two sorts of unconscious thoughts lies in the ease with which they can become conscious. When the topic turns to the Eiffel Tower, the 'unconscious', or latent, beliefs about the topic, smoothly pass into conscious awareness. Freud called beliefs, which are easily 'capable of becoming conscious', 'preconscious' beliefs.[18] By contrast, Freud's interest lay in those unconscious beliefs which, he claimed, 'cannot become conscious' because 'a certain force opposes them'.[19] These beliefs are so shocking or painful that something stops them from making the journey, which the preconscious beliefs find so simple. Instead of slipping into the field of awareness, they are turned aside – they are repressed. Thus, the secret beliefs, unlike the 'ordinary' preconscious ones, *cannot* become conscious, for they are constantly being driven away.[20] It is these types of unconscious beliefs which form the subject matter of psychoanalysis, and which Freud sometimes, for sake of convenience, called the 'properly' unconscious beliefs.

The theoretical implications of this distinction are immense. The secret beliefs are to be distinguished from the ordinary preconscious ones because they have been repressed, not because they are unconscious. Thus, the quality of being repressed, rather than that of being unconscious, characterizes the beliefs that psychoanalysis aims to uncover. As Freud wrote in 'The ego and the id', 'we obtain our concept of the unconscious . . . from the theory of repression'.[21] There is a

---

[16] 'The unconscious', *PFL* 11, p. 168.   [17] Ibid.
[18] 'The ego and the id', *PFL* 11, p. 352.   [19] Ibid.
[20] At least, they cannot become conscious unless they are 'subject to considerable expenditure of effort', ('New introductory lectures', *PFL* 2, p. 103).
[21] *PFL* 11, p. 353.

further implication. The Freudian unconscious is not to be considered as a pre-existing 'thing' which we are born with and which holds our ordinary conscious selves in some sort of permanent thrall. We have to create our unconscious. Unless we do something – unless we repress or push aside thoughts – we won't have an unconscious. In this respect, the unconscious has to be created by an activity. The big claim of psychoanalysis was to have discovered this previously overlooked activity, which creates the unconscious realm of hidden secrets.

The secrets of Elisabeth von R

'Studies on hysteria' is the first book in which Freud used the concept of repression (*Verdrängung*). When working with Breuer on the book, Freud had not yet formulated many of the ideas which were to characterize psychoanalytic thinking. In fact, he was not yet using the term 'psychoanalysis'; he and Breuer still called their method of treatment 'catharsis'. At that time, also, Freud had no theory of infant sexuality, no Oedipus Complex, no superego or id, nor even a worked out theory of instincts. All that was to come later. A second edition of 'Studies' was published in 1908, by which time many of the elements of Freud's mature thinking were in place. In his preface to the second edition, Freud distanced himself from the early work. But he did not disown it. He had no wish to eliminate 'evidence of my initial views'. He wanted readers to realize that 'the developments and changes in my views during the course of thirteen years of work have been . . . far-reaching'. Nevertheless, 'Studies' contained 'the germs of all that has since been added to the theory of catharsis'. He could give no better advice to anyone who was interested in the development of psychoanalysis than 'to begin with 'Studies on hysteria' and thus follow the path which I myself have trodden'.[22]

As Freud noted, the germs of psychoanalysis are all there in 'Studies', especially in the sections written by Freud. Not only is there the concept of repression, but also the idea that repression plays a decisive role in the origins of neurosis. 'Studies', in both its clinical and theoretical sections, claimed that hysteria had hidden psychological causes. The outward symptoms could be traced to secret thoughts or experiences, of which the patient was not consciously aware. These thoughts or experiences, having been denied access to consciousness, had been converted into neurotic symptoms. If the doctor were to restore the patient to health, drugs would be inefficacious. Instead, the doctor needed to discover the

[22] Breuer and Freud, 'Studies on hysteria', *PFL* 3, pp. 49–50.

hidden, repressed thoughts, and bring them to the conscious awareness of the patient. Only then would the symptoms desist. To achieve this happy outcome, the patient would have to collaborate in the task of recovering the lost thoughts. Patients must talk at length, emptying the contents of their thoughts, while the doctor would have to listen attentively for the subtle clues which would indicate where the crucial hidden element was to be found. Talk, therefore, was to be the medium for the cure.

There was a crucial difference between the theories expressed in 'Studies' and those of mature psychoanalysis. This concerns the nature of what is to be repressed, rather than the act of repression itself. In this early work, Freud and Breuer believed that traumatic events caused neurosis. In the opening section of the book, they claimed that 'external events determine the pathology of hysteria to an extent far greater than is known and recognized'.[23] A painful event occurs, which the patient cannot deal with. Freud and Breuer wrote that 'a normal person' might be able to work through the memory of a traumatic event, bringing about 'the disappearance of the accompanying affect'.[24] However, other people can find the events so traumatic, and the memories of such events too painful to recall, that they cannot come to terms with the past. Then, the memories may disappear from conscious awareness. In a passage, which marks Freud's first published use of the word 'repression', he and Breuer claimed that, in such instances, 'it was a question of things which the patient wished to forget, and therefore intentionally repressed from his conscious thought and inhibited and suppressed'.[25]

Freud, at the time of 'Studies'' publication, but after he had treated the patients described in that work, was being drawn to his controversial theory of infant, sexual abuse. In 1896, in the year following the appearance of 'Studies', he was to deliver his lecture, 'The Aetiology of Hysteria', in which he outlined the theory that all hysteria was caused by a repressed experience of sexual assault occurring in infancy.[26] This was very different from the later theorizing, which denied that the roots of neurosis lay in what Freud and Breuer had called 'external events'. According to the mature Freud, the roots were to be found in fantasies and repressed wishes, especially children's erotic fantasies about their parents.

The case of Elisabeth points the way to this future direction of psychoanalytic theorizing, for, as will be seen, Freud diagnosed her repressed thoughts to be erotic fantasies, rather than memories of

---

[23] Ibid., p. 54.   [24] Ibid., p. 59.   [25] Ibid., p. 61.
[26] The paper, its relations to Freud's later work and its present status in Freudian controversies are discussed below in chapter 6.

traumatic events. Elisabeth had come to Freud, complaining of a number of ailments, most principally pains in the leg, which often prevented her from walking. She had consulted other doctors, who had been unable to find any physical cause for her symptoms. Freud suspected a case of hysteria, but, initially, he treated her legs 'with high tension electric currents', but without, as he reported, expecting to effect a cure by such a method.[27] If the cause of her symptoms was psychical, then a psychological cure was required.

In another respect, the case of Elisabeth was an indicator of things to come. Breuer had used hypnosis to extract hidden memories from his patients and Freud initially had followed his example. However, Elisabeth was one of several patients who had resisted Freud's attempts at hypnosis. It seems that she took pleasure in demonstrating that the young doctor was unable to put her to sleep. The doctor had to devise other conversational ways to guide the patient to the painful areas of the past. In this way, commented Freud, 'I arrived at a procedure which I later developed into a regular method and employed deliberately.'[28] At this time, Freud had not yet developed the practice of seating patients on a couch.[29] He was, however, moving towards the technique of free association. He would put his hands on Elisabeth's forehead and ask her to remember everything she could, letting her thoughts wander.

So Elisabeth spoke to Freud about her background, her past life and her present hopes. She was, as Freud reported, an intelligent and independently minded young woman.[30] She was 'greatly discontented with being a girl' and was 'full of ambitious plans'.[31] Elisabeth had hoped to avoid the conventional fate of a young, fairly well-to-do woman – marriage to a young man with suitable prospects and good family background. Nevertheless, she was also impelled by a strong sense of family duty. She put aside her own hopes for a career, as the family underwent 'many misfortunes and not much happiness'.[32]

Elisabeth's father had died following a long illness. Elisabeth had dutifully born the brunt of the sick-nursing. Her leg pains had begun during this period. Her mother then required a serious eye-operation. Elisabeth's views on marriage were confirmed by the experiences of her oldest sister, whose husband appears to have been a most unpleasant man. This husband was the source of much family friction, especially

---

[27] Ibid., p. 205.
[28] 'Studies on hysteria', p. 206.
[29] Roazen (1992) suggests that Freud developed the use of the famous psychoanalytic couch because he felt uncomfortable being watched by his patients (p. 123).
[30] Appignanesi and Forrester (1993, pp. 108f) give details of the patient's actual name and family background.
[31] 'Studies on hysteria', p. 207.   [32] Ibid., p. 202.

relating to money matters. However, her second oldest sister had married happily and Elisabeth believed this sister's husband to be the ideal spouse. The young couple had one child, but Elisabeth's sister, who did not enjoy good health, became pregnant again. Her heart was unable to take the strain of a second pregnancy. News reached Elisabeth that her sister was ailing. Although rushing immediately from Vienna to her sister's home in a summer resort, she arrived too late. The young woman had already died. Afterwards, Elisabeth's symptoms worsened.

As Freud asked Elisabeth about her thoughts, so he would frequently find that she had difficulty in replying. He would ask what was in her mind, and she would reply that nothing was. She would say this following a long period of silence 'during which her tense and preoccupied expression of face nevertheless betrayed the fact that a mental process was taking place in her'.[33] So Freud came to suspect that the denials and the silences indicated hidden thoughts: perhaps she found them 'too disagreeable to tell' or perhaps 'she tried to suppress once more what had been conjured up'.[34] Whatever the reason, the denials were not to be taken at face value; they offered clues to the secret causes of the problem. In this suspicion, Freud was moving towards the psychoanalytic concept of 'resistance', whose importance will be discussed later.[35]

The secrets, which were being simultaneously hidden and denied by Elisabeth's silences, were, according to Freud's interpretations, erotic desires. Initially, when sacrificing herself to nurse her father, Elisabeth was having to put aside her own desires. Freud suggested that 'her duties to her sick father came into conflict with the content of her erotic desires which she was feeling at the time'. And so she 'repressed her erotic idea from consciousness and transformed the amount of its affect into physical sensations of pain'.[36] But this was just the beginning. The real crises were to come later and were focused around Elisabeth's repressed feelings for the ideal husband of her second oldest sister.

Freud suggested that Elisabeth had been in love with the young man, but this forbidden, shameful love was repressed from conscious awareness. Her pains became ways of keeping the feelings secret from herself. She enjoyed going for walks with the young man. Yet, she complained of pains when she walked. The pains even prevented her from walking. Freud asked Elisabeth what might have brought on the pain. She gave 'the somewhat obscure reply that the contrast between her own loneliness and her sick sister's married happiness . . . had been painful to her'.[37]

---

[33] Ibid., p. 223.   [34] Ibid.   [35] See below chapter 7.
[36] 'Studies on hysteria', p. 235.   [37] Ibid., p. 220.

Freud suspected that this was by no means the full story. The pain was an expression of repressed desire. He pushed Elisabeth to talk of issues, which clearly she did not wish to explore. Above all, he wanted her to talk about the day of her sister's death. How had Elisabeth felt 'at that moment of dreadful certainty', when she knew that her sister was dead? Freud wanted to know about her guilt at being unable to nurse the sister as she had nursed her father. And a further source of guilt was revealed. At the very moment of seeing her sister lying on her death-bed, a thought had passed through Elisabeth's mind. It forced itself 'irresistibly upon her once more like a flash of lightning in the dark: "Now he is free again and I can be his wife" '.[38]

This was the conclusive proof for which Freud was searching. In the moment of extreme emotional tension, as Elisabeth was looking at the body of her sister, the repressed desire – the love of her brother-in-law – had forced its way into consciousness, from which it needed to be repressed. And so she had pushed aside the thought. The memory had remained forgotten until Freud's incessant promptings had overcome her resistance. And, then, Elisabeth still denied that she loved her brother-in-law. She accused Freud of trying to force her to make the admission. Her pains returned. She wept.

The tears and recriminations in the consulting-room were a prelude to a happy ending. And how Freud loved happy endings to his case-histories. The hidden thought is revealed as the cause of the symptoms. And once the culprit is exposed, so the misdeeds can be undone. The symptoms eventually abate, as the repression is unravelled. The young woman can return to a normal life.

Freud adds a marvellous postscript. He hears in the spring of 1894 that Elisabeth has been invited to a ball. He manages to obtain a ticket. And, there, the doctor watches the patient, who could hardly walk eighteen months earlier, 'whirl past in a lively dance'. We can picture her, smiling at the young man, with whom she is dancing, hardly giving the middle-aged doctor a second glance. And he smiles to himself, paternally. Even better still, reports Freud, she has 'by her own inclination' married someone 'unbeknown to me'.[39] A happy ending indeed.

Repression's inevitability and forms

The case of Elisabeth presents a number of important aspects which illustrate the Freudian theory of repression, relating to the basic nature of repression. First, there is an issue which must be cleared up,

---

[38] Ibid., p. 226.   [39] Ibid., p. 230.

otherwise it might lead to misunderstandings later. It is easy to imagine that Freud considered repression to be an enemy force. After all, the goal of psychoanalysis was to undo the painful consequences of repression. Elisabeth was to be cured by exposing the repression, by which the shameful thoughts had been repressed. Yet, the unpicking of a particular form of repression is not to be equated with the total undoing of repression. Freud, in general, was not anti-repression. His own routines were built upon a rigid self-discipline.[40] He strongly believed in the necessity of repressing instincts and impulses in order to maintain an ordered, civilized and moral life.[41]

Freud, despite what some critics during his life-time claimed, was not advocating a life of instinctual pleasure, in which the repressed desires of the id would be released from repression. Elisabeth might have unconsciously loved her brother-in-law during her sister's lifetime. Freud would not have advocated that she should have pursued this love, wrecking the structure of the family. She would have had to come to terms with the love, recognizing its existence and then pushing it from her mind. In the famous phrase, which he used to describe the aims of therapy in the 'New introductory lectures', written in the final years of his life, Freud declared 'Where id was, there ego shall be'[42] The ego, which, as will be discussed, was the mechanism of repression, should hold sway. The demons, through self-knowledge, would be rationally controlled and, perhaps, repressed again.

Elisabeth might whirl past in the delights of the dance. But life, for Freud, could not be an extended dance. Pleasure, accordingly, must be allied to duty. Significantly, Freud's comment about the dancing whirl is followed immediately by his announcement of her marriage – the truly happy ending to his tale. Of course, Freud recognized that in marriage the erotic desires could be (and should be) satisfied. Yet, for Freud, very much a man of his time and class, marriage was much more (or less) than erotic satisfaction. As his own love letters to his fiancée Martha indicate, marriage was to be founded on duty, service and quiet contentment.[43] Elisabeth may have been whirling past on her way to marriage. Nevertheless, marriage, the end-point of Freud's story of Elisabeth, and, indeed of his understanding of a woman's life, was not to be a whirl. It was service to the husband, who himself should have even higher duties.

[40] For more details, see below chapter 4.
[41] His defence of repression as a social philosophy is to be found most strongly in 'Civilization and its discontents'.
[42] 'New introductory lectures', *PFL* 2, p. 112.
[43] See below, chapter 7.

The point is a wider one than Freud's somewhat dubious views on love, marriage and women. The psychoanalytic attitude towards repression is double-edged. On the one hand, particular forms of repression are to be exposed, especially in the consulting-room. On the other hand, repression is not to be abolished, but to be set in place. Hence, the ageing Freud made an apparently shocking remark about the outcome of treatment in one of his last works, 'An outline of psychoanalysis'. He declared that the aim of treatment was to strengthen the ego in its battle with the id. However, the outcome was, he wrote, 'a matter of indifference'.[44]

It might seem odd that Freud, who spent so much of his life devoted to the curing of patients' ills, should finally declare himself to be indifferent to the outcome of treatment. However, the phrase was not a betrayal of all those hours of therapy. What Freud meant by the remark was that it did not matter whether the self-knowledge, which psychoanalysis should bring, 'results in the ego accepting, after a fresh examination, an instinctual demand which it has hitherto rejected, or whether it dismisses it once more, this time for good and all'.[45] One might translate these late remarks back to the early case of Elisabeth. Having discovered that she loved her brother-in-law, it did not matter whether she accepted this knowledge, coming to terms with her erotic feelings; or whether 'for good and all', she dismissed the knowledge from her mind. In the latter case, she would push aside the troubling thoughts, repressing them finally. Thus, the outcome would not be an unrepressed psyche, but further repression, this time reasonably and effectively established. Either way, Freud would be recommending that Elisabeth should get on with her life, freeing herself from the demands of a doomed attraction.

Regarding the formal nature of repression, the case of Elisabeth illustrates something of theoretical importance, especially in relation to later intellectual disputes between psychoanalysts. Psychoanalytic theorists have distinguished between two forms of repression. One aims to push away a shameful thought which pops into the mind. The other seeks to prevent the thought from becoming conscious in the first place.

Elisabeth was repressing in the first sense, when she experienced the thought about her brother-in-law at her sister's death-bed. She briefly, but consciously, entertains the idea that he might now be free to marry her. Then the thought has to be repressed in a piece of deliberate, or

---

[44] 'An outline of psychoanalysis', *PFL* 15, p. 413.
[45] Ibid.

motivated, forgetting.[46] She deliberately wants to push away the thought which flashed into her mind. She must not only forget the idea, but she must forget that she has deliberately forgotten it.

However, there is more to Elisabeth's repression than the pushing aside of a troublesome thought. In a sense, this pushing aside was merely a piece of repair work to compensate for the momentary failure of a long-term repression. Freud claims that Elisabeth had been in love with her brother-in-law for a while without realizing her feelings. It was only in the extreme emotion of seeing her sister lying dead that the repressed feeling gained access to her conscious mind. Previously, this love had been so secret that even she was unaware of it. The pushing aside, or repression, of these feelings must have been taking place routinely and, most importantly, unconsciously. Elisabeth could not have been aware that she was driving away an idea, of which she seems to have had no conscious knowledge. Or, as Freud put it, with regard to her feelings of love 'she was in the peculiar situation of knowing and at the same time not knowing'.[47] She knew unconsciously, but not consciously – and, as Freud recognized, this is a peculiar state to understand.

Before going any further, it should be noted that there is a terminological controversy regarding these two forms of repression. Theorists, both supporting and criticizing psychoanalytic theory, have engaged in lengthy debates about how the word 'repression' should be properly used. Much hinges on the idea whether the term 'repression' should be confined to the form of repression, which supposedly occurs unconsciously. According to some theorists, the driving away of a conscious thought should be called 'suppression' rather than 'repression'. In their view, Elisabeth would have 'suppressed' her shameful thought on the death of her sister, rather than 'repressed' it. Similarly, the patient, who pushes away a troubling desire for 'good and all', is not repressing the desire, but 'suppressing' it.

Freud's daughter, Anna, in her influential book *The Ego and the Mechanisms of Defence*, made the case for distinguishing between repression and suppression. She argued against classifying conscious repression as a form of repression, claiming that in proper repression, the ego, as a rule, 'knows nothing of the rejection of the impulse or of the whole conflict which has resulted'.[48] When Elisabeth was disgusted with herself for entertaining the idea about her brother-in-law being free, and

---

[46] See Erdelyi (1990) and also Bower (1990) for arguments on why it is useful to consider the Freudian concept of repression as a form of 'willed forgetting'.

[47] 'Studies on hysteria', p. 236.

[48] A. Freud (1968), p. 9.

when she managed to forget the distressing episode, she was suppressing. However, when she was unaware of feelings of love, then she, or rather her ego, was engaged in the activity of repressing.[49]

Some of psychoanalysis's persistent critics also follow this line, insisting that 'real' repression must be completely unconscious. The critics' motive could not be more different from Anna Freud's. The critics, like Anna Freud, will also cite the authority of Freud senior to substantiate their view that correct repression is always unconscious.[50] The critics, despite posing as the guardians of the 'true' Freudian concept of repression, uphold their definition as part of an argument to demolish the credibility of psychoanalytic theory, not to build upon the work of its founder. Their aim is to show that repression does not occur. They admit that people can drive away thoughts – to deny that would be silly. However, they claim that 'real' repression is something different, for repression, if it is to deserve the name, must be totally unconscious. Having insisted on this, the critics move to demonstrate the implausibility of unconscious repression. By so doing, they hope to dismiss the very basis of psychoanalytic theory.[51]

[49] There is another terminological debate about the concept of 'repression' and, again, Anna Freud takes a position, which is not being followed here. In the present work the term 'repression' is used in a general sense, covering the various ways which people might have for 'pushing aside' thoughts. This is the sense in which Freud used the word in *Studies*, and also in later works, such as his essay 'Repression'. According to this usage, particular ways of concealing desires from the self, such as projection, sublimation, denial etc, are all forms of repression. Anna Freud, in common with a number of psychoanalytic theorists claims that 'repression' should not be used to denote the general category, for it represents one way of pushing aside threatening thoughts: it is, thus, a particular means of psychological defence, on a par with sublimation, projection etc. Anna Freud argued that the correct general term should not be 'repression', but 'defence mechanisms' (*Abwehrmechanismen*), with repression being one type of defence mechanism. She cited the authority of Freud for defining 'repression' narrowly, claiming that this corresponds to his usage in early works. She argues that Freud replaced 'defence' in his middle period by 'repression', but later 'reverted to the old concept of defence' (pp. 42–3; see also Frosh, 1997, pp. 21f for a discussion of Freud's use of 'defence'). One reason for resisting Anna Freud's definition here is to avoid using the term 'defence mechanism'. The problem lies with the term 'mechanism' (although, see Sackheim, 1983, for a discussion of the problems of confining repression to 'defence', omitting the issue of offence). The present argument stresses the importance of understanding repression in terms of the activities of persons, rather than in terms of hidden mechanisms which operate mysteriously within persons (see also, Schafer, 1976, who argues that psychological defence is an activity not a mechanism).

[50] For example, Holmes (1990) quotes Freud's essay 'Repression' to support the view that the term 'repression' should be reserved for instances 'in which threatening material is relegated to the unconscious before it is consciously recognized as stressful' (p. 86); he claims that the evidence from laboratory experiments fails to find evidence that this sort of repression occurs.

[51] Erwin (1996), one of Freud's most persistent critics, makes this move in his tendentiously named *A Final Accounting*. He rejects the idea that repression can be

The present analysis uses 'repression' to cover both the conscious and unconscious forms of driving away thoughts. There is no need to cite the passages from Freud to justify this definition; this task has been undertaken by others.[52] Certainly in 'Studies', Freud uses the term 'repression' in the wide sense, most notably describing Elisabeth's driving away of her bedside thought as repression. As has already been quoted, the very first Freudian use of the 'repression' comes in a passage referring to a thought being 'intentionally repressed' (however, the editors of the *Standard Edition* add a footnote to assure readers that Freud did not really mean 'intentional', but that he merely wished to imply that the repression was motivated, without making any implication of '*conscious* intention').[53] Freud's use of repression in this wider sense is not confined to his early writings. As will be seen, when the mature Freud returned to discuss the case of Elisabeth, he continued to describe her pushing aside the bedside thought as an instance of repression.

There is a further reason for not adopting the definition of 'repression', which is advocated today by Freud's critics. They hope to push psychoanalytic theory into a conceptual corner, by demonstrating the implausibility of such unconscious repression. For them, the idea of repressed love, or any other repressed feeling, is implausible: how can we unconsciously push aside feelings which we don't know we have? However, it will be argued later that the idea of unconscious feelings, such as those apparently held by Elisabeth, is not so absurd as the critics

defined as 'intentional forgetting', on the grounds that 'there is nothing distinctively Freudian about this process' (p. 222). Regarding the idea that we might deliberately forget uncomfortable thoughts, or displace anger onto innocent targets, Erwin comments 'we do not need sophisticated experimental designs and fancy statistical tests to confirm such commonsense assumptions', because 'they have, in most cases, already been amply warranted by commonsense observations' (p. 190). Far from taking this as a confirmation of Freudian ideas, he takes this as a refutation. 'Real' Freudian repression is preventative, for which, he claims, there is no evidence. Another critic, Grünbaum (1989) recognizes that repression is the corner-stone of Freudian theory (p. 5) and also argues that Freudians should not claim that the concealment of conscious thoughts should be called 'repression' (pp. 199–201). Sachs (1992) criticizes Grünbaum on this point, especially for ignoring Freud's arguments in 'Psychopathology of everyday life'. Sachs claims that if one accepts the occurrence of tendentious forgetting then Freud's discussion of examples is reasonable (p. 324). Crews (1995) is another critic who 'defends' the concept of repression from being weakened to cover conscious repression. He criticizes Erdelyi, who advocates the broader concept, accusing him of reducing repression to something 'pea-sized', by 'radically trivializing its function in Freud's psychodynamic system' (p. 272). Crews insists that repression must be understood in its unconscious forms, and claims that 'the full-blown psychoanalytic concept of repression can be seen to lack appreciable *independent* support' (p. 248, emphasis in original).

[52] Most notably see Erdelyi (1990), who provides a useful and scholarly demonstration of Freud's differing uses of the term 'repression'.

[53] 'Studies on hysteria', p. 61n, emphasis in original.

would have us believe.[54] In fact, it is not particularly mysterious, at least once adjustments are made to Freud's theory of consciousness, and once repression is understood in terms of language, rather than in terms of hidden, inner processes. Then, it becomes easier to understand how Elisabeth could love unconsciously, and how she could simultaneously know and not know this love. The sort of pushing aside, involved in this simultaneous knowing and not knowing, is not so different from the deliberate sort, which Freudians and critics alike admit to being very much a part of psychological life.

The gap in Freud

If the process of repression is the corner-stone of psychoanalytic theory, then one would expect that the greater part of Freud's writings would be devoted to elucidating how people accomplish the task of repression. But he has surprisingly little to say directly on the subject. His interest is in the causes and effects of repression, rather than in the repression itself. This can be seen in his account of Elisabeth. It may be objected that the case of Elisabeth is an early report, written when the details of psychoanalytic theory had yet to be worked out. In later writings one might be expected to find the gap closed. Years later, when he discussed the case again, the gap still remained.

Freud, with characteristic intellectual honesty, was prepared to admit his ignorance about the processes of repression. In the 'Introductory lectures', written when he was over sixty and more than twenty years after he had seen Elisabeth, Freud posed three basic questions about repression: 'What kind of mental impulses are subject to repression? by what forces is it accomplished? and for what motives?' He then made an extraordinary admission: 'so far we have only one piece of information on these points'. We only know, he conceded, that repression 'emanates from forces of the ego', and that these forces are 'responsible', at least in part, for repression. Apart from that, he added, 'we know nothing more at present'.[55]

It is easy to overlook the crucial gaps in the case reports, because they contain so much stunning detail. In presenting the case of Elisabeth in 'Studies', Freud commented that his account differed from the customary medical report: he was giving 'a detailed description of mental processes such as we are accustomed to find in the works of imaginative writers'.[56] This is certainly true: we have the whirl of the dance, the

---

[54] See below, chapter 7.
[55] 'Introductory lectures', *PFL* 1, p. 339.
[56] 'Studies on hysteria', *PFL* 3, p. 231.

walks with the brother-in-law, the drama in the consulting-room as the doctor tells the patient his hypothesis about the secret love. Nevertheless, the details have their limitations. The descriptions of the patient's mind seem to stop just at the moment when Freud begins to describe how the patient represses disturbing information.

Freud described the early onset of Elisabeth's symptoms, when she was nursing her father. He suggested that her duties conflicted with her erotic desires. Freud claimed that 'under the pressure of lively self-reproaches she decided in favour of the former, and in doing so brought about her hysterical pain'.[57] The description skips over things. We are not told exactly the nature of her self-reproaches. More crucially, Freud does not say how the decision to nurse her sick father is related to the bringing on of the pain; not does he discuss how the pains lead to the repressing of the erotic desires, whose content is left tactfully vague. As regards the ways that a moral reproach can be converted into physical pains, Freud was frank: 'I cannot, I must confess, give any hint of how a conversion of this kind is brought about.'[58]

The same gap occurs when Freud discusses how Elisabeth's love for the brother-in-law was pushed away from reaching consciousness. Freud writes that Elisabeth 'succeeded in sparing herself the painful conviction that she loved her sister's husband by inducing physical pains in herself instead'. Whenever this conviction 'sought to force itself on her . . . her pains came on, thanks to successful conversion'.[59] A medically sounding term, 'conversion', is employed as if to explain the process, but, as Freud concedes, nothing is known how such conversion could take place. We do not know, nor apparently did Freud, how Elisabeth was able to induce the pains. Thus, what she did, in order to succeed in repressing the disturbing thoughts, is left unclear.

Similarly, there is a crucial gap in Freud's dramatic description of Elisabeth at her sister's death-bed. He describes her approaching the house of tragedy, and he depicts the shameful thought as a flash of lightning in the dark. But it is not clear whether Freud's description of the thought – 'now he is free again and I can be his wife' – is taken directly from Elisabeth's words; or if it is Freud's summary; or his conjecture. If they were Elisabeth's words, it is unclear whether she was explicitly paraphrasing for Freud's benefit the thought or whether she was claiming that these were the exact words which shot through her mind. But, most importantly, Freud breaks off his description. He does not say what happens next; he does not say what exactly Elisabeth might have felt, when these words flashed through her mind. Nor does he

[57] Ibid., p. 235.   [58] Ibid., p. 237.   [59] Ibid., p. 227.

discuss how Elisabeth pushed the thought aside, apparently forgetting it until Freud prompts her. In short, the process of repression is omitted in the story, which claims to be retelling the details of mental processes.

When Freud later re-told the story, he added more details about the repression.[60] In 1909 Stanley Hall, the notable American psychologist, invited both Freud and Jung to Clark University, in Massachusetts, to deliver a series of lectures. Here at last was the first sign of the international academic recognition, for which Freud craved. The lectures, which Freud delivered, were to be published as 'Five lectures on psychoanalysis'. To this day, this small book remains a wonderfully clear and compelling introduction to psychoanalytic ideas. In the second lecture, Freud presented the notion of repression. He explained how neuroses might result when unpleasant experiences are driven from consciousness, only to re-emerge as pathogenic symptoms. Freud said how he had given the name of 'repression' to the forces of resistance, which prevented the forgotten material 'being made conscious' and which must 'have pushed the pathogenic experiences in question out of consciousness'.[61] Rather than confine himself to theory, or reporting a confusing variety of cases, Freud told his audience that he would relate a single case 'in which the determinants and advantages of repression are sufficiently evident'.[62] He apologized that he would have to abridge the case history and omit 'some important underlying material'.[63]

Freud described Elisabeth's troubled history, focusing on the bed-side scene. He recounts the thought which flashed through Elisabeth's mind. The wording is slightly changed from the account in 'Studies': 'Now he is free and can marry me.'[64] Then, according to Freud, an act of repression occurred:

We may assume with certainty that this idea, which betrayed to her consciousness the intense love for her brother-in-law of which she had not herself been conscious, was surrendered to repression a moment later, owing to the revolt of her feelings.[65]

[60] For a general discussion of the way that Freud, as he developed his theories, reconstructed his early case histories, see Borch-Jacobsen (1996).

[61] Freud (1963), p. 48. Freud explained repression with the use of the metaphor of a disturbance in a lecture-hall. Should someone disrupt the lecture by behaving in an unruly manner, then other students would eject the recalcitrant individual. Similarly, the ego ejects disturbing thoughts. The metaphor, along with the example of Elisabeth's death-bed scene, makes it plain that, here at least, Freud considered the willed forgetting of conscious thoughts as a prime example of repression.

[62] Ibid., p. 49   [63] Ibid.

[64] Freud (1963), 'Five lectures', p. 49. The English translations of Elisabeth's thought in 'Studies on hysteria' and 'Five Lectures' reflect the differences between the two texts in the original German: see *Studien über Hysterie*, p. 222 with *Über Psychoanalyse*, p. 22 in Gesammelte Werke, vols. 1 and 8).

[65] Freud (1963), p. 49.

Again, Freud does not describe how exactly Elisabeth represses the idea. His interests are in tracing the origins of the repressed thought, and then showing the neurotic effects.

Freud's phrasing is both curious and revealing. He writes that we may *assume* that repression occurred, as if he had no further evidence. The shameful thought was 'surrendered to repression a moment later owing to the revolt of her feelings'. The passive tense is used to describe the action of repressing: the thought is somehow 'surrendered' up to repression.[66] The phrase suggests that something automatic happened, with repression being a reaction, occurring beyond the actions of Elisabeth herself.[67] On the other hand, there is the phrase 'the revolt of her feelings'. She has feelings, but Freud does not detail precisely what she felt. He does not reconstruct her state of mind after the flashing of the shameful thought. He adds that Elisabeth had completely forgotten 'the odious egoistic impulse that had emerged in her', until 'she remembered it during the treatment'.[68] How she managed to forget such a dramatic thought is also unclear.

It is as if the repression takes place by magic. The shameful impulse is there one moment. And the next, it's gone, surrendered up to an irresistible mental force. Then, magically, it is transformed into symptoms.[69] The metaphor of magic is not inappropriate. In 'The question of lay-analysis', Freud wrote that nothing takes place between the analyst and the patient 'except that they talk to each other'.[70] Sceptics, he urged, should not scoff that psychoanalysis is nothing but words, for words can have the power to heal. In ancient times 'the word was magic – a magical act'. It is no surprise, continued Freud, that the word has today 'retained much of its ancient power' and that, even in modern times, talk occasionally seems to exert magical powers.[71]

---

[66] James Strachey's English translation reproduces the German original in this respect: '*Durch den Aufruhr ihrer Gefühle im nächsten Moment der Verdrängung überliefert wurde*' in Freud *GW* 8, p. 22.

[67] Linguists have discussed in detail how the passive tense can be used to minimize the sense of personal agency (Fairclough, 1992 and 1995; Fowler et al., 1979; Kress, 1988).

[68] Freud (1963), p. 50.

[69] Roustang (1997) makes a similar point vis-à-vis the concept of sublimation, which is a particular form of repression. He argues that Freud fails to explain how 'through its own development the sexual transforms itself into the non-sexual' (p. 28). In consequence, Freud cannot account for the origins of sublimation nor say where the 'gift' for this form of repression comes from.

[70] *PFL* 15, p. 287. In the passage, Freud imagines a critic of psychoanalysis, scoffing 'so it is a kind of magic, you talk and blow away the ailment'. Freud urges this imaginary sceptic not to 'despise the *word*' (p. 287, emphasis in original).

[71] Ibid., p. 288. The same ideas about the word and magic are also to be found in the 'Introductory lectures' (*PFL*, 1, pp. 41–2).

The words, uttered in the dialogue between analyst and patient, bring back the forgotten memory, as if by an act of magic. If words possess the power to work this psychological conjuring trick, then perhaps they were responsible for the original disappearing act. Maybe, Elisabeth said something to herself – some sort of psychological 'hey presto' – to make the odious thought disappear and to keep it hidden from the conjuror herself. And there the thought must remain, hidden from conscious awareness, until Freud's verbal 'abracadabra' – with perhaps a flourish of the hand upon the brow – did the returning trick to the astonishment and extreme discomfort of Elisabeth.

Two voices of Freud

Freud was well aware how his case reports differed from the standard medical reports of the day. 'It still strikes me as strange', he wrote in the report of Elisabeth, 'that the case histories I write should read like short stories and that, as one might say, they lack the serious stamp of science'.[72] Freud was, perhaps, being too self-deprecating. His case histories rhetorically bear the stamp of science. The opening and concluding sections of 'Studies' are highly theoretical, freely using the medical terminology of the day. Moreover, the case-histories, sandwiched between the outer layers, are not devoid of theory. As has been seen, the technical terms can intervene at opportune moments. Thus, 'conversion' and 'surrendering to repression' convey a medical precision, which belies elision and vagueness.

Scholars have often commented that Freud's writings are marked by two rhetorical voices – the voice of the scientist and the voice of the humanist.[73] Freud can use technical language, which most certainly aims to convey the serious stamp of science. Roy Schafer, for instance, has referred to Freud's 'mixed physiochemical and evolutionary biological language'.[74] In this language, Freud writes of forces, instincts, energies and so on. This is the language of his theoretical, 'metapsychological' writings, in which he attempted to map out the dynamic relations between the structures of ego, id and superego.[75] It is also the language used in the quotation, which was cited earlier, when Freud

---

[72] 'Studies', p. 231.
[73] See, for instance, Schafer (1976); Spence (1982 and 1994); Mahony (1987); Marcus (1986).
[74] Schafer (1976), p. 3.
[75] Freud wrote that a 'metapsychological presentation' aimed to depict 'a psychical process in its dynamic, topographical and economic aspects', ('The unconscious', *PFL* 11, p. 184).

claimed that little was known about 'the forces of the ego' and how mental impulses are subjected to repression.

Freud's metapsychological works depict battles between psychic entities of the mind. Thoughts are surrendered or subjected to repression. Repressing is not seen as an activity that people perform. The language that Freud uses to describe these inner processes is very different from what Schafer calls Freud's 'action language'. This, above all, is the humane language of the case reports, in which Freud depicts with his novelist's skills the characters of actors in their human dramas. We get to know people such as Elisabeth. We read about them doing things in their lives. We catch a glimpse of the doctor, watching the young girl at a dance – not his ego responding to outer perceptual stimuli.

The two voices are not sharply divided between the metapsychological writings and the case-histories. Dry and technical though the metapsychological writings might be at times, human examples are not far away. After all, Freud defended his theoretical writings, by stressing that abstract concepts must always refer back 'to the material of observation from which they appear to have come'.[76] The consulting-room provided the place of observation. Throughout his working life as a psychoanalyst, Freud maintained a heavy load of patients. He was unlike today's successful academics, who find that time for rudimentary work, such as lecturing and tending to the laboratory, diminishes as they rush between important conferences and committees. Freud never forsook the rigours of the consulting-room for ostensibly more important tasks. Even in his last year in London, exhausted by cancer, exile, and old age – and even though he still believed he had vital messages to deliver to an uncaring world – he was regularly seeing three to four patients a day.[77] Such was his continuing interest in human lives.

If the metapsychological writings contain human examples, so the case-histories testify to Freud's love of scientific speculation, or what he described as the 'intellectual pleasure' of science.[78] Sufficient quotations from the case of Elisabeth have already been given to show how Freud, even in the same sentence, can veer from descriptions of patient's actions to technical terms. We hear about Elisabeth's moral feelings, her shock and then her surrendering to 'repression' and 'conversion'. Constantly, Freud is switching between his novelist's and scientist's voices.[79]

---

[76] 'Instincts and their vicissitudes', *PFL* 11, p. 113.
[77] Jones (1957); Gay (1995), Schur (1972).
[78] 'Formulations on the two principles of mental functioning', *PFL* 11, p. 41.
[79] A further example of this can be given. In describing Elisabeth's pains, Freud writes that 'I could not help thinking that the patient had done nothing more nor less than look for a *symbolic* expression of her painful thoughts' ('Studies', *PFL* 3, pp. 221–2, italics in original). Thus, he describes Elisabeth, her thoughts and actions. In the very

In the switching of voices, the problem of repression can appear to slip away, as if it has been resolved. Yet the problems remain. How can I keep something secret from myself? How can Elisabeth be unaware of her feelings? If she deliberately pushes them from her mind, then she must be aware that she is pushing them away. It is easier to use a language which suggests that the pushing away is somehow happening to her in some ill-defined way, rather than she is accomplishing the self-deception. Thus, Freud, in his scientific voice suggests that the repressing then can be ascribed to a mental agent, namely the ego.

Significantly, when Freud in 'Introductory lectures' admitted ignorance of the operation of repression, the one piece of information that he claimed was known was that it 'emanates from forces of the ego'.[80] It was as if the ego operated silently behind the ordinary conscious individual. Elisabeth herself was not repressing her distressing thoughts, but her ego was doing the unpleasant business. When the troubling thought comes into the mind – as it did during the emotional circumstances of the death bed scene – then, as Freud wrote in 'Studies', 'the ego is obliged to attend to this sudden flare-up of the idea and to restore the former state of affairs by a further conversion'.[81]

Similarly, when Elisabeth was going for walks with her brother-in-law – or not going for them because of the pains in her leg – she, herself, was not repressing the feelings of love. The hidden ego was accomplishing the business. Freud often used the metaphor of the watchman to illustrate the operation of repression. In the 'Introductory lectures', he described the unconscious as resembling a large entrance hall; consciousness was a small, narrower drawing-room which adjoined the hall. The thoughts of the unconscious jostled each other trying to enter this small room. On the threshold of this room 'a watchman performs his function: he examines the different impulses, acts as a censor, and will not admit them into the drawing-room if they displease him'.[82]

If this image of the ego is translated to the case of Elisabeth, then it suggests that the crucial psychological action is always being performed by an actor within the ordinary actor – a watchman, or dedicated servant, lodged unobtrusively within the psyche of the person. We can imagine Elisabeth in the summer before her sister's death. She is

next sentence, he switches voice: 'the fact that somatic symptoms of hysteria can be brought about by symbolization of this kind was already asserted in our "Preliminary Communication"' (p. 222). Elisabeth disappears as the agent in this second sentence. Freud uses the passive tense; 'symbolization', rather than a person appears as the causative agent of the medical condition.

80 'Introductory lectures', *PFL* 1, p. 339. See above, p. 27.
81 'Studies', p. 239.
82 Freud, 'Introductory lectures', *PFL* 1, p. 336.

spending time, getting to know her brother-in-law. She develops feelings of love, but these never disturb her conscious awareness. As she is walking with him, talking with him, or resting in bed alone in the evenings, her unconscious ego is going about its business. It has guessed how revolted Elisabeth would be if she were aware of her feelings and how such feelings would endanger the whole family. It sees unpleasure and danger beyond immediate pleasure. So silently, like a faithful but neglected family servant, it turns back the emotions from the ante-rooms of consciousness. 'You cannot disturb the mistress', this part of the ego repeatedly tells the forces of love. In consequence, the young woman is unaware of the instinctual forces which her sister's husband has stimulated within her. But all the vigilance and energetic service of the hidden ego are powerless when she sees her sister lying dead. The repressed desire momentarily breaks through. Then, the repair work of deliberate repression is required. The hidden ego assists to calm the disturbed mistress, sweeping up the psychic mess, acting as the unnoticed, unthanked domestic servant.

Too many egos

The idea of the hidden ego seems, at first sight, to solve the problem of repression, especially unconscious repression. But the apparent solution is not a genuine one. The problems remain, but, as it were, at a remove. The hidden ego has no independent reality – it cannot be observed. Nor can one say how it might operate.[83] Most importantly, one might ask how has it acquired its skills? How has Elisabeth's hidden ego learnt exactly how to protect her mistress? The idea of the unconscious ego – or the hidden 'I' within the 'I' – creates considerable conceptual difficulties. One writer has referred to the 'paradoxes of the ego'.[84] Basically, these paradoxes revolve around the problem of the ego (or the 'I') doing things unbeknown to itself, as if there is a hidden person within the person, or an ego within the ego.[85] In fact, the problem may

---

[83] See Thalberg (1983) for a pointed discussion of the problems with Freud's attribution of agency to the ego, with regard to Freud's idea that the ego censors dreams when we are asleep.

[84] Frosh (1997).

[85] In broad terms, this is the problem of the homunculus. Daniel Dennett (1991), in an interesting discussion of the problem, denies that all uses of homunculus in psychological theory create conceptual difficulties. However, the acceptable uses of the homunculus-type metaphors normally refer to lower order processes. Freud's unconscious ego resembles a mental director of operations, or what Dennett calls 'a central meaner'. It is this very notion that Dennett argues against.

be worse. Beside an unconscious and a conscious ego, Freud's theory may, indeed, assume even more egos.[86]

The idea of the hidden ego does enormous theoretical damage to Freud's own theoretical schema. At its simplest, the schema depicts a conflict between conscious and unconscious life. The ego is the structure of consciousness, most principally comprising the sense of self.[87] As Freud stated ironically in 'The question of lay analysis', each one of us assumes that we have an ego (or, more literally a 'self') 'without being a philosopher, and some people even in spite of being philosophers'.[88] The ego, in Freud's view, is engaged in constant battle with the forces of the id, a mental region 'more extensive, more imposing and more obscure than the "I"'.[89]

If the ego were to stand for the conscious part of the mind (together with the preconscious), and the id for the unconscious, matters would be fine. However, Freud claims that repression is accomplished by the ego and that it does this unconsciously. The net result is conceptual difficulty. The ego cannot be equated with the conscious 'I', for part of its duty is to protect the conscious 'I'. Thus 'the ego' is both the watchman and the 'I', whom the watchman supposedly protects. Freud's difficulty is compounded because he assumes that the process of repression, which is conducted by the ego, often is unconscious. In such instances, the ego as censor must inspect the desires before letting them enter consciousness. The conscious 'I' must not become aware of what the censor is doing, or even that such censorship is taking place.

In consequence, the ego cannot possibly be equated with the ordinary conscious agent. On the contrary it has two parts: the ordinary conscious agent, and an unconscious ego, faithfully protecting that agent. Freud, in 'The ego and the id', in discussing these matters, commented that we have found ourselves 'in an unforeseen situation'. The ego,

---

[86] Sackheim (1983) makes a convincing argument that Freud's theory of the process of self-censorship itself involves a dual model of the ego. Freud's theory assumed that the world is apprehended directly by the perceptual apparatus. This, too, is the work of the ego. Then the ego-as-censor inspects the information which the perceptual ego has provided. Accordingly there must be three egos: the perceptual ego; the interpretative ego and the conscious ego.

[87] Some commentators suggest that Freud has been ill served by his English translators. The original German for the ego is *das Ich*, literally 'the I' (see, for example, Bettelheim, 1986; Parker, 1998a). Such commentators claim that terms such as 'ego' and 'id' go against Freud's deliberate choice of what he called 'simple pronouns' to describe the major elements of mental life ('Question of lay analysis', p. 105). For a historical analysis of Freud's use of *das Es* (the id), see Bos (1997). However, Freud's problems regarding the ego are not to be solved by switching to 'the I'. His theory of repression still depends on a hidden 'I' behind the everyday, ordinary 'I'.

[88] 'Question of lay analysis', *PFL* 15, p. 295.

[89] Ibid.

having both conscious and unconscious functions, must be seen as split, for an important part of it 'and Heaven knows how important a part' is 'inherently unconscious'[90] There is a hidden 'I' behind the ordinary 'I', which the ordinary 'I' knows nothing about.

The idea that repression emanates from the unconscious part of the ego fails to solve the problem of repression, for, as was seen, Freud was unclear how the ego operated, in order to repress. This failure adds to the theoretical confusion. Moreover, it hands a weapon to Freud's critics. The central concept of psychoanalysis is seen to describe a mysterious task, performed by an unseen, hidden part of the mind. It is little wonder that the critics today have insisted on guarding Freud's concept of unconscious repression and then triumphantly proclaiming to find little supporting evidence for it.

However, there is a way out of the muddle. This involves returning to Freud's other voice, in which he describes the actions of people, rather than their egos. Over twenty years ago, the American psychoanalyst Roy Schafer advocated this move. He argued that psychoanalysts should avoid Freud's scientific language, which makes egos, ids and other mental structures the prime actors in psychic dramas.[91] Analysts, according to Schafer, should try to speak plainly about people, rather than 'engage in speculation about what is ultimately unutterable'.[92] By so doing, the language of psychoanalysis would become less mystifying.[93]

Schafer's argument is directly applicable to the notion of repression. We should, he suggests, speak of repression as an action, rather than 'as a mechanism with structural and energic attributes'.[94] Repression, in consequence, should not be described in terms of the unconscious ego repelling mental forces. Thus, some of the phrases, which Freud used to describe Elisabeth's repression, are best avoided. Ideas are not 'surrendered' up to the process of repression. Instead, people repress ideas. We would need to say how Elisabeth could fail to recognize her love for her

---

[90] *PFL* 11, pp. 355–6.

[91] However abstract and unreal the language of Freud's metapsychology, Schafer says that the problem is worse in the writing of later psychoanalysts. In particular, he claims that the work of Melanie Klein and the English school has 'carried the reifications of metapsychology to a grotesque extreme' (p. 3). It is arguable whether Kleinians have, in fact, reached the grotesque extreme. Lacanians arguably have better qualifications for that title.

[92] Schafer (1976), p. 10; see also Spence (1982 and 1994).

[93] Other psychoanalysts have also advocated the abandonment of Freudian mechanistic language. For example, Kohut (1984), in his self psychology, suggests replacing talk about 'defence mechanisms' with talk about 'defensiveness' (pp. 114f). However, the language which Kohut uses, including his concept of 'defensiveness' is by no means the 'action' language, as envisaged by Schafer, for it retains too many concepts which refer to inner processes of the mind rather than the activity of persons.

[94] Schafer (1976), p. 206.

brother-in-law. Elisabeth, and not some unseen inner mechanism, was pushing aside the disturbing thoughts.

At first glance, this seems to set psychoanalytic theory an impossible task. The language of deliberate actions must be used to describe actions that cannot always be deliberately performed: how can Elisabeth deliberately drive away ideas, which she denies possessing? And how can she be unaware that she is deliberately doing such a thing? Nevertheless, as will be suggested, the circle can be squared. As so often is the case, Freud himself provides a clue. In discussing Elisabeth, Freud draws attention to the ways that she devoted herself to sick-nursing her father and other members of her family. The routines of nursing would have taken her mind from disturbing thoughts: 'Anyone whose mind is taken up by the hundred and one tasks of sick-nursing which follow one another in endless succession over a period of weeks and months will, on the one hand, adopt a habit of suppressing every sign of his own emotion, and on the other, will soon divert his attention away from his own impressions, since he has neither time nor strength to do justice to them'.[95]

Routines may provide a means of pushing disturbing thoughts from the mind, and, as such, they may offer a clue to the skills required for repression. Routines often fall between wholly conscious and unconscious actions. When we act routinely, we might know we are performing the routine but we are unaware of all we do. Our mind might be on other things. As will be argued in subsequent chapters, the routines of language play a major part in repression. If language can be shown to be routinely expressive and repressive, then the central concept of psychoanalytic theory, may cease to appear so mysterious. Its inner gap may even be filled.

[95] 'Studies on hysteria', *PFL* 3, p. 232.

3   Thinking, speaking and repressing

When on the trail of the unconscious, it is easy to overlook the obvious. If one is searching for the processes of repression, then one might imagine that the clues are always to be found in the obscurest places – in dreams, in the oddities of neuroses, in startling slips of the tongue. Freud, however, argued that ordinary social life depended upon repression. That means that people are repressing as they go about their everyday business. If so, then the clues might be sought in ordinary, rather than extraordinary, activities. It would be a mistake, therefore, to isolate the depth psychology of psychoanalysis from the surface psychology of ordinary life.

One of the great strengths of Freud's metapsychological writings is that he attempts to link his psychology of unconscious thinking with a theory of consciousness. However, the strength is also a weakness. As will be shown in this chapter, his theory of consciousness is the root of many difficulties. It is directly related to the gap in his concept of repression. In order to reformulate Freudian ideas about repression, it is necessary to begin with the surface psychology, on which so much of the depth psychology depends.

Therefore this chapter will critically examine Freud's theory of consciousness. Following the arguments of the previous chapter, his theory will be taken to task for using the language of mechanistic science, positing the agencies of hidden structures such as the id and ego, rather than using the language of human action. Moreover, Freud's theory of consciousness grants language a peripheral role. This, it will be suggested, is a major mistake. Repression depends on the skills of language: we push away disturbing thoughts in much the same way as we avoid troublesome topics in conversation. To appreciate this, it is necessary to see the extent to which unrepressed thoughts are constituted in language. Hence, one requires a surface psychology which puts language at the centre of human thinking.

For this reason, the present chapter contains a lengthy detour into the psychology of ordinary thinking, together with a recommendation for recent attempts to produce a 'discursive psychology', based on analysing the details of talk. The discursive approach, if stretched a little, can provide the basis for understanding repression. Psychological constructs, however, are not to be piled on top of each other, as if building a free-standing, but empty, sky-scraper. As Freud well appreciated, theory only serves a point if it can house human lives. Consequently, the present chapter will re-examine one of Freud's most famous case-histories – the story of the patient who has come to be known as the 'Rat Man'. The patient's internal thinking can be seen to comprise of dialogues, thereby exemplifying the discursive nature of thought. Moreover, the patient uses rhetorical devices to repress unwelcome thoughts. Freud, of course, uses language to tell the story. His language is not straightforward. It, too, seems to miss out things, to repress elements. Both doctor and patient, thus, illustrate the repressive aspects of language.

Freud's theory of consciousness

Any satisfactory theory of the unconscious must also be a theory of consciousness. To understand how a thought might be repressed, or pushed from conscious awareness, we must be able to say what happens when a thought is not repressed. The philosopher, Donald Davidson made a similar point in an essay about Freud. He suggested that our ideas about irrationality cannot be totally separated from our ideas about what is rational, for 'irrationality is a failure in the house of reason'.[1] It is easy for a psychoanalytic theorist to pay lip-service to such an eminently sensible principle, but then to ignore it. The temptation is always to assume that ordinary, conscious thinking is unproblematic, and that unconscious thinking presents the intriguing mystery which deserves all the attention. However, that would be a serious mistake.[2] To understand why there might be gaps in Freud's theory of repression, it is necessary to look at his ideas about ordinary, unrepressed thinking.

Basically, Freud's theory of mental processes, as outlined in his metapsychological works, addresses the question 'how do ideas become conscious?', rather than tackling the question 'how do we repress thoughts?' He assumed that unconsciousness was the 'natural' state for thoughts. The key problem for a psychological theory of the mind was to show how an idea could make the difficult journey from unconsciousness into conscious awareness. This emphasis fitted his clinical practice.

[1] Davidson (1983), p. 289.
[2] See, for instance, the arguments of Brearley (1991); Cioffi (1991) and Bouveresse (1993).

Freud sought to discover what thoughts were being blocked from the conversations in the consulting-room: what, for instance, Elisabeth was concealing from herself and from her doctor. He also wanted to discover the necessary therapeutic techniques for undoing the blockage, allowing the unconscious thought to flow into conscious awareness. Thus, the practice of therapy depended on solving the problem of how to bring the unconscious thought into consciousness.

In formulating his theory of thinking, Freud translated the particular therapeutic problem into a general statement about the relations between consciousness and unconsciousness. His position was a humane one, stressing the similarity between the neurotic's way of thinking and that of supposedly normal people. The neurotic, whose repressed thoughts had to be coaxed to the surface of consciousness, was not portrayed as thinking in ways different from the normal person. Our 'normal' conscious thoughts, like those of the neurotic, have travelled from the unconscious realm of the mind.

Freud's metapsychology was based on the assumption that the unconscious played a major role in thinking. As he wrote in his essay 'The Unconscious', 'the more we seek to win our way to a metapsychological view of mental life, the more we must learn to emancipate ourselves from the importance of the symptom of "being conscious"'.[3] Most of Freud's metapsychological works were written after 1910. 'The Ego and the Id' did not appear until 1923. However, many of the ideas about the dynamic functioning of mental processes can be found in the latter part of 'Interpretation of dreams', which was published in 1900. There, Freud argued that it was 'essential to abandon the overvaluation of the property of being conscious'.[4] The unconscious was more important than the conscious realm of mental life, for it was 'the larger sphere, which includes within it the smaller sphere of the conscious'. The reason why the unconscious was the larger, and more important, sphere was that 'everything conscious has an unconscious preliminary stage'.[5]

Freud justified this position in terms of his notion of the 'preconscious'.[6] The vast majority of a person's thoughts and beliefs would be, at any given moment, 'unconscious', latently waiting to be used. Freud typically talked of the preconscious (*Pcs.*) as a topographical area of the mind. When a thought is consciously used, it has to travel from the preconscious realm of the unconsciousness into the full glare of conscious attention. In this way, conscious thinking is based on unconscious

[3] 'The unconscious', *PFL* 11, p. 197.
[4] 'Interpretation of dreams', *PFL* 4, p. 773.
[5] Ibid.   [6] See above, chapter 2, pp. 15f.

thought.[7] In 'Interpretation of dreams', Freud drew a parallel between this normal pattern of thinking and what happens in dreams. A wish, which is censored during day-time, 'seeks to force its way along the normal path taken by thought-processes, through the *Pcs.* (to which it partially belongs) to consciousness'.[8] Only during the night-time, when the censorship of the ego is relaxed, can the forbidden wish successfully undertake the journey, and, then, only in disguise. Again, the argument stresses the similarity between 'normal' (or unrepressed) thinking and that which is subject to repression. The crucial difference is that the normal thought has no barrier to circumvent.

Freud conceded that not all the contents of consciousness could be described in this way. Perceptual experiences seem to enter conscious attention directly, without having to be fished out of the preconscious.[9] But, according to Freud, perceptual experience was not to be equated with proper thinking, for generally 'thinking in pictures' was only 'a very incomplete form of becoming conscious'.[10] Most conscious thinking, by contrast, was verbal.

Regarding the role of language in thinking, Freud took an interesting, but ultimately misguided, step. He claimed that deeply unconscious thoughts are essentially non-verbal, but words become attached to unconscious thoughts as a means of successfully passing into consciousness. In 'Interpretation of dreams', he suggested that the preconscious system needed to have qualities 'which could attract the attention of consciousness'. The necessary qualities were verbal: 'it seems highly probable', he argued, that the preconscious system obtained the necessary qualities for transition to consciousness 'by linking the preconscious processes with the mnemic system of indications of speech'.[11]

Much the same idea can be found in 'The ego and the id', where Freud discussed the difference between preconscious and repressed thoughts. The role of language was crucial, he argued, for 'the real difference' between a repressed unconscious idea and a preconscious one was that 'the former is carried out on some material which remains

---

[7] In 'A note on the unconscious in psychoanalysis', Freud wrote that 'every psychical act begins as an unconscious one, and it may either remain so or go on developing into consciousness, according as it meets with resistance or not'. (*PFL* 11, p. 55).

[8] 'Interpretation of dreams', *PFL* 4, p. 728.

[9] As Sackheim (1983) has pointed out, modern cognitive psychology does not accept Freud's assumption that the perceptual apparatus passively receives an accurate impression of the outside world. Interpretation, and thus the possibility of bias, is involved at the earliest stages of perceptual processing (Bruner, 1992; Neisser, 1976; Stevenson, 1993; Greenwald, 1980 and 1992). See Erdelyi (1990) for a discussion of the relations between Freud's theory of perception and contemporary cognitive science.

[10] 'The ego and the id', *PFL* 11, p. 359.

[11] 'Interpretation of dreams', *PFL* 4, p. 730.

unknown, whereas the latter (the *Pcs.*) is in addition brought into connection with *word-presentations*'.[12] Freud went on to suggest that the question 'How does a thing become conscious?' would be most advantageously recast as 'How does a thing become preconscious?' Freud then answered his own question: 'Through becoming connected with the word-presentations corresponding to it'.[13]

These ideas underline the essentially wordless nature of the id. Instinctual impulses – primeval in their origin – are generated. They can only push their way to conscious awareness by means of words. There is another implication of this theory. A shift of focus has been accomplished. Repression, supposedly the corner-stone of psychoanalytic theory, is not placed at the centre of the metapsychological ideas of mental processes. The key question has become 'how does an idea become conscious?', as if the notion of an unconscious idea were unproblematic. The problem has become the thrusting *into* consciousness rather than the pushing *away* from consciousness. One might say, with more than a hint of mischief, that the theoretical structures of the metapsychology succeeded in pushing away the pushing away, or repressing the issue of repression.

Problems with Freud's metapsychological model

Freud's metapsychological model of the mind has a number of problems, preventing it from providing a suitable psychology for understanding thinking. Certainly, some of the terminology is old-fashioned, not sharing the computing and information-processing metaphors of today's cognitive science. Yet, curiously, the underlying model of mental activity is not that out-of-date. Several psychologists have pointed out the resemblance between some of the models in contemporary cognitive psychology and Freud's metapsychology. When Freud writes about preconscious ideas becoming conscious, he is, it is said, talking about the same issues as cognitive psychologists, discussing how information is accessed from 'memory-stores'.[14] Sympathizers of psychoanalysis have been pleased to note such similarities. They claim that the parallels demonstrate the continuing relevance of Freud's ideas.[15]

This is not the position taken here. Quite the reverse, the parallels with today's cognitive psychology are sufficient to raise doubts about the adequacy of Freud's metapsychology. In fact, the sort of criticisms,

---

[12] 'The ego and the id', *PFL* 11, p. 358, italics in original.
[13] Ibid.
[14] See, most notably, Erdelyi (1990 and 1996) and Conway (1997).
[15] For example, Jones (1993).

which can be raised against much cognitive psychology can equally be addressed to Freud's theory of consciousness. Particularly, both Freud and cognitive psychologists tend to concentrate on depicting hypothetical internal processes; and, most crucially, both ignore the centrality of language in human thinking.[16]

Certainly, Freud's metapsychological writings, despite the precision of their technical terms, have an abstract quality, positing hypothetical structures of the mind. Freud took what he called 'a topographical point of view', talking of the structures of the mind as if they were located in space.[17] Thus, the 'preconscious' is spoken of as if it were an entity, which exists somewhere in the brain. And similarly 'the unconscious' appears as a structure which has its place. The same is true of the 'memory organization packets' and 'information-stores' of contemporary cognitive science.[18]

The problem for both Freud and today's cognitive theorists is that these mental structures are not actually mapped onto a neurophysiological basis. Freud cautioned against presuming that the preconscious and unconscious could be identified with an actual anatomical structure in the brain. As he wrote, 'every endeavour to think of ideas, as stored up in nerve-cells and of excitations as migrating along nerve fibres, has miscarried completely'.[19] Yet his writings do not exclude the possibility of discovering the neurophysiological location of thinking. In 'The ego and the id', he drew a diagram, suspiciously resembling the human brain, to depict the relations between ego and id.[20] The ego, with its links to the perceptual apparatus, is on the surface of the system, while the id is diagrammatically located well below. Similarly, the diagrams of cognitive science today share a similar ambiguity. Authors might specifically deny that they are depicting actual physiological processes, but they use a terminology which implies that the depicted processes may link up with neurophysiological structures.[21]

This all matters for a simple reason. Freud's metapsychology, like contemporary cognitive science, suggests that the real psychological

---

[16] For criticisms of cognitive psychology from the perspective of discursive and social constructionist psychology, see Billig (1996); Edwards (1997); Gergen (1994); Harré and Gillett (1994); Potter (1996); Potter and Wetherell (1987); Shotter (1993b).

[17] 'The unconscious', *PFL* 11, p. 174.

[18] Shotter (1993a) puts the matter well in his critique of the language of Freudianism and of cognitive psychology. He suggests that Freudians are engaging in a counterfeit way of talking when they speak of the id, ego and unconscious as if speaking of real things. These terms, he argues, give a sense of reality to wholly fictional worlds (pp. 138f).

[19] *PFL* 11, p. 177.

[20] *PFL* 11, p. 363. See Sulloway (1980) for a detailed account of the influence of biological principles on Freud's thinking.

[21] For analysis of this rhetoric in both Freud and cognitive science, see Soyland (1994).

action is going on within the head. Moreover, the action is being carried on by the unseen structures of the mind. Outwardly in daily life, we hear people acting, talking, going about their daily business. But this is only the outward manifestation of their interior mental processes. To use Freud's terminology, the person is able to talk, because unconscious ideas in the preconscious have been associated with word-presentations and reached a sufficient level of excitation, in order to reach the system of consciousness (a modern cognitive psychologists may say that the appropriate 'mental model' has been accessed from the 'memory-store' and been given semantic form).

Once psychologists talk of the person in this way they are breaching the principle outlined in the previous chapter: this principle states that we should attribute actions to people rather than to hypothetical mental structures.[22] It is hard to see how Freud's metapsychology, for example, could illustrate the pattern of interaction to be found in his consulting-room. In the case history of Elisabeth, we read of the dialogue between patient and doctor. Freud tells Elisabeth that he suspects her of being in love with her brother-in-law. It adds nothing to say that Freud's preconscious idea was at this moment sufficiently stimulated and associated with appropriate words that it slid into conscious awareness and, then, out aloud into consulting-room. To understand why Freud said what he did, and when he did, we need to look at the interaction with Elisabeth, his suspicions and his theories. We do not need to hypothesize about the location of his preconscious and the stored residues of 'word presentations'.

This relates to a major problem with Freud's metapsychology (which again is paralleled in cognitive psychology). Although Freud claims that most human thinking is verbal, language is of secondary importance in his model of consciousness. Words are seen to be attached to thoughts, rather than forming thoughts. Perception and the unconscious are, in his scheme of things, essentially non-verbal. Language becomes, as it were, a means of moving the non-verbal impulses of the unconscious into the outer surface of conscious awareness. In consequence, depth psychology is committed to looking beyond language, stripping away the 'mere' words, in order to find the 'real' thoughts or impulses.

Freud called his metapsychology 'dynamic' as well as 'topographical'. By this he meant that the structures of the mind not only had a location with respect to each other (for instance, the ego being the outer layer and the id being deeper); but also that the structures were in dynamic relations to each other. Once the metapsychology is taken seriously,

[22] See above, pp. 35f. and also Schafer (1976).

then thinking is to be seen in terms of the relations between pre-conscious, unconscious and conscious etc., as if these structures are doing the thinking. But, of course, none of these regions, however, can be identified as an actual entity, just as cognitive scientists cannot actually produce an 'attitudinal schema' or 'frame of reference' for inspection. The existence, operation and mutual interaction of these inner structures must all be inferred from the outer actions of the person.

In this regard, Freud's metapsychology fits a dominant trend in western theorizing about thinking during the past three hundred years. His theory is 'Cartesian' in that it treats thinking as a series of unseen processes occurring within the individual thinker's mind. A good visual illustration of this view is provided by Rodin's famous statue, *Le Penseur*. Rodin depicts the thinker (of course, a man) sitting naked on a rock. His head rests on his hand. He is not looking at anything, nor is he speaking. All his attention is focused inwards. There he sits alone and silent, lost in his own thoughts, abstracted from social life. By his nakedness, he carries nothing that can link him to a particular cultural group or historical period. We don't know what he is thinking about, but, from the state of his body, we might presume it's not a sexual fantasy. There's serious business going on inside Le Penseur's skull. But we're not privy to the secret.

There is a very important difficulty with the Cartesian model of thinking, whether it appears in the form of Freud's metapsychology of consciousness or in cognitive psychology's account of mental processing. Because thinking is a hidden process, which unfolds in the head of the individual and which can never be directly observed by others, it is difficult to see how children could ever learn to think. One cannot copy Le Penseur, except by taking off one's clothes and sitting quietly on a rock.

Furthermore, and crucial to psychoanalytic theorizing, it is difficult to see how children could learn to repress. Perhaps Le Penseur, like Elisabeth, has been struck by a shameful thought, against which his whole moral being rebels. We might imagine that he is driving the thought away, as Elisabeth did. But what are these skills of repression and where did they come from? If they are hidden, internal processes, operated by the unseen ego, then we cannot acquire them by observing others. We may watch Le Penseur repressing his disturbing thoughts. Even if we study him for hours, all we see is his outer form. We glimpse no repression, which we might be able to copy.

So where did Elisabeth acquire the ability to repress thoughts, when the need arose? Freud's metapsychology gives few clues, especially since it is constantly examining the passage to conscious awareness rather the activity of pushing ideas from consciousness. In a general sense, his metapsychology points in the wrong direction. Look inside the head, it says; ignore the superficiality of words. However, as Freud himself recognized, and as he himself so supremely exemplified, much thinking is verbal. And this may provide a clue about the skills of repression: they might be bound up in the business of talk. But to explore this possibility, one needs a psychology that puts language at the centre of human thinking.

Speech and thought

What is required is a psychological approach, which, in contrast to Freud's metapsychology, does not distinguish sharply between language and thought. The basic idea is not new. The Eleatic Stranger, in Plato's dialogue, *The Sophist*, asserted that 'thought and speech are the same: only the former, which is the silent conversation of the soul with itself, has been given the special name of thought'.[23] There is an important psychological consequence from taking such a position. Thinking, as Wittgenstein stressed in his later philosophy, is not to be considered as a hidden, unobservable and silent process, occurring within the head of the individual. In contrast to what Cartesian philosophers have assumed, thinking can be outwardly observed in conversation.[24] This is something taken seriously by the new movements in social constructionist and discursive psychology.[25] This new psychological approach will be outlined. Afterwards, it will be possible to return to the topic of repression, in order to suggest how the skills necessary for repression might be contained in wider skills of language.

For social constructionists, language is primary. It does not merely provide labels attached to our perceptual impressions. Language permits us to enter into the life of culture. Nor is language merely to be conceived as a system of grammar. As the Russian thinker Mikhail Bakhtin and his *alter ego* Vološinov argued, language is based on the

---

[23] Plato (1948), 'The sophist', 263e. By tradition the Eleatic Stranger is thought to represent Zeno.

[24] As Wittgenstein claimed, it is wrong to distinguish between speech and action for 'words are deeds' (1992), p. 46e. See Cavell (1993) for a reinterpretation of Freud that specifically advocates a Wittgensteinian approach over a Cartesian one.

[25] For excellent outlines of the social construction project, see Gergen (1994a and 1994b); Harré (1987); Sampson (1993); Shotter (1993a and 1993b); Wertsch (1991); Michael (1996). For discursive and rhetorical psychology, see Antaki (1994); Billig (1991 and 1996); Edwards (1997); Edwards and Potter (1993); Harré and Gillett (1994); Parker (1992); Potter (1996); Potter and Wetherell (1987).

practical tasks of conversation.[26] The project for discursive psychology, then, is to examine how we use language in social life. In so doing, this psychology seeks to show how our thinking is constituted through language.

Every day, in conversation we hear and formulate utterances, which, in their detail, have never been made before. Linguistic creativity depends, above all, on the rhetorical skills of argumentation, most principally, on the practices of justification and criticism.[27] If speakers merely were to agree with one another, there would be little thinking within language. Our use of language would resemble the communication-systems of other species. The bee, who communicates to other bees where pollen might be, receives no disagreement from its audience. Bees cannot challenge communicators critically, forcing them to justify their statements. No bee can say 'You say there's pollen over to the west, but surely there's better pollen to the east.' Nor can the challenged bee reply in self-justification: 'No, the pollen to the east is not so flavoursome, as you imagine', and then open up a buzzing discussion about pollen, directions and flavour.

For all this, more is required than the bee can hope to provide. Only humans have the necessary skills.[28] A discussion, which pushes a dialogue into new directions, depends upon speakers' possessing the syntax of negation – they must be able to say 'no', as well as 'yes'. In addition, reasons must be given to justify the 'no' and to criticize the previous speaker's 'yes'. The ability to justify and criticize does not mean accessing a store of ready-made formulations. New utterances have to be spontaneously created for each new discursive situation, so that the justifications and criticisms fit the present context.[29]

In the continually creative activity of justification and criticism, we can hear the activity of thinking. As people discuss issues, even in banal,

[26] See, for example, Bakhtin (1986) and Vološinov (1973). For arguments suggesting that Bakhtin was the genuine author of Vološinov's book, *Marxism and the Philosophy of Language*, see Holquist (1990). For discussions of the ways that Bakhtinian ideas have been incorporated into constructivist psychologies, see, *inter alia*, Billig (1997); Shotter (1993b, especially chapter 6); Shotter and Billig (1998); Sampson (1993); Wertsch (1991).

[27] For the importance of justification and criticism, see Perelman and Olbrechts-Tyteca (1968); Billig (1991 and 1996); Antaki (1994).

[28] Chimpanzees can be taught the rudiments of sign language, but, even so, they appear unable to acquire the skills to handle negatives, justify and criticize, which are so necessary for human conversation (Edwards, 1997).

[29] Ethnomethodologists stress the extent to which utterances are indexical, or refer to the context in which they are uttered (Garfinkel, 1967; Heritage, 1984). As such, utterances are, in the words of conversation analysts, 'occasioned' (Edwards, 1997). Since occasions differ from one another, even in minute ways, then utterances have to be newly formulated for each occasion Billig (1991).

seemingly boring conversations, they are engaging in complex, co-ordinated creation.[30] Even those who like to ride verbal hobby-horses, pontificating on familiar subjects, will be producing novel utterances with subtle changes of emphasis, wording or intonation.[31] It is wrong to suppose that each utterance is only an outward sign of the thought processes, which must be occurring silently and internally within the speaker's head. In discussions, turn and counter-turn can occur too quickly to assume the spoken words to be merely the surface manifesta-tion of the 'real' thought, which has to be formulated before the utterance is made. Often we hear ourselves saying something in re-sponse, only discovering what our thoughts are as we speak. The thinking is not hidden, but is happening out there in the conversation.

If the Cartesian position has difficulty explaining how children might learn to think, the discursive position faces no such problem. From an early age, children hear conversations. By living in worlds filled with dialogue, they acquire the rhetorical skills to justify and criticize. In this, they learn how to participate in the collective thinking of conversation. Thus, they learn to think.

But what about silent thought? Surely not all thinking is to be located in the burble of dialogue. It might be suggested that *real* thinking goes on when everyone stops talking. However, it would be a mistake to overestimate the difference between the thinking, which occurs out-wardly in dialogue, and the thinking which occurs in isolated silence. As the Eleatic Stranger implied, thinking is an inner conversation: to use the phrase of the Russian psychologist Lev Vygotsky, it is 'internal speech'.[32] As was argued by Vološinov, who, according to some, was Bakhtin writing under a *nom de guerre*, inner speech resembles 'the alternating lines of a dialogue'.[33] In order to conduct such an inner dialogue, we must have first acquired the rhetorical skills to converse with others.[34]

We can imagine Le Penseur having an internal debate. Perhaps his voice of conscience is debating with his voice of desire. He wants to get off the rock to buy an ice-cream, but he tells himself, repeating the

---

[30] Conversation analysts, by examining the details of banal conversations, have shown the detailed richness of seemingly trivial remarks (e.g. Atkinson and Heritage, 1984; Drew, 1995; Nofsinger, 1991; Tannen, 1984).

[31] Billig (1991, chapter 8).

[32] Vygotsky (1978 and 1988); see also Wertsch (1991).

[33] Vološinov (1973), p. 38. Wittgenstein's position is similar. He, like the Eleatic stranger, suggested that inner conversation is based upon outward dialogue: 'the close relation-ship between "saying inwardly" and "saying" is manifested in the possibility of telling out loud what one said inwardly, and of an outward action's *accompanying* inward speech' (Wittgenstein, 1953, p. 220).

[34] Billig (1996).

words of his doctor, that he should cut down his fat-intake. 'But I worked hard this morning, I deserve a treat' says the internal voice of desire. 'But that would be weakness, which would threaten the whole diet' replies the critical voice of conscience. Round and round the voices go. Were there no debate, Le Penseur would already be on his way to the ice-cream parlour. The point is that Le Penseur, even if he is seated alone, is not abstracted from social life and the world of dialogue. Because Le Penseur is a member of the dialogic species, he is 'the thinker'. Chickens or guinea-pigs, seen at rest with downcast head, would not be recognized as thinkers.

A cognitive psychologist, at this point, might put in an objection. Surely, the dialogic perspective exaggerates the importance of language in thinking. Not all the contents of the human mind are language-based. Of course, this is true in a simple sense. As Freud recognized, we register visual and auditory perceptions in ways which are not dependent on language. Thus, we can recognize shapes and sounds; babies do this before they can speak. But if humans can recognize patterns and shapes without language, then so too can chickens and guinea-pigs. Experimental psychologists have historically paid enormous attention to skills, such as 'pattern recognition' or 'object perception', that humans share with other species. By contrast they have paid far less attention to the sort of uniquely human thinking that requires words: for instance, thinking about morality, politics, the course of our lives, the characters of others, what will happen tomorrow. All these matters are beyond the thinking capacity of wordless creatures. Not only can we think quietly about such issues, but we can, and regularly do, talk of them with others. As will be seen, such topics provide the sense of morality, from which the need to repress emerges.

Cognitive psychologists might attempt to translate human dialogue into models of auditory recognition and response. They might even use notions from Freud's metapsychology to do this. After Freud had suggested to Elisabeth that she was really in love with her brother-in-law, she became angry. She accused Freud of talking her into the suggestion – she could never have been capable of such wickedness. We could, then, ask how Elisabeth was able to access the precise words from her memory-store of words and, then, how the accessed words were articulated into audible sounds.

We might, then, believe that we would be on the trail of Elisabeth's thoughts. But we wouldn't be. Quite the contrary, we would be avoiding those thoughts, or rather we would be mistaking their locus. They did not exist within an internal schema or mental model; nor within the processes of the conscious ego. They were being produced in the developing conversation. No hypothetical mental model would compare with the depth, subtlety and intricacy of the utterances, breaking the silence in Dr Freud's consulting-room.

If we wanted to know what Elisabeth and Freud were thinking at that time, we would need to have listened to what they were saying, as justification and criticism followed each other in a tense, fraught spiral. Today, we can only reconstruct scraps of the dialogue from Freud's own account, which, of course, cannot be trusted as being either complete or impartial. Of one thing we can be sure. Freud and Elisabeth were saying things, which neither had ever previously said or heard. Both were on the edge of discovery. It is hard to think that the stationary head of Le Penseur was producing a more creative burst of thought than did that volatile dialogue when Elisabeth argued with her doctor.

Opening up and closing down dialogue

So far, one might be pardoned for supposing that the detour into discursive psychology has taken several decidedly anti-Freudian turns. It has been suggested that human thinking should not be considered in terms of hidden processes, but should be examined in relation to the outward skills of rhetoric. These skills are continually on display in conversation. This psychology does not appear to delve into the hidden psychological hinterland, which forms the basis of the Freudian vision. Quite the reverse, the person, as it were, has been turned inside-out: what was considered to be individual, internal and hidden is shown to be social, external and observable.[35]

Generally, it must be admitted that discursive psychologists are uncomfortable with the notion of consciousness. They prefer to talk about the structure of conversation, rather than the speakers' interior life.[36] Certainly, discursive psychologists do not explain conversational interventions in terms of the speakers' motives, let alone their inner

---

[35] The assumption of 'hearability' is crucial for conversation analysis. Instead of assuming that speakers have private understandings, conversation analysts assume that speakers' understanding of each other's turns are outwardly 'hearable' in the conversation (Antaki, 1994; Drew, 1995; Edwards, 1997; Potter and Edwards, 1990; Heritage, 1984). In this sense, the understanding is outwardly displayed in the transcript of the conversation, and analysts should recognize understanding from what has been audibly displayed as understanding.

[36] Conversation analysts avoid making motivational assumptions about speakers, often explicitly warning against deriving suppositions about speakers' internal states from the outward structure of talk (Drew, 1995). In practice, this means that conversation analysts, rather like behaviourists, seek to use an analytical language which avoids mentalistic concepts. For example, they write about speakers 'doing agreement' rather than 'wishing to agree' (for discussions of these issues, see Antaki, 1994; Edwards, 1997; Edwards and Potter, 1992).

egos. If consciousness is not a topic for discursive psychology, then unconsciousness is doubly out of bounds.[37] It is as if this psychology is declaring that there is no secret mental life: all can be heard, if one listens closely enough. Moreover, speakers know what they are doing: they do not have secrets hidden from themselves.[38]

The detour into discursive psychology seems to have taken us to a terrain, which is not only flatter than the Freudian hinterland, but which has a more cheerful, welcoming aspect than the gloomy crags and crevices of the psychoanalytic landscape.[39] Rhetorical skills enable us to open up topics, whether in social debate or in private conversation. Because we can do more than merely say 'yes', or express a preference for agreement, we can, and do, go forward dialogically.[40] Matters, which were unspoken and unthought, become objects of speech and, thereby, of thought. Thus, we have an image of people as Socratic debaters, pushing the limits of conversation back with their probing conversational gambits.[41] In this celebration of argumentative skills, there is no hint of Freudian cynicism to tell why people may not take advantage of their skills of intellectual exploration and why they may be crippled by secrets, which they dare not admit to themselves.

There is another side – a side, which tends to be ignored by psychologists who admire the creativity of argumentative rhetoric.[42] If we humans possess the rhetorical skills to open up matters for discussion, then so we are equipped with the abilities to close down matters discursively. For every rhetorical gambit to push debate forward, so there must be analogous rhetorical devices which permit discursive exploration to be curtailed. Routinely, we are able to change the subject, pushing conversations away from embarrassing or troubling topics.

We might assume that, for everything which is said, other things are

[37] See Billig (1997) for details about how conversation analysts appear to rule out Freudian explanations.

[38] Conversation analysts often assume that speakers are knowledgeable participants in dialogical and social life. For example Boden writes that conversation analysts assume that 'human beings are knowledgeable agents in the production (and reproduction) of their lives and their history' (p. 13). It is precisely this assumption that psychoanalytic theorists dispute.

[39] For more details, see Billig (1997).

[40] Foppa (1990) has called the creativity of dialogue as 'topic progression'. What this means is that dialogues do not stay constant, but develop topics.

[41] This image is particularly prevalent in rhetorical psychology, e.g. Billig (1991 and 1996).

[42] It is certainly ignored in my *Arguing and Thinking* (Billig, 1996). That book displays a theoretical one-sidedness, despite arguing for the necessity for psychological theory to be two-sided. The book, in its enthusiasm for argumentation, concentrates on the way that the rhetoric of argument opens up topics for thought. It does not consider how the same rhetoric might provide the means for avoiding argument, or for repressing matters from the agenda.

not being said. This is not to say that the other things are necessarily being hidden, nor that speakers are deliberately stopping themselves saying certain things. The point is simpler. No speaker can be making two utterances at once. Every utterance, which fills a moment of conversational space, is occupying a moment which might have been filled by an infinity of other utterances. These potential utterances will now never be said, at least in that specific context. As Roland Barthes wrote, 'the *said* must be torn from the *not-said*'.[43] Barthes might then have gone on to say that 'the said', having been uttered, creates the 'not-said' (or what in French, is referred to as *le non-dit*).

The idea of the 'unsaid' provides a clue about the rhetorical nature of repression. 'The said' and 'the unsaid' are intimately linked: to say one thing implies that other things are not being said. If language provides the rhetorical skills for opening up lines of talk, then it also provides the skills for creating the unsaid. More than this, language provides the means for closing down areas of talk. The opening up and closing down must proceed simultaneously, so that dialogic creativity and avoidance, far from being polar opposites, might be closely linked in practice.

From this, there is a short step which takes us back into Freudian terrain. When listening to certain dialogues we might entertain suspicions about the speakers' patterns of opening up and closing down topics. In particular, we might suspect that avoidances are occurring, as Freud suspected that Elisabeth was avoiding talking about her feelings towards her brother-in-law. Traces of the avoidance should be audible, even in long silences between uttered words. As the conversation seems to lurch towards a topic, which will disturb the speakers, so the speakers might steer around the unspoken obstacle, putting the dialogue safely back on course.

Analysts of conversation have shown how speakers use particular linguistic devices for opening up topics for discussion. Little words can be so important for the task. For instance, the speaker who wishes to disagree, but also to keep the conversation going, may be faced with a dilemma. Too forceful a disagreement may be heard as aggressive or rude and, in consequence, may threaten the continuation of the dialogue. On the other hand, too ready an agreement will fail to move the conversation to a discussion. Often speakers will resolve the dilemma by prefacing comments of disagreement with markers of agreement.[44] If one speaker feels the other has missed the point, they can use the

---

[43] Barthes (1982), p. 129, emphasis in original.
[44] See, for instance, Pomerantz (1984). See also Brown and Levinson (1987) for a discussion of the ways in which speakers may use 'indirect' ways of expressing disagreement or 'hedging' refusals to comply with requests.

rhetorical device of starting their critical reply with 'Yes, but . . .'[45] In this way, the speaker expresses agreement in order to dismiss the previous speaker's argument, thereby moving the point of conversation towards the topic, which the speaker claims to be the 'real' issue.

This rhetorical device simultaneously moves the discussion *towards* a particular topic, while redirecting the conversation *away* from another. This is not accidental, for a conversational move *towards* is simultaneously a conversational move *away from*. Conversation analysts have shown that speakers have conventional ways of signalling changes of topic. Typically they use a brief word or two as a 'discontinuity marker'.[46] 'Anyway' or 'but' can function in this way. Such markers alert conversationalists 'not to try to look for any connection between what they have just been talking about, and what he or she is about to say'.[47] Without the marker, listeners would assume that the present utterance is in some way connected with the previous one: the assumption of relevance has been called one of the basic maxims for conversation, which conversationalists tend to take for granted.[48] 'Yes, but . . .' can be used as a discontinuity marker. The previous speaker's remark is acknowledged by agreement ('yes'), and then the topic is redirected ('but, what about . . .').

Changing the topic of conversation is not necessarily a sign of repression, but further signs might be suggestive. An observer might suspect that the movement *away* is dominating the movement *toward*, especially if the speaker continually changes the subject when a particular topic is mentioned. The observer might surmise that the speaker is not fully aware of what they are doing, so that the avoidance appears automatic rather than deliberate. Perhaps, the speaker shows outward signs of resisting any invitations to talk on the avoided topic. And, maybe, what the speaker actually talks about betrays tell-tale signs of the topic they seem to be avoiding.

Freud suspected Elisabeth of such motivated, but not deliberate, avoidance. She constantly resisted opening up the matter of brother-in-law for discussion. Her pains would arrive at an opportune moment to break up the dialogic flow. Freud as the outsider began to suspect that Elisabeth was not fully aware of what she was doing. He entertained these suspicions because of what Elisabeth was saying. As such, her repression was not taking place behind the words, which Freud heard. It

---

[45] For details, see Billig (1991), especially pp. 177ff.
[46] See, for example, Drew (1995) and Schiffrin (1987).
[47] Drew (1995), p. 75 (see also Levinson, 1983; Schiffrin, 1987). Significantly, such markers are not used if the conversation has flagged and a speaker is breaking a silence by introducing a new topic (Bergmann, 1990).
[48] See Grice (1975) and also Sperber and Wilson (1986).

was being accomplished by these words. Also, her own conversational attention, and, thus her thoughts, were being directed by these shifts. Elisabeth, not her hidden ego, was doing all this. More generally, speakers' egos do not change topics and then deny doing so. Speakers themselves do this, by what they say and by what they leave unsaid.

Replacement and repression

At its simplest, repression might be considered as a form of changing the subject. It is a way of saying to oneself 'talk, or think, of this, not that'. One then becomes engrossed in 'this' topic, so 'that' topic becomes forgotten, as do the words one has said to oneself in order to produce the shift of topic. This forgetting is helped by the fact that the discontinuity markers are themselves small, eminently forgettable words.

It can be presumed that thinkers can only accomplish shifts in their 'inner speech' because they have been speakers, successfully accomplishing topic-shifts in dialogue. On the other hand, the shifting of topic need not be confined to the words that one says to oneself. Actual conversations with other speakers can be brought into play, so that the repression, rather than being confined to the inner dialogues of the isolated individual, is part of outward social life. Two rhetorical elements are required for successful shifting – whether in external or internal dialogue. First there are the small words of the discontinuity markers, which indicate that such shifting is occurring. The second requirement is another topic to move towards. 'Anyway' should not be followed by silence. A replacement topic is needed, if attention is to be shifted.[49]

This second requirement may seem so obvious that it is hardly worth stating. However, the necessity for replacement can be overlooked, especially if repression is seen as an internal process, which is aimed at driving away a particular thought. Sometimes Freud made this mistake, particularly when he discussed repression in terms of censorship. In 'Interpretation of dreams' Freud described how dreams were censored, so that disapproved thoughts were omitted or disguised. He claimed that 'this censorship acts exactly like the censorship of newspapers at the

---

[49] Freud and psychoanalytic theorists generally have talked of 'displacement' rather than replacement. The term 'displacement' invokes Freud's hydraulic model of mental energy. It suggests that the energy, which lay behind the thought to be repressed, is drawn off and used in the replacement thought. Because the present analysis seeks to dispense with the assumptions of Freud's hydraulic model the term 'displacement' will be avoided. On the other hand, the term 'displacement' suggests something important for a Freudian theory of repression: the replacement topic will in some non-obvious way be connected with the topic to be repressed. Thus, there will be a symbolic link between the replaced and the replacing thoughts.

Russian frontier, which allows foreign journals to fall into the hands of the readers whom it is its business to protect only after a quantity of passages have been blacked out'.[50] As the French psychoanalysts, Laplanche and Pontalis, have pointed out, Freud, in describing repression as a form of censorship, was doing more than use a metaphor: the 'literal sense' of censorship is 'present' in Freud's understanding of repression. This is why Freud said that repression functions 'exactly' like the censors of the Austro-Hungarian Emperor.[51]

Freud's analogy between repression and political censorship, nevertheless, breaks down. The Austro-Hungarian censors left black passages in those Russian papers which they permitted to cross the borders. In so doing, they betrayed their handiwork to the world. Successful repression, by contrast, covers its own traces.[52] There are no blanked spaces in conscious experience, or in the internal dialogues of inner speech. The mind does not switch itself off, like a radio being unplugged. Instead, other things must be thought about and, perhaps, the avoided thought comes to express itself subtly and indirectly in these substituted topics.

In this respect, mental censorship resembles the work of the modern, totalitarian censor, who uses more sophisticated methods than did the crude employees of the Austro-Hungarian emperor. The sophisticated censor replaces offending articles, thereby covering up the signs of censorship.[53] So it is with repression. Elisabeth, having driven away the thought of her brother-in-law being free to marry her, must find other things to occupy her attention. She cannot have a blanked out mind. She has aches and pains to preoccupy her and she can talk of these at length with other members of her family. When Freud brings up the uncomfortable topic of her loving the brother-in-law, then Elisabeth starts talking of her pains. Suffering pains in silence would not have been sufficient to distract Freud. She must outwardly display the pain, preferably in talk, thereby diverting the flow of the doctor's words.

Should the repression occur in an inner dialogue, then the thinker must follow up an inwardly spoken discontinuity marker with a

---

[50] 'Interpretation of dreams', *PFL* 4, pp. 676–7.

[51] Laplanche and Pontalis (1983), p. 66. See also Jacobus (1996) for a feminist analysis which applies Freud's metaphor of censorship to his case of 'homosexuality in a woman'.

[52] Actually Freud recognized this aspect of repression. In 'Analysis terminable and interminable', he claimed that repression, rather than acting as a censor merely deleting an offending passage, should put in its place a substitute passage that said exactly the opposite (*SE* 3, p. 236).

[53] Galasinski and Jaworski (1997), analysing the tactics of the official censors in communist Poland, comment that 'the censor is not only in a position of a gatekeeper of some information, she or he is also a gatekeeper of the very fact of gatekeeping' (p. 354).

replacement topic of thought. It would a mistake to think that 'real' repression is internal, or even that there is a sharp distinction between internal mental life and external social life. The topic, which is used as a replacement, need not be confined to the interior dialogue: it can become part of an external conversation. Repression stands a better chance of success if it involves outer dialogue. That way, other people can be enrolled into its accomplishment. It is even better still if the repression becomes sedimented into habits of life, so that repression becomes a repeated, habitual dialogic activity. How this might occur will be illustrated by one of Freud's most well-known cases.

The case of the so-called 'Rat Man'

In 1909 Freud wrote his paper 'Notes upon a Case of Obsessional Neurosis', which described the case of the patient, who was to become known in psychoanalytic circles as 'the Rat Man'. Psychoanalysts have long recognized the importance of the case. It has been variously described as 'a classic of psychoanalysis',[54] 'one of Freud's most taught and written about cases',[55] and a case that is 'known to every analyst'.[56] The patient was a twenty-nine year old lawyer and army reservist. The patient started having regular sessions with Freud in October 1907, and the treatment continued for over a year.[57] Patrick Mahony in his book *Freud and the Rat Man* has revealed the real name of the patient – Ernst Lanzer.[58]

The case was particularly important in the development of Freud's ideas about obsession. Freud believed that obsessives show the content of their minds more clearly than other types of neurotic. As he wrote in 'Notes', unconscious mental processes, in the case of obsessional neurosis, break through into consciousness 'in their pure and undistorted form'.[59] For present purposes, the case can be used to illustrate two points. First, Freud shows the extent to which the patient's thinking took the form of internal dialogues. If the patient's conscious obsessions reflect unconscious mental processes in their pure and undistorted

---

[54] Weiss (1980), p. 203.

[55] Kiersky and Fosshage (1990), p. 107.

[56] Lipton (1992), p. 1182.

[57] Mahony (1986) points out that it is difficult to estimate exactly how long the treatment continued, for Freud, in his published report, seems to have exaggerated the length of the treatment and possibly the success of the outcome (see also, Sulloway, 1992).

[58] Ibid.

[59] 'Notes upon a case of obsessional neurosis', *SE* 10, p. 228. References to the case are taken from the Standard Edition, rather than the Penguin Freud Library, because the latter does not include Strachey's version of the 'process notes'. References to the full text of the process notes, published by Elza Hawelka, are given as 'Hawelka (1974)'.

form, then the latter may not be quite as non-verbal as Freud's metapsychology assumed. Second, Freud described the strategies, which the patient used to control his inner voices. Often, these were rhetorical strategies.

For Freudian scholars, the case is special for another reason. It is the only one for which Freud's 'process notes' have survived. Freud was in the habit of writing notes in the evenings about his day-time sessions with patients. Freud usually destroyed the notes after each case had been completed or when he had finally written up any published report. For reasons which have not been established, he failed to destroy the first part of his notes for Ernst Lanzer's case. Most of the notes were first published in 1954, in the Standard Edition of Freud's works.[60] James Strachey, who edited and translated the Standard Edition, omitted the first seven proper sessions, while including the introductory meeting. He justified the omission on the grounds that those parts had been 'reproduced by Freud almost *verbatim* in the published version'.[61] As will be seen, the justification does not altogether hold up. For twenty years Strachey's English translation of the abbreviated notes was the only published version; the notes were not included in the German edition of the *Gesammelte Werke*. In 1974, the notes were published in full, in an edition that gave the original German text alongside a French translation.[62]

Freud seems to have written the process notes as a personal *aide-mémoire*, drawing upon them heavily when he came to compose the official report in the summer of 1909, several months after the treatment must have finished. As Strachey pointed out, much of the case report is heavily based, often almost word for word, on early sections of the process notes. Freud's note-taking in the case of Lanzer was therefore simultaneously a means of remembering and a preparation for telling the public story. The published report, however, shows crucial changes and omissions from the notes.[63] These differences give hints as to Freud's working methods, showing how he was developing his interpretation of the case.

One word of caution must be sounded. The notes cannot be accepted as a true record of the therapeutic sessions. Some of Freud's admirers

---

[60] The Standard Edition of the Collected Works contains the notes for the preliminary session on 1 October 1907. It then omits the first seven proper sessions, recording the eighth session (10 October). The record continues until 20 January 1908.

[61] Strachey (1955), p. 254.

[62] Hawelka (1974); Hawelka's edition includes excellent editorial notes.

[63] Hawelka (1974) in the editorial notes accompanying the full text usefully points out the divergences between the published case history and the original notes. Mahony (1986) has provided careful and insightful analyses of some of these divergences.

have praised his phenomenal memory, and he himself occasionally called it 'phonographic'.[64] It was easier to have a reputation for 'phonographic' memory before the days of tape-recorders. Nowadays, when the precise details of verbal recall can be checked, few people would be bold enough to claim phonographic recall. Psychological studies have shown that claims to remember verbatim typically involve small changes of words, especially the grammatical tidying up of reported speech.[65] Freud's process notes, although mostly written on the very day of the treatment session, are not verbatim records of what was said between doctor and patient. Even while he was listening to the patient, Freud was selecting some matters to remember and some to forget, always interpreting as he did so. It is simply not the case, as Lacan has suggested, that the first seven sessions 'are reported to us in full'.[66] Quite apart from anything else, it only takes five minutes to read aloud the longest of Freud's reports of these fifty-minute sessions.[67] Thus, the bulk of the dialogue must be treated as being lost. What remains, even in the process notes, is always a summary, designed to illustrate the story that Freud was in the process of constructing.[68] That story reveals Freud's state of mind, even more than it does that of his patient.

Anyone writing today about the case is faced with an immediate problem: what to call the patient? Freud did not use the term the 'Rat Man' in his writings. In the case history, he invented a pseudonym, but he scarcely used it.[69] The patient is called 'Lieutenant H', and his first name is given as 'Paul'.[70] Strachey, in translating the process notes,

---

[64] 'New introductory lectures', *PFL* 2, p. 33 (see also Mahony, 1986, p. 139).

[65] These issues are discussed at length in Edwards (1997).

[66] Lacan (1977), p. 78. Lacan's comment can be treated as symptomatic of his approach which promises to accord centrality to the role of language but which consistently avoids analysing the details of speech. The same duality can be seen in the work of those influenced by Lacan. For example Blades (1989), analysing the case of 'the Rat Man', claims 'that language itself must be taken as the subject of inquiry' (p. 102), but does not raise issues about the details of the dialogue between Freud and the patient, nor does she refer to the detailed differences between the process notes and the case history. In her account, Hawelka's edition of the process notes is ignored.

[67] Lipton (1992) points this out.

[68] Freud played down the problems of recording the conversations of the consulting-room. In the case of Dora, he claimed that he was 'writing from memory after the treatment was at an end'. However, the details were still fresh in his mind and 'thus, the record is not absolutely – phonographically – exact, but it can claim to possess a high degree of trustworthiness', 'Dora', *PFL* 8, p. 38.

[69] Freud in the course of his career showed a growing reluctance to invent pseudonyms for his patients, preferring to leave them anonymous. The earlier reports, such as those in the 'Studies on Hysteria' employ pseudonyms freely, as do the reports of 'Dora' and 'Little Hans'. Freud's growing reluctance to invent pseudonyms is seen in later reports such as those of the so-called 'Wolf man' and the 'Case of homosexuality in a woman'. The patients are left completely unnamed.

[70] 'Bemerkungen über einen Fall von Zwangsneurose', *GW* 7, p. 398 (*SE*, p. 174).

offers 'Lorenz' as the pseudonym for the patient's family name; for the sake of consistency, he alters the reference to Lieutenant H to 'Lieutenant L' in the case history.[71] Hawelka, in his edition of the process notes, changes the real family name in the original manuscript to 'Lehrs', while keeping Ernst as the first name. Consequently, there are a variety of names – pseudonymous or real – that could be used for the patient. If we wished to be formal, he could be either 'Lieutenant' or 'Dr' Lehrs/Lanzer/Lorenz/H/L.

Then, there is the sobriquet by which the patient has become famous, but which Freud did not use in his writings. The nickname, however, is best avoided. As will be seen, the term 'Rat Man' says as much about psychoanalysts' interest in the case, as it does about the patient's own obsessions. From the start, analysts, including Freud, have been obsessed by the rats, whereas the patient's outward preoccupations were elsewhere. The nickname itself, as will be seen, conveys an interpretation of the case, which has become sedimented into psychoanalytic folklore.

If the nickname will not do, then there is still the problem of choosing between real name and pseudonym. And if, following psychoanalytic tradition, a pseudonym is selected, then which pseudonym should it be? To be consistent with the case of Elisabeth, the pseudonym in the Standard Edition will be used here. So Ernest Lanzer will be 'Paul Lorenz'. To prevent him acquiring greater status than Elisabeth, whose role as an early patient in constructing psychoanalytic theory should not be underestimated, he will, for the most part, be plain 'Paul', rather than 'Dr' or 'Lieutenant Lorenz'.[72]

Obsessions, inner voices and dialogue

Freud described Paul as a youngish man. In the course of the treatment, Paul turned thirty, and, thus, reached the age at which Freud had married Martha. But Paul was far from acquiring the settled career and domestic responsibility that Freud had at an equivalent age. Paul had only just passed his examinations to become a lawyer, his studies having been delayed by his mental condition. He was clearly a disturbed man, beset by inner voices which commanded him to do various bizarre things and which threatened dire consequences if they were not obeyed. He lived in fear lest failure to obey his inner compulsions would result in harm to those he loved. In particular, he feared that a 'young lady',

[71] 'Notes upon a case of obsessional neurosis', *SE*, p. 172.
[72] On the creative role of Freud's early patients, especially women patients, see Appignanesi and Forrester (1993).

whose identity he was initially reluctant to reveal to Freud, would suffer for his failures to comply precisely with the commands. Paul also expressed fears for his father, whom Freud was surprised to discover had been dead for several years.

Paul's obsessions came to him in the form of inner conversations. For example, there was an episode when his young lady went to nurse her sick grandmother while Paul was in the middle of studying for his law exams.[73] He suddenly received the inner command to cut his own throat. As he hurried to the cupboard to fetch his razor, he had the countervailing sanction that he must first go and kill the grandmother. He told Freud that he fell to the ground in horror.

Freud's interpretation also took the form of reconstructing an internal dialogue between different voices. He suggested that the outburst expressed the patient's annoyance with the old lady for causing his beloved to be absent. Freud wrote that there came over him something 'which, if he had been a normal man, would probably have been some kind of feeling of annoyance with her grandmother: "Why must the old woman get ill just at the very moment when I'm longing for *her* so frightfully?"'[74] Freud thus portrays the feelings, not as an internal state beyond words, but as a verbal complaint. In the case of Paul, the 'normal' annoyance was jacked up to a murderous intensity. This feeling was, according Freud's interpretation, immediately followed by the command: 'Kill yourself as a punishment for these savage and murderous passions!'[75] Initially these thoughts were unconscious, in Freud's view, but as they passed into consciousness, their order was reversed with 'the punitive command coming first, and the mention of the guilty outburst coming afterwards'.[76] It should be noted how easily Freud slips into describing these apparently unconscious thoughts in terms of an inner dialogue. In fact, it is hard to see how Paul could have entertained such precise thoughts, whether consciously or unconsciously, without words.

Paul told Freud about the strategies that he developed to cope with his inner voices. He formulated a number of techniques, which were essentially rhetorical. One such 'defensive formula' was 'a rapidly

---

[73] 'Notes upon a case of obsessional neurosis', *SE* 10, pp. 187f.
[74] 'Notes upon a case of obsessional neurosis', p. 187, emphasis in original.
[75] Ibid., p. 188.
[76] Ibid. Freud's interpretation suggested that, in the 'normal' person's internal argument, the last word would have gone to the voice of guilt, which would have silenced the aggressive wish. In this respect, it was not only the intensity of the anger which differentiated the 'normal' from the obsessive; it was also the failure of the repressing argument. In the case of the obsessive, the voice of restraint, not having the last word, remains unanswered.

pronounced *"aber"* ('but') accompanied by a gesture of repudiation'.[77] He attempted to use this formula of dismissal in the dramatic episode, which was to form the core of the case and which gave rise to the patient's psychoanalytic nickname.

Paul told Freud a complicated story about events on a recent army manoeuvre. He had lost a pair of pince-nez and had gone to a post-office to telegraph for a replacement. The new pair had promptly arrived and had been collected by a fellow officer, who had paid the necessary charges at the post office. Later that evening Paul had been talking to two fellow officers, one of whom was his commanding Captain. By all accounts the Captain delighted in telling stories about cruelty. On that particular occasion, he told of a particular torture, apparently practised in the far East. It involved strapping a pot filled with rats onto a victim's anus. Paul, as Freud reported, had great difficulty in finishing the story. He became so upset in the telling of it, that Freud had to coax him gently to complete that tale and describe the punishment.

Paul told Freud what he had felt when he had originally heard the Captain's story: 'at that moment the idea flashed through my mind *that this was happening to a person who was very dear to me'*.[78] Freud suspected, not least by the expression on his face, that the expressed fear concealed an unexpressed wish. As often happened, Paul's fear was followed by a command, or 'sanction', which he needed to fulfil in order to prevent the fear (or suspected wish) from being realized. He attempted to dismiss both the fear and sanction by his usual formula. Almost out loud, he repeated 'but' with the gesture of repudiation, adding, for good measure the phrase 'whatever are you thinking of?'.[79] Freud reports that the defensive formula was successful, at least for a brief while. At this point, the process notes and the case history differ in their account of the defensive formula. The differences are slight, in that they hinge on the interpretation of the word 'both' (*beider*); but nevertheless they are revealing.

The process notes mention the fear and the command; then they mention Paul's defences which worked successfully against *both* for a while. In the context, 'both' refers to the fear and the sanctions which are said to have occurred simultaneously (*gleichzeitig*).[80] In this way, the process notes indicate the temporary success of the defensive formula in driving away *both* the fear that the rat torture was happening to the loved

[77] 'Notes upon a case of obsessional neurosis', *SE* 10, p. 224 (see also, p. 294).
[78] Ibid., p. 167, emphasis in original.
[79] 'Notes upon a case of obsessional neurosis', *SE* 10, p. 167.
[80] Hawelka (1974), p. 46 (the page numbers refer to those for Hawelka's edition as a whole, not those which he specifically ascribes to Freud's text).

one *and* the command which had to be performed to prevent the fear from being realized. The process notes also record Paul 'did not mention what the sanctions were that came to him at the same time'[81] The absence of any more information also suggests that Freud did not ask him about the sanctions.

The wording of the case history not only differs but it also contains a crucial addition. The case history mentions the ideas, which came into Paul's head and also the defensive formulae. Freud comments that 'he had just succeeded in warding off *both* of them'.[82] At this point, Freud added a passage, which is not in the process notes. He states that 'this "both" took me aback, and it has no doubt also mystified the reader', because up to this point 'we have heard only of the rat punishment being carried out on the lady'.[83] Freud recounts that he questioned Paul who was then forced to admit of a second idea – namely, 'the idea of the punishment also being applied to his father'.[84] The process notes contain no mention either of this question and answer, nor of Freud being taken aback by 'both'.

The difference between the texts is perplexing and indicative. We can imagine Freud, late in the evening at his desk, going over his process notes, as he writes up the case history. Now he is convinced of the central role of Paul's relations with his dead father, something he was unsure about in the early sessions. As he rereads his notes after a year, he is taken aback by 'both'. It must refer to the father, he thinks. He searches his memory, trying to recall the original scene. He reconstructs his questioning Paul and the latter's reply – something that had not seemed significant in the evening when he wrote the original notes. As he thinks back, so Freud trusts his recollections as being almost phonographic. Then, as he comes to write his final draft, Freud carelessly transposes his feeling of being taken aback from the time when he re-read his notes to the original session.

Naturally, there is no way of verifying this account – or, indeed, whether Freud's questioning about the meaning of 'both' and Paul's answering actually occurred or whether Freud imagined it later. The issue, however, is not one of accuracy, as if the original events can be

---

[81] Ibid.
[82] 'Notes upon a case of obsessional neurosis', *SE* 10, p. 167.
[83] Ibid. Actually, Strachey alters the word order to emphasize that Freud was expressing surprise at the 'both', which appears in the previous sentence. In Strachey's translation, not only is 'both' brought towards the end of that previous sentence, but it is repeated in the next sentence. The original German has Freud being stopped in his tracks by the plural, rather than specifically by 'both' ('*Der Plural machte mich stutzig*', ('Bemerkungen', *GW*, p. 392). There seems little doubt that Strachey, by altering the word order, was elucidating the meaning of the original text.
[84] 'Notes upon a case of obsessional neurosis', *SE* 10, p. 167.

now be determined. Nor need the issue be whether the case history has distorted original events, which are better presented in the process notes. Above all, what matters is the account, which Freud gives in the published case history. He is directing the reader's attention to the story of rats. 'Both' now refers exclusively to that story. The attention is taken away from the countervailing sanction. The case history glosses over Freud's ignorance of the sanction – as well as his failure to question Paul on the point. The text conveys, but does not state, that these are unimportant matters. The reader is to be 'mystified' by the story of the rats. In this way, the case history directs attention *towards* the supposed cause of the repression, and *away* from other aspects, which include the actions of repression and Freud's comparative lack of interest in these actions.

'But' may have been temporarily effective as a defensive formula, but the idea of the rat torture was not easily dismissed from Paul's mind. The rhetorically repressed thought returns with a vengeance. That evening, the captain had told Paul that he needed to repay 3.80 kronen (a comparatively small sum) to Lieutenant A, who had paid the post office for the cost of the pince nez. Back come the obsessions: unless he pays the sum, then his loved one(s) would suffer the awful punishment. Then things start to go seriously awry.

It turns out that Lieutenant A had not paid the sum in question. It was another lieutenant, who had paid the 3.80 kronen (or maybe it was the woman who worked in the post office). Paul faces a dilemma. He feels that the Captain's command must be fulfilled to the letter: he must personally pay Lieutenant A, who, then, must give the money to Lieutenant B, to whom the sum is really owed (or perhaps B should hand the money over to the woman in the post office). Paul starts devising frantic schemes, involving railway journeys, the post-office assistant and the two Lieutenants. Even Freud can't quite follow the plans. One can only guess the surprise of the two Lieutenants had they been asked to break their respective journeys in order to return with Paul to the post office in order to execute a complex passing of 3.80 kronen from one to another.

Paul's strategy of uttering 'but' to himself has not been successful, except for the brief moment after the telling of the story. As soon as he sees the story-teller again, he is haunted by fears and commands. In fact, his defensive formulae generally seem to be unsuccessful. Paul subtly changes them – something he would be unlikely to do were they largely successful. Freud recounts that, during the course of treatment, the patient started accentuating the second syllable of *aber*, making it sound like *abwehr* (defence) 'a term which he had learned in the course of our theoretical discussions of psychoanalysis'.[85] His defence strategy involves an inner dialogue. He speaks sharply to himself, even gesturing to himself. He even calls out 'defence', but the word fails to provide one.

It is not difficult to see why the formula should be ineffective. In terms of his inner dialogue, it provides the rhetoric for a shift of topic. He is saying to himself 'stop thinking of these things'. He uses 'but' as if it were a 'discontinuity marker', which is about to introduce a shift of topic. But all he does is to indicate discontinuity – to signal a dialogical move *away* without a replacement topic to move *towards*. He even scolds himself for his thoughts. 'What are you thinking of?' he says in a way which does not invite reply. He merely leaves a blank in his inner conversation.

Freud reports that, on other occasions, Paul also tried to drive away troubling thoughts by devising prayers to say to himself. Again, this tactic was unsuccessful. As soon as he stopped reciting his prayers, the offending thought would appear, even turning the positive prayer into its opposite. For instance, if he said 'May God protect him', then a final 'not' would insinuate itself, after the formula had been uttered. As Freud comments, 'his original intention, which had been repressed by his praying, was forcing its way through in this last idea of his'.[86]

At best, these formulae only accomplish repression for little more than the moment in which they are being uttered. They provide no shift of thought or attention. Moreover, the unfortunate Paul would find himself desperately repeating the formula, in order to prevent the thoughts returning the very moment he ceased his self-directed utterance. By themselves the formulae failed to provide the self-distraction, which is so necessary for the successful accomplishment of repression.

Conversations and distractions

Paul may not have successfully driven away his disturbing thoughts by his use of 'but'. Nevertheless, some of the thoughts, which the 'but' was attempting to repress, may themselves have offered a more successful example of repression. After hearing the rat story, Paul sought to push the fear and the sanction from his mind. Yet, the sanction, when translated into the project to repay Lieutenant A, becomes, at least for a while, a means of repression. It totally absorbs the young man's energies and thoughts. As he becomes preoccupied with his schemes, so his mind is distracted from all thoughts of rats.

Dialogues were central to the schemes. Paul becomes involved in

[85] Ibid., p. 225 (see also p. 294).   [86] Ibid., p. 193.

some pretty odd conversations with his fellow officers. He needed to speak to the various lieutenants, in order to persuade them to come to the post office. There were also his internal dialogues, as Paul turned scheme after scheme around in his thoughts. He tells Freud about his anguished inner debates. Having found out that he did not owe the sum of money to Lieutenant A, he argued with himself whether he still needed to fulfil the captain's command to repay A. Just before the end of the army manoeuvres, he spent a terrible night in turmoil. Was his vow to repay Lieutenant A cancelled, now that he knew that he no longer owed the money to A? 'Arguments and counter-arguments had struggled with one another', reported Freud.[87]

The following day was his final opportunity to pay A. To do this, he would have to co-ordinate a series of complex railway journeys, as well as persuading A to accompany him to the post office, which was three hours journey away from the place where they were quartered. Again, there was an internal debate. Should he approach A? Would he make a fool of himself if he did so? On the other hand, was he being cowardly by trying to avoid 'the unpleasantness of asking A. to make the sacrifice in question and of cutting a foolish figure before him'?[88]

The schemes, in one sense, are a success in that they take his mind off the image of the rats. Their success, however, is brittle. The thoughts, which ostensibly he wishes to drive from conscious awareness, are never far from the schemes. In fact, he does the very thing to ensure that he has to talk of the rats: he consults Dr Freud.

On one level, the visit to Freud fits with Paul's schemes. Paul says that he only consulted Freud because he wanted a medical certificate which would explain that his mental health would be seriously affected unless Lieutenant A accepts the sum of 3.80 kronen. He would show the certificate to A, who would be sufficiently impressed that he would accept the money. Freud firmly told Paul that he has no intention of being used in this way.

On another level, Paul must have known that he would have to tell Freud about the rats, in order to obtain the certificate. He was not ignorant of Freud's type of treatment. He had read an extract from Freud's theory of dreams and also 'The psychopathology of everyday life', which he said reminded him of his own turn of thoughts.[89] In fact,

---

[87] Ibid., p. 170.   [88] Ibid., p. 171.

[89] Again, the process notes differ from the case history. In the latter, Freud downplays what the patient had known about psychoanalysis: 'he had read none of my writings, except that a short time before he had been turning over the pages of one of my books and had come across the explanation of some curious verbal associations which had so reminded him of some of his own "efforts of thought" in connection with his ideas that he had decided to put himself in my hands' (*SE* 10, pp. 158–59). Freud delicately

he knew enough to talk spontaneously during the first session about his sexual experiences. Freud records that Paul himself began the second session by announcing that he would speak of 'the experience which was the immediate occasion of my coming to you'.[90] He then proceeds to tell about the manoeuvres, the pince-nez and then the Captain's story. By coming to Freud, Paul is ensuring that he will recount the thoughts, which apparently he is trying to hide from himself.

There is a further reason why the repression is on the verge of collapse, even as it seems to be succeeding in distracting the young man. The distraction is only possible because the schemes are fiercely difficult to operate. Had it all been simpler and had Paul repaid the money immediately to Lieutenant A, he would be back with time on his hands to brood about his fears. The scheme is only able to overwhelm his thoughts, because it cuts across ordinary social conventions. As Paul is well aware, he is making a fool of himself in front of his fellow officers. He is trying to enrol them into something which is absurd. The more preoccupied Paul becomes, the odder he appears. And he knows this. A friend, with whom he stays after the army manoeuvres, tells him that he needs help. And so he comes to Dr Freud, telling himself that all he seeks is a certificate.

The failure of Paul's schemes offers clues about the conduct of more successful repression. Others can be enrolled in the replacing activity, so that those attempting repression are not left alone with their thoughts. Moreover, the chances of success are greater if the activity is neither quickly completed nor at variance with social customs. What Paul required was something to take his mind off the disturbing thoughts – an activity which would be bolstered by the support of others and embedded in accepted social customs. His own prayers, which he had devised and would repeat on his own, offered little defence. But had he thrown himself into the rituals of an organized religion, with regular shared prayer sessions, time-consuming rituals and religious leaders warning against the sinfulness of errant thoughts, he might have been provided with routine activity and support for his distraction.

Certainly Freud thought that there was little psychological difference between the rituals of neurotic obsessions and those of organized

conveys the impression that the patient had little knowledge of psychoanalysis (he has not read the book, only turned its pages) but just enough to have chosen to come to Freud. The process notes specify which book the patient had seen – *The Psychopathology of Everyday Life* (Hawelka, 1974, p. 63). Freud in the notes also mentions that, in the second session, the patient 'praises me discretely and mentions that he had read an extract from my theory of dreams' (Hawelka, 1974, p. 53). This sentence did not find its way into the published case history.

[90] 'Notes upon a case of obsessional neurosis', *SE* 10, p. 165.

religion. He elaborated the parallel in an essay, 'Obsessive actions and religious practices', published in the year in which he began seeing Paul. In that essay, Freud claimed that the personal obsessions of neurotics and the communal rituals of religion owed their origins to similar psychological roots. Although the former were of a 'private nature' as compared with 'the public and communal character of religious observances', there was an inner psychological similarity: both start as defensive actions to renounce impulses.[91] The origins are forgotten, as the business of conducting the rituals takes over. In consequence, as Freud argued, 'it cannot be denied that in the religious field as well there is a tendency to a displacement of psychical values, and in the same direction, so that the petty ceremonials of religious practice gradually become the essential thing and push aside the underlying thoughts'.[92] In both cases, thus, ritual becomes a means of repressing: the more absorbing the ritual, then the more successful is the repression.

What this means is that repression is not confined to the head of the solitary individual but can be collectively accomplished in shared behaviour. The rituals of religion may not be unique in this respect, but other shared practices could be sites for the accomplishment of repression. The habits of conversation are a case in point. What is customarily said may also routinely create the unsaid, and, thus, may provide ways for accomplishing repression. For the present, a general point can be stressed: language, or rather dialogue, provides the means of repression. Because we possess the little words to effect shifts of topic, we can move dialogues, including our inner conversations, from awkward to safer matters. We can say 'but . . .' or 'anyway . . .' to ourselves, just as we can utter those words to fellow conversationalists.

There is no reason to suppose that the discourses of psychoanalysis are uniquely free from gaps and avoidances. The exposure of repression is accomplished through dialogue. And this dialogue must create its own unsaid matters. As Freud points in one direction – telling his readers to 'look over here' – so he is silent on other matters. The direction, in which the psychoanalytic story of Paul points, is towards the rats. As Freud wrote, 'the rat-story becomes more and more a nodal point'.[93] While Paul was still being treated, Freud spoke of the case at the first International Conference of Psychoanalysis, held in April 1908 at Salzburg. He kept his audience in rapt attention for over four hours. Shortly after the talk, psychoanalysts began referring to Paul as 'the Rat

---

[91] 'Obsessive actions and religious practices', *PFL* 13, p. 33.
[92] Ibid., p. 40.
[93] 'Notes upon a case of obsessional neurosis' *SE* 10, p. 292.

Man'.[94] Later psychoanalysts, as they reinterpret the case, continue to give the rats pride of place, even quoting in full the Captain's story, as retold by Freud.[95] One Lacanian theorist has commented that the story of the pince-nez 'pales into insignificance beside the highly charged story of the rat torture'.[96] Thus, psychoanalysts readily tell the story, which the young man could hardly bring himself to finish.

Every time Paul is called 'the Rat Man', so there is more pointing, routinely and unwittingly accomplished. One might imagine what nickname Paul's fellow officers would have devised. Given how absurd his behaviour was becoming, the young man might easily have become known as 'the Pince-Nez Man'. If there were to be a 'Rat Man' in these circles, it would have to be the Captain. For the officers, as they gossiped about the bizarre antics of Paul, and as they smirked behind his back, the rat story must have paled into insignificance beside the saga of the pince-nez.

One can ask whether Freud and later psychoanalysts, in pointing towards the rats, are also unwittingly pointing away from other topics. Are there matters which even the great exposer of repression is avoiding as he exposes? The gaps between the process notes and the published case history are suggestive, as Freud covers his traces about what he might have forgotten to inquire about, or as he stretches the evidence around the theory a little bit more completely.

There are other curious gaps in his report about Paul. Most notably, Freud had just published his essay comparing religion with obsessional neurosis. Yet, in the case history, he does not quote this essay. Nor does he refer readers to consult the essay, should they be interested in the parallels. The failure to refer to the essay would be understandable if religious rituals were irrelevant to Paul's obsessions. But clearly they were important. Paul uses prayers as a means of repression. The case history's brief references do not hold together. Freud reports that Paul was 'devoutly religious' until he was fourteen or fifteen, before he 'developed into the free-thinker that he was today'.[97] However, when Freud describes how Paul formulates his prayers to ward off the inner voices he refers to the 'revival of his piety'.[98] He hardly appears as the free-thinker of Freud's earlier description.

---

[94] Mahony (1986), p. 18. Ernest Jones describes Freud's talk and its reception in his biography (see Jones, 1955, p. 47).

[95] See, for instance, Shengold (1980) and Kiersky and Fosshage (1990). Mahony (1986) quotes in detail from the pornographic novel from which the Captain is likely to have taken the torture story (p. 13).

[96] Schneiderman (1993) p. 45.

[97] 'Notes upon a case of obsessional neurosis', SE, p. 169.

[98] Ibid., p. 193.

Freud glosses over the religious issue: we are told nothing about Paul's devoutly religious period, despite the importance of childhood in Freud's general theorizing and in his interpretation of Paul's obsessions. The process notes record that Freud and Paul had talked about the infantile element in religion. Paul had told him how, as a child, he had taken pleasure in Bible stories, although the punishments meted out to the various characters had appeared obsessive.[99] This exchange comes in one of the early sessions, where the process notes appear almost verbatim in the published report. It is omitted from the case-history. This cannot be a chance omission: it is a careful excision. Later, in the process notes, Paul describes an incident in 1903, when he must have been twenty-five: he goes to a church and falls to his knees in a state of religious piety.[100] This reference, too, fails to make the journey from the private process notes to the conscious attention of the public readership.

It is as if the religious element is being skirted around. 'Obsessive Actions and Religious Practices' also has delicate gaps. Freud stresses how religious ritual can be obsessive, but he forebears to detail the obvious example: the practices of orthodox Judaism, which had irritated him since he was an adolescent. The published case history of Paul removes those give-away signs in the process notes, that would have enabled readers to recognize Paul's Jewish background. After Paul tells of the incident in the church, it appears that Freud had asked him about converting to Christianity and whether his father would have objected – something Paul specifically denied.[101] None of this was included in the case history. Freud does not discuss how Paul's self-made prayers might be related to his earlier religious devotions, and whether these latter practices had involved Jewish rituals.[102] The links were all there, should Freud have shown his customary keenness to make connections. It would have been simple to argue that Jewish religious culture had left its imprint on Paul. The inner commandment – to repay Lieutenant A – is interpreted literally, as if it were a Talmudic injunction based on a strict interpretation of the letter of the law.

But Freud pursues none of this. Always, we, as readers, are being directed to look elsewhere, towards the rats.[103] Yet, as will be argued in

[99] Hawelka (1974), p. 53.
[100] 'Notes upon a case of obsessional neurosis', *SE*, p. 301.
[101] Ibid., p. 302.
[102] Weiss (1980) points out that Paul's prayers seem to be a mockery of Jewish prayers; Weiss also comments on the case history omitting the Jewish references in the process notes.
[103] Mahony (1986) points out that Freud fails to discuss the Jewish themes contained in the symbolism of rats; Freud does not examine connections with the German word *raten*, which was associated with paying in instalments – Jews in Vienna were being popularly linked with this method of payment (p. 96).

chapter 8, in regard to the case of Dora rather than that of Paul, there is evidence that Freud's pointing towards the inner life of his patients was accompanied by a shared avoidance of looking too closely at the precarious position of Jews in Vienna. Certainly, he did not want his psychology to be dismissed as being merely a 'Jewish psychology', with all the contempt that would have implied in the Austro-Hungary of those times.

The avoidances do not undermine Freud's originality. They may even have been necessary if Freud were to point to aspects of mental life which others overlooked. Freud, in forming his growing group of sympathizers into the professional organization of psychoanalysis, was devising new habits of interpretation. These habits continue to this day. Subsequent analysts have also looked through the pince-nez to notice the rats. The routine labelling of the patient as 'the Rat Man' is part of the interpretative habit, diminishing Paul's humanity as it elevates psychoanalytic explanation. The attention is to be drawn to the supposed causes and consequences of repression. The means of the repression seem insignificantly paler when compared with the vivid stories of instincts, neuroses and torture. But the little words, which are so easily forgotten, but which are so crucial for changing the topic of speech, should be heard to play their necessary part in the stories of repression.

4   Language, politeness and desire

When Paul, the so-called 'Rat Man', was uttering his defensive formulae to himself, hoping to ward off his inner voices, he was demonstrating the links between language and repression. There are two ways of looking at such links. In the first place, the links might be considered to be rather loose. Language, it might be thought, provides a means for accomplishing repression. But what is to be repressed exists outside language. This would certainly fit in well with Freud's vision of the battle between the id and the ego, between biology and civilization. Accordingly, the 'civilized' person uses language in the constant battle to keep at bay the biological desires, which stand outside, and which threaten to topple, the moral order. Paul's urge to kill his girlfriend's grandmother and his fantasies of performing shameful acts with women would have been expressions of instinctual longings. The instincts of sex and aggression – indeed, the roots of desire itself – would, on this account, lie outside language.

There is another way of looking at the links between language and repression. This is not to locate the objects of repression necessarily outside the realm of language. Paul, in attempting to dismiss his thoughts, would not, as it were, be attempting to push away alien objects. Instead, the objects of repression – his complex and often precise desires – would themselves be formed in language. More than this, the psychic battleground may not be dominated by the conflict between language and wordless instinct. Instead, the battleground may be within language – between what is permissible to be said (and to be thought) and what is impermissible.

The present chapter will explore these tighter links between language, desire and repression. It will be suggested that language does not merely offer a means of repression: it demands repression. The roots of repression do not necessarily lie in biologically inborn desires, which make their presence felt in the earliest stages of infancy, before language is acquired. Because we speak, we have desires which must be repressed. If these desires, which are evoked by language, are not repressed then language, and the moral order, would be threatened. No other species has language, and no other species needs to develop habits of repression. This is no quirk of fate, but language is fundamentally both expressive and repressive.

Although the position developed here departs from Freud in many respects, there are also similarities. It is assumed that social life makes demands on us: we have to comply with moral expectations. With social constraint comes the desire to kick against restriction, but this desire must be routinely pushed from awareness. Habitual social constraint can be seen, above all, in the practice of conversation. In order to talk with others – to partake in the skills of dialogue – we need to have done more than acquire suitable vocabulary and grammar. We must be able to practise routinely the social codes for politeness. This involves routinely repressing the countervailing desires to rebel with rudeness.

In outlining these ideas, a word of caution should be sounded. Language, contrary to what many linguists imply, is always more than a system of grammar and word meanings. It is a spoken activity, which forms the basis of social life. The social world, like human inner thoughts, is saturated with language. As the Russian theorist of language Vološinov argued, speech 'permeates our behaviour in all its aspects'.[1] Should one wish to speak biologically about these matters, one might say that we are the language species, equipped with an instinct to talk.[2] In this respect, language is not to be opposed to our bodily existence; it is part of it, as we use our bodies in dialogic activity on which social life depends.

In the previous two chapters, theoretical ideas about repression have been illustrated with Freud's case-studies. Thus, incidents from the cases of Elisabeth von R and Paul Lorenz figured prominently in the arguments about the importance of repression and its linguistic forms. Here, the choice of examples will shift slightly from Freud's cases to the case of Freud himself. As he listened to his patients, as he sat at home with his family, and as he wrote for hour after hour, so Freud was exemplifying something that he took to be the general condition of humanity: the great exposer of repression was routinely practising repression in his daily life.

Freud's puzzle

At the heart of Freud's vision of society is an image of conflict. The demands of civilized life, Freud suggested, conflict with the instinctual

[1] Vološinov (1976), p. 88.   [2] Pinker (1994).

demands of human biology. The human being is fuelled by sexual and aggressive instincts, which are essentially anti-social in their aims. These instincts have to be curtailed if humans are to live orderly social lives, and are to show a modicum of civilized behaviour. As Freud wrote in an essay, which was first published in 1908, 'our civilization is built up on the suppression of instincts'.[3] He was to be increasingly preoccupied by this theme. 'Civilization and its discontents', written towards the end of his life, developed the notion that instinctual happiness conflicts with social order. The higher the level of civilization, the greater the amount of renunciation, which is required: 'If civilization imposes such great sacrifices not only on man's sexuality but on his aggressivity, we can understand better why it is hard for him to be happy in that civilization'.[4]

The conflict between instinct and civilization is one of the grand visions of Freud's psychology. In Freud's view, a sense of tragedy hangs over the human condition. We cannot escape from, nor rest easily with, our biological inheritance. If our instincts were allowed to flow without impediment, there would be no morality, no sense of conscience, no kindness. The instinctual inclinations are so strong that they must not only be resisted but renounced, so that the temptations, which they pose, are be driven away from consciousness. The result is that morality and security are achieved at the cost of natural happiness.

The grand vision creates a puzzle. Social life continues, day by day, hour by hour, minute by minute. If the social world depends on instinctual repression, then the activity of repressing must also continue hour by hour, minute by minute. As life rolls on outwardly, so there must be an unseen accompaniment of repression. Yet, it is unclear how such repression can be routinely accomplished.

Freud recognized the puzzle without solving it. Repression, he acknowledged, had to take place constantly. He wrote that 'the process of repression is not to be regarded as an event which takes place *once*, the results of which are permanent'. Instead, repression 'demands a persistent expenditure of force'.[5] Significantly, Freud depicted this continual repression in terms of hydraulic forces, battling within the inner reaches of the psyche. As was argued earlier, such a notion puts the processes of repression well beyond the reach of observation. The hydraulic metaphor suggests a rigid distinction between the outward conduct of social life and the inner processes of repression. Social life is conducted between conscious, sentient beings: repression is supposedly occurring inwardly, without those beings knowing what is happening.

---

[3] '"Civilized" sexual morality and modern nervous illness', *PFL* 12, p. 38.
[4] 'Civilization and its Discontents', *PFL* 12, p. 306.
[5] 'Repression', *PFL* 11, p. 151, emphasis in original.

The two sets of processes – the social and the repressing – unfold in parallel, without any seeming connection. The result is that repression is portrayed as a mysterious, almost self-contained process, unconnected with the actual details of social life, which supposedly relies on its constant performance.

Perhaps there is something about the activity of daily life, that enables repression to be constantly renewed. The case of Paul Lorenz provides a clue. As he was speaking to his fellow officers, attempting to persuade them to comply with his schemes to repay the postal charges for his pince-nez, so he was driving an unwelcome thought from his mind. His schemes were a diversion. His behaviour, which was bizarre to the point of being socially disruptive, shows how more conventional actions might also function to keep disturbing thoughts from consciousness. Freud made allusion to this, when he suggested that Elisabeth, in carrying out the demanding duties of a sick-nurse, was successfully pushing away her disturbing erotic inclinations.[6]

Social life comprises complex norms, customs and habits: the way we greet people, make entrances and exits, ask questions, offer answers and so on, are all bound by intricate codes, which we follow as matters of habit.[7] The sociologist, Norbert Elias attempted to give a sociological and historical context to the ideas of Freud's 'Civilization and its discontents'. He argued that modern civilization demands increasing self control, which must be exercised spontaneously and unthinkingly. The greater the complexity of the social order, 'the more complex and stable control of conduct is instilled in the individual from his (sic) earliest years as an automatism, a self-compulsion that he cannot resist even if he consciously wishes to'.[8] The result is that self-restraint becomes 'as it were, "second nature"', practised routinely without second thought.[9] This self-restraint is necessary if we are to follow the intricate rules of conduct, which govern practically every action in daily life.

In 'Totem and taboo', Freud offered a great insight about moral rules. He suggested that strict codes of morality are signs of forbidden desire. After all, as he wrote, 'there is no need to prohibit something that no one desires to do, and a thing that is forbidden with the greatest emphasis must be a thing that is desired'.[10] When he wrote those words,

---

[6] See chapter 2, p. 37.

[7] The work of Erving Goffman provides a marvellous introduction to the sociology of everyday life (e.g., Goffman, 1959, 1976 and 1981).

[8] Elias (1982), p. 233.

[9] Ibid., p. 235. A similar notion is expressed in Pierre Bourdieu's concept of 'the habitus', which ensures that formal rules and explicit norms are 'internalized as a second nature' and thereby practised routinely (1990, p. 57).

[10] 'Totem and Taboo', *PFL* 13, p. 126.

Freud had in mind the explicit codes of taboo, such as the prohibitions against incest, or the elaborate rules devised by 'primitive peoples' to honour their kings. Such rules, argued Freud, were indications of the desire to commit incest and to murder kings. And these desires, he believed, reflected instinctual, biological tendencies.

The question is whether the same logic can be applied to the informal codes of everyday life. If our daily actions are hedged by codes of behaviour, then are these signs of repressed urges? Are, for example, the daily practised codes of greeting and bidding farewell keeping in check urges, which threaten the very codes of social interaction? Freud imagined that the rules of social life were curtailing primal instincts, as if the instincts existed before the social rules. However, there is no need to make this assumption. The social rules may not merely, or even primarily, be curtailing inborn temptations: instead they might be creating their own restrictions, and thereby their own temptations.

A trivial example might illustrate this. Freud, as he delivered his 'Five lectures on psychoanalysis' to the American audience, illustrated the notion of repression by using the metaphor of students attending a lecture.[11] Anyone in the audience making a disturbance will be ejected by others. In the same way, according to Freud, disturbing thoughts are ejected from consciousness through repression. Whereas Freud, in his metaphor, concentrated upon the ejection of the badly behaved listener, we might ask what keeps ordinary members of an audience silently in their seats. They will be accepting codes of social behaviour, which they have internalized as 'a second nature'. They do not have to think deliberately about entering the lecture-hall, sitting down, opening their note-book, and maintaining a certain level of quiet as the lecturer begins to speak. All this is done routinely, automatically, indeed compulsively in the given situation. Even if the lecturer is talking rubbish, the audience of students will normally maintain a pose of relative quiet. One might predict that the constraints on their behaviour will create opposing desires – to shout out, walk out, make noise or whatever. But ordinarily these desires have to be curtailed. More than this, the disruptive desires should be pushed from conscious attention if satisfactory 'lecture-attending' behaviour is to be produced. If they are not, the desires might spill over into action, with disastrous consequences, not merely for the conduct of the lecture, but also for the individual. Suppose one student were to give way to feelings in a crowded lecture hall – shouting out and banging on the desk. Imagine if it had happened

---

[11] Freud (1963), p. 50.

in Freud's historic lecture at Clark University. Everyone would look round; there might even be titters of laughter. An embarrassing scene would have been created. Maybe, the interrupter might afterwards say words to the effect 'I don't know what came over me; I could have died of shame.' The very thought of such shameful embarrassment will normally keep in check any such urge, which might momentarily surface as the lecturer drones on and on.

Thomas Scheff has argued powerfully that fear of shame keeps social interaction in place. He suggests that shame 'is probably the most intensely painful of all feelings'.[12] More often than not, this emotion follows the infraction of 'minor' social rules, rather than major crimes. Shame is especially felt by those who have interrupted the smooth flow of social life – when they have said the wrong thing, gone out with their clothes unbuttoned, failed to answer a letter, been inadvertently rude to a colleague etc. These are the sorts of moments whose later recall brings about sleepless nights, a flush to the face and the mirth of others. Through fear of shame, the desires to disrupt social life are kept in place.

The logic of 'Totem and taboo' would suggest a direct relationship between constraint in everyday life and the desire to break through that constraint.[13] This is not necessarily a conflict between social order and biology. The urge to shout out in a quiet, formal lecture is not an instinctual desire, which is genetically transmitted from generation to generation. The temptation is created by the social conditions of restraint, as the existence of social rules itself provokes the possibility of shameful desire. The more ordered the life, the more such desires must be curtailed. And, as a psychoanalyst might suspect, the greater the curtailment, the more that the temptations will nag away beneath the apparent calm of social order.

---

[12] Scheff (1990), p. 169. See also Scheff (1997). In arguing for the importance of the motive to avoid shame as the factor lying behind the maintenance of social life, Scheff explicitly draws on the work of Helen Lewis, who has reinterpreted some of Freud's basic ideas in terms of the motives of shame and guilt (Lewis, 1983).

[13] Experimental social psychologists, following the lead of Festinger et al. (1952), have attempted to investigate the conditions under which people will engage in socially forbidden behaviour. It has been suggested that when people are 'deindividuated', the normal social constraints will be loosened (Zimbardo, 1969; Diener, 1980). Significantly, such theorists predict that the state of deindividuation and the performance of the normally forbidden behaviour will be experienced as pleasurable. The notion of deindividuation shares a common history with Freud's analysis of social behaviour in his 'Group psychology and the analysis of the ego': both explicitly draw on Le Bon's analysis of crowd behaviour (see Farr, 1996; Moscovici, 1985; Reicher, 1982).

An ordered life

Freud himself must have well understood the relations between temptation and an ordered, respectable life. His daily habits were founded
upon a tight, disciplined schedule, which permitted him to explore
intellectually the psychology of temptation. He would rise at seven,
beginning his sessions with patients at eight, punctually on the hour. At
exactly one o'clock, he would leave his consulting room, to walk across
the apartment to the dining-room, where he would join the rest of the
family for lunch. As soon as he sat down at the head of the table, and not
a moment before, the maid would arrive with the meal. Ernest Jones
provides a wonderful description of Freud at the dinner table, surrounded by his family. He would say little, concentrating on his food
and the conversations of others. If one of the children were not present,
Sigmund would point silently at the vacant chair with knife or fork.
Martha, from the other end of the table, would explain the absence.
Sigmund, with a nod of his head, would then continue eating.[14]

After lunch Freud would take an afternoon stroll and then resume
seeing patients promptly at three. When his consultations were completed, he would have his supper, followed by another walk or a family
game of cards. Then the evening's work would begin – writing up case-
notes, preparing manuscripts, editing journals and so on. Typically, he
would finish work and prepare for bed at one in the morning. Sundays
were different, of course, but they too had an established pattern. In the
morning Freud would visit his mother, and, in the evening, attend to his
correspondence.[15]

The ordered existence depended on the collusion, or rather the
dedication, of his wife. Martha ensured that the household ran with
clock-like precision so that nothing would interrupt the work of
Sigmund. Everything possible was done to smooth his daily journeys
from bedroom to consulting-room, to dining-room, back to his desk and
eventually to bed. He hardly needed to think about domestic details:
'She laid out his clothes, chose everything for him down to his hand-
kerchiefs, and even put toothpaste on his toothbrush.'[16]

Freud wrote sympathetically about the ceremonial rituals which
obsessives create for their daily lives. In the essay 'Obsessive actions and
religious practices', he described what he called 'the bed ceremonial' of
a typical obsessive:

---

[14] Jones, 1955, pp. 426–7; see also Roazen, 1974, pp. 77f.
[15] See Gay (1995, pp. 156f) for a description of Freud's routine.
[16] Roazen (1974), p. 79. See also Roazen (1973) chapter 2.

The chair must stand in a particular place beside the bed; the clothes must lie upon it folded in a particular order; the blanket must be tucked in at the bottom and the sheets smoothed out; the pillows must be arranged in such and such a manner, and the subject's own body must lie in a precisely defined position. Only after all this may he go to sleep.[17]

Obsessives cling to such rituals, becoming distressed with the slightest deviation from the familiar pattern. The rituals, according to Freud, serve a psychological purpose. By devoting themselves to the minutiae of their personal routines, obsessive persons keep troubling thoughts at bay.

Freud commented that the obsessive's personal ceremonies, such as the bed ritual, did not differ greatly from the rituals of 'normal' life: 'In slight cases the ceremonial seems to be no more than an exaggeration of an orderly procedure that is customary and justifiable.'[18] Freud's own domestic life seems to represent the sort of customary, justifiable pattern, which, in his opinion, is only a slightly scaled down version of an obsessional routine. We do not know how Sigmund, at the end of a long day, which was dominated from early morning until past midnight by stories of sexual temptation, prepared for bed. We don't know his ritual. There probably was one: the rest of the day was planned meticulously to run according to a precise pattern. We can use Freud's own ideas to speculate about the thoughts, which his bed ritual might be pushing aside, as Sigmund eased his tired body into bed next to the sleeping Martha.

Discipline and the containment of desire marked the dialogues, which Freud habitually conducted in his consulting-room. For most of his professional life, he would spend eight hours a day, six days a week, in consultation. Even when engaged in writing major works of theory, where his imagination was excitedly leaping forward, Freud spent the better part of the working day listening to patients. That is how he earned his living to support his household, to clothe his wife and children, and to pay the domestic servants who brought the meals to the dining-room at the stroke of the clock.

Freud's ambivalent feelings towards his daily burden of patients can be glimpsed in the letters, which he wrote to his friend Wilhelm Fliess between 1887 and 1904. Sometimes he wrote with excitement about a new patient or the course of an existing treatment. Typically these would be cases which aided his scientific work. For example, he told his friend that he had all the elements of an explanation of hysteria and obsessional neurosis, 'but I have not yet put the pieces of the puzzle in the right place'. Fortunately, Freud went on, he had 'daily opportunities

[17] 'Obsessive actions', *PFL* 13, p. 32.   [18] Ibid.

to be corrected or enlightened'. One current patient 'ought to clear up a few disputed points for me' and 'another man (who does not dare go out in the street because of homicidal tendencies) ought to help me solve another puzzle'.[19] These were the moments when the patients were promising to tell him what he wanted to hear. One can imagine how he anticipated those hours, concentrating all his attention on what his patients were telling him.

At other times, concentration must have been an effort. He was hearing things which he had heard many times before or which were tangential to his current interests. He wrote to Fliess at one point in 1895, that 'I am up to my neck in the infant paralyses, who do not interest me at all.'[20] Or perhaps the patients were not co-operating in the way he might have hoped. Sometimes he expressed mixed feelings: 'Mrs M will be welcome; if she brings money and patience with her, we shall do a nice analysis.' The next sentence makes it plain that the 'nice analysis' will be nice for the doctor: 'If in the process there are some therapeutic gains for her, she too can be pleased.'[21] But if she fails to bring patience, then the doctor, too, will feel impatient. It is precisely such impatience, not to mention boredom, that had to be suppressed in the analytic hour.

Freud confided in Fliess during low moments, when his patients were particularly burdensome: 'When I am not cheerful and collected, every single one of my patients is my tormentor.'[22] Such thoughts had to be pushed aside, as he listened to, and talked with, the patients. He admitted to Fliess that he 'really believed he would have to give up on the spot', but he had found a way out 'by renouncing all conscious activity so as to grope blindly among my riddles'. Sometimes, especially when Freud's intellectual work was not progressing well, the devices would seem to fail. In March 1898, he wrote to Fliess that 'my way of life, the eight hours of analysis throughout eight months of the year, devastates me'. His productivity was suffering; he felt 'just plain stupid', as if 'buried in a dark shaft'. What is more, as he confessed, 'I sleep during my afternoon analyses.'[23]

After the long analytic hours had been completed, there was more repression to be done. Thoughts about his patients and his own lack of scientific progress had to be dismissed during the moments of relaxation. 'In my spare time', he wrote to Fliess, 'I take care not to reflect on it.' Instead, 'I give myself over to my fantasies, play chess, read English

---

[19] Freud (1985), p. 148.
[20] Ibid., p. 150.   [21] Ibid., p. 107.   [22] Ibid., p. 404.
[23] Ibid., p. 303. Sulloway (1992) points out that the editors of the 1950 edition of Freud's letters to Fliess suppressed this confession.

novels; everything serious is banished.' In consequence, he vegetated harmlessly 'carefully keeping my attention diverted from the subject on which I work during the day'. He concluded that 'under this regimen I am cheerful and equal to my eight victims and tormentors'.[24]

Freud's bitter humour is apparent. He can call his patients 'tormentors' because his friend will understand the irony. Years later, he wrote to a new recruit to the psychoanalytic profession: 'That you have become an analyst is the right punishment for you.'[25] As Freud's own book on humour showed, jokes are not merely jokes.[26] Or rather, because a joke is only a joke, it can express a deeper truth. Freud both expresses and retracts his hostility towards his patients, who were paying him for his precious, and precisely measured, time but who often disappointed him. The tormentors are also victims. And again Freud is using irony, in order to say the unsayable. Fliess knows not to take the 'torment' inflicted by the patients too seriously; he would not be over-concerned by the patients' victimization at the hands of their brilliant doctor. Freud, in following his daily routines, has formed defences to prevent his admitting the torment too openly and too frequently. Bitter irony in a letter to Fliess, written on a Sunday, is different from yawns or gestures of impatience slipping out during weekday therapy.

The conversations with the tormentors have to continue, six days a week, for week after week. The impulse to tell patients to collect their hat and coat, if they have nothing more interesting to say, has to be repressed again and again, until it ceases to be thought in the daily routines of therapy. The unthinking must become a habit, so that codes of behaviour are maintained. Otherwise the carefully maintained world would start to totter. If the patients are insulted, then the income would dry up. The scientific work would be threatened. The close order of domestic routine would disintegrate. And who knows what other thoughts – what other conversations – would fill the threatening void?

Language and dialogue

Language was at the centre of Freud's world. There were the conversations with patients, requiring his disciplined attention. Then there were the words to be put on paper, carefully chosen to persuade a sceptical public. Even when relaxing on a Sunday, there were the conversations with mother. Afterwards, it would be back to the desk in the cluttered study, in order to put pen to paper again, to write to friends such as

---

24 Ibid., p. 404.
25 Quoted by Roazen (1992), p. 301.
26 'Jokes and their relation to the unconscious', PFL 6.

Fliess. Again words had to be chosen with care. It would be embarrassing if Freud were to address Fliess too directly. On the other hand, if the tone were too formal, offence would be caused. Intimacies, phrased in a tone of irony, steered between the Scylla of openness and the Charybdis of stuffiness. Hence the patients were victims and tormentors.

None of this is peculiar to Freud. He would have been following conventional norms, which simultaneously permit dialogue while restricting what should be said. The restrictions, like all restrictions, create their own temptations, which are stifled by routine. This is the condition of language itself. Constraint and desire are to be found in the details of language, in the small words and micro-pauses of conversation. These can be observed in the results from studies which analyse the fine details of conversation.

It might seem obvious to say that language is based in the practical activity, of talk. However, the point needs stressing, given the emphasis that formal linguists have placed upon grammatical structure, rather than on the actual practices of conversation. Linguists have followed de Saussure's distinction between the formal structure of language (*la langue*) and the actual utterances that people make (*la parole*). Structural linguists have seen their task to uncover the hidden, deep structure of language, from which particular utterances are supposedly derived. In consequence, they have often tended to treat actual utterances, or *la parole*, as mere surface reflections of the deeper, more significant underlying structure. By contrast, the present approach, and that of discursive psychology generally, is firmly on the side of *la parole*,

Formal linguistics has had a profound impact on the development of psychoanalysis through the work of Jacques Lacan and his followers. In the hands of Lacanians, the abstract theory of language, which lies at the heart of formal linguistics, has produced an abstracted theory of repression. Lacan expressed his position in a famous phrase: 'the unconscious is structured like a language'.[27] Since Lacan does not specify what the 'structure of language' is, it becomes doubly difficult to understand what possibly could be the structure of something as unobservable as 'the unconscious'.[28] It is no coincidence that Lacan and his followers

---

[27] Lacan (1979), p. 20.
[28] Roustang (1990) has pointed out that Lacan's slogan is inherently ambiguous because 'we never know exactly what the words "structure" and "like" mean' (p. 113). In terms of Saussure's distinction between *la langue* and *la parole*, Lacan is on the side of the former (Billig, 1997c). Forrester (1990), however, makes an interesting case for saying that Lacan's approach to language, at least in his early writings, is based on recognizing the pragmatic aspects of using language. What does seem undeniable is that Lacan does not get down to analysing the details of utterances, in the way recommended by linguistic philosophy, discursive psychology or pragmatic linguistics.

have produced some of the most obscure writings in the history of psychoanalysis; their texts are littered with technical terms which seem to bear little relation to the activities and words of actual people. In fact, Lacan's patients hardly appear in his texts.[29]

Both the style and theoretical position of Lacanian psychology are avoided here. 'Language' is not treated as if it were a thing with an underlying structure – and, as if that hidden structure were what really matters. Similarly, the present position avoids considering the unconscious as if it were an object. Instead, the emphasis is on activities, rather than things. Accordingly, language is something which is used, particularly in speech. The unconscious only exists to the extent to which people repress. To understand what people do when they repress, we have to understand what they do when they talk. Grand statements about 'structures' are of less use than close observation of details.

In this regard, the present position is of a piece with the approach of Mikhail Bakhtin, although it parts company with Bakhtin's, or rather Vološinov's, total dismissal of Freudianism.[30] In contrast to those formal linguists who seek to uncover the hidden structure of language as a total entity, Bakhtin urged linguists to look at actual talk, or what he called 'concrete utterances'. It was all very well devising complex theories about the nature of language, but, fundamentally language is something which is used. If one wishes to understand language, one must observe the business of talk: 'After all, language enters life through concrete utterances . . . and life enters language through concrete utterances as well.'[31] Utterances are typically made in conversations or dialogues and, thus, 'real-life dialogue' is the 'simplest and most classic form of speech communication'.[32]

Typically, a speaker's utterances are not merely the unmediated expression of an inner thought, but are formulated to be heard by a particular audience. The speaker's words will be part of ongoing dialogues, for 'any speaker is . . . a respondent to a greater or lesser degree'. After all, as Bakhtin wrote, no speaker is the very first person to disturb 'the eternal silence of the universe'.[33] Thus, to cite Bakhtin again, the speaker 'is oriented' towards the reactions of the hearers.[34] Freud will speak differently to Fliess, than to Martha or to his mother. What he says, and how he says it, will change, depending on whom he is speaking

---

[29] Billig (1997c) refers to the 'depopulated' nature of Lacan's psychology.

[30] See in particular, Vološinov (1976 and 1994). Vološinov argued forcefully that Freud neglected the cultural construction of mental states. However, Vološinov did not attempt to move from a negative critique to a positive consideration of how repression might be related to the practical activity of speech.

[31] Bakhtin (1986), p. 63.

[32] Ibid., p. 75.   [33] Ibid., p. 69.   [34] Ibid.

to and what that person has just said. Utterances are not a direct outpouring of the inner psyche, but they belong to particular contexts: 'Every concrete utterance always reflects the *immediate* small social event.'[35]

Bakhtin's idea of studying actual conversation in detail has only really become possible with the widespread use of recording devices. In the past twenty-five years, conversation analysts have examined the micro-processes of talk, by studying in detail the transcripts of recorded conversations.[36] By and large, this programme of research has confirmed what Bakhtin supposed. What is said reflects the context of dialogue. Participants, in their utterances, subtly orientate themselves to the responses of others. Perhaps the most striking finding of all has been to demonstrate the remarkable richness of even brief, seemingly banal, snatches of conversation. Again and again, studies reveal that the sort of daily exchanges, which we take for granted in our daily life, are accomplishments of great complexity.

Participants in dialogue have much to do, even when engaging in seemingly stereotypical forms of speech. Ways of greeting and saying goodbye, or asking routine questions and supplying answers, involve dialogic minuets, which need to be performed with skill and timing. Each participant has to encourage the other to provide the requisite type of response. As one analyst has put it, 'conversation is guided by a sociability norm such that participants agree to mutually uphold each other's claims, evaluations, offers, invitations and so on'.[37] Talk cannot be simple if speakers are to maintain this sociability. They must coordinate their interventions to keep a dialogue going and, for this, there must be complex codes to regulate participants' dialogic behaviour.

Dialogue has a basic condition, which is absolutely crucial to the conduct of talk: participants alternate between being speakers and listeners. This means that they must be able to coordinate the movement between listening and speaking. Participants cannot all take the floor at once; nor can they all be silent listeners. As Bakhtin wrote, that 'the boundaries of each concrete utterance as a unit of speech communication are determined by a *change of speaking subjects*, that is, by a change of speakers'.[38]

Conversation analysts have given much attention to the organization

---

[35] Vološinov (1973), p. 86, emphasis in original.
[36] For general accounts of conversation analysis, see, *inter alia*, Drew (1995); Heritage (1984 and 1988); Atkinson and Heritage (1984); Nofsinger (1991).
[37] Buttny (1993), p. 44.
[38] Bakhtin (1986), p. 71, emphasis in original.

of 'turn-taking systems'.[39] It is crucial that speakers recognize when one another's turns of speaking and silence are coming to an end. Without shared norms for signifying the end of speaking turns, there would be a babel of competing voices or mute silence; participants will be speaking when they should be listening and *vice versa*. Moreover, turn-taking has a wider significance. If conversation permits social life to continue, then turn-taking systems are vital for social life. As one conversation analyst writes, 'turn taking and the sequenced structuring of action' lie 'at the heart' of social interaction.[40] Intonation, pitch, speed of delivery, gaze and much more can all be used by speakers to indicate that they are coming to the end of their turn and that they are ceding the floor to another speaker. Contrariwise, speakers must be able to pause while speaking in such a way that they indicate that the turn is not completed and that more is to come despite the momentary pause. All this is habitually practised as second nature.

There is a wider implication. Because norms for turn-taking are essential for talk, they are, in a very real sense, a linguistic universal. No language community can do without them.[41] As Erving Goffman noted, in all spoken interaction 'conventions and procedural rules come into play which function as a means of guiding and organizing the flow of messages'.[42] Thus, some sort of social order must be built into the very conditions for talk. Freud, as has been mentioned, suspected that rules indicate the presence of temptation and desire. This raises an intriguing possibility. Because talk depends on the constant practice of order and restraint in some form or another, the very conditions of language may create hidden temptations, which need to be routinely repressed, if conversation is to be successfully and routinely accomplished.

Politeness and morality

The codes of appropriate talk, which permit dialogue to occur, can be considered as norms of politeness. If they are infringed, then speakers will feel that social and moral infractions have occurred. As some linguists have stressed, politeness in some form or another is essential

---

[39] See Nofsinger (1991) chapter 4. See also Schegloff and Sacks (1974) and Sacks, Schegloff and Jefferson (1978) for classic studies of turn-taking. See also Schegloff (1995) for a more recent study.

[40] Boden (1994), p. 53.

[41] Formal linguists, being more concerned with *la langue*, than *la parole*, tend to ignore turn-taking when they consider linguistic universals. For example, Aitchinson (1996) discusses ten possible features common to all language. She includes grammatical and phonological features, but does not consider pragmatic aspects, such as rules for turn-taking.

[42] Goffman (1976), p. 33.

for dialogue.[43] For instance, when speakers are coordinating their turns in dialogue, they must demonstrate that they are yielding and taking up the conversational space according to the requisite norms. In this respect, as one analyst has written with just a touch of exaggeration, 'every instance of communicated language exhibits politeness'.[44]

Not only are there systems of turn-taking, but a host of other norms enable dialogue to take place. There are norms governing the asking and answering of questions. For instance, if questions are asked, then listeners should feel an obligation to provide answers.[45] The way that questions are to be asked is governed by codes of appropriateness. Can the speaker outrightly ask for the information, or must the request be dressed up with extra phrases, so that the speaker approaches the point indirectly? As has been pointed out, all languages permit direct and indirect questioning.[46] In many cultures, politeness requires that questions, addressed to strangers or to social superiors, must be posed indirectly. Too much directness will make a question appear like a command and will be seen as being inappropriately rude.[47] For example, English speakers, asking for directions from a stranger, would normally be expected to phrase their question indirectly, by prefacing it with phrases such as 'excuse me', 'I wonder if you could . . .' or 'I'm sorry to trouble you' etc. Some analysts have said that the norm of sociability is supported by a 'preference for agreement'.[48] If the listener is to refuse a request, a straightforward 'no' is not expected. The refusal has to be hedged with explanations, justifications, apologies and so forth. To refuse outright would usually be interpreted as impolite, so 'markers' of politeness customarily accompany refusals.[49]

All language communities have codes for talking, together with ways of showing disapproval when such codes are infringed. In this sense politeness is universal.[50] So is the possibility of rudeness. Transgressing the codes for politeness carries a severe moral evaluation: it is a source of shame and censure. Speakers who constantly break the codes of turn-taking – interrupting when they should be silent, remaining silent when

---

[43] According to Chilton (1990), 'politeness formulations are universal and pervasive in everyday intercourse, largely conventionalized and often benign' (p. 222).

[44] Grundy (1995), p. 130.

[45] Conversation analysts have devoted considerable attention to 'adjacency pairs', showing how one turn is connected with an adjacent one, such as a question and answer, or invitation and acceptance, or compliment and receipt (see Nofsinger, 1991, chapter 2, Heritage, 1984 and 1988).

[46] Thomas (1995), p. 124.

[47] See Brown and Levinson (1987).

[48] See, for instance, Pomerantz (1984); Bilmes (1987); Nofsinger (1991).

[49] Firth (1995).

[50] Brown and Levinson (1987); see also Tracy (1990).

they should be answering, being direct when they should be indirect etc. and etc. – are likely to be judged in moral terms. They will be found arrogant, disrespectful or generally rude. As the sociologist Harold Garfinkel has suggested, conversations are a form of practical morality.[51] If codes of talking are broken, not only is the immediate conversation threatened, but so is the cultural morality of social interaction.

'Politeness' should not be misunderstood in this context. It does not refer to a particular type of conversation. The 'polite conversation' is often seen as one which runs according to the particular requirements of Western bourgeois norms of *politesse*. Nevertheless, it is wrong to think of politeness in this narrow, culturally specific way. There are widely differing codes of politeness even within a single culture or, indeed, a single family. What is considered appropriate, or polite, in one cultural context may be considered impolite in another. Sigmund may have been permitted to ask a question by pointing to the empty chair with his fork. Martha would have recognized this as a turn which demanded a reply.[52] No one else at the table would have been allowed to ask the question in such a way. The privilege was reserved for the man sitting at the head of the table. Certainly, none of the children, let alone the maid, would be expected to pose a question by such a gesture of cutlery, dispensing with the conventional codes of indirectness.

One might predict that Sigmund's use of the fork was no simple transgression of politeness. Sigmund's pointed question, too, would have followed expected codes. He would have had to wait his turn, in order to be noticed; his gesture would be precise; food would have been removed from the eating implement. One might predict that the other members of the family would be able to tell whether the gesture, and accompanying movement of head, indicated a hint of criticism. Although Sigmund's wordless questions might have been considered rude, if performed by others in the room or by himself in other company, even this action was hedged by its own routine codes of accomplishment. Sigmund would respond to Martha's explanation for the absence: as Ernest Jones reports, Sigmund 'would nod and silently proceed with his meal'.[53] In so doing, he demonstrates that he has accepted Martha's explanation as an adequate account. The nod, followed by a resumption of eating, also signals the end of the brief sequence. The nodding is required of Sigmund, otherwise Martha

[51] Garfinkel (1967).
[52] West (1995) suggests that women have particular competencies for ensuring the smooth running of dialogue. The silent Sigmund with his fork raised and Martha conducting the conversation with family and guests well fits the image.
[53] Jones (1955), p. 427.

might feel obliged to offer further explanation.[54] In this context, were Sigmund to resume his eating, without making his nod, he would be transgressing the family's accepted codes. Martha is owed the slight movement of the head. Such are the codes of politeness even within this routine, which outsiders might consider to infringe the codes of bourgeois *politesse* and which was said to be 'a source of embarrassment to strange visitors'.[55]

Certainly, codes of politeness vary across cultures. What is polite in one culture may be impolite in another. Although many cultures deem it polite to formulate requests for information indirectly, this is by no means universal: in some cultures indirectness can be considered impolite.[56] Martha might take it amiss were Sigmund one day to replace his directly pointing fork with an indirect, coldly uttered 'I wonder, my dear, if you could be so kind as to inform me, where young Anna might happen to be this lunchtime.'[57] One observer has suggested that Freud's development of psychoanalysis was a reaction against the so-called 'rude', direct speech of Eastern European ghetto Jews, in favour of the more restrained, quieter styles of bourgeois Christian patterns of speech.[58] However, one should beware of any contrast, which takes the conventions of Western bourgeois talk as representing in an absolute sense the 'correct' form of politeness, besides which other forms of talk are 'impolite'.[59] The noisier, direct forms of talk, which appear impolite to the upholders of bourgeois *politesse*, have their own codes and moral sanctions.[60]

---

[54] Using the terminology of conversation analysis, one might say that Sigmund and Martha's sequence has structure of two overlapping adjacency pairs. First there is the question accomplished by the pointed cutlery and Martha's answer, explaining the absence of the child. The explanation, then, acts as the first part of a further pair: explanation and receipt of explanation.

[55] Jones (1955) p. 426.

[56] Compare, for example, the codes of the Akan in Ghana, in which indirection is practised (Obeng, 1997) with the codes of Israelis where indirection is considered inappropriate (Katriel, 1986).

[57] Brown and Levinson (1987) discuss the impolite, face-threatening uses of 'over-politeness'.

[58] Cuddihy (1987).

[59] Brown and Levinson (1987). The cross-cultural evidence presented by Brown and Levinson qualifies any idea that 'politeness' is a comparatively late development of western society, as Elias (1982) argued. Even, in the so-called 'uncivilized' mediaeval times, when rough manners seemed unexceptional, there must have been intricate codes of talk, especially since talk would have expressed subtle differences of social rank.

[60] The idea that traditional East European Jewish speech lacked rules of politeness or turn-taking is itself a reflection of the assumptions of bourgeois *politesse*. Schiffrin (1984) showed that the speech patterns of Jews in North America differed substantially from non-Jews; among Jewish speakers argument can be a form of sociability. Within this pattern there were codes for conducting argument and 'doing disagreement' (see also Horowitz, 1996).

Even forms of talk, which apparently breach norms of politeness, will have their own norms, which can be demanding for the participants. The psychoanalytic conversation offers a case in point. The type of therapeutic dialogue, which Freud invented, may have been freed from many of the constraints which affected the sort of 'polite conversation' to be heard in Freud's living-room. Topics, which were taboo in polite society, even in the Freuds' living-room, were expected to be talked about in the privacy of the psychoanalytic consulting-room. When a visitor to the Freuds explained a slip of the tongue, Martha pointedly said 'we never hear such things'.[61]

As Sigmund turned from the dining-room across the foyer and down the corridor to the consulting-room, he was not moving from a world of restraint to one of dialogical freedom, where anything and everything could be uttered. The psychoanalytic conversation made strict demands on patient and doctor. Freud hoped his patients would speak in particular ways. They should cooperate in bringing to light early memories and he hoped that patients, such as Mrs M, would show patience in this endeavour. To be sure, patients would be expected to talk about the sort of sexual matters, which might be kept from living-room talk. They would also talk about themselves more than would be appropriate in standard 'polite' talk. The dialogues had a peculiar physical setting, which emphasised the rather unbalanced pattern of communication. The patient would lie on a couch, watched by, but unable to see the person to whom their remarks were addressed. In the early years, Freud might also put his hands on the patient's forehead. The patient was not expected to reciprocate by touching the doctor.

Patients might need to be told what was expected of them dialogically. In the report of the case Paul Lorenz, Freud described the opening of the first proper session. He explained to Paul how they would talk. The patient had to pledge himself 'to the one and only condition of the treatment – namely, to say everything that came into his head, even it was *unpleasant* to him, or seemed *unimportant* or *irrelevant* or senseless'.[62] Freud was telling the young lawyer that the standard codes of conversation should be laid aside. What would normally count as irrelevant would be relevant for these types of conversation.[63] In ordinary conversation it would be rude to say the first thing to come into one's head. But, in this situation, to 'orientate' to the demands of the

[61] Roazen (1974), p. 80.

[62] 'Notes', *SE*, p. 159, emphasis in original. The 'process notes' are somewhat different, mentioning two, not one, conditions: 'After having communicated to him the two principle conditions of treatment, I left him free to begin' (Hawelka, 1974, p. 33).

[63] Grice (1975), in a famous analysis of conversation, lists 'relevance' as one of the basic maxims of conversation, which speakers assume others to be following.

doctor at his desk, the patient on the couch is allowed longer turns of talk and is freed from the standard demand to be relevant. The irrelevant thought (or what would be considered irrelevant in ordinary dialogical settings) becomes supremely relevant for this conversation. After the young lawyer had agreed to the conditions, Freud reports that he 'gave him leave to start his communications with any subject he pleased'.[64] The patient, who already knew something of Freud's work, was aware that some subjects were more relevant than others in this setting. Without apparent prompting from Freud, he was soon talking of his early sexual experiences.[65]

One can imagine the preliminary exchange, in which the doctor explains the conditions for their dialogue. The doctor would be speaking, the patient listening.[66] Perhaps the patient was nodding, or indicating with a chorus of 'yesses', that he was assenting, as the doctor outlined the conditions. Then the doctor would wait for the patient's formal agreement: almost certainly, more than a quick nod of the head would be expected. Perhaps, the doctor asked a question to check that all was fully understood, and the patient replied in the affirmative. In short, the doctor and patient would be following accepted and widely practised codes of dialogue in order to establish the new codes.

The new codes could not be entirely new. Old patterns of dialogue and turn-taking would still be evident. Studies of conversation in the therapeutic situation show that therapists continually give signs to patients, in order to achieve the putting aside of conventional turn-taking. For instance, therapists might utter little 'um's' and 'mm-hm's' to indicate that the patient should continue talking, when, in other conversations, it would be time to yield. In this way, the 'ums' become understood as signs that the therapist is yielding their turn to speak. There is nothing remarkable in such use of 'um' or 'mm-hm'. The therapist is using a conventional rhetorical device, which can be heard to function in just this way in other contexts and whose significance would be instantly, but not necessarily consciously, recognized by the patient.[67] The 'ums' and the 'mm-hms' have another function. They indicate to the patient that the therapist is still paying attention, and has not fallen asleep, as Freud did during the bleak moments of 1898.

In short, the therapeutic dialogue runs on its own continually prac-

---

[64] 'Notes', *SE*, p. 159.   [65] Ibid., p. 160.

[66] One might note that it is the doctor who sets the rules for the conversation and thus, as Forrester (1990) has argued with insight, the psychoanalytic dialogue is an exercise in the doctor's power over the patient.

[67] Czyzewski (1995) reports that the use of 'mm-hm' enables the therapist to indicate that longer pauses by the patient are to be tolerated, as well as indicating that the speaker should continue.

tised and reinforced codes, which determine the conventions of speaking and listening. Not only must therapists listen but they must be heard to be listening. Anything else would be impolite. Freud's new codes of dialogue made demands on patient and doctor alike. There could be no dialogic freedom from codes.[68] As Freud confided to his friend Fliess, he hoped that the patients would be up to the task. And he worried about his own patience to endure the discipline of this type of conversation. It is small wonder that, after a hard morning's listening, Sigmund, during his hour of refreshment, would abandon the discipline of words, in order to pose questions by means of his cutlery.

Habits of restraint

If the idea of code-free conversation is an illusion, then dialogue can be said to show three features, which emphasize that speakers are constrained in what they say.

(1) In virtually every utterance, the influence of complex rules can be detected. The discursive devices of politeness show the extent to which utterances are not merely expressions of thought, but are orientations to others, following cultural patterns for appropriate speech.

(2) The codes for appropriate speaking are practised habitually. Although speakers might at times deliberately weigh their words and consciously emphasize certain aspects, the bulk of what they do is second nature. We are not aware of every nod we make as listeners, or of every signal contained in pitch and intonation. We can practise the rules of turn-taking, and other codes of conversation, without specifying them explicitly.[69] Therapists may not be aware of all the 'ums' that they utter without second thought. The sociologist, Pierre Bourdieu, in discussing the role of habit in everyday life, comments that 'it is because agents

[68] Modern therapeutic groups will have their own codes of talk, even when they are claiming to set aside all conventional restraints. Wodak (1996), in discussing a particular therapeutic group, comments that the rules of speech within the group differ from those of everyday conversation. According to Wodak, 'routine forms of politeness . . . are not considered necessary' for 'emotions may be shown'; also 'very intimate topics are dealt with at length, and everyone gets their turn' (p. 178). Routine politeness might be set aside, but, clearly, there cannot be a vacuum. Another system of turn-taking and norms of speech must be in place in order to ensure that everyone gets their turn. Thus, there would need to be rules, which might be explicitly explained to newcomers and these function as forms of politeness in the particular therapeutic setting. There would also be ways of indicating disapproval, if a speaker were preventing another from having what would be considered their rightful turn (for analyses of discourse in therapeutic groups, see Edwards, 1997; McNamee, 1996; Riikonen and Smith, 1996).

[69] Garfinkel (1967). Central to Garfinkel's analysis is the idea that we cannot specify the background assumptions of our habitual behaviour.

never know completely what they are doing that what they do has more sense than they know'.[70] This is particularly true of dialogic actions, where so much is performed routinely or unconsciously.

(3) Dialogue, although bound by rules and norms, is not merely a routine performance. Day by day, speakers say new things, producing utterances which, in their precise details, have never been spoken before. Speakers must be able to manage the familiar rules in new situations. Perhaps, as Freud was explaining the conditions of the psychoanalytic conversation to Paul Lorenz, he was repeating something he had said many times previously to new patients. Nevertheless, the precise words would be different. Freud, like most speakers, would be monitoring the effect of his words as he spoke, adjusting them accordingly in ways which he would not have been able to specify completely, if asked afterwards. The familiar preface would be adapted for the occasion. As the new patient told his story, Freud would be hearing things, which he had never previously heard. Accordingly, he would need to make his familiar responses, such as the minimal 'ums' and 'mm hms', in new contexts.

If the habits of politeness attend every utterance, and if these habits are also habits of morality, then an interesting possibility arises. As was mentioned earlier, Freud claimed that morality indicates the presence of desire. Perhaps this observation can be applied to the routine practice of conversation. In dialogue speakers are continually constrained to follow rules of politeness – to be attentive, to reply when questioned, to be direct, to be indirect and so on. It can all take an effort, which must appear as effortless routine. Politeness often, but not invariably, demands the use of indirectness, so that polite utterances are frequently longer than rude ones.[71] Thus, a greater expenditure of effort is typically required to formulate the appropriately polite utterance.

One might suspect, following the logic of Freud's observation, that dialogic constraint, practised as second nature, will evoke the countervailing desire to be conversationally free – to say what one will, to interrupt with abandon and so on. Such desires must be routinely curtailed, or pushed aside, if conversation is to continue. Yet, as Freud suggested, the possibility of moral censure indicates the probability of immoral desire. Why, to paraphrase Freud's point in 'Totem and taboo', might shame and moral censure be attached to infringements of codes of questioning and turn-taking, if no one ever desired to break those codes? And why might the censure be experienced with an intensity which seems out of proportion to an offence of such triviality as an over-

---

[70] Bourdieu (1990), p. 69.   [71] Thomas (1995), pp. 155f.

loud voice, an overly quick reply, the omission of a single syllable of gratitude?

Freud himself admitted to having the urge to disobey the social constraints of everyday politeness. In 'Interpretation of dreams', he drew a parallel between the sort of dissimulation which occurs in dreams and the sort of dissimulation which the conventions of politeness demand in daily life. In the case of dreams, the wish has to disguise itself. Freud suggested that just the same happens in social life, especially when one person 'possesses a certain degree of power which the second is obliged to take into account'. He continued: 'The politeness which I practise every day is to a large extent dissimulation of this kind.'[72] Sigmund could not insult his paying patients, who were providing his means of subsistence. Similarly he had to watch his tongue with the medical establishment, which at the time held the power to block his professional advancement.

Freud, in talking of his daily dissimulation, had in mind the sorts of things which he consciously checked himself from saying. He might wish to complain directly to the authorities, especially when he suspected that university promotion had been denied for what he called, in 'The interpretation of dreams', 'denominational considerations'.[73] Instead, he bore his injuries with public silence, speaking politely to his superiors. This daily politeness would be accomplished as a rich, complex, ingrained habit, whose details would be reproduced beyond conscious awareness. Freud would not have been aware of his every gesture – his every nuance of deference – which his words and body were conveying. One might say that the bulk of Freud's politeness – even his dissimulation – was being reproduced unconsciously.

Freud believed that underlying desire was revealed in those moments when usual constraints were relaxed. Hence, he detected the presence of unspoken desire in jokes, dreams and slips of the tongue. The same signs of desire may be shown in those moments when conversational smoothness seems to be in trouble and repair-work is called for. The possibility of misunderstanding haunts dialogue. Participants can monitor their contributions, but still things can go wrong. Questions can be heard as criticisms and *vice versa*. Analysts of conversation have paid particular attention to the way that conversational repairs are made. As one analyst has written, 'it is important for our understanding of each other that we can fix these flaws before they lead to more serious and fundamental problems'.[74] To stop conversations collapsing into

[72] 'The interpretation of dreams', *PFL* 4, p. 223.
[73] Ibid., p. 218.
[74] Nofsinger (1991), p. 124.

mutual embarrassment, competent speakers have an 'impressive range of repair'.[75] They can use devices of 'self-repair' to correct their own infractions or 'other-repair' to draw attention to the infractions of other speakers in ways that invite correction, avoid embarrassment and, thereby, set the dialogue back on track.[76] By skilful use of repairs, 'conversational death' can be averted once a tricky situation threatens to unfold.

There is a particular example of repair work, which has been much examined by conversation analysts. It occurred in a conversation as one speaker suggested that the other had not brought a great deal of fruit cake.[77] The remark is met by silence from the other speaker. The listener by remaining silent (by withholding even a nod of the head) communicates that the remark was being understood as a criticism. The original speaker then 'backs down' and reverses the original statement, to suggest that a little cake can go a long way. Face has been saved all round.[78] The conversation can continue.

Conversational analysts typically devote their attention to the repair work itself, rather than the intervention which has necessitated the repair.[79] Like the joke or the disturbing dream, the remark, which must be repaired, might express a rebellion against the very sort of restriction, which the repair sets back in place. In the example of the fruit-cake, the first speaker calls back the potentially offensive remark, in order to repair the dialogue. Might one say that the speaker has revealed the desire to make an uninhibited criticism? However, this desire, having been momentarily released, then has been pushed aside by the structures of routine politeness. In this way, the dialogic structures of conventional conversation ensure the repression of the disruptively rude desire.[80]

With unconsciously practised politeness comes the temptation of disruption. However, there are routines to curtail the temptation. If a disruptive remark slips out, there are conversational devices to effect repairs. Speakers find themselves using these repairs as second-nature, automatically without conscious intent. The temptations may, like the ornate details of the polite routines themselves, exist just outside the margins of conscious awareness. As the routines of social life unfold

---

[75] Boden (1994), p. 148.

[76] See, for example, Schegloff, Jefferson and Sacks (1977) and Pomerantz (1984).

[77] The example comes from Pomerantz (1984) and is analysed by Nofsinger (1991) and Potter and Wetherell (1995).

[78] See Brown and Levinson (1987) for an account of the relations between 'face-work' and the customs of politeness. They discuss also why self-repair may be preferred to 'other-repair' (p. 38).

[79] See Billig (1997a) for further details.

[80] Conversation analysts certainly do not tend to make inferences about desires and suppression: see, for example Drew (1995); Potter and Wetherell (1987).

with mechanical smoothness, so might a mirror image of temptation be reproduced. Sigmund develops routines of listening, which keep him from insulting his patients; Martha habitually and promptly answers the pointing fork. In both cases, smooth dialogic routines are set in place, so that between the adjacent pairs of question and answer, or of utterance and response, there is little space for disruptive wishes intrude. Nevertheless, it might be suspected that unexpressed temptation lurks within those well practised dialogic routines.

Temptation and rudeness

To put the matter simply: the demands of politeness create the temptation of rudeness. The respective origins of politeness and rudeness can be seen to be closely linked. Politeness is not a biological imperative, for 'pleases' and 'thank-you's' are not wired into the infant's genetic make-up. The routines of dialogic politeness must be taught to the young child. If politeness is routinely taught, as it must be for the skills of conversational turn-taking to be acquired, then rudeness also must be taught. One cannot have one without the other. Each time adults tell a child how to speak politely, they are indicating how to speak rudely. 'You must say *please*' . . . 'Don't speak when others are speaking' . . . 'You mustn't use *that* word.' All such commands tell the child precisely what rudeness is, pointing to the forbidden phrases as surely as Sigmund pointed to the empty chairs at the dinner-table.

With English speakers, at least, the teaching of politeness (and rudeness) can be heard as adults instruct children about appropriate turn-taking. Significantly, this instruction can take place before the child has acquired the formal grammatical features of language. This is illustrated in the following example, taken from a recorded dialogue between a seventeen-month-old boy and his mother.[81] The infant, Mark, is unable to utter a single clear word. He and his mother are playing with a toy telephone. The mother says 'How are you?' and Mark replaces the receiver on the hook. The mother then responds: 'That's very rude. You've hung up.' Mark then lifts the receiver to his ear again. The mother continues with the pretend conversation: 'Hello. Have you had your dinner?'

The investigator, studying Mark and his mother, points out that the infant is being taught how to take turns in dialogue, even before he can formulate his own utterances: 'Part of what is learned is simply the sequencing of vocalizations in dialogue, even in the absence of mean-

---

[81] For full details, see Edwards (1978).

ingful verbal communication.'[82] In this example, the teaching of turn-taking is directly related to the teaching of politeness and rudeness. The mother playfully teaches politeness, by indicating what is rude: 'That's very rude', she says. If this sort of this dialogue is repeated again and again, the young child will not only learn how to take turns in conversations (including mock telephone conversations); but by the time the child is old enough to put the lesson into routine practice, he will be armed with a considerable knowledge of rudeness.

The mother, in teaching politeness, provides a model of rudeness. She does not speak in a way which would be acceptable if addressed to an adult. In fact, adults typically address children in ways which would be considered rude (even very rude) if their utterances were part of adult conversations.[83] When talking to children, adults as a rule make direct demands (or more precisely, they issue unhedged commands). They will often refuse children's requests with an unelaborated 'no', without offering mitigating explanations. If then asked to justify an outright refusal, they will not necessarily engage in delicate repair work, but may counter with 'Because I say so.'[84] The result is that adults, and particularly parents, routinely demonstrate to children the very sort of talk which they do not want the children to use, especially when the children speak to adults.[85] Thus, adults unwittingly ensure that the child acquires a well-stocked armoury of rudeness.

Rudeness can be used as a weapon in order to undermine authority. Children are, of course, regularly, faced with authority. Children regularly hear adults telling them what words mean and how they should talk. If children are to learn to speak appropriately, they must accept the dialogic authority of older speakers. Children must assume that adults provide reliable information about language. As one developmental psychologist has commented, if children regularly reject what adults tell them about word meanings, they 'would have little hope of achieving mastery over language'.[86]

It is easy to suppose that children enthusiastically adopt the lessons of their elders and betters. Barbara Rogoff, in her insightful book *Apprenticeship in Thinking*, depicts children as willing apprentices, being guided

---

[82] Ibid., p. 451.

[83] This point should not be generalized across cultures (Ochs and Schieffelin, 1984 and 1995).

[84] This can be contrasted with the example of the fruitcake conversation, in which a self-repair is made (see footnote 77). The participant, who hears the speaker's words as a criticism, does not retort 'that's very rude', but withholds assent until the other speaker offers a 'self-repair'.

[85] See Aronsson (1991) and Billig (1997a) on this point.

[86] Robinson (1994), p. 357.

by adults in 'skilled, valued sociocultural activity'.[87] However, this is a somewhat rosy view of the relations between children and adults. All is by no means sweetness and enlightenment in the world of the developing child. To be sure, children must accept the adults' definitions of meaning and the accepted patterns of speaking. But the acquisition of language gives the child weapons of rebellion, which can be turned back on the figures of authority. The lessons in politeness can be returned as exercises in rudeness. And they regularly are.

The work of Judith Dunn, investigating the interaction between mothers and young children in England, is particularly revealing.[88] Her results show that the acquisition of meaning by children (or its imposition by parents) is by no means a smooth process. The whole business more closely resembles Freud's image of the impulsive child reacting against the demands of civilization than it does the image of the willing apprentice entering into the spirit of learning. Between the ages of two and four, the child regularly confronts the mother, deliberately resisting her authority. Dunn calculates that at this stage, there are, on average, eleven conflict episodes per hour.[89]

Children resist, tease and delight in forbidden pleasures. As Dunn's research shows, children typically show a fascination with bodily functions, gaining enjoyment from what they have been told is dirty. If they are told not to talk of bodily smells, bottoms or genitalia, then, penny to a pound, these are just the topics which they will discuss with relish. Above all, children rebel with humour, turning language round on adults, mis-using words for fun. Dunn reports that at the age of two children regularly laugh as social and linguistic rules are broken, especially by themselves. Dunn points to 'the pleasure and excitement the children show as they deliberately repeat the forbidden act'.[90] The use of naughty words brings particular fun. In Dunn's study, one young girl commented that her mother didn't allow her to use the term *piggyface*. Then, with great enjoyment, she kept on repeating 'Mr Piggyface' again and again.[91]

The 'Piggyface' episode illustrates something general. What has been forbidden becomes an object of desire and pleasure. Only because the girl was told not to utter 'Mr Piggyface' did she derive such pleasure from saying it repeatedly. It is not a pre-existing biological pleasure.

---

[87] Rogoff (1990), p. 39.
[88] See, for instance, Dunn (1988, 1991 and 1994); Dunn and Munn (1987). Dunn's main study examined in detail conversations between second-born children and their mothers in forty families. She recorded the same children at 18, 24 and 36 months. She has also examined children at other age points.
[89] Dunn (1994).
[90] Dunn (1988), p. 18.   [91] Ibid., p. 157.

There was nothing intrinsic to the sound itself which marked this word as a particular source of enjoyment. The pleasure derives from the prohibition. Later on, she will encounter the pleasures of swear words, which must not be politely spoken. Today, such rude words primarily refer to bodily functions, which, as the child has learnt, should not be spoken of freely. In former times, and in other cultures, the forbidden words might mock sacred deities.

A paradox attends the teaching of correct codes of speaking. The parent invariably informs the child about rudeness, as an unforeseen consequence of instructing the child in the ways of politeness. Thus, the child learns what must not be spoken. Temptation is created, for, as Freud recognized, prohibitions create their own desires. In this way, the child is provided with a forbidden world of discursive pleasures, just as it acquires the duties of social constraint. If, in this context, one wants to talk of the creation of 'the unconscious', then it is a dialogic unconscious.

Jokes and the return of the repressed

Children are given licence, at least in contemporary Western society, to speak with a freedom, which is denied to adults. In Dunn's study, mothers did not always reprimand children, who made childishly impolite utterances. Sometimes, the mothers, too, might smile.[92] Children can be tolerated to butt in and ask direct questions, which adults would fear to pose (except when speaking to children). It's only a child talking, after all. But childish talk – such as chanting 'poo-poo' or 'Mr Piggyface' – must be outgrown. To become a mature conversationalist, the person must absorb the appropriate codes of politeness and practise them routinely. The pleasures of rudeness, one might say, need to be repressed.

Yet is it right to talk of *repression* in this context? Repression implies the persistence of pleasure. Perhaps the delight in chanting 'poo-poo' and 'piggyface' is confined to the earlier stages of life. The joke grows flat and the pleasure is diminished as we grow older. If this were the case, there would be no reason to say that the pleasures are repressed. Rather they would be outgrown, just as adults may outgrow the preference for sweet things. We do not need to say that the pleasure for sherbet is repressed and displaced, in the adult world, onto Camembert or avocado.

In the case of rudeness, by contrast, there are signs that the childish

---

[92] Ibid., pp. 156f.

pleasures linger, continuing to offer tempting release from the burdens of adult constraints. Freud claimed that what is repressed returns in the 'parapraxes' of social life, such as lapses of memory and slips of the tongue. As far as the temptation of rudeness is concerned, humour is especially interesting. In his book 'Jokes and their relations to the unconscious', Freud suggested that 'our enjoyment of the joke' indicated what is being repressed in more serious talk.[93] Sex and aggression are the themes most commonly expressed in what Freud called 'tendentious' jokes. Of course, the joke is marked off from normal ways of talking. Speakers outwardly display that 'they are only joking, ha-ha', as they make utterances which would be impermissible in ordinary, serious discourse.[94]

Comic heroes frequently disrupt the patterns of restrictive politeness. A common thread runs from Diogenes of Sinope, living in his tub, through to Groucho Marx and John Cleese. Their displays of rudeness are not greeted with moral outrage, but with shared signs of delight. Audiences find pleasure in the character who sweeps aside shame and social rules. Even Alexander the Great was said to have joined in the fun, when he was insulted by Diogenes. Sometimes, as with John Cleese's character of the hotelier, Basil Fawlty, the constraints of politeness are turned into weapons of rudeness with great comic effect: 'thank-you-so-much', he proclaims in a parody of politeness to the guests, whom he insults.[95]

It might seem curious that displays of rudeness, which ordinarily will be treated as shocking breaches of morality, are greeted with pleasure in the context of humour. Freud claimed that the pleasure indicates the persistence of a renounced desire: 'To the human psyche all renunciation is exceedingly difficulty, and so we find that tendentious jokes provide a means of undoing the renunciation and retrieving what was lost.'[96] According to Freud, in daily life we have to check our 'insulting tendencies'. However, the desire to insult finds expression in humour, so that 'tendentious jokes are especially favoured in order to make aggressiveness or criticism possible against persons in exalted positions who claim to exercise authority'.[97]

Comic heroes are figures of identification because they have the courage to utter the rudeness, that we fear to display. Our laughter betrays the wish to be released from the constraints of social custom,

---

[93] 'Jokes and their relation to the unconscious', *PFL* 6, p. 138.
[94] Mulkay (1988).
[95] See Brown and Levinson (1987), pp. 229–30 for a discussion of the ways that overpoliteness can become a means of insult.
[96] 'Jokes', *PFL* 6, p. 145.   [97] Ibid., p. 149.

which demands the daily displays of politeness.[98] The freedom from social constraint is localized, contained within the joke. The joke is 'only' a joke, and our laughter simultaneously confirms and over-steps the constraint. Inhibitions are released within the joke, but pleasure is safely contained, as the audience vicariously enjoys the display of insult. Yet, as Freud appreciated, the whole business of laughter and the pleasures of humour only make sense if there is a wish which stretches beyond the moment of humour: otherwise why would the comic figure be greeted with delight rather than outrage? As Vološinov suggested, the joke is a conspiracy against social order. The good joke needs a listener and 'its aim is not only to bypass a prohibition, but also to implicate the listener via laughter, to make the laughing listener an accomplice'.[99] Those 'stinky-poos', which caused such amusement to the children studied by Judith Dunn, continue to be visible in adult jokes.[100]

Children, however, must learn that there is 'a time and a place' for jokes. Ordinarily the codes of politeness must be maintained. The tempting pleasures of rudeness must be pushed aside, in favour of the sequences of dialogic politeness. The very thought of rudeness will disrupt the smooth running of ordinary dialogues. Shame will be involved, if rudeness is not curtailed. One sociologist has recently described everyday interactions as 'polite exchanges, aimed at avoiding embarrassment'; but if 'the social fabric and person's moral esteem be torn temporarily, this damage is repaired with excuses and justifications'.[101] Most people can recall occasions, when they let slip the wrong word, causing dialogue to come to an embarrassing standstill, breaking what Thomas Scheff has called 'the social bond'.[102] The mere recall of

---

[98] Poetry, too, can fulfil a similar function. A survey reported that the most popular poem in Britain was Jenny Joseph's 'Warning'. This poem describes what the poet will do as an old woman. Age will free her from customary social constraints. As the poet says, for now, she has to wear sensible clothes and 'not swear in the street'. But, when she is old, she will sit on pavements, wear outrageous clothes and learn to spit (*Guardian*, 12. 10, 1996). The sheer popularity of the poem indicates the extent of the taboos, whose rupture is celebrated. An old woman breaking the taboos, after a lifetime of conformity, poses no threat to the social order. Readers of the poem confirm the social rules as they vicariously enjoy the fantasy of breaking them.

[99] Vološinov (1976), pp. 58–9.

[100] In the United States, Howard Stern broadcasts regularly to an audience of eighteen million listeners. His show trades on making the sort of rude insult (whether sexual, lavatorial or racial) which ordinarily is considered beyond the limits of respectable conversation. His collaborator, Robin Quivers, describes his success: 'All of us remember a time when we were children and we had the freedom to say whatever we wanted and then it got beaten out of us by society. So when we're driving along and we're having a thought and Howard voices it, it just reminds us what it was like to be free' (quoted in *Guardian*, 17. 3. 1997).

[101] Brown (1994), p. 236.

[102] Scheff (1990 and 1997).

such episodes can produce sensations of shame out of all proportion to the actual offence. Better not to think of those moments; better not to relive the shame and embarrassment – it is more comfortable to drive such thoughts away and think of other things.

More than mere *politesse* is at stake in the performance of dialogic politeness. In talking politely and in showing ourselves to be socially competent speakers, we are reproducing ourselves as tolerant, moral, sympathetic selves. We are showing consideration for other speakers, making repairs, phrasing our demands sensitively, etc. We are reinforcing the morality of our community and reproducing our own social bonds. Intolerant, rude, hurtful possibilities (and desires) are routinely driven from conscious awareness. The mere thought of being rude – of criticizing directly, snapping back, discarding the constraints of dialogic organization – raises temptations. If interaction is to proceed routinely and if we are to display, in our utterances, those innumerable small signs of politeness, of which we are hardly aware, then temptation must be far from our conscious thoughts. We must concentrate on the dialogic business in hand, for there is so much to do, and to avoid, in every utterance.

Dialogic repression in action

Repression can be seen to be dialogic, for dialogue involves both the creation of desires and their routine repression. Moreover, as was suggested in the previous chapter, language provides the means of repression. Dialogic repression can be seen to operate at different, but interrelated, levels, whether in the mind of the isolated individual or in shared practices of discourse. Paul Lorenz engaged in bizarre conversations, as a self-distraction from his own troubling inner voices. For him, the outer dialogue became a means of escaping the inner dialogue. But this outer dialogue itself demanded further skills of politeness, which he, in opportuning his fellow officers to join his schemes of repayment, was constantly in danger of infringing.

The disciplines of dialogic politeness can themselves provide further means for repression. Speakers might share patterns of talk which permit the accomplishment of repression. By avoiding certain topics or lines of questioning, they can collaborate to keep disturbing thoughts from being uttered. The shared patterns may be common to a general culture or ideology.[103] On the other hand, the patterns of avoidance may

---

[103] See Billig (1997b) for an analysis of conversations by English families on the monarchy, in which the issue of race is avoided. Racist desires that the Royal Family will not marry non-whites, were projected onto an amorphous public or an anonymous

be narrower in scope. Individual families may have their own patterns of conversation, developing their own variants of wider, social patterns of dialogic repression. We do not know how the Freuds managed not to talk of psychoanalytic issues in their living-room, but the dialogic gap would have to be accomplished in some way.[104]

Freud himself seems to have overlooked the significance of dialogic routine as a form of shared repression. As has been mentioned, in the case of Elisabeth he pointed to the importance of routines for driving away unwelcome erotic thoughts.[105] He also viewed the routines of religion as a form of repression. But the details, not to mention the dialogic aspects, did not particularly interest him. Both the importance of dialogic routines and Freud's own comparative lack of interest are illustrated in his famous case of Dora, which Freud described in 'The fragment of an analysis of a case of hysteria', and which will be discussed in detail later.[106]

Dora was a young woman of nineteen. Her domineering father had insisted that she needed to be treated by Freud, because she was showing the conventional signs of 'hysteria'. It did not take long for Freud to realize that her family life was based upon an intricate pattern of deceit. Dora's father was having a protracted affair with a younger woman, who was the wife of his friend Herr K. The father had been selfishly manipulating family arrangements so the lives of the two households would overlap as much as possible. In this way, he and young Frau K would have further opportunities for consorting together. Herr K, rejected by his wife, had been turning his attentions to young Dora. He had been pursuing her since she was fourteen. For his part, he was contriving to spend as much time as possible in her company.

Freud writes that the situation was made for self-deception. Dora's mother was apparently choosing to ignore the obvious. Herr K did not want to enquire too much about the relationship between his wife and Dora's father. Dora's father did not want to know about Herr K's feelings for his daughter. As Freud wrote, Dora's father was 'one of those men who know how to evade a dilemma by falsifying their judgement upon one of the conflicting alternatives'. Freud specifically

'them'. The details of their talk gave signs of unease with the issue, as the topic was quickly changed or avoided.
[104] Martha's role in restricting psychoanalysis in the household should not be underestimated. Apparently, late in life, Martha confided to the analyst and family friend Marie Bonaparte, that she had been surprised and shocked by her husband's work. When Marie Bonaparte reported back the comment to Freud, he responded 'my wife is very bourgeois' (Ferris, 1997, p. 352).
[105] See above, chapter 2, pp. 36–7.
[106] See chapter 8 for a detailed discussion of the case.

commented on Dora's father that if someone had pointed out to him that his daughter faced danger 'in the constant and unsupervised companionship of a man who had no satisfaction from his own wife', the father would no doubt have replied that 'he could rely upon his daughter, that a man like K. could never be dangerous to her, and that his friend was himself incapable of such intentions'. In this way, both Dora's father and his old friend Herr K 'avoided drawing any conclusions from the other's behaviour which would have been awkward for his own plans'.[107]

The lives of the two families were based on a fragile social order. Certain topics were not to be spoken about, if polite routines of dialogue were to continue. Freud did not especially ask Dora about the conversational routines of the family life. He saw his task to uncover Dora's hidden, repressed desires, rather than discovering how repression was accomplished in the daily routines of her family life. Anyway, Freud assumed that repression took place within the head, not outwardly in conversation. Yet, as Freud noted, the family were showing patterns of avoidance. This enabled Herr K 'to send Dora flowers every day for a whole year while he was in the neighbourhood, to take every opportunity of giving her valuable presents, and to spend all his spare time in her company, without her parents noticing anything in his behaviour that was characteristic of love-making'.[108]

Freud's statement is extraordinary, not least because he fails to enquire how Dora's parents could actually fail to notice Herr K's behaviour. What did they have to do in order to achieve their failure of apprehension? It cannot simply be a perceptual failure, as if they do not see Herr K and his flowers arriving at their house day after day. It is a dialogic failure, or, rather, it is a dialogic accomplishment. No one talks about the matter. Questions are not posed: no one asks why he is always calling. But an absence is not sufficient on its own. The social space must be filled by patterns of routine.

There are a host of unanswered, and now unanswerable, questions. How did Dora's parents react when Herr K called, carrying his expensive gifts? How did they greet him? Did he ask to see Dora? How was Dora summoned? Presumably routines of greeting developed over the year. Did the maid take Herr K's coat? Did she tell her master and mistress who had called? And did they come to greet their dear friend? Perhaps the adults exchanged brief words about the weather, while Herr K was waiting awkwardly for the arrival of Dora. Did Dora's father, then, have the effrontery to ask after Frau K? Perhaps that was another

---

[107] 'Fragment of an analysis', *PFL* 8, p. 66.   [108] Ibid.

topic of dialogic avoidance. Maybe, jokes were cracked. We can imagine Dora's older brother calling out 'Your lover's here again, ha-ha.' If such family jokes were routinely uttered, then the joke repressed the truth that it seemed to express. It was only a joke after all.

It may be that nothing was said about Herr K's demeanour. But nothing could only be said because other things were spoken. A total silence would have been pointed. It would have pointed accusingly to Herr K and his wrapped presents. Other words must fill the space of silence.

When Freud sought to describe the processes of repression, he often resorted to metaphors, especially those about energies and forces. He even talked about the wishes being denied access to rooms, being kept in hallways, and then returning to sneak into the room of consciousness under disguise.[109] The idea of repression being illustrated by the metaphor of a family house is striking, for it emphasizes the place where important repressions are formed. Perhaps an even more vivid image of repression (and its return) would be conveyed by adding figures to the setting, in order to depict repression as a scene of polite interaction. We can imagine the scene of Herr K, standing in the hallway with a bunch of flowers. Everyone is talking politely to him. He is smiling, and so are his friends. We can't quite hear what they saying; but it appears to be nothing consequential – perhaps they are exchanging jovial words, accompanied by gentle displays of laughing. Then someone opens a door, and, with a slight bow, he walks through. Nothing untoward has been said.

[109] 'Introductory lectures', *PFL* 1, p. 89. See above, chapter 2, p. 33.

5   Oedipal desires and Oedipal parents

Repression might be the basic idea of psychoanalytic thinking, but, as Freud developed his ideas, he became increasingly convinced that the Oedipus Complex provided the central theory. With the discovery of this complex, he believed that he held the key to understanding human behaviour. As he wrote in 'Totem and taboo', not only did the complex constitute 'the nucleus of all neuroses', but 'the beginnings of religion, morals, society and art converge in the Oedipus Complex'. All the problems of social psychology, he continued, were proving soluble 'on the basis of one single point – man's relation to his father'.[1] It was because of the Oedipus Complex, argued Freud, that the child becomes 'civilized'. If humans did not undergo this experience as children, they would develop little moral or social sense. Thus, Freud made big claims for the Complex.

At root, the Oedipus Complex is a theory about the way that children acquire a conscience and moral sense. The Complex, according to Freud, explained the need to repress. Without a conscience, there would be little requirement to drive away shameful thoughts. Indeed, without a sense of shame, there could be no shameful thoughts. As Freud wrote in his essay 'On narcissism', 'for the ego the formation of an ideal would be the conditioning factor of repression'.[2] Only a person with moral standards – an image of the 'ideal' – can be offended by their own thoughts. Elisabeth was shocked by her momentary desire for her dead sister's husband: as Freud said, her whole moral being revolted against the idea. Paul punished himself for the inner voice which told him to murder his girlfriend's grandmother. Neither Elisabeth nor Paul would have felt the need to push aside their thoughts, had they not possessed an internal sense of morality.

But why should people torture themselves with feelings of guilt and shame? Why should they acquire the moral voice in the first place? The answers, according to Freud, lay in the mysteries of the Oedipus

[1] 'Totem and taboo', *PFL* 13, p. 219.
[2] 'On narcissism', *PFL* 11, p. 88.

Complex. His arguments for the Complex will be examined closely in this chapter and they will be found wanting in several respects. Freud's ideas about the origins of morality will be examined in relation to the details of his famous case of Little Hans, which he felt provided direct evidence for the truth of the Oedipal theory.

As will be argued, this case, too, shows a familiar gap. Repression, although playing a central role in both the theory and the case, again is left unaccounted for. The child, whose psychological development is charted with vivid and careful detail, suddenly is able to repress. Repression just seems to happen. However, the details of the case permit us to go further, in order to tie the origins and practice of repression to language. Freud, in his report, includes records of conversations between Hans and his parents. These dialogues evoke the family atmosphere of those distant times. In addition, they provide clues, which Freud overlooked, about how Hans was picking up the need to repress and the skills to do so. These clues all point to the parents.

As will be seen, the Oedipal theory continually draws attention to the child's desires. The case can be re-read to point in the opposite direction. Hans is picking up skills of talk from his parents. He is acquiring moral precepts from them as he converses with them. He does not have to wait for the full-blown Oedipus Complex to acquire this. The roots of repression are contained within this talk.

To pursue these notions, the focus of attention must be decisively shifted from the Oedipal child to the Oedipal parents. Freud saw the young boy's words as symptoms of deeper, essentially non-verbal processes. The present argument is different. If the child is to acquire the habits of repression, then these habits will be learned from adults through conversation. What the adults say to the child is even more important than what the child says. Consequently, the case will cease to be Little Hans's story. It will become just as much the story of his parents, who, it will be suggested, were practising habits of repression. It is also a story about Freud, who was no distant bystander. Freud was constructing the Oedipal story, which the parents were imposing on the child and which depicted the child, not his parents, as possessing desires requiring repression. The Oedipal story itself was therefore part of the repression practised by the parents.

The Oedipal story

When Freud collaborated with Breuer to write 'Studies on hysteria' he had not yet hit upon one of the hallmarks of later psychoanalytic thinking – namely, the idea that the origins of adult neuroses are to be found in the desires of childhood. The cases of Elisabeth and Paul are different in this respect. Freud sought the origins of Elisabeth's neuroses in events of her adolescence. He portrayed her experiences, while nursing her sick father, as the pivotal moment of the case. By the time, Freud came to analyse Paul, he was convinced that early childhood held the key to the adult condition. Accordingly, Freud sought to connect Paul's adult obsessions to his early relations with his father. In this, he was seeking to find an Oedipal explanation of Paul's condition.

Although sometimes Freud described the Oedipus Complex in intricate terms, he also summarized the basic Oedipal situation succinctly, especially in his more popular writings – and especially in relation to the young boy. The Complex, he wrote, arises from the young boy's erotic love for the mother between the ages of two and five, together with 'the attitude of rivalry and hostility towards the father'.[3] Originally in the very early stages of life, the infant shows 'auto-eroticism', but soon it takes the mother as its 'love-object'. The sexes may diverge in their attachments: 'Boys concentrate their sexual wishes upon their mother and develop hostile impulses against their father as being a rival, while girls adopt an analogous attitude'.[4] It was the situation of the boy, especially his relation with the father, that occupied Freud's attention: he never seems to have sorted out the position of girls in his own mind.[5] The boy wants the father out of the way, and, consequently, finds himself having two extreme, but related, wishes: 'to kill his father and take his mother to wife'.[6] Yet, the boy loves the father. He worries that the father can read his mind. He imagines the father's anger, on discovering his son's murderous impulses. Perhaps, the father would, as an act of revenge, attempt to castrate his son, who was now a rival for the mother's love. All this goes on in the son's imagination.

At this stage, usually during the child's fourth or fifth year, the Complex reaches its climax. A successful resolution is possible. In his imagination the son becomes the father: if he *were* the father, then he would be able to possess the mother. Thus, the son identifies with his father. The successful solution comes at a psychological cost. The child's ego is split. Part of it becomes the ego-ideal, or the superego, which is the imagined stern voice of the father, now internalized, as the

[3] 'Two encyclopaedia articles', *PFL* 15, p. 143.
[4] 'An autobiographical study', *PFL* 15, pp. 219–20.
[5] Indeed, Freud wavered in his belief whether girls went through a complex which was the mirror image of the Oedipal situation, or whether the whole business was less fraught with girls.
[6] 'Introductory lectures', *PFL* 1, p. 243.

child's own stern voice of conscience. This superego acts as 'a critical agency within the ego', becoming the 'chief influence in repression'.[7]

The result is not the possession of the mother but the curtailment of instinct. The voice of conscience – the superego – turns on the instinctive desires, demanding their repression. These impulses have become shameful in the child's mind and now must be pushed aside, dismissed from conscious awareness. The hostility towards the father and erotic feelings for the mother are repressed. Then follows the latency period, which lasts until puberty. During this time 'the *reaction-formations* of morality, shame and disgust are built up'.[8] In this way, the Oedipal situation lays down the basis for morality and creates the necessity for repression.

Freud did not hesitate to make sweeping claims for the Oedipus Complex. In 'The introductory lectures', he claimed it to be 'a regular and very important factor in a child's mental life', adding that in his view 'there is more danger of our under-estimating rather than over-estimating its influence and that of the developments which proceed from it'.[9] The complex, he asserted, has the greatest importance 'in every human being' for it determines 'the final shape' of the individual's erotic life.[10] Freud confidently asserted that the Oedipus Complex affected 'every human being', because he was firmly of the opinion that the complex was rooted in the human biological condition. In an essay published in 1924, he stressed this theme. Although the majority of people 'go through the Oedipus Complex as an individual experience', he wrote that it is nevertheless a phenomenon 'which is determined and laid down by heredity'.[11] He argued, in another piece, that the Oedipus Complex was 'the psychical correlate of two fundamental biological facts'.[12] These two factors were: the long period of the human child's dependence on adults and the presence of sexual desires during this period of dependency. Thus, the child could not escape the Oedipal situation, regardless of cultural background or the situation of the family.

Because the child's impulses are seen as being instinctual, the adults are not responsible for awakening them. Freud even suggested that the parents might be the victims, as the infant child tries to seduce them. In 'The introductory lectures', Freud described how the young boy might 'make actual attempts' at seducing the mother. Freud also alluded to the 'coquetry' of the young girl towards her father.[13] The possibility of

[7] 'Group psychology and the analysis of the ego', *PFL* 12, p. 139.
[8] *PFL* 15, p. 220.   [9] 'Introductory lectures', *PFL* 1, p. 244.
[10] 'Two encyclopaedia articles', *PFL* 15, p. 143.
[11] 'The dissolution of the Oedipus complex', *PFL* 7, p. 315.
[12] 'A short account of psychoanalysis', *PFL* 15, p. 181.
[13] 'Introductory lectures', *PFL* 1, pp. 376–7.

adults desiring the child are downgraded.[14] The child, in consequence comes over as the seducer, who cannot help blindly following a pattern of desire imposed by biology.

The Oedipal story depicts a sequence of events which culminate in the creation of the super-ego. The story suggests that the moral sense is set in place almost at a single go, as the child internalises the voice of the father. Yet, as will be seen, matters are more complicated and more gradual. Even the pre-Oedipal child is a speaking subject, constantly participating in conversations which convey, and themselves represent, a moral order.[15] One might suppose that, unless children have been taught some sort of incipient morality, they would be unable to develop the fears that they supposedly hold at the height of the complex. Why else would the boy imagine that the father would be unwilling to share the mother's affections? Also, the internalized voice of the father is a moral voice. Presumably the child has been hearing this voice for a while: why else would the child take such moral tones to represent the voice of the father? This may be connected with another difficulty in the Oedipal story. Freud's story does not explain how the child, or its newly created superego, is able to repress the shameful wishes, when the occasion demands. The skill just appears. Perhaps, the key lies in the moral voices that the child has been hearing.

As always, the details of Freud's cases offer possibilities for reinterpretation. In the case of Little Hans, Freud leaves a record which allows us to do something that he did not do: to study the little words in the record of the conversations with Hans. This means examining not so much the words supposedly uttered by the child, but those of the adults, most notably the Oedipal parents, and most remarkably of all, those of the Oedipal discoverer, Freud himself.

[14] This can be seen in the passage of the 'Introductory lectures', in which Freud described the infant as a seducer of parents. Freud did not ignore the possibility that adults might 'seduce' (or abuse) children. In the 'Introductory lectures', he raises the possibility in a single sentence, only to dismiss it: 'We must not omit to add that the parents themselves often exercise a determining influence on the awakening of a child's Oedipus attitude by themselves obeying the pull of sexual attraction, and that where there are several children the father will give the plainest evidence of his affection for his little daughter and the mother for her son.' The phrasing itself downplays the adult feelings and responsibility – adults are 'obeying' the pull of sexual attraction and this manifests itself in 'greater affection'. The single sentence raises no spectres of actual seduction, as if harmless favouritism is the sole outcome of adult sexual desires towards children. The sentence is followed by a theoretical dismissal: 'But the spontaneous nature of the Oedipus complex in children cannot be seriously shaken by this factor' (p. 377). The proviso does not subvert the main story: the objection is taken into account in order to be discounted.

[15] Shweder, Mahapatra, and Miller (1990), examining the talk between children and adults, have commented that the internalization of adult moral standards is a process 'that does not wait patiently for an Oedipus Complex to develop' (p. 192).

Little Hans and the theory of Oedipus

Originally, Freud derived his theory of the Oedipus Complex from the analysis of adults. His method was to encourage adults to talk of their childhood memories, going as far back as they could into their remembered pasts. From analyses, conducted in the late 1890s and early years of the twentieth century and, of course, from his own famous self-analysis, which he started shortly after the publication of 'Studies on hysteria', Freud became convinced of the reality of the Oedipal situation. He was not, however, to use the actual term 'Oedipus Complex' until 1910.[16] Freud was aware that his theory could be easily criticized on methodological grounds because it was based on adult recollections about what happened in childhood. The theory lacked evidence directly taken from the analysis of children.

Around 1905 and 1906, Freud was particularly keen to remedy this situation. Martha had adamantly refused to let him psychoanalyse their own children.[17] So he turned to the small group of followers, who met regularly at his house each Wednesday evening and who were to form the nucleus of the Vienna Psychoanalytic Society. Freud encouraged those with young children to keep records, watching out for any Oedipal developments. Max Graf, a music critic interested in using psychoanalysis to study art, duly obliged.[18] His wife had introduced him to Freud and psychoanalysis. A few years earlier, when she was still single, she had been treated by Freud.[19] Max, but not his wife, joined the all-male Wednesday group, as one of its earliest members.[20] He even appears to have began psychoanalysing his wife.[21] A year after Max

---

[16] Laplanche and Pontalis (1983), p. 283.

[17] See Isbister (1985), p. 160.

[18] Many years later, shortly after Freud's death, Max Graf was to publish a fascinating reminiscence of his relations with Freud and of the early history of the psychoanalytic movement (Graf, 1942).

[19] It is not clear why Freud treated Hans's mother. In the case report of Hans, Freud merely mentions that Hans's 'beautiful mother fell ill with a neurosis as a result of a conflict during her girlhood' (*PFL* 8, p. 298).

[20] Graf seems to have accepted the sexist views of the times in general and the psychoanalytic circle in particular. He is reported in the minutes of the Vienna Psychoanalytic Society, as saying that studying was harmful for women (15 May 1907: reported in Nunberg and Federn, 1967). It was to be a few years before the first women joined the group (Appignanesi and Forrester, 1993).

[21] Freud wrote to Jung in February 1910 that he had thought it 'quite impossible to analyse one's own wife', but 'Little Hans's father has proved to me that it can be done' (Freud and Jung, 1991, p. 174). Freud and Graf seem to have taken it for granted that, if there is to be analysis between spouses, the husband should analyse the wife, rather than vice versa.

became a regular member, the Grafs' son, Herbert, was born.[22] A daughter was to be born three years later.

The Grafs decided to raise their son according to psychoanalytic precepts. Max, in his notes, paid particular attention to his son's interest in sexual matters. He passed these notes regularly to Freud. When Freud came to write about the young Graf, in 'Analysis of a phobia in a five year old boy', he quoted extensively from the father's notes, especially the records of conversations between Hans and his parents. In these notes, the young boy emerges as an intelligent child, ready to debate and question his parents. In Freud's words, he was 'a cheerful, good-natured and lively little boy'.[23]

In the published account, Freud was to change the boy's name from Herbert to Hans. Now that the real name as well as the pseudonym are known, the modern writer about the case is faced with the same problem that was discussed in relation to the so-called 'Rat Man': by which name should the patient be called?[24] Whereas Ernst Lanzer had, by accident, more than one pseudonym, as well as a nickname, matters seem much simpler in the case of the Graf boy. He has become known as 'Hans', his only pseudonym. So it would seem sensible to keep the first name by which he became known in psychoanalytic circles, while maintaining his real, non-pseudonymous family name.

In deciding to give Herbert the pseudonym 'Hans', Freud was doing more than merely selecting a name which resembled the original, in that both share the same first letter. He must have been aware that his choice of name was not entirely innocent. He was using a name, which Max had almost chosen for his son and which had symbolic importance for the father. Both names, 'Hans' and 'Herbert', were symbols of the father's illicit sexual desires, as Max Graf admitted in Freud's presence. While Freud was still collecting regular reports on the case – on 8 April 1908, to be precise – Max Graf talked about the significance of his children's names at one of the Wednesday meetings of the psycho-analytic group in Freud's house. The minutes of the meeting record him saying that both his children had names beginning with 'H' (Herbert and Hanna). As a student he had been infatuated with his cousin Hedwig, and had written the initial 'H' everywhere, apparently 'taking pride in the especially beautiful way he wrote it'. He had considered naming his son 'Hans' or 'Harry'. Even after his marriage,

---

[22] Jones (1955) dates Graf's membership from 1902 (p. 9).
[23] 'Analysis of a phobia', *PFL* 8, p. 170.
[24] See above, chapter 4, pp. 58–9.

Max Graf had continued to think 'with great intensity' about his 'old sweetheart'.[25]

Freud, in the case history, mentions none of this. At its simplest, Graf's admission shows the atmosphere of the family and hints at the troubled relationship between Max and his wife. The marriage, in fact, was to end in divorce, as Freud recorded in a postscript, written in 1922 for a later edition of the case-history.[26] One might speculate whether Max's wife was aware of the significance of the letter 'H'- and, indeed, whether she knew that her husband was talking of these private matters to his male psychoanalytic friends. She might not have been best pleased to discover that her children's names commemorated an earlier, and surreptitiously continuing, passion. One might hope that Max would not have told her too much about his continuing 'intense' thoughts for his old love.

Freud's silence is perhaps unsurprising. Given that Frau Graf would read the report, and would know that it described her Herbert, then it would have been tactful not to mention Max's remarks, told confidentially man-to-men. But there is more than tact being shown to a colleague and fellow male. Freud could argue that the extra information was not relevant to the story. Nor would it be, if one assumes that the secrets of the parents are not relevant to uncovering the secrets of the child's mental life.

On the other hand, if the skills of repression are based on skills of avoidance, then the keeping of family secrets may not be quite so irrelevant. The boy was growing up in an environment of secrecy. His very name symbolized a secret wish, probably not to be discussed openly between mother and father. All this becomes relevant if one asks where the child learnt to hide – even from himself – his own forbidden sexual desires.

Freud's pseudonym for the boy has become the name routinely used by psychoanalytic writers. The boy, now, *is* Little Hans. This, too, is symbolic. Every time the name is used unproblematically, without reference to the secret symbolism omitted in Freud's report, so we continue to look in the direction that Freud was pointing. We look to the child for the hidden desires. We continue to assume that it is the case of Little Hans, and not that of his parents. The pseudonym, thus, has become a shared routine of concealment, in which the unwitting support of later generations has been enrolled.

---

[25] Nunberg and Federn (1967), p. 368.
[26] 'Analysis of a phobia', *PFL* 8, p. 305.

Hans's Oedipal story and repression

Oedipal themes dominate Freud's report of the case.[27] The notes sent by Graf themselves emphasize such themes, and Freud organized them in order to highlight Hans's love for his mother and his aggressive feelings towards his father. The report is rich in detail, containing subsidiary themes, such as Hans's concerns with childbirth and with defecation. The central message is clear. Freud described Hans as 'a little Oedipus who wanted to have his father "out of the way", to get rid of him, so that he might be alone with his beautiful mother and sleep with her'.[28]

Freud did not analyse Hans, in the sense that he analysed his adult patients. The analysis was carried on at a distance, as Freud examined the reports which Hans's father brought. Apart from one occasion, the boy did not come to his consulting-room. The reports, which no doubt were supplemented by discussions with Graf, were sufficient for Freud to declare many years later that he 'never got a finer insight into a child's soul'.[29] He was to refer to the case as providing the necessary proof for the Oedipal hypothesis. In the second edition of his 'Three essays on the theory of sexuality', Freud commented that 'it is gratifying to be able to report that direct observation has fully confirmed the conclusions arrived at by psychoanalysis'.[30] Similarly, in 'The sexual theories of children' he was to assert that the case offered 'irrefutable proof of the correctness of a view towards which the psychoanalysis of adults had been leading me'.[31] Freud believed that Hans's case illustrated universal aspects of child psychology. As he wrote in 'Totem and taboo', Hans, in regarding his father 'as a competitor for the favours of his mother' was displaying the 'typical attitude of a male child'.[32]

The early parts of the case history seek to establish Hans's awakening sexuality. The earliest of the father's notes, which Freud included in his report, depict episodes in which the young boy shows an interest in

---

[27] The case has, of course, become notable in psychoanalytic circles and, as such, has been the object of reinterpretation: see, for example, Glenn, 1980; Silverman, 1980; and Ornstein, 1993a. The case, however, has not attracted the same amount of attention as other major cases such as Dora and the 'Rat Man'. For example, Marcus (1984), in his book on the culture of psychoanalysis, devotes full chapters to those two cases, but Little Hans gets only a single, cursory mention. Whole books have been devoted to the cases of Dora, the 'Rat Man' and the 'Wolf Man'. There is no equivalent for Little Hans.

[28] 'Analysis of a phobia', PFL 8, p. 269.

[29] Jones (1955), p. 294.

[30] Freud PFL 7, pp. 111–12. The first edition was originally published in 1905, before Hans's phobia with the horses.

[31] PFL 7, p. 192.   [32] PFL 13, p. 189.

sexual matters, and especially in his parents' genitalia. We read about young Hans asking his mother whether she has a 'widdler' (or more accurately a 'wi-wi-maker'). The notes describe Hans's interest in young girls and particularly in his baby sister. Above all, Hans seems to be preoccupied by widdlers. Freud comments that 'his interest in widdlers was by no means a purely theoretical one: as might be expected, it also impelled him to touch his member'.[33] When Hans was three and a half, his mother found him with his hand on his penis. 'If you do that' she told him, 'I shall send for Dr A to cut off your widdler.'[34] Freud comments that these examples help to confirm that 'much if not most' of Hans's behaviour is 'typical of the sexual development of children in general'.[35]

The case history develops other Oedipal themes. We read that Hans wanted to share his mother's bed, and he became increasingly jealous of his little sister. The main focus of his jealousy is his father. Although hated as a rival, this was, nevertheless, the same father 'whom he had always loved'.[36] A crisis develops in Hans's life. When he is four, he develops a phobia of horses. He will not leave the family house for fear of encountering these terrifying animals. Something has upset the cheerful, bright young boy, turning him into a fearful neurotic. Hans's father no longer merely delivers weekly reports to Freud, but he turns to the doctor for advice. At this point, he brings the child to Freud for a consultation.

Freud and Hans's father believe that sex lies at the root of the boy's problem. They explain the fear of horses according to the Oedipal hypothesis. They suggest that Hans's love for his mother, which has been increasingly thwarted since the birth of his sister, is being accompanied by aggressive feelings towards his father, his rival for a place in the maternal bed. Hans also fears that his father might be able to read his mind. Hans supposedly imagines that his father would retaliate by castration if he only knew what he, Hans, was thinking. The sight of female genitalia fuels this fear: in Hans's mind, females, such as his mother and baby sister, have already been castrated. However, Hans loves his father, as well as fearing and hating him. Hans 'solves' this complex of feelings by repressing the aggression and directing it onto horses, which he associates with his father (having noticed the big 'wi-wi-makers' of these animals). Once the fear and aggression are projected onto horses, Hans can resume loving his father, and he internalizes the paternal image as the voice of conscience. Hans is then on his way to the calm of the latency period.

[33] 'Analysis of a phobia', *PFL* 8, p. 171.
[34] Ibid.   [35] Ibid.   [36] Ibid., p. 291.

Hans began to show his fear of horses, and his unwillingness to go out in the street, at the beginning of January 1908. When his mother said that she would take him to the park, he started crying. Eventually she persuaded him to go. On the return home, again he showed signs of distress; 'after much internal struggling' he told his mother that he was afraid a horse might bite him.[37] On the same day, Freud reports, his mother asked him 'Do you put your hand to your widdler?'[38] Hans answered that he did so, every evening in bed. The following day, before his afternoon sleep, he was told not to put his hand to his widdler.

Stopping Hans putting hand to widdler was not sufficient for the parents. The desire was as bad as the action. In March, while Hans's phobia about horses was still at its height, Hans's father told him one morning: 'You know, if you don't put your hand to your widdler any more, this nonsense of yours'll soon get better.' Hans then denied that he touched himself any more. 'But you still want to', accused his father. Hans demurred, adding that 'wanting's not doing'. That was not sufficient excuse for the father: 'Well, but to prevent your wanting to, this evening you're going to have a bag to sleep in.' Hans's father reports that the boy's spirits were lifted. He was less afraid of horses and said 'Oh, if I have a bag to sleep in my nonsense'll have gone tomorrow.'[39]

The episode is revealing. To a modern reader, it indicates the obsession of the parents with masturbation. It also shows the parents' belief that Hans's fear of horses was connected with his desire to masturbate – rather than to any induced guilt about masturbating. The desire must be stopped, as Hans is told by his father. In so doing, the father is telling Hans to repress, push aside, the desire. But he doesn't tell Hans how to do this. All he does is offer a sleeping bag. If Hans sleeps in this bag, then the troublesome thought will automatically be banished. How or why this magical disappearance will occur is not explained. The boy does not ask. Nor does Freud comment on the matter.

The omissions are symptomatic of a wider omission, regarding the processes of repression. Freud relates the onset of Hans's phobia to an increasing anxiety that his mother might leave him. Hans says he wants his mother to 'coax' (cuddle) him. According to Freud, Hans's affection for his mother had 'become enormously intensified' and that this 'was the fundamental phenomenon in his condition'.[40] He then asserts that this increased affection 'suddenly turned into anxiety – which, as we should say, succumbed to repression'.[41]

The phrasing is similar to Freud's description in the 'Five lectures' of Elisabeth, at her sister's deathbed, pushing her shameful thought about

---

[37] Ibid., p. 187.   [38] Ibid.   [39] Ibid., p. 193.
[40] Ibid., p. 187.   [41] Ibid., p. 188.

her brother-in-law from awareness. Then, he described the thought as being 'surrendered' (*überliefen*) to repression. Hans's anxiety 'succumbs' (*unterliegt*) to repression. In neither case is there any description of what goes on in the person's mind, to describe how the surrendering or succumbing actually occurs. It is as if an outside force – the repression – takes hold of the mind. This is reinforced by the description Freud gives in summarizing the case of Little Hans. He writes that 'we have seen how our little patient was overtaken by a great wave of repression'.[42] Again, repression is something that happens to people, not something they do. And again, the actual moment of repression, let alone the action of repressing, is left undescribed.[43]

A child has to learn the mysteries of the world. Hans is to learn that touching his widdler makes him frightened of horses. He doesn't seem to question this explanation. He must also learn to banish the desire to touch his penis. If he sleeps in a bag, then the desire will disappear. Again he doesn't question. Hans just has to lie there, and the thoughts will disappear. And so they do. He enters the latency period: the obsessions with horses and widdlers apparently pass. He must have learnt to repress.

But how has he learnt to do so? His father has not taught him. Apart from the bag business, he has no help or advice to offer. It seems that either repression is magical – like a conjurer making balls disappear from a velvet bag; or, it spontaneously occurs as a force of nature. There is, however, a third possibility. The child learns from adults, who are spontaneously practising repression. They cannot talk of it – they cannot pass on tips – because they, too, are largely unaware of what they are doing. The child, in acquiring these habits, which are going on all around him, also acquires this unawareness. If this is the case, then, to understand childish repression, we should not go further back into the life of the child. We should look up, in order to notice what the adults are doing.

Castration and parental desire

The Oedipal story focuses on the young child's desires. The parents, by contrast, seem devoid of desire. The case-history of Hans begins with the little boy's interest in sex, and this is conveyed as something that spontaneously occurs. The resulting sequence of events seems to unfold

[42] Ibid., p. 295.
[43] Because of this gap, it is hard to agree with commentators who claim that Freud in his case reports actually specifies the processes of repression; see, for example Ornstein (1993a), who recognizes Freud's failure to take into account the actions of the parents.

with an inevitable momentum which the parents are powerless to stop. They are the objects of Hans's desires and fears. Nothing they do, according to the logic of the narrative, is responsible for the events. Freud stressed that Hans's 'excellent and devoted' mother should not be blamed in any way for Hans's phobia: she had little choice for 'she had a predestined part to play, and her position was a hard one'.[44] She was a mother, who, like all mothers, could not escape being the object of her young son's desires.

'Why don't you put your finger there?', Hans asks his mother after a bath, as she powders round his penis. Because it would be 'piggish' and 'not proper', she replies. 'But it's great fun' declares Hans without shame.[45] Freud was to describe Hans's words as an attempt 'at seducing his mother'.[46] The mother, of course, was not to be blamed 'for having precipitated the processes of repression by her energetic rejection of his advances'.[47]

The parents' reactions are presented as being, as it were, a natural backdrop against which the child's inbuilt desires are displayed. Hans's parents are not devoid of desire. One particular desire is expressed again and again: they want to prevent their son masturbating. While Hans is still three and a half, the mother can be heard uttering a threat of castration: Dr A will be summoned to cut off the widdler, if Hans does not stop playing with it. The incident, for Freud, reveals childish desires, rather than adult ones. In so doing, he suggests the parent could do little else but threaten such violence, when faced with the offensive desires of the child.

In other works, too, Freud wrote about the threat of castration as if it were a normal part of the universal Oedipal process. For instance, in 'Outline of Psychoanalysis', he describes the Oedipal situation as one 'which every child is destined to pass through'.[48] The boy begins to show signs of sexuality. The mother realizes that she cannot allow him to touch his penis. Her prohibitions have little effect. At last she makes the severest threat of threatening to remove the continually touched organ: 'Usually, in order to make the threat more frightening and more credible, she delegates its execution to the boy's father.'[49] She says she will tell the father and he will cut the penis off.

Freud, in his Oedipal account, does something very interesting and

[44] 'Analysis of a phobia', *PFL* 8, p. 190.
[45] Ibid., p. 182.   [46] Ibid., p. 188.   [47] Ibid., p. 190.
[48] 'Outline of Psychoanalysis', *PFL* 15, p. 422.
[49] Ibid., p. 424. In the 'New introductory lectures', he wrote that a boy's castration anxiety is initially grounded in realistic fears, for 'people threaten him often enough with cutting off his penis during the phallic phase, at the time of his early masturbation' (*PFL* 2, p. 119; see also 'Introductory lectures', *PFL* 1, p. 416).

symptomatic. He traces the origins of the boy's castration complex – the fear that the father will castrate him – to the young boy's erotic desires for the mother. He does not relate them to the mother's threats. Or, at least, the mother's threats are not seen as the cause of the complex, for they are the inevitable result of the boy's self-touching. In this, Freud is assuming that the particular parental reaction – that of threatening castration – is universal, rather than reflecting harsh patterns of child rearing current in Vienna.[50]

Freud downgrades the importance of parental words, which, unlike those of their children, are not seen as signs of desire. By overlooking the parents' words, Freud overlooks something else in the case of Hans: the extent to which the overt emergence of sexuality is accompanied by moral discourse. The examples offered in the case history bear this out – as Hans demonstrates his interest, so the parents, most notably the mother, indicate disapproval. She threatens castration; she tells him it is 'piggish' and 'not proper' to touch the penis. In this way, Hans receives lessons in morality.

Freud, then, relates Hans's problems, and those of other children to inner desire, not to outer lesson. Always, it is back to Hans. Mother and father, too, blame Hans. Their actions – threatening violent punishment against a small child for touching himself – are not described in the language of desire. In this story, it is only the child who has aggressive desires. It is as if the adults are projecting their own desires onto that bright, lively boy, who, coinciding with the adults' growing obsession with his widdler, becomes afraid to leave the house.

Projecting aggression onto Hans

The idea of parental projection suggests a solution to the problem of how Hans might learn to repress. If the parents are projecting their desires onto Hans, then this would be seen in their patterns of explanation. They deny having desires, which might be attributed to them, and they attribute such desires to Hans. As such, projection is a pattern of talk. With the parents using such talk in front of the boy. Hans is being brought up in a discursive environment, in which a form of repression is being practised routinely. The Oedipal child is being taught by Oedipal parents.

The record of the conversations, reproduced by Freud, shows that the very desires, attributed to Hans, can just as plausibly – and, in some cases, even more plausibly – be attributed to the parents. Moreover, the

---

[50] For more on the patterns of child rearing, especially the acceptance of harsh parental violence, see Wolff (1988).

parents deny having such emotions, either explicitly or implicitly by the way that they point the accusing finger at their son. Freud, in telling the Oedipal tale, tacitly supports such denials.

There is a case for saying that the son is accused of desiring to commit the sort of aggressive behaviour which the parents engage in.[51] As his father makes the charge, so he, with Freud's support, discounts the actual aggressive actions committed by the adults in Hans's life. One charge is that Hans feels aggressively towards his baby sister. The report suggests that the mother regularly beats the baby. Hans specifically says he doesn't like hearing Hanna scream when Mummy whacks her 'on her bare bottom': Hans expresses no pleasure, nor wish to participate in the scene.[52] Yet, Freud still writes about Hans's 'undisguised expression of his death-wish against his sister', without specifying the possible effects of his regularly witnessing violence against the infant.[53]

In questioning Hans, the father tries to elicit answers, which will express a desire to be violent. At one time, the father asks Hans 'Which would you really like to beat? Mummy, Hanna or me?' Hans replies 'Mummy'. He is then asked how he would like to beat her, and he replies 'with a carpet beater'. In the notes to Freud, the father adds in parenthesis that 'his mother often threatens to beat him with a carpet-beater'.[54] Hans, having been encouraged to express a wish to hurt, repeats a wish that he has often heard expressed by the parent against him. There is a further example. The father has been talking about horses with Hans and asks: 'Would you like to beat the horses as Mummy beats Hanna? You like that too, you know.'[55] Hans, in his reply, avoids all mention of liking. He says that horses do not mind being beaten. The father adds a note saying that he had told Hans this once, to prevent him from being disturbed by seeing horses whipped.

These conversations show Hans declining to express a liking to beat. He repeats what he has heard, and also returns a threat made by his mother. These responses are taken as evidence for his aggressive desires. The actual actions and more forceful threats of the adults are, as it were, pushed aside. They are not seen as indicating aggressive desires against children. As we know, in Vienna at that time, violence was regularly practised against children in the name of discipline. It was a 'normal' accepted part of child-rearing, despite several well publicised cases in

---

[51] Erich Fromm accused Freud of ignoring the violence of Hans's parents. He claimed that the report showed Freud had switched from being an advocate of the child to a defender of the parent (Fromm, 1970).

[52] 'Analysis of a phobia', *PFL* 8, pp. 232–33.

[53] Ibid., *PFL* 8, p. 272.

[54] Ibid., p. 241.   [55] Ibid., p. 239.

which beatings had led to children's death.[56] Still, it is the child wishing
to hurt the adult, rather than vice versa.

The father also accuses Hans of wishing to hurt him. Freud partici-
pates in this accusation. When Hans is brought to Freud's consulting
room, the doctor gently tells the boy that he 'was afraid of his father,
precisely because he was so fond of his mother'.[57] He mentions that he
had told Hans's father this. He tells Hans that he is not blaming him and
that other little boys feel the same. At this point the father interrupts. He
is wanting to establish that he has done nothing to provoke Hans's fears:
'Have I ever scolded you or hit you?', he asks. Hans replies, offering not
quite the answer the father was seeking to elicit: 'Oh, yes! You have hit
me.' The father denies the charge: 'That's not true.' The father,
according to Freud, then recollected that Hans 'had quite unexpectedly
butted his head into his stomach, so that he had given him as it were a
reflex blow with his hand'.[58] Freud accepts the father's account of the
episode, which puts the blame firmly on Hans. Freud interprets the
episode as a further example of the boy's 'hostile disposition' towards
the father.[59] By contrast, Freud does not discuss the father's possible
hostile disposition towards his son.[60]

The son has heard his father denying ever hitting him. And he hears
his father, when challenged, describe the episode in a way that rhetorically puts the blame on Hans. The innocent father has been provoked:
not guilty, pronounces the doctor. Thus, when the father hits Hans, the
story becomes further evidence of Hans's aggressive desires. We may not
know the inner wishes of the three participants of the dialogue; nor can
we know what really happened. But we do know that Hans hears adult
rhetoric. He hears how a story may be told, so that blame can be
deflected and responsibility denied.[61] Hans hears the rhetoric of denial

---

[56] For a discussion of the routine violence used in the treatment of children in fin-de-
siècle Vienna, see Wolff (1988). Wolff makes the point that, despite the publicity given
to several cases in which children were actually beaten to death by their parents, there
was an avoidance of general debate on the topic, as if the implications were being
repressed. Wolff uses the court reports published in *Neue Freie Presse*, the daily Viennese
newspaper read by Freud.

[57] 'Analysis of a phobia', *PFL* 8, p. 204.

[58] Ibid.   [59] Ibid.

[60] Freud adds that it is 'remarkable' that the father at first had not connected this episode
with the boy's neurosis: after all, it clearly expressed the boy's Oedipal hostility. Freud
does not probe why such a 'remarkable' omission had taken place: why should Max
Graf have apparently forgotten something so crucial?

[61] Discursive psychologists have paid great attention to the way that speakers reformulate
events in order to make rhetorical cases, especially relating to the allocation and denial
of blame. See, for example, Antaki (1994), Edwards (1997) and Edwards and Potter
(1992).

and projection, and this offers him, as it were, a guide for dealing with his own psychic conflicts.

Oedpial parents and the projection of sexual desire

In the Oedipal interpretation of Little Hans's case, much is made about Hans's wish to share his mother's bed. There is little doubt that Hans enjoyed getting into bed with his mother for a cuddle. But that does not mean that he was jealous of the father. If anything the record suggests that there is more reason to suspect the father of being jealous of Hans, rather than vice versa. Later, it will be suggested that the father specifically instructs Hans to 'admit' his jealousy. For the present, it is sufficient to show how Graf and Freud construct a tale of Hans's jealousy.

The Oedipal story depicts the young boy filled with a sexual energy, which is waiting to burst upon the mother. At the time, Freud and his colleagues worried about mothers' showing too much affection towards their sons, lest they stimulate the sexually primed boy. Just a few weeks before Little Hans began to show his fear of horses, his father had attended a Wednesday session, in which Isidor Sadger had, according to the minutes, argued that 'the most significant and most severe traumata are inflicted on the infant by excessive demonstrations of affection'.[62] Although Graf criticized Sadger on several points, having felt the lash of Sadger's critical tongue the previous week, he does not seem to have taken issue with him on that particular matter.

Graf seems to have brought his psychoanalytic fears home with him. Following the birth of Hanna, Hans had been moved into a room of his own. Still he kept coming back to his parents' bedroom and Max Graf strongly disapproved. Above all, he disliked Hans getting into bed with Mummy.[63] The father gave psychoanalytic justifications for his disapproval. Herr Graf told his son 'as long as you come into our room in the mornings, your fear of horses won't get better'.[64] Graf often directed his criticism against his wife, whom he claimed showed the boy too much affection. As Freud wrote, 'his father accuses her, not without some show of injustice, of being responsible for the outbreak of the child's neurosis, on account of her excessive display of affection for him and her too frequent readiness to take him into her bed'.[65]

Max Graf may have disapproved of his wife's affectionate treatment of Hans, but, it seems, with little effect. At one stage, he reports, that Hans

---

[62] Nunberg and Federn (1967), pp. 271.
[63] 'Analysis of a phobia', *PFL* 8, pp. 186, and 190.
[64] Ibid., p. 209.   [65] Ibid., p. 190.

'always' comes through to their bedroom, and 'my wife cannot resist taking him into bed with her for a few minutes'. His description of his wife's behaviour contains more than a hint of blame: she cannot 'resist', as if the action is one that should be resisted. Again, there is no attribution of desire. He does not suggest, heaven forbid, that his wife might actually want to give Hans a cuddle.

Graf reports that he warned his wife not to let Hans into bed with her, 'and she answers now and then, rather irritated, no doubt, that it's all nonsense, that after all one minute is of no importance, and so on'. He comments that 'then Hans stays with her a little while'.[66] It appears, therefore, that Hans witnesses this disagreement, seeing his father lose the argument regularly. We are not told exactly what mother and father say. The father's text is vague: 'and so on', he writes, suggesting that the details of the mother's words are of little importance.

There are other intimacies, which the son shares with the mother, and from which the father, much to his expressed disapproval, is excluded. At one point, as the father is conducting his psychoanalytic interrogation of the boy, it becomes clear that Hans, but not the father, knows what colour knickers the mother was wearing that day. When asked how he knows this, Hans is evasive. The father has his suspicions: 'I asked my wife whether Hans was often with her when she went to the WC.'[67] The question implies that the father is excluded from this intimacy. The mother's reported reply, which offers a justification, suggests that she has heard the question as another accusation. In admitting her 'misdemeanour', she exculpates herself: ' "Yes", she said, "often. He goes on pestering me till I let him. Children are like that" '.[68]

Once more, it is Hans's fault. He wants all this intimacy. He has the desires, whether loving or jealous, and the parents present themselves as victims of this desire.

The Oedipal tale suggests that two males are competing for the love of one woman. In the case of Little Hans, the situation is symbolized by the bed. Hans is supposedly jealous of his father, because he shares the mother's bed. The German text suggests that Max and his wife had separate beds.[69] There is little evidence in the reported conversations that Hans objects to his father being in the mother's bed. Following the father's denial that Hans could have witnessed the couple having sexual relations, it is possible that Hans has never seen his father in mummy's bed.[70] But we do know that the father often sees Hans in mummy's bed; and that he objects regularly; and that the woman dismisses his objec-

[66] Ibid., p. 201.   [67] Ibid., p. 219.   [68] Ibid.   [69] *GW* 7, p. 306.
[70] 'Analysis of a phobia', *PFL* 8, p. 292.

tions; and, that Hans often receives the forbidden cuddles. So who can be said to be the jealous male?[71]

Where is Freud in all this? He too is encouraging the idea of Hans as the spurned, jealous male. Surely, Freud cannot be jealous too; surely he is not hankering after Frau Graf, with whom he used to share the formal intimacy of his consulting-room, before she married Max. Yet, there are signs. If Freud, rather than Hans, had been the target of analysis – if his behaviour and words had been psychoanalytically scrutinized – then such signs would not be easily ignored. Twice in the report, for example, Freud describes Frau Graf as 'beautiful'.[72]

What Freud does not say is as revealing as what he does. There is the business of the rocking-horse. The symbolic nature of horses is important in Freud's explanation of the case. Freud discusses at length Hans's horsy games. For example, Freud mentions Hans playing with a new maid, who let him ride on her back: 'He always calls her "my horse" and holds on to her dress with cries of "Gee-up"'.[73] Hans has a rocking-horse. We don't know whether he played with the rocking-horse during the period when he was afraid of horses. Was he also afraid of the toy horse? We are not told. In fact, in the case history we are not told anything at all about the rocking-horse. It is from an article, written by Max Graf many years later, telling of his experiences with Freud, that we learn that his son had been given a rocking-horse on his third birthday.[74]

Freud knew of the horse, because it was Freud himself who had given it to Hans. He had carried it up four flights of stairs to the Graf's apartment, to deliver it personally. Yet, he fails to mention the toy. It is a strange omission, to say the least. A psychoanalyst would treat the omission as significant. For present purposes, the question is not 'what did Freud unconsciously intend by the gift?' The question is what would Freud, as a psychoanalyst, believe that such a gift could signify, at least if it had been given by someone else? And that leads to a further question:

---

[71] Another instance of possible projection can be given. As further evidence for Hans's sexual desires, the report claims that Hans likes having his knickers unbuttoned and his penis taken out so he can widdle. Freud quotes the father's report: 'On walks it is mostly his father who assists Hans in this way; and this gives the child an opportunity for the fixation of homosexual inclinations upon him' (*PFL* 8, p. 184). Freud does not ask why, at this point in the notes, the father abandons the customary first person singular ('I') and lapses into awkward impersonal speech, referring to himself as 'his father'. Is he embarrassed to be telling of unbuttoning Hans's knickers and why is he quick to talk of Hans's homosexual inclinations? Is the stilted language a sign of repressed and projected desire? Freud, so quick to spot Hans's desires, does not ask these questions. He is telling a story of Hans's desires, omitting those of the parents.

[72] Ibid., pp. 269 and 298.

[73] Ibid., p. 193.   [74] Graf (1942), p. 474.

'What might Freud have thought, according to the logic of his own theories, that he was omitting by failing to mention the rocking-horse?'

According to Freud's ideas at the time, a horse was not a neutral symbol. Neither Freud in his report nor Graf in his reminiscence mention that Freud, in one of the Wednesday meetings at which Graf was present, asserted that the horse was a symbol of sexual intercourse.[75] He made the remark in November 1907, just weeks before Hans was to develop his fear of horses. Although no longer a young man himself, Freud carried the large gift up the stairs to the Graf's appartment. And this act also has sexual significance for Freud. In a footnote added for the 1910 edition of 'The interpretation of dreams', he suggested that 'the rhythmical pattern of copulation is reproduced in going upstairs' for 'we come to the top in a series of rhythmical movements and with increasing breathlessness and then, with a few rapid leaps, we get to the bottom again'.[76] We can imagine Freud carrying an object, which he believes to be a symbol of sexual intercourse, to the Graf's home – to the home of the young mother, whom he calls 'beautiful'. He becomes increasingly breathless as he approaches the apartment. If he could see himself, Freud would have a ready interpretation.

The point is not to turn Freud's own methods on himself, in order to discover whether he might have had unconscious, or barely conscious, feelings for Frau Graf. The point is that his own methodology, had it addressed the subject, should have led him to suspect such feelings. The issue is the Oedipal story itself. The case report exemplifies a central theme in Freudian thought: it is instructing the psychoanalytic reader to look at the desires of the child, for there, so it says, lies the key to psychological problems. A habit of interpretation is being constructed. The actions of adults are to be explained in terms of the desires of the child and not *vice versa*.

So it is with the rocking-horse. It would appear to be centrally relevant to the story, which Freud is telling. Yet it is omitted, to be forgotten as the story passes into psychoanalytic culture. We, the readers of the case history, are to remember Hans, running with fright from the sight of horses with big widdlers, or riding on the back of his nurse. We are not invited to imagine Freud climbing the stairs to the Graf household with a rocking-horse in his arms, the father of psychoanalysis introducing the symbol of sexual intercourse into the house of the child. It is not relevant to the story which Freud is telling. The omissions of adult desire are, in the broadest sense, repressions. Adults tell Hans this same story, as they

[75] Nunberg and Federn (1967), p. 250.
[76] 'Interpretation of dreams', *PFL* 4, p. 472n.

speak to him accusingly about his desires. Oedipal adults are creating the Oedipal child.

The morality of looking and justifying

It is still necessary to show, in detail, how the child, in acquiring a moral voice, also acquires the rhetoric of repression. This means examining what the adults are saying to the child, in order to see in their words the simultaneous practice of discursive instruction and the pushing aside of awkward topics. Particular attention should be paid to the moral language used by the parents. Developmental psychologists have shown how caretakers, especially mothers, routinely use moral concepts when talking to children from a very young age.[77] Judith Dunn, describing her detailed study of mother-child talk, comments that 'the moral order of their parents' world was conveyed to the children again and again in the repeated events of their daily lives'.[78] Thus, Hans's sense of morality is not something which would come to him suddenly at the culmination of the Oedipal drama. Right from the earliest conversations, he should be hearing, and responding to, moral discourse. Often this morality will not be expressed directly. It will be contained within the practice of talk, for, as was argued in the previous chapter, conversation itself is bound by moral codes, which must be enacted if dialogue is to take place.

Several incidents from Hans's case study will be examined in detail, in order to show that Hans, while ostensibly showing the desires of the Oedipal boy, is being implicitly instructed in what should be said – and, most importantly, what should not be said.[79] In this instruction are the roots of repression, and, thereby, the creation of what might conveniently be called 'a dialogic unconscious'. The clues lie not so much in the words that Hans utters, but in those that he hears. What especially count are the largely unnoticed discursive details; and, here, some of the practices of conversation analysis can be helpful.[80]

[77] See, for example, the studies of Shweder and Much (1987) and Much and Shweder (1978).

[78] Dunn (1988), p. 73.

[79] A further example of Hans being explicitly taught moral rules is included in Billig (1998).

[80] At first sight, it would seem inappropriate to use the techniques of conversation analysis for analysing the reported conversations in Freud's account of Little Hans. These techniques are properly applied to the accurate transcription of conversations, which themselves have been recorded (Potter and Wetherell, 1987). Without recording devices, the sort of accuracy, which conversation analysts typically require, cannot be expected. Freud's report of the conversations between Hans and his parents is very different from the transcriptions presented by conversation analysts. Freud's accounts do not contain those details, such as hesitations, repetitions and ungrammatical features, which a note-taker typically misses and which need to be recorded

First to be considered is an incident reported early in the case report. Freud intended the episode to illustrate Hans, in his pre-Oedipal stage, showing a lively interest in sexuality. Also, it reveals the mother imposing moral and discursive requirements without conscious, or explicit, teaching, as she attempts to direct the dialogue along appropriate paths. The incident occurred when Hans was about three and three-quarters. He was looking on intently while his mother was undressing for bed. The following exchange is reported:

'What are you staring like that for?' she asked
HANS I was only looking to see if you'd got a widdler too.
MOTHER Of course. Didn't you know that?
HANS No. I thought you were so big you'd have a widdler like a horse.[81]

We are not told what the mother said next.

In this episode, as in others, Freud is not interested in what the parents say, but in what the episode signifies about Hans's inner thoughts. Accordingly Freud passes over two features which reveal much about the Graf household. First, Hans also asks his father whether he has a widdler, because he had 'never seen it when you were undressing'.[82] At that time, Hans had been sharing his parents' bedroom, and clearly had been in a position to observe both parents dressing and undressing. The question indicates the coyness of papa Graf.

Second, Hans also asks his father whether Mummy has a widdler. Herr Graf gives a totally different answer than his wife: 'little girls and women . . . have no widdlers: Mummy has none, Hanna has none and so on'.[83] Freud has advised Graf to give 'Hans some enlightenment in the matter of sex knowledge', particularly by 'informing him that his mother and all other female beings (as he could see from Hanna) had no

---

electronically if they are to be preserved in a textual account (see, for instance, Atkinson and Heritage, 1984; Jefferson, 1985; Schenkein, 1978). The dialogues in Freud's report read like literary productions. The speakers talk in clear, easily readable grammatical sentences. These are dialogues which have been tidied up. The tidying up (and, more generally, the textual editing) raises a second methodological problem, for it has been accomplished by one of the participants (the father) who has a vested stake in the interpretation of the dialogues. There is further editing by Freud, who also has a rhetorical interest in using the dialogue to persuade the reader of a theoretical story. These difficulties would be crucial if the aim of reanalysis were to recover the hidden dynamics of Hans's mind. On the other hand, the notes reflect adult interpretations of those dialogues. These interpretations are important evidence if the intention is to reconstruct the sorts of things which adults were thinking and saying. If repressed themes still slip into the edited stories, like the repressed images in reported dreams, then this should give more, rather than less, confidence in pointing to the possibility that dialogic repression may be being unwittingly practised in conversation.

[81] 'Analysis of a phobia', PFL 8, p. 173.
[82] Ibid.   [83] Ibid., p. 194.

widdler at all'.[84] Freud is concerned with the effect that receiving such information will have on Hans's castration complex.[85] He is not so bothered about the effect of the father confidently denying what the mother confidently asserts. He is more interested in the strangeness of Hans's fantasies, than in the oddities of the adult world in which Hans is living.

Freud interprets the staring in terms of Hans's search for knowledge about the mystery of hidden genitalia. However, in the exchange between mother and son, much more appears to be going on. The mother is not merely answering the boy's question, as if neutral facts are being passed from adult to child. There is an implicit, and complex, teaching of morality; this is not just a morality of sexuality, but a morality of looking, justifying and knowing.

The mother's initial question ('what are you staring like that for?') indicates that Hans was being asked to justify what he was doing at that moment. As one conversation analyst has remarked, accounts are needed 'when the event becomes recognized by interactants as no longer routine and ordinary, but instead, problematized or unusual'.[86] To use the terminology of conversation analysis, the mother's question offers Hans a conversational 'slot' in which he can offer an account to defend himself. Without a defence – without an answer – he is open to accusation, even punishment. The mother's question, therefore, characterizes Hans's looking as something not quite proper.

In the original German, the verb *schauen* (look) is used rather than 'stare', so that Hans was being asked why he was looking *in that way* (*Was schaust du denn so?*) The mother, thereby, conveys that Hans was looking in a manner that was neither usual nor socially acceptable, unless he could provide good reason.[87] The English translator, by using the word 'stare' emphasizes this understanding of the question: it is rude to stare, unless one has good reason (and can justify oneself). Children must learn the culturally appropriate morality of gazing and not gazing.

[84] Ibid., p. 191. Freud also advised Graf to tell his son that his fear of horses was 'a piece of nonsense' and that 'the truth was, his father was to say, that he was very fond of his mother and wanted to be taken into her bed'. The boy should be told that his fear of horses was connected with his interest in widdlers and that he was quite right in thinking that 'it was not right to be so very preoccupied with widdlers' (p. 191). Thus, Hans is to learn a curious mixture of conventional morality (it is wrong to think about widdlers), psychoanalytic theory of causation (desire for the mother's bed as a cause of fear) and peculiar anatomy (women have no widdlers).

[85] Ibid., p. 198. The disagreement between Max Graf and Sadger at the Wednesday meeting in December 1907 seems to have concerned the desirability of telling children about sex. Sadger, supported by Freud, was on the side of openness. Graf urged reticence (see Nunberg and Federn, 1967, pp. 270ff.).

[86] Buttny (1993), p. 24; see also Antaki (1994) and Much and Shweder (1978).

[87] 'Analyse der Phobie eines fünfjährigen Knaben', *GW* 7, p. 247.

Hans was no exception. An episode in a restaurant, occurring a little later, finds Hans taking furtive glimpses at a young girl, becoming embarrassed if caught looking directly.[88] He has by now realized that it can be wrong to stare.

Hans's reply, as presented in Freud's text, was that 'I was only looking to see if you'd got a widdler too.' Freud accepts the remark as revealing Hans's state of mind while he stared at his mother undressing. From a discursive point of view, Freud might have been too trusting: the explanation might have been formulated *post hoc* to counter the critical question.[89] The question of what was in Hans's mind as he stared can be put aside. The issue is what happens as Hans is speaking to his mother – what is the mother conveying and what is Hans understanding.

Hans indicates by his reply that he has understood the moral challenge which his mother has posed. Judith Dunn has shown that as children develop language so they learn to use justifications to avoid disapproval.[90] So Hans justifies his staring. 'Only' (*nur*) is the operative word, which marks the response as a defence. As other analysts of conversation have noted in their data, a speaker 'disclaims the blameworthiness' of an action by adding 'only' or 'just'.[91] If Hans used *nur*, we can take this as a sign that he heard his mother's question as a challenge inviting a justification. Of course, we cannot trust Hans's father to have produced a word-perfect transcript – perhaps he added the '*nur*'. But if he did, that is also significant. It implies that the father hears, or understands, Hans's reply as a justification, thereby as confirming the mother's question as a moral challenge which has been answered.

The mother responds by taking Hans's explanation as a question, as if he has asked whether she has a widdler. The original German text (but not the English translation) emphasizes the point by placing a question mark at the end of Hans's reply.[92] Naturally, replies the mother. By treating Hans's self-justification as a question, she is, in effect, treating it as a satisfactory answer to her challenge. No blame is forthcoming. He has accounted for himself by offering an acceptable explanation for his inappropriate looking. He is to be answered, not chastised.

[88] 'Analysis of a phobia', *PFL* 8, p. 181.
[89] In social life, rules are frequently formulated post hoc. This is one of the most important claims of ethnomethodology (Garfinkel, 1967; Heritage, 1984; Wieder, 1972). See Pontecorvo and Fasulo (1995) and Stirponi and Pontecorvo (in press) for parental examples in family discourse.
[90] Dunn (1991).
[91] Shweder and Much (1987), p. 206; for unanalysed examples of this move, see, inter alia, Brown and Levinson (1987), p. 237; Dunn (1988), p. 33; Wellman and Bartsch (1994), p. 345.
[92] '*Ich schau' nur, ob du auch einen Wiwimacher hast?*' ('Analyse der Phobie', *GW* 7, p. 247).

Again, matters are not quite so straightforward. Hans's justification might be treated as enabling his question to pass as permissible, but then the mother questions its asking. She does not merely answer in the affirmative – 'naturally' as if the answer should be obvious; she adds an expression of surprise that her son did not know. It is not for us to express surprise that she should be surprised that a three-year-old boy should not know something which neither her husband nor the eminent psychologist would seem to know. Instead, we should ask what she is doing dialogically with her expressed surprise.

The mother is inviting further justification and, through her questioning, she is controlling the direction of the dialogue.[93] Hans now has to provide a further justification – why he doesn't know what should be obvious. He gives a reason: he would have thought that Mummy, if she had a widdler, would have one as big as a horse's (unlike, presumably, a rocking-horse). The implication is that since he can't see a huge widdler, commensurate with Mummy's size, then he is perplexed whether she has one. We do not know her response – whether she laughs, tells him not to be silly, or changes the subject entirely.

Her answers dialogically point to a change of subject. She implies that the information is obvious. Having given him the information, there is no need to stare. If he stares again, he will be accountable and his previous justification will no longer hold: he will now possess the information which excused the original staring. His quest has not been entirely successful. He has looked, but has not seen Mummy's widdler. His visual search was turned into a verbal search. His question has been answered; indeed it has been dismissed by being answered.

Suppose Hans had been staring at his mother's hands. What are you staring at, she asks. I was only looking to see if you had a wedding-ring. We can imagine his mother holding out her hand to show the ring. She might even say 'didn't you know this was my wedding-ring?' But in the case of her widdler, she displays nothing. Hans learns that this is not something to be displayed to him. Moreover, her questioning of his question is preparing him to realize that it is neither respectable to try to glimpse the mother's widdler nor even to ask about it. His question has been answered. More than that: the question has been questioned. The mother is closing the matter. And Hans has not been shown what he said he was looking for.

The world into which Hans is being taught to enter is a strange one. He is to learn that some things are to be hidden, physically and dialogically. Not only is there implicit instruction in the morality of

---

[93] See McTear (1985), pp. 66f, for a discussion of such control.

staring and the morality of not displaying, or touching, genitalia; there is rhetorical instruction. Hans, already participating in conversations of justification and accusation, is learning subtler rhetorics. The mother is demonstrating how to answer a question while leaving it unanswered; or rather she is showing how to change the unanswerable question into one which can be answered and thereby dismissed. In this way, the mother is showing how to repress rhetorically. The lesson cannot be explicit: the mother cannot say 'Did you notice, Hans, what I just did with my question?' That would be rhetorically self-defeating. Besides, the mother may not have been consciously aware of what her words were dialogically accomplishing, as she unhesitatingly and proficiently uses her rhetoric.

Hans, who will need to learn how to repress awkward desires, has been participating in a dialogue, guided by an adult using language to hide or silence the awkward question. These are rhetorical arts which he, in time, will acquire in order to use in conversations. Moreover, they are arts which he can use in his own internal dialogues. The arts need not be completely successful; the dismissed topic can still return. Hans will continue to be perplexed by the widdler which his mother possesses naturally, which his father says she does not possess and which he must now not look for directly.

Talking of giraffes and dismissing Mummy's chemise

By participating in family discourse, Hans is learning what are acceptably polite forms of reply, as well as what will be accepted as reasonable justifications.[94] The teaching of such skills is double-edged. The dialogical skills, which parents and caretakers impart, can be turned back on themselves. As Judith Dunn's work displays, children use their growing abilities to argue in order to challenge the authority of their parents.[95]

An episode occurred at the height of Hans's phobia, which is, of course, the period identified by Freud as the peak of his Oedipal situation. Although Hans had been told not to come into his parents' bedroom during the night, one night, towards the end of March, he came into his parents' bedroom unexpectedly in the middle of the night. His parents asked him why he had done this. Hans replied that he would tell them the following morning. The next morning Hans was carefully questioned, and Max Graf recorded the dialogue in shorthand.[96] Hans, in answer to his father's questioning, claimed that there had been two

[94] See, for examples, of such learning Bonaiuto and Stirponi (1996).
[95] Dunn (1988); for more references to Dunn's work, see the previous chapter.
[96] 'Analysis of a phobia', *PFL* 8, p. 199.

giraffes in his room – a big giraffe and a crumpled giraffe. Hans said he took the crumpled giraffe from the big one and the big one had called out. He then had sat down on the crumpled one.

Hans's father, as a devoted follower of Freud, immediately sees sexual significance in the story. He takes the big giraffe to represent himself, with its long erect neck symbolizing the paternal phallus, of which Hans is supposedly jealous. The crumpled giraffe, which Hans wants to hold or possess, is the mother. The big giraffe cries out, because he is jealous when Hans possesses the crumpled giraffe. Max Graf sees the fantasy as arising from enlightenment about sex which he had given Hans earlier. Thus, according to the father, Hans 'was seized in the night with a longing for his mother, for her caresses, for her genital organ and came into our bedroom for that reason'. The whole business was, accordingly 'a continuation of his fear of horses'.[97] Freud agrees with Graf's interpretation.

More is going on than either Freud or Hans's father openly discuss. At one point in the interrogation about the giraffes, Hans asks his own questions, which are abruptly dismissed:

HE . . . Why are you writing that down?
I Because I shall send it to a Professor, who can take away your 'nonsense' for you
HE Oho! So you've written down as well that Mummy took off her chemise, and you'll give that too the Professor too
I Yes. But he won't understand how you can think that a giraffe can be crumpled up.[98]

In asking his questions, Hans raises an issue which appears not to have been mentioned earlier: he mentions that mummy had removed her nightdress. When Hans asks whether Daddy will tell the professor about mummy taking off her chemise, his father replies 'yes'. He then changes the subject abruptly. It doesn't appear that the father did specifically send this information to Freud, except by way of including Hans's question in his notes. Freud certainly does not discuss the mother without the chemise.

The father's answer is rhetorically interesting. He simultaneously answers and dismisses Hans's question by saying 'yes, but . . .' As has been discussed earlier, this is a powerful rhetorical device of argumenta-tion.[99] By saying 'yes but' the speaker appears to concede a point, as if expressing agreement and so implying that the topic need not be debated. The 'but' then dismisses the agreement as if irrelevant or

[97] Ibid., p. 201.   [98] Ibid., p. 200.
[99] See above chapter 3, pp. 52f.

unimportant, as it prefaces the introduction of a new issue for talk. As such, the 'yes, but' achieves the sort of shift of topic, which was discussed above in chapter 3. The father, by using this rhetorical device in answer to Hans, banishes Hans's question from the argumentative agenda.

A young child like Hans is learning the techniques of conversation. He will learn how to change topic, by using little words such as 'yes, but'. It would appear from the father's notes, which Freud reproduces, that Hans, in a conversation, which took place a month after the giraffe dream, was using these devices to counter questions from his father. Hans has said that he wants to give birth to babies. His father tells him that it is impossible, because, as Hans well knows, boys cannot have babies. Thus, the father seems to have caught out Hans with having contradictory thoughts. Hans simply dismisses the objection: 'Well, yes. But I believe they can, all the same'.[100] Hans's father starts a new line of questioning. He asks about the name of an imaginary girl, whom Hans fantasizes playing with. Hans has successfully used 'yes, but' to dismiss the awkward question. He's been learning well.[101]

Such rhetorical skills of dismissal cannot be taught explicitly. As soon as attention is drawn to such small words, their rhetorical effect is undermined. Their use is acquired through practice and non-conscious imitation. As Sir Frederic Bartlett showed many years ago, we seldom recollect the little words which we hear or use. We might recollect the 'gist' of a story, but the little words, which act as the necessary glue, without which conversation falls apart, are not memorable in themselves.[102]

Such rhetorical devices provide a clue about how children learn to repress. The child learns the rhetoric of dismissal, or topic-shifting, as used in conversations. The rhetoric of argument can be turned inwards to permit and prevent internal debate. As was discussed in chapter 3, Paul Lorenz attempted to dismiss his unwelcome inner voices by saying

---

[100] 'Analysis of a phobia', *PFL* 8, p. 254. 'Yes' and 'but', although separated by several words, appear in the original German: '*No ja, ich glaub's aber doch*' (*GW* 7, p. 330).

[101] In fact, 'yes, but' is used by both father and son in the sleeping-bag conversation, shortly before the giraffe episode. The topic is masturbation and Hans denies that he still touches his widdler. 'But you still want to' counters his father. Hans, then replies, '*Yes*, I do. *But* wanting's not doing' (emphasis added). His father counters with a further 'yes but': 'Well, but to prevent your wanting to, this evening you're going to have a bag to sleep in' (1990, p. 193). In the original German text, the father's 'yes but' is less clear, for he omits the expression of agreement (*GW* 7, p. 266).

[102] See Bartlett (1932) for the classic demonstration of the way that exact phrasings are rarely recalled (see also Hunt and Love, 1982; Neisser, 1981). For a discussion of what might count as 'the gist' of a story, and how the gist itself can be a matter of debate, see Edwards (1997).

'but'. His failure did not arise from the rhetorical weakness of the small word 'but', but from his inability to provide a new topic to which the 'but' could point. Hans knows not merely to counter his father's awkward question with a 'no' or even a simple 'but'. His 'but' leads to a justification, which would be hard to counter and which moves the dialogue onto a slightly different point of focus. 'But' he says to his father, if I want to believe that boys can have babies, why shouldn't I be left to my own thoughts? If 'but' can repel his father's questioning, then so might it grant him peace of mind, when, in his own internal dialogues, disturbing questions are raised. If the train of thought unfolds as quickly as the dialogue with his father, then he is unlikely to remember using the little word, which rhetorically can achieve so much, so habitually and so unobtrusively.

How to love Mummy really

Parents, in talking to children, may appear to have the power to define the meanings of words and the appropriateness of responses. Yet, as they do so, they can be challenged. If, as some developmental psychologists suggest, challenge is necessary for the child's cognitive development, then so, too, it might be for parental development in learning to formulate *post hoc* justifications for the moral rules that they are imposing.[103] The mother had never previously faced a child staring and asking whether she has a widdler. She had to formulate new answers. In this way, the parent, as much as the child, discovers the moral rules of discourse.

This is important theoretically, for Freud described the Oedipal situation as being predestined, with the mother having little alternative but to play her part. The story suggests that the child cannot avoid the inborn feelings of instinct. Foremost amongst these instinctual feelings is the child's love for the mother. Freud presumed that a young boy, such as Hans, does not have to be taught to love the mother. Such love emerges naturally, at a psychic level deeper than language. As will be argued later, human emotions are not wordless. Love has its discursive and moral aspects.[104]

Freud was oversimplifying matters when he portrayed the boy's love for the mother spontaneously and inevitably coming into conflict with the demands of morality. The following incident suggests that the love for the mother cannot be taken for granted. Hans has to be taught how

---

[103] See Dunn (1988), Dunn and Munn (1987) and Dunn and Slomkowski (1995). More generally, see Shantz and Hartup (1995) and Valsiner and Cairns (1995).

[104] The discursive aspect of emotions is discussed in more detail in chapter 7.

to love his mother appropriately, because, as will be seen, he can love his mother too little, rather than too much. Again, for this teaching words are vital. The mother, far from being a passive object, can be a demanding teacher in matters of the heart.

During the summer, when Hans was four and a half, the family stayed at an inn in Gmunden. Hans became friendly with the innkeeper's and the neighbours' children. Most of these children were slightly older than Hans. The Grafs noticed how Hans would like to kiss some of the older girls. He was particularly fond of the innkeeper's fourteen-year-old daughter, Mariedl. One evening at bedtime, Hans said that he wanted Mariedl to sleep with him. When told that this was not possible, he replied 'Then she shall sleep with Mummy or with Daddy.'[105] Hans was told that Mariedl must sleep with her own parents, whereupon according to Hans's father, the following dialogue took place:

HANS Oh, then I'll just go downstairs and sleep with Mariedl.
MOTHER You really want to go away from Mummy and sleep downstairs?
HANS Oh, I'll come up again in the morning to have breakfast and do number one.
MOTHER Well, if you really want to go away from Daddy and Mummy, then take your coat and knickers and – goodbye![106]

Hans's father reports that Hans took his clothes and went towards the staircase, 'but, it need hardly be said, he was fetched back'.[107]

The episode seems not to fit the Oedipal story. Supposedly consumed with desire for his mother, he is chasing after another girl, seeking to enter her bed and willing to forsake his mother's. In this exchange, the mother is using a way of talking, whose detailed rhetoric Hans has not yet grasped. As such, he is given a lesson in the language of love.

In the exchange, communication between mother and son had not gone smoothly. Hans has misunderstood his mother's remarks. Mummy had said 'goodbye' and Hans takes his leave. But she did not mean 'goodbye' – she was not giving permission for Hans to take his things and go. The father presumes that an adult would have understood what Hans fails to. This is indicated by the added comment that 'it hardly needs to be said' that Hans was fetched back. He presumes (but spells out the presumption to make absolutely certain) that his reader, who is Freud, would understand that the uttered goodbye was not, in fact, to be understood as a goodbye. Freud, by including the father's comment, also conveys in his turn that the readers of the case history should grasp that the goodbye was not 'really' a permission to leave.

---

[105] 'Analysis of a phobia', *PFL* 8, p. 180.
[106] Ibid.   [107] Ibid.

The mother's words, in their literal sense, appear to be asking Hans what he wants to do and then bidding him goodbye. Do you want to go from Mummy? she asks. He does. So goodbye. As discourse analysts have stressed, talk about wishes is not usually to be understood literally as reporting inner events. Speakers perform complex discursive actions with the language of wanting.[108] In this case, the mother is not merely asking about Hans's desires. She is unsuccessfully trying to do something: not only is she seeking to stop Hans from going, but she is attempting to stop him from wanting to go.

There is an extra word in her question, whose import Hans misses. She is asking whether he 'really' (*wirklich*) wants to go. In this context, 'really' functions rhetorically as the opposite of the 'only' (*nur*) which Hans had used to justify his staring. While 'only' mitigates, 'really' in this context increases the rhetorical stake. The mother is not talking about mere whims, unimportant feelings (i.e. 'I *only* want to see her for a moment'). She is talking 'real' feelings. A 'goodbye' is not just (only) a goodbye; it might really be goodbye.

In answer to the mother's question whether he *really* wants to go away from Mummy, Hans seems to offer a denial, which mitigates the going away. 'Oh', he replies (original German: '*No*'), claiming that he would be returning in the morning for breakfast and lavatory. The returning is offered as evidence that he does not 'really' want to go. The mother's next remark indicates that she does not accept Hans's recitation of his early morning needs as sufficient evidence that he 'really' does not want to go away. The discourse of real love is not to be justified in such stark pragmatic terms. Something else, beyond the statement of an early return, is required to show he 'really' does not want to go. And this Hans fails to grasp. A conversational opening has been created for him to proclaim his feelings – his real feelings – for his mother. 'No I don't want to really leave you and so I won't go to Mariedl' is sort of the preferred response, which an adult, it hardly need be said, would recognize.[109] Instead of talking about feelings, Hans gets down to the practicalities of taking his clothes. The mother's questions have elicited the wrong responses.

We do not know what was said when Hans was fetched back – whether his mother pursued her questioning and whether Hans, in reply, said how much he loved Mummy. Perhaps there were kisses and cuddles, of the sort Herr Graf would disapprove and which, according

[108] On this point, see, for example, the discursive analyses of Edwards (1997); Edwards and Potter (1992); Potter and Wetherell (1987); Wetherell and Edley (in press).

[109] On preference structure and preferred answers, see Bilmes (1987); Pomerantz (1984); Nofsinger (1991); Horowitz (1996).

to the official story, only Hans wants. Nor can we know. But we can say that Hans apparently misunderstood the discourse of real love. If so, then Hans had not yet learnt to recognize the rhetorical import of 'really' and to react accordingly.

Hans must also learn that talk of love is not straightforward. Lovers, as Roland Barthes has so elegantly portrayed, can appear to say the opposite of what they mean and that this is the meaning of their words.[110] Mummy, far from granting permission, was making a threat. If he didn't really love Mummy, then she doesn't care if he goes – he can go – goodbye – Mummy doesn't love him. Hans is meant to cry, throw his childish arms around Mummy and declare his love. She is wooing him with threats. Hans is fetched back to love her.

If the mother's words carry an implicit threat, this is to teach Hans not to want to sleep with other girls: he belongs to mummy. In this respect, Hans is being taught, through words, how to love his mother. This love is not merely the wordless and inevitable eruption of an inner instinctive force. His mother has a part to play. She recruits anxiety to teach him the lesson. Hans, at least to begin with, fails to spot the threat, because the meanings of words seem to have been turned around. If in the discourse of 'real' love, words do not really mean what they appear to, then all this has to be learnt. It's a curious world, this 'real' world of adults.

Oedipus, jealousy and denial

The Oedipal situation is founded upon images of jealousy. According to Freudian theory, the boy's jealousy of the father, and the later repression of this jealousy, unfolds naturally.[111] The vocabulary of jealousy, just like the vocabulary of love, has to be acquired. Hans has to learn the meaning of the term. However, he does not learn the word as an interesting exercise in semantics. He must learn the word in the context of the family and the stories told within the family. As has been pointed out, in the narrative politics of families, there is no equality: parents have more power than children to determine the family stories.[112] Hans has to learn the family narrative being told by the adult Grafs: namely that he is the jealous one. The word 'jealous' is not to be applied to Daddy, who objects to Hans being in Mummy's bed; nor is it to be applied to

---

[110] Barthes (1990).
[111] For a discussion of the centrality of envy in Freud's theory of moral and social behaviour, see Forrester (1996). For a feminist critique, see Brennan (1992).
[112] For the notion of 'narrative politics' in families, see Ochs and Taylor (1992).

Mummy, who objects to Hans wanting to go to Mariedl's bed. It is to be applied to Hans.

Parents, in teaching children the language of emotions, impose their definitions of the emotions. This occurs right from an early age. One study, looking at mothers talking to babies, found that the majority of statements , which mothers addressed to their babies, were descriptions of the babies' states or feelings. Thus, from birth – and certainly before the infant can understand, let alone reply – the child is being told what it is feeling. From these imposed definitions, the child learns to use the language of emotions.[113]

Max Graf's record contains signs that Hans, in learning to use the word 'jealous', is being guided to apply it principally to himself. In this way, semantic and moral training coincide with the imposition of the Oedipal explanation. Accordingly, Hans is not merely to be described as jealous in the father's reports, and in Freud's theory. He himself has to learn that his behaviour (and, by implication, not that of his father or mother) is the prime example of 'jealousy'.

Elements of this can be detected in one episode recorded by Graf. The father is asking Hans directly about his feelings. Are you fond of Daddy? Oh yes. The father then directs his questions towards eliciting Oedipal answers. He reports the dialogue:

I You're a little vexed with Daddy because Mummy's fond of him.
HANS No.
I Then why do you always cry whenever Mummy gives me a kiss? It's because you're jealous.
HANS Jealous, yes.
I You'd like to be Daddy yourself.
HANS Oh yes.
I What would you like to do if you were Daddy?
HANS And you were Hans? I'd like to take you to Lainz every Sunday – no, every weekday too. If I were Daddy I'd be ever so nice and good.
I But what would you like to do with Mummy?
HANS Take her to Lainz, too.
I And what besides?
HANS Nothing.[114]

The exchange represents a further example of the power of parents in conversation. The father is asking questions, whose form is designed to

---

[113] Sylvester-Bradley and Trevarthen (1978). These researchers found that the majority of statements made by mothers were utterances using the second person, 'you', rather than being statements about what 'I' (the mother) was feeling. See also Rogoff (1990, pp. 68–9) and Kuebli, Butler and Fivush, (1995). This research bears out the general point made by Wittgenstein that 'psychological language' (or the grammar of emotional language) is not learnt by introspection.

[114] 'Analysis of a phobia', *PFL* 8, p. 248.

restrict the child's range of answers.[115] When Hans denies feeling 'a little vexed', the father's next question indicates that he does not accept the denial: 'Then why do you always cry . . .' In this case, the father does not permit Hans to answer but he gives the 'correct', or desired, answer to his own question. This answer is a criticism of Hans's previous answer: it is because you are 'jealous', he says, using an unambiguous statement, which carries a moral evaluation.[116]

The utterance resembles an ostensive definition: the father is telling Hans what jealousy is, as if Hans is unsure of the meaning of the concept. Elements of imposition and acquisition can be seen in the extract. The original German text suggests an ambiguity, which is glossed in the English translation. The word 'jealous' (*eifersüchtig*) is only used by the father, whereas the English translator has Hans repeating the word.[117] In German, it is a long word, unlikely to be used by a young child. Hans's reply to his father's statement is more equivocal in the German. Hans neither says the German equivalent of 'jealous' nor 'yes', as the English translator implies; instead, he says *Das schon* ('a bit').

A short while later, the father asks Hans whether he was jealous while on holiday at Gmunden. Hans says no (again without actually using *eifersüchtig*) and explains that at Gmunden he had his 'things', and a garden and other children. The explanation would make sense if Hans were hearing *eifersüchtig* as a synonym for 'unhappy'. Hans's father does not probe the point nor question whether having toys (things) is 'really' a good reason for not being 'jealous' as opposed to being 'unhappy'. It is easy for adults to 'hear' a child's ambiguous use of language as being appropriately meaningful, only questioning the child's use of adult language in the case of an obvious break-down. The example provides its own evidence. The English translator, despite being in possession of a written text, 'hears' Hans using the word 'jealous', which, textually at least, is the father's word, but which both father and translator impose on the boy.

The father is not merely imposing a category of interpretation. He is attempting to impose a narrative, which identifies Hans as the jealous son, seeking to take the father's place in order to possess the mother sexually. The direction of his questions is recognizable for anyone who knows the Freudian story, which Hans did not. The son, in his answers to the questions, does not oblige. When asked what he would do if he

---

[115] See McTear (1985).
[116] Chapter 7 discusses in detail the moral implications contained in the use of emotion words, such as 'jealous'.
[117] *GW* 7, pp. 324–5.

were Daddy, he does not talk beds and mummies. He adds 'and you were Hans'. His answer does not so much convey what he would do as Daddy, but what Hans would like to receive from Daddy. He says that he would be 'nice and good', and take the family for treats to Lainz every Sunday. The father does not pursue this line, but rhetorically dismisses the theme – it is not what he seeks to hear. He ignores the criticism implicit in the son's remark: that he should be a 'nice and good daddy', giving everyone, especially Hans, treats. He wants to know what Hans would do with Mummy – nothing, says Hans.

A few days earlier the father had been asking Hans why he wanted to come into bed with Mummy. His questions were phrased to invite Hans to express aggression against his father. Hans mentioned that he didn't like Daddy scolding him. 'What do I really scold you for?' the father asked. Hans said he didn't know but that Daddy scolded him 'because you're cross'. But that's not true, replied the father. Hans stood his ground: 'Yes, it *is* true. You're cross.' He is blaming his father for being aggressive, not 'nice and good'. The father does not accept this, and, uses psychoanalytic theory, to recruit his reader onto his side, to explain the reason for Hans's (unbelievable) assertion, which the father inter-prets as a projection of the boy's aggression: 'Evidently, therefore, my explanation that only *little* boys come into bed with their Mummies and that *big* ones sleep in their own beds had not impressed him very much.'[118] It is back to Hans's jealousy and the mother's bed.

In the father's account, offered to Hans and to Freud, and later to general readers in the form of psychoanalytic theory, the father himself is not angry or jealous. The problem is not that he seems 'always' to lose the argument with his wife, as his son triumphantly takes his place in the bed. Nor, in this account, is he repressing and projecting denied feelings. That is what his son does; and so do all sons. Questions are omitted in this account: how do Hans and all those other boys learn to repress and project? Who teaches them? Who can they copy? The omission of such questions – one might say their dialogic repression – is part of the story being told to Freud, to readers and, above all, to Hans.

Further implications

The details of the conversations, presented by Freud and by Hans's father, indicate how much Hans, and indeed all children, have to learn and how, in their everyday conversations with caretakers, they are being implicitly instructed. At one level they are being instructed in the use of

---

[118] 'Analysis of a phobia', *PFL* 8, pp. 242–3, emphasis in original.

language. This instruction does not solely, or even principally, consist in being told the meaning of nouns, such as 'jealousy'. Such definitions are part of wider interaction. Little words, such as 'only', 'yes, but' and 'really', whose practical use has to be acquired, are crucial. Above all, the child, in participating in dialogue, is being told all the time about appropriate questions and answers, turns and responses. In this way, the child is being instructed into the conventional morality of ordinary interaction.

From a psychoanalytic point of view, one of the most important aspects of dialogue, which a child learns, is the ability to dismiss topics rhetorically. Hans hears his parents appearing to answer questions, while leaving them unanswered; he hears them changing the topics of discussion. He, too, can be heard to acquire the small words, which enable topics to be changed. These are rhetorical devices which can be applied to his own internal thoughts. His parents, thus, are providing the means of repression. Perhaps, also, by creating anxieties, such as invoking threats of castration and implying a withdrawal of love, they are also providing the occasions for repression.

What emerges from this re-examination is somewhat different from Freud's portrayal of the Oedipal situation. The growth of morality, shame and repression is closely tied to the conduct of ordinary, everyday situations. Hans is being told about morality through dialogue. However, the very conduct of dialogue itself involves the practical exercise of morality. As the child talks to his parents, he must learn to talk appropriately.

This dialogic perspective raises a key question, which has so far remained to one side, but which is crucial for any cultural approach to the issue of the unconscious. This is the issue of universality. One must ask whether the dynamics of Little Hans's repression indicate something general about childhood or whether they belong to the specific cultural milieu of his time and place. Certainly, the accumulating anthropological evidence suggests that the Oedipal situation, as described by Freud, is not culturally universal.[119] This is to be expected if repression is closely allied to dialogue. Different cultures have different ways of talking, especially to children.[120] It is not merely that the content of talk varies from culture to culture, but so does its rhetoric. If there are cultural variations in what children hear, and if the inner life reflects the dialogic world in which the child is immersed, then one should expect differences of inner life. Regarding the Oedipal situation, one should not

---

[119] See, for instance, Levine (1990); Shweder (1991); Roland (1996) and, more generally, Kirschner (1996).
[120] Ochs and Schieffelin (1984 and 1995).

underestimate the extent to which Oedipal parents create the Oedipal child.

On the other hand, one might suppose that repression is universal, at least in general terms, for the activity of speaking in dialogue demands repression. Although there will be vast cultural differences in the dialogic codes for polite talking, all cultures will need such codes to enable dialogue to take place. As was suggested in the previous chapter, if children learn politeness, they must also learn rudeness. All speaking communities will have things which are to be left unsaid. Consequently, one can hypothesise that dialogic repression is universal, although what is to be repressed, and how it is to be repressed, will vary culturally.

Freud's case of Little Hans is revealing, for, almost a hundred years later, it appears to be a report from another culture. Enough detail is provided to give a feel of the characters. Many of their words seem strange. The routine acceptance of violence against children and the obsession with curtailing signs of masturbation belong to other times. But other topics, such as the insecurities and jealousies of the characters, are familiar. One thing, above all, is not out-dated. The child has to pick up habits of talk and behaviour from adults. If we want to understand the deeper thoughts of the child, we should be listening critically to the words of the adults. In their comments to the child will be the signs of what is to be left unspoken and how it is to be so left. The adult words provide both child and analyst with clues to the acquisition of repression.

6   Remembering to forget

If a person is said to have repressed an experience or a wish, then they are unable to recall it. The experience or wish has, in some sense, been forgotten. However, not all forgetting can be said to involve repression, although Freud sometimes considered that it might be.[1] The person, who represses something, is suspected of having a motivation to forget. As such, repression has been said to comprise wilful or willed forgetting, although the willing may be said to occur unconsciously.[2] The child, in the Oedipal situation, has an interest in forgetting shameful desires. In the light of the previous discussion of Little Hans, one might also say that the parents, too, have reasons for overlooking their own desires, and projecting them conveniently onto the child.

Yet, this leads back to the dilemma of repression. How can one intentionally forget something? The moment one concentrates on accomplishing the forgetting, one is surely remembering the very thing which is to be forgotten. As was shown in chapter 2, Freud attempted to resolve the dilemma by postulating an unconscious ego. This hidden 'I' supposedly goes about the business of repression, concealed from the awareness of the conscious 'I'. Such a theoretical move, however, provides no real solution. Instead, it makes repression seem mysterious and unobservable.

The present approach seeks to avoid the problems of a hidden 'I', by linking repression to the use of language. The gain is at the expense of another problem. If the skills of repression are rooted in the skills of language, then they have to be acquired. As children learn to talk, so they acquire the ability to change topics, and thereby to repress. Because repression is a form of forgetting, then this implies that the child has to learn to forget. Here the argument seems to be slipping gently off the path of reasonableness. Surely, forgetting denotes the absence of

---

[1] This was one of the famous, and most controversial arguments of 'Psychopathology of everyday life'.

[2] On repression as motivated forgetting, see, for example, Erdelyi (1990) and Bower (1990).

learning. When something is learnt, it is remembered. How can one remember to forget? To talk of forgetting as something which has to be learnt, then is perverse.

However, the bluff reasonableness, which supposes that forgetting and remembering are simply opposites of one another, overlooks the psychological complexity of the phenomena. This chapter will argue that remembering and forgetting are psychologically bound together. Because we can remember, so we can be said to forget. More than this, successful remembering, in a real sense, involves forgetting. One cannot have one without the other.

As always, to plunge into the depths of the unconscious without first clarifying consciousness is to invite theoretical trouble. If repression is a form of forgetting, then its nature cannot be understood without first grasping the 'ordinary' relations between remembering and forgetting. Common-sense views of 'ordinary' remembering and forgetting can be misleading. It is easy to suppose that both activities are innate and essentially non-linguistic, occurring 'naturally' and spontaneously. In the case of remembering, the 'natural' process works to the child's benefit, while forgetting produces an unfortunate deficit. However, the common-sense view is a simplification. In important respects, human remembering is based on acquired skills, rooted in language. If remembering is an acquired skill, then so, in a non-trivial sense, is forgetting. We have to learn how to forget in appropriate ways.

To substantiate these ideas it will be necessary to look beyond the theories of Freud and to draw upon concepts and empirical findings from modern psychological research. Recent ideas about memory then can be applied to Freud's cases and to the problems of repression. The case of Little Hans continues to reveal more than Freud specifically emphasized. The conversations between Hans and his parents will be used to show how the child was being implicitly taught how to remember and also how to forget. Other examples from Freud's writings also will be used to show how repression, as a form of forgetting, might occur. In all this, it is helpful not to overdramatize the secret and extraordinary nature of repression. 'Ordinary' remembering and forgetting are extraordinary enough.

Orthodox psychoanalysts may have qualms about accepting one implication of the present position. If repressing depends on skills of language, then it cannot occur before the child is old enough to practise such skills. There are, therefore, good reasons not to trace repression and the unconscious all the way back to the earliest moments of infancy, when the child would have neither the means nor the motives to repress. Instead, by treating repression as a social skill, to be acquired in the course of development, especially moral development, the cultural and ideological dimensions can be emphasized.

Freud and the continuing battles of memory

Today, it is not possible to discuss these matters merely as interesting, intellectual points of theory. A painfully intense debate is taking place with consequences that directly affect the lives of thousands of people. Not only is the issue of repression, as depicted in classic Freudian theory, at stake, but so are the probity of Freud himself and the moral implications of the Oedipal theory. This debate concerns the sexual abuse of children.

One of the great contributions of the feminist movement has been to confront the issue of child sexual abuse, especially that committed by fathers. In the last twenty years, shocking evidence has been produced, showing not only the extent of such abuse, but also how psychologists, social workers and the public in general have colluded to hide and ignore the evidence.[3] Psychoanalytic theory has been indicted in this collusion. Freud's Oedipal theory depicted the child as the seducer of the adult, and, in so doing, overlooked adult desires for the child.[4] Adults, who reported sexual stories from infancy, could easily be interpreted by psychoanalysts as remembering their own repressed fantasies, rather than reporting memories of actual abuse. Freud, it is said, was originally aware of the extent of childhood sexual abuse, or what he more delicately called the 'seduction' of the child. In early work, most notably in a lecture delivered to the Viennese Society for Psychiatry and Neurology in April 1896, he claimed that child abuse was the principle cause of adult neuroses.[5] However, for reasons, which are still vehemently contested a hundred years later, he turned away from his Seduction Theory towards the theory of infant sexuality. Critics accuse Freud of moral cowardice: instead of acknowledging the scandalous reality of parents 'seducing' their children, he shifted his attention to the less contentious notion of children's fantasies of seducing their parents.[6]

In the wake of well publicized exposures of childhood sexual abuse, a

---

[3] See, for example, the ground-breaking work of Judith Herman (1981 and 1992).

[4] Jeffrey Masson(1984 and 1990) has probably been the foremost instigator of the accusations against psychoanalysis.

[5] Much of the credit for bringing this paper to the foreground must be given to Masson and Herman. Herman (1992) calls the paper 'a brilliant, compassionate, eloquently argued closely reasoned document' (p. 13).

[6] This charge is made by both Herman and Masson. It has gained wider currency in feminist writings generally. For a detailed analysis of the reasons that Freud gave for abandoning the Seduction Theory, see, in particular, Israëls and Schatzman (1993).

disturbing phenomenon has occurred, especially in the United States. Thousands of persons, principally but not exclusively adult women, have come forward, claiming to have suddenly recovered memories of childhood abuse, which have been forgotten, or repressed, in the intervening years. Such has been the extent of this phenomenon that it makes sense to talk of a Recovered Memory Movement. Therapists have offered specialist services to help victims recover such buried memories of childhood trauma. Best selling books have been published to help survivors recognize symptoms of unsuspected abuse and to recover the forgotten memories.[7] Families have been destroyed as adult children accuse ageing parents. As one observer has commented, the recovery of such forgotten episodes constitutes 'a social epidemic that has affected thousands of American families during the 1990s'.[8]

There has inevitably been a reaction. Parents, denying the accusations brought by their children, have claimed that the alleged memories are fabrications, the products of vulnerable personalities, egged on by zealous therapists. In consequence, the claims of 'recovered memories' are counter-balanced by the so-called 'False Memory Syndrome'.[9] It is claimed that the parents are victims of a social madness, which is only to be compared with the mania for witch-hunting two centuries ago. There has been a counter to the counter-charge, asserting that no such 'syndrome' as 'the False Memory Syndrome' actually exists and that the label itself serves to exculpate the guilty. And so the argument continues bitterly and irreconcilably.

An enormous volume of popular, academic and quasi-academic writings now exists on the topic.[10] Much of the debate focuses on the status of the recovered memories. Are the 'recovered memories' genuine memories, which have been repressed over time, as others, including social workers and psychiatrists, were unwilling to listen to stories of abuse? Only now, when the social climate has changed, can such memories be faced. Or are some of the 'memories' not really memories at

---

[7] The most notable of such books has been Bass and Davis's *Courage to Heal* (1994), which has been estimated to have sold over three quarters of a million copies.

[8] Schacter (1996), p. 249.

[9] See, in particular, Pendergrast (1995) for a critical account of the Recovered Memory Movement by a parent accused of abusing his child.

[10] For academic accounts, which take the Recovered Memory side, see, in addition to the works of Herman already cited, Harvey and Herman (1994) and Terr (1994). For psychological criticisms of this position, stressing the way that 'memories' may have been fabricated, see Ofshe and Watters (1994) and Loftus and Ketcham (1994). For more popular criticisms, see Crews (1995), who appears more concerned with demolishing psychoanalysis than with the victims of child abuse. For an analysis of the social background to the issue, see Burman (1996/7), who sees the debate as a reflection of wider postmodern conditions.

all? It is being contended that, along with genuine stories of abuse, some vulnerable personalities, under the guidance of committed therapists, and in response to a climate which values 'victimhood', are now being encouraged to construct 'memories' of events which never occurred.

No blanket answers can be given to these general questions. It is certainly not the intention to come down firmly on one side or the other. Yet, the issue cannot be avoided. Both sides of the Recovered/False Memory debate have made claims about Freud's theories of repression and about Freud himself. Several questions need to be considered. Is it feasible that memories can be repressed and then remembered under therapeutic circumstances? Certainly, Freud thought so. But if his theory is to be reinterpreted in terms of language, then does this mean that repression is more likely, or less likely, to occur in the way that the Recovered Memory theorists suggest? And more generally, how do remembering and forgetting occur?

Then, there is the issue of Freud himself. In the previous chapter the Oedipal theory was criticized for ignoring the issue of adult desires. Does this mean, as some of Freud's critics are now suggesting, that we should reverse Freud's own intellectual development, in order to turn from the Oedipal theory back to the Seduction theory? In so doing, should we criticize Freud for retreating from cases of actual abuse in order to concoct myths about infantile fantasies? Again, the issues should not be avoided, even if they are not to be satisfactorily resolved.

The position taken here is that repression does not generally operate in the ways suggested by the Recovered Memory theorists. But this certainly does not mean that all remembered stories of once forgotten childhood sexual abuse are to be treated as erroneous fabrications. It is possible to repress, or push the unpleasant from conscious memory. How this is done can only be understood if one accepts that suggestion and 'fabrication' are involved in 'ordinary' remembering, rather than being the distinguishing marks of 'false memories'.

Above all, the sort of forgetting involved in repression is based on acquired skills, which are too complex to be practised by infants. Freud's principle mistake, then, was to search for the roots of repression too far back in childhood. This, too, has implications for the charges levelled against Freud in 'the memory wars'.[11] Freud, in seeking to confirm the Oedipal theory, often searched for the hidden memory behind the overt memory. However, even when Freud was supposedly accepting stories of childhood abuse, he was searching for some earlier scrap of memory, which had been lost in the processes of repression.

[11] The term is used by Schacter (1995) and is the basis for Crews's (1995) book.

This drive to the earliest moments of infancy, so common in psycho-analytic theory and practice, constitutes a serious problem. It overlooks the learnt nature of remembering and, thus, locates the origins of forgetting in a time before the child has learnt to forget, or repress, properly.

Freudian repression and infantile amnesia

This chapter will be presenting a series of interlocking arguments about the nature of remembering and forgetting. We can start with a form of forgetting which affects us all. We remember little, if anything, from our earliest years. As Freud wrote in Lecture Thirteen of the 'Introductory lectures',

> You are all familiar, of course, from your own experience, with the remarkable amnesia of childhood. I mean the fact that the earliest years of life, up to the age of five, six or eight, have not left behind them traces in our memory like later experiences.[12]

Modern psychological research has confirmed the reality of infantile amnesia. Adults remember nothing which occurred before they were two or three and very little before the age of six.[13]

Freud's account of the Little Hans case contains an interesting post-script added in 1922, thirteen years after the case history was first published. Freud recounts how he had recently met Hans again, having not seen him since he was child. Hans by then was 'a strapping youth of nineteen', who, by his own admission, 'suffered from no troubles or inhibitions'.[14] He remained on good terms with his parents who were now divorced. Freud added that 'one piece of information given me by little Hans struck me as particularly remarkable'. Hans said that when he read Freud's case history 'the whole of it came to him as something unknown; he did not recognize himself; he could remember nothing', apart from a dim recollection about a vacation journey to Gmunden.[15] Freud noted that the analysis, in common with the rest of the memories, 'had been overtaken by amnesia itself'.[16]

What Freud found remarkable was not that Hans had forgotten so much of his childhood, but that the amnesia covered the analysis. Freud had given the topic of infant amnesia much thought. He believed that infantile amnesia could best be explained by the hypothesis of repres-

---

[12] *PFL* 1, p. 236.
[13] See, for instance, Schacter (1995, chapter 8); Nelson (1993); Fivush et al. (1997); Kihlstrom (1996). Even traumatic events occurring in earliest infancy are subject to the general infantile amnesia (Goodman et al., 1994).
[14] 'Analysis of a phobia', *PFL* 8, p. 304.
[15] Ibid.   [16] Ibid., p. 305.

sion. The child's earliest desires, whose repression supposedly resulted in infant amnesia, played a significant role in Freudian theory. All later neuroses and desires should be traced back to the desires, which were repressed in early childhood. Freud discussed the problem in the second of his 'Three essays on the theory of sexuality' published in 1905. In these essays, Freud claimed that sexuality, is present in the earliest years of childhood, and then disappears after the resolution of the Oedipus Complex, lying dormant until re-awakened by the onset of puberty. The disappearance of sexuality during childhood was, he argued, directly related to the phenomenon of the 'peculiar *amnesia* which, in the case of most people, though by no means all, hides the earliest beginnings of their childhood up to their sixth or eighth year'.[17]

The result, according to Freud, is a paradox. We forget the events which occur during the period of life when our capacity for remembering is at its sharpest. We have, Freud wrote, 'good reason to believe that there is no period at which the capacity for receiving and reproducing impressions is greater than precisely during the years of childhood'.[18] What happens, Freud suggested, was that the memories are actually retained in the brain with all their original sharpness. However, these stored memory-traces become unavailable to conscious awareness.

Freud made a parallel between infantile and hysterical amnesia. Hysterical amnesia, he suggested, 'occurs at the bidding of repression' and is 'only explicable by the fact that the subject is already in possession of a store of memory-traces which have been withdrawn from conscious disposal'.[19] And so it was with infantile amnesia. The earliest memories had not been destroyed as such, but were repressed from conscious awareness. The reason these experiences have been repressed is closely tied to the repression of sexual urges. In consequence, infantile amnesia 'turns everyone's childhood into something like a *prehistoric* epoch, and conceals from him the beginnings of his own sexual life'.[20] But, according to Freud, what seems to be forgotten is, in a real sense, still remembered: conscious forgetting is accompanied by unconscious remembering.

Freud's theory of the unconscious posited that what is repressed neither decays nor lies dormant. The repressed desires are dynamic, seeking their way back to consciousness. In the case of infantile amnesia, what is repressed becomes expressed in what we later like to consider to be our earliest memories. However, these consciously recalled 'earliest memories' conceal, and reveal signs of, even earlier repressed experi-

---

[17] 'Three essays', *PFL* 7, pp. 89–90, emphasis in original.
[18] Ibid., p. 90.   [19] Ibid., p. 91.
[20] Ibid., emphasis in original.

ences. This was Freud's hypothesis of 'screen memories', which he outlined in a paper published in 1899 and developed in 'Psychopathology of everyday life'.[21] He suggested that 'a person's earliest childhood memories seem frequently to have preserved what is indifferent and unimportant'.[22] As later he was to write in 'The introductory lectures', the few memories, which are preserved from childhood, 'do not necessarily correspond to the important experiences of childhood years'.[23] Yet, one must ask why such insignificant memories have survived the general oblivion. Freud's answer was that they expressed the earlier, repressed experiences, just as dreams express hidden desires. Such memories are like screens, on which earlier memories are projected in distorted form. These screen memories are to be distrusted. The so-called earliest childhood memory is not a 'genuine memory-trace, but a revision of it, a revision which may have been subjected to the influences of a variety of later psychical forces'.[24]

The early 'screen memories' are of the utmost importance in Freud's account of the way in which psychoanalytic treatment works. As he argued 'in every psychoanalytic investigation' it was possible to explain the earliest of childhood memories in terms of being screens for even earlier experiences.[25] The analyst should seek to discover the earliest repressed desires, for until these hidden secrets are revealed no full cure is possible. As he wrote, 'in psychoanalytic treatments we are invariably faced by the task of filling up these gaps in the memory of childhood'. He continued: 'In so far as the treatment is to any extent successful – that is to say, extremely frequently – we also succeed in bringing to light the content of those forgotten years of childhood.'[26] The screen memories, therefore, provide the route to recovering the forgotten and decisive experiences of early life.

The earliest memories which a person can consciously recall offer clues which must be interpreted, in order to reach the psychological buried treasure sought by the psychoanalyst. Freud's case histories provide numerous examples of the analyst asking for, and then interpreting the hidden significance of screen memories. For example, in the case of Serge Pankejeff, the so-called 'Wolf Man', Freud constantly treated the patient's earliest recalled memories as screens for even earlier

---

[21] See 'Screen memories', SE 3.
[22] 'Psychopathology of everyday life', PFL 5, p. 83.
[23] 'Introductory lectures', PFL 1, p. 236. In 'Screen memories', Freud claimed that 'what is important is suppressed and what is indifferent is retained' (SE 3, p. 306).
[24] 'Psychopathology of everyday life', PFL 5, p. 88.
[25] 'A childhood recollection from "Dichtung und Wahrheit"', PFL 14, p. 325.
[26] 'Introductory lectures', PFL 1, p. 237.

repressed desires.[27] For example, the patient recalled early memories of his governess, telling of the occasion when they were out walking and her hat blew away in the wind. In Freud's view, such a trivial memory could only be preserved in conscious awareness if it expressed a deeper, repressed meaning. Freud suggested that the remembered image 'pointed to the castration complex'.[28]

The patient in the 'Wolf Man case' also provided one of the most famous screen memories in psychoanalytic history. He recalled a dream, in which six or seven white wolves were sitting on a walnut tree. He had this dream repeatedly until his eleventh or twelfth year. He seems unclear when he first had the dream – whether he was 'three, four, or at most five years old at the time'.[29] Freud interpreted the dream as encapsulating a memory of a scene which had occurred when the child was probably only a year and a half. According to Freud, the infant must have suffered the trauma of awakening in his cot and witnessing his parents having intercourse. Freud felt able to give precise details about the scene which the infant supposedly had seen and then repressed.[30]

According to Freud, the patient had no conscious recollection of witnessing the 'primal scene'. His repeated dream, which he clearly remembered, was a screen for an earlier repressed memory. By skilful interpretation, which treated the dream's manifest content as a cipher for the forgotten experience, Freud was able to recover the buried memory. At least, he was able to 'recover' it to his own satisfaction. It appears that the patient did not accept the interpretation, never himself believing that he had witnessed the scene so carefully reconstructed by Freud.[31] Some later critics have sided with the patient, pointing out that Freud's reconstruction contains internal implausibilities.[32]

The repressed memories of infancy, according to Freudian theory, resurface in adult dreams. In the 'Introductory lectures', Freud provided an example from his own self-analysis. He reported dreaming of a one-eyed man of small stature whose head was sunk into his shoulders. He claimed that he was able to deduce from the content of the dream that the man was probably a doctor. He suspected that the image was a trace of an early memory. Freud asked his mother about the appearance of

---

[27] Again, there is the problem of what to call Freud's patient. Freud neither gave the patient a nickname nor pseudonym. His real name was Serge Pankejeff. In his case there is more justification, than in the case of Paul Lorenz, for using the nickname. It is said that in later life, Pankejeff would answer the phone by saying 'Wolf Man speaking' (Mahony, 1984; Ferris, 1997).

[28] 'From the history of an infantile neurosis', *PFL* 9, p. 247.

[29] Ibid., p. 259.   [30] Ibid., pp. 268–9.

[31] See Sulloway (1992).

[32] See, for example, Mahony (1984) and Crews (1995).

the doctor, who had delivered him and whom he had not set eyes upon since he was three. He learnt from her that the doctor did in fact have the characteristics of which he dreamt. His mother also told him something else of significance, 'which I myself had forgotten' but which Freud did not divulge to his readers in the 'Introductory lectures'.[33] Another buried memory had been successfully exhumed.[34]

The outlines of Freud's theory of infantile amnesia are plain. The early memories are retained, rather than erased. To use the language of Freud's model of memory, which he outlined in 'The interpretation of dreams', the mind retains the original 'memory-trace' (or '*Mnem.*)', left by the perceptual experience, but the memory-trace cannot enter consciousness. Modern cognitive scientists might express the same point by saying that the engram is preserved in the memory-system, but cannot be accessed or retrieved. In circuitous ways, the memory-traces seep back into consciousness. So-called earliest memories, then, are covers for what has been repressed at an even earlier stage, as a consequence of shame being felt for the vivid sexual and aggressive desires of the Oedipal stage. These repressed memories continue to haunt the adult psyche, whether in recalled memories, dreams or in the symptoms of neuroses. Because the original traces, or memories, have not been erased, they can be recovered in the course of careful therapeutic work. Once they are exposed, the adult problems – or the haunting of the psyche – will be alleviated.

This theory of repression is essentially the same as that which can be found in much contemporary 'Recovered Memory' work. As the experimental psychologist John Kihlstrom has argued, recovered memory theorists tend to assume three basic Freudian assumptions: (a) present symptoms are caused by past traumatic experiences, occurring in childhood; (b) the memories of these traumas are lost to conscious awareness, but are retained unconsciously within the mind; and (c) successful psychological treatment depends on the restoration of such memories to conscious awareness, and that it is the task of trained therapists to assist in this recovery of memory.[35] Kihlstrom has also commented that some of the recovered memory theorists crudely read off 'memories' of abuse from overt symptoms, as if, for example, a patient's neurosis is an infallible sign of enforced infantile incest. He comments that 'this vulgar

---

[33] 'Introductory lectures', *PFL* 1, pp. 237–8.
[34] Kihlstrom (1996) argues that the term 'exhumed memory' provides a better metaphor than 'recovered memory'.
[35] See Kihlstrom (1996). The assumptions of repression are held widely, not only by therapists, but also by laypersons (Garry et al., 1994).

Freudianism – even Freud admitted that sometimes a cigar is a cigar – epitomizes the present-day doctrine of the return of the repressed'.[36]

There are differences between the ideas of current recovered memory theorists and those of classic psychoanalysis. Most obviously, memory theorists and orthodox Freudians disagree on the cause of repression. For orthodox Freudians, the roots of repression lie in infantile desires, which are common to all humans. The recovered memory theorists, on the other hand, concentrate on memories which are repressed as a result of sexual abuse. Although they claim that such abuse is much more frequent than had previously been suspected, they do not claim that it is by any means universal. Moreover, many recovered memory theorists see repression as a biologically based reaction to trauma, although the evidence for this has been contested.[37] In this, the recovered memory theorists resemble the Freud of 'Studies on hysteria', which, too, suggested that the origins of repression lay in external trauma.[38]

Freud, in effect, was putting the blame for infantile repression on the child's desires. If Little Hans developed a phobia of horses and if ultimately he were to forget this, it was because of his 'uncivilized' desires for his mother and his murderous feelings towards his father. Of course, Hans was said by Freud to be morally blameless because he was acting out a biological inevitability. The recovered memory theorists decisively shift the locus of blame from the child to the adult, especially to the male adult. In doing this, they point accusingly at the dangers of Freudian theory. The Oedipal idea, it is said, encourages analysts to suspect that, when victims report memories of sexual abuse, they are only indulging in childish fantasies.

On another point, however, Freudian and recovered memory theorists find themselves grouped uncomfortably together. Outsiders may doubt whether the memories, which both claim to recover in the course of therapy, may be veridical. Even the patient, as in the 'Wolf Man' case, can suspect the interpretations of the therapist. Perhaps the memories, which are reconstructed, are not memories at all. Freud asked his

---

[36] Kihlstrom (1997), p. 103.
[37] See, for example, the arguments of Terr (1994) and van der Kolk and Fisler (1995), and, more generally, those of Courtois (1997). Both Terr and van der Kolk suggest that repression is liable to occur when individuals dissociate themselves from their bodies during repeated traumatic experience of abuse. The memory, then, is not integrated into the normal memory system. There may even be chemical releases, emitted as a reaction to stress, which also affect the way that the memory is stored. For a critical examination of this account of repression, and the lack of fundamental supporting evidence, see Schacter (1995), chapter 9 (see also Goodman and Quas, 1997, for a critique of the idea that amnesia is more likely to follow repeated childhood sexual abuse, rather than a single occurrence).
[38] See above chapter 2, pp. 18f.

mother about the appearance of the doctor. He does not seem to ask whether she had ever spoken to him about the one-eyed doctor. It is possible that Freud was dreaming of a figure whose strange appearance he had heard about in the course of family conversations. In that case he would not be remembering infant experiences of the doctor but his dream would be expressing, or recalling symbolically, later acts of the imagination.

Critics claim that this can easily happen in the course of therapy aimed to recover memories of abuse. The adult 'memories' might reflect earlier forgotten dreams or acts of imagination. They might even be concocted by the promptings of the therapist. As experimental psychologists have demonstrated, people can genuinely claim to have vivid memories of events which never occurred. They can generate their own illusory memories spontaneously or the idea can be implanted by the suggestions of others.[39] Whatever the origin, the detail of the memory and the sincerity with which it is held are insufficient to guarantee the veracity of the memory-claim.

If a patient recovers false memories in the course of therapy, then one might query whether the activity should be properly classed as one of 'remembering'. When Serge Pankejeff was telling Freud of his often repeated childhood dream about wolves, he might be said to be remembering something from his past. Whether he was remembering a particular occurrence of the dream, or remembering the dream in general might be questioned, but not that he was remembering.[40] Suppose he had shared Freud's theoretical enthusiasm for treating such memories as screens and he had followed Freud's leads in reconstructing the scene of the hot summer's afternoon from his infancy. Suppose, then, that Pankejeff came to believe Freud's account that the whole family had apparently gone for a siesta and that he had awakened in his cot to witness parental intercourse, performed not once but three times, seeing the genitals of both his parents, as they engaged in sex from behind.[41] Perhaps, under Freud's promptings, the patient claims now to remember the previously forgotten scene. Perhaps he starts to offer details, as the 'memory' floods back. He now remembers the colour of

---

[39] See, for instance, Loftus (1993); Loftus, Feldman and Dashiell (1995); Lindsay (1994). Even what are called 'flashbulb memories' of highly 'memorable' events can be shown to be inaccurate, despite being recalled in detail (Neisser, 1982; Neisser and Harsch, 1992). Moreover, people can claim to 'remember' saying things that they never actually said (Parks, 1997).

[40] Cognitive memory theorists distinguish between memories for specific and repeated events, claiming that different levels of information processing are involved (see, for instance, Conway and Rubin, 1993).

[41] Such is the detail of the Freud's reconstruction: see 'History of an infantile neurosis,' *PFL* 9, pp. 268–9.

the wall-paper, the sounds of his parents and so on. But supposing there are good, independent reasons for believing that the event never could have happened. It would be like the case of the experimental psychologist Ulric Neisser, who claimed that he could remember accurately from his boyhood hearing the news about the bombing of Pearl Harbour, but, as he shows, the details are so wrong that the memory must be a later fabrication.[42]

In that case, one might wonder how to describe the conversation between Freud and the so-called Wolf Man. Surely the two of them were not recovering 'memories', if the events which are 'remembered' did not occur. If the patient were adding details – which, of course, he did not do – then would we be right in saying that he is 'remembering', although this is what he himself might be claiming to do? Is something else going on in the conversation besides remembering? As the recovered/false memory debate illustrates, much can hang on the way the activity is described – whether it is called 'remembering' or 'fabricating'. Yet, this implies that 'remembering', or genuinely remembering the past, is a straightforward psychological activity and that the problems arise when the past is inaccurately recalled after being seemingly forgotten. However, one cannot specify how a memory might be recovered from repression or how it might be vividly fabricated by suggestion, unless one has a clear notion of what might be involved in remembering. For this, it is necessary to consider the psychological nature of remembering and forgetting.

Learning to remember explicitly

Freud's explanation of infantile amnesia is basically unsatisfactory. He does not account for the fact that virtually everything which happens in the first few years of life is lost to later recall. If shameful desires need to be repressed, then this does not account for the fact that 'innocent' memories too are swept along with the general forgetting. Perhaps, a Freudian might reply that during the Oedipal stage the desires are so strong, so preoccupying, that they dominate the whole life of the child. Unless everything goes, then the memory of these desires will still remain in conscious awareness. But such a defence is hardly convincing. Little Hans's fear of horses was only part of his life. He had other interests, other routines and other delights. Yet by the time he was nineteen, all had gone. Even the analysis, conducted by his father under the guidance of Freud, was caught up in the amnesia. This seemed to

[42] Neisser (1982).

have perplexed Freud. Why should the analysis, which supposedly was unmasking the processes of repression and helping the child to cope with troubling desires, also be repressed?

In an important sense, Little Hans's amnesia, like that of all children, was not total. During the years, which he could not later recall, he was developing and learning. What he learnt would remain unforgotten. The dialogues, noted by his father and reported in Freud's case history, testify to the child's development of language. His vocabulary is growing. As was suggested in the previous chapter, Hans can be heard to learn the meaning of words such as 'jealous'. He is learning to produce socially adequate answers to adult questions. In this, he is learning the lessons of appropriate, or polite, dialogue. What is learnt may last a lifetime, but the specific circumstances, when the learning took place, are forgotten. Hans will continue to use and understand the word 'jealous', but he will be unable to recall how he acquired this knowledge. Not just 'jealous', but the origins of practically all the familiar words, which he will continue to use in later life, will be lost in this fog of amnesia.

If the general amnesia of childhood cannot be satisfactorily explained by Freud's notion of repression, then another explanation is required. A much simpler one will be offered. Remembering is not based on fishing out a stored memory-trace from the mind, and then playing it back in consciousness. Modern memory theorists stress that 'memories' are not simply stored in the brain, passively awaiting to be accessed, so that the original experience can be re-experienced in pristine fullness. As one team of experimental psychologists has recently commented, the very metaphors of 'storage' and 'retrieval' are misleading; moreover 'the idea that memory is like a videotape recording (never seriously believed by psychologists but occasionally endorsed by others) is even more misleading'.[43] Instead, memories have to be formulated and constructed. As will be argued, language plays an important role in this. Until the child acquires sufficient linguistic skills then this type of remembering is not possible. To put it simply, infantile amnesia occurs because the child in its earliest years has not yet learnt how to remember.

Memory researchers often use a distinction, proposed by the neuro-psychologist Daniel Schacter, between two types of memory: explicit and implicit memory. Explicit remembering occurs when the person is aware that they are remembering something. When we remember implicitly we are not aware that some piece of information has been retained. According to Schacter 'implicit memory is an unintentional,

---

[43] Roediger, McDermott and Goff (1997), p. 144.

nonconscious form of retention that can be contrasted with *explicit memory*, which involves conscious recollection of past experiences'.[44] In the experimental paradigms, which are designed to test implicit learning, a person claims not to have seen a particular stimulus previously, whilst it is demonstrated that their unremembered prior familiarity affects present responses. Thus, there is evidence of remembering without a conscious awareness of such remembering.[45] Implicit remembering, can occur from birth.[46] Within days a child has often learned to recognize its mother's face. Sights and sounds are recognized, procedures of movement acquired and so on. All this is implicit remembering, for infants, in acquiring these skills, are not consciously aware that they are remembering – they cannot claim to remember anything. However, by their responses they are showing 'nonconscious effects of past experiences on subsequent behaviour and performance'.[47] This sort of learning is also to be observed in non-humans, whose behaviour can be modified by past experience.

In the case of explicit remembering, language is typically involved. It is for this reason that some psychologists prefer the term 'declarative memory' to 'explicit memory'.[48] We engage in explicit remembering when we tell stories about the past, displaying what psychologists are now calling 'autobiographical memory'.[49] Rats, cats and babies cannot engage in such story telling. They cannot declare their memories, although they can act in ways that lead observers to presuppose that they have learnt from, and thus remembered, past experience implicitly. When Pankejeff was telling Freud about his recurring childhood dream, he was engaging in explicit remembering, and, as is typical of autobiographical accounts, he attempted to date the past events: the dreams must have occurred between the ages of three and eleven, he suggested. Similarly, when Freud, in the 'Introductory lectures', was narrating his dream of the one-eyed doctor and his subsequent conversation with his mother, again he was engaging in explicit remembering. He was explicitly recalling events from the past. One can see why the videotape metaphor of remembering is so misleading. When one is engaged in such remembering, one is not re-experiencing the past in a literal sense. Pankejeff did not re-dream his dream in the present as he had done

---

[44] Schacter (1993), p. 387. See also Schacter (1995) chapter 6 and Schacter et al. (1997).
[45] See, for example, Schacter et al. (1995 and 1997) for discussions of such 'priming' effects.
[46] Schacter (1995) chapter 6.
[47] Schacter et al. (1995), p. 19.
[48] See, for instance, Squire (1995).
[49] On 'autobiographical memory', see, for instance, Thompson et al. (1996); Conway and Rubin (1993).

when a child. Second time around, he has doing something very different. He was talking about the dream, constructing a coherent narrative, locating the events in a story about past time.

Experimental psychologists, testing the operations of explicit memory, typically ask their subjects to recall which stimuli they may have been shown previously; or they ask the subjects whether they have seen a particular stimulus before. As such, these sorts of experiments require dialogic interchanges between experimenter and subjects, even if the conversations are of a restricted nature.[50] Experimental subjects would not be able to perform such tasks if they were not told what to do and did not give indications that they had understood the instructions.[51] In consequence, the paradigms for testing conscious, or explicit, re-membering are not transferable to animals or to new-born infants.

To follow the instructions experimental subjects must be familiar with what can be called 'the grammar of remembering'.[52] They must be able to perform the activities which are understood as being 'remembering'. As Wittgenstein stressed, psychological words stand in need of outward criteria.[53] 'Remembering' cannot consist of replaying an internal, private video. If it did, then there could be no concept of 'remembering' in the public vocabulary: 'What we deny is that the picture of the inner processes gives us the correct picture of the idea of the use of the word to "remember"'.[54] Psychological subjects, when asked whether they remember seeing a particular stimulus, are not being asked to replay an internal video.

What is true of the restricted experimental situation is doubly true of autobiographical remembering, especially that which occurs sponta-neously in the course of conversation. Language proficiency is required to tell tales of the past and to recognize that one is 'remembering' when one is telling such tales. This is why some psychologists have claimed that memory can be studied by examining how participants talk of memory, giving particular attention to 'the situated uses of words such as "remember", "forget", and so on'.[55] Only humans with appropriate narrative skills can have autobiographical memory. Infants, who have

---

[50] For detailed arguments on this point, see Edwards (1997); Edwards, Middleton and Potter (1992); Trabasso (1997).

[51] Gardiner and Java (1993) claim that experimental results can be affected depending on whether subjects are asked whether they 'remember' or 'know' a given stimulus (pp. 169f).

[52] On the grammar of remembering, see Eder (1994) and Shotter (1990).

[53] Wittgenstein (1953), remark 580.

[54] Ibid.

[55] Edwards (1997), p. 282.

not yet acquired these skills, including the 'grammar of remembering', cannot be expected to remember autobiographically. At best they can remember implicitly.[56]

Studies, which examine conversations between young children and adults, illustrate how children learn to remember through dialogue. It has been shown that children are much more likely to recall those aspects of past events, which have been spoken about by parents.[57] Mothers, in talking to children about past events, convey to them what is 'memorable' – in other words, what features are appropriate to recall.[58] If details of past events are not forthcoming, mothers will often ask guiding questions to prompt appropriate responses. In this way, they provide discursive guides for what cognitive psychologists call 'retrieval cues'. In a literal sense, adult speakers are demonstrating to children how to 'interrogate' the past.[59] Children acquire the appropriate narrative skills for remembering: these skills involve not merely the retelling of past events but also the constructions of the narratives themselves. Consequently, children learn to retain memories by formulating them as narratives.[60] The child practices these skills of remembering in the course of conversations with adults, with the result that the remembering is frequently not accomplished by the child alone but jointly with the adult.[61] This practice of remembering in conversation continues through life.[62]

As always, dialogic skills can be internalized to become the skills of solitary thinking. The sorts of questioning, which parents use to guide children to remembering past details, can be applied to individual reminiscing.[63] The psychologists Martin Conway and David Rubin describe how an experimental subject can construct an autobiographical memory of the past. If subjects are asked to recall a memory when given the cue word *cinema*, and they do not have an immediate answer, they may pose questions of themselves: 'when did I go to the cinema a lot?' and they may then answer their own question *'when I was a student?'*[64] In

---

[56] For an excellent discussion of these issues, see Nelson (1993).
[57] See Tessler and Nelson (1994); Nelson (1993).
[58] See, for example, Edwards and Middleton (1988); Middleton and Edwards (1990); Fivush and Kuebli (1997).
[59] Middleton and Edwards (1990); Saywitz and Moan-Hardie (1994).
[60] See Thompson et al. (1996), pp. 10f.
[61] See Trabasso (1997); Edwards and Middleton (1988) and Middleton and Edwards (1990).
[62] See Edwards and Middleton (1986); Billig (1990); Billig and Edwards (1994) for examples of conversational remembering.
[63] See, for instance, Nelson (1993).
[64] Conway and Rubin (1993), p. 111.

such an instance, external dialogical skills, having been internalized as inner speech, become a means of constructing memories.[65]

What all this implies is that the skills of explicit remembering are bound up with the skills of language and, therefore, they are learnt skills. Before the age of five, children have not tended to acquire such skills. Perhaps they can tell broad stories about regular happenings; but often they are unable to distinguish between the novel events, which adults find memorable, and ordinary events, which adults consider unworthy of recall. As Katherine Nelson has written, 'in early childhood everything is novel, therefore nothing is memorable'.[66] Implicit remembering may occur daily, before the child has acquired the skills to remember explicitly. However, the narrative skill of memory cannot be satisfactorily post-dated to weave together earlier experiences into narratives of remembrance.[67] Memories are best retained when the child possesses the narrative skills at the time of the experiences. The result is that earlier experiences are lost in amnesia, or, at best, survive as fragmented images, which cannot be easily located in time and place.[68]

Freud was correct in pointing to the unparalleled capacity for memory in the earliest years. Throughout infancy the child has much to acquire, including the whole complex business of language and talk. Never again will the person be able to acquire so many diverse linguistic skills as they do between the ages of one and five. The lessons learnt then will stick for life. But the paradox is that, until these skills are learnt and retained the child, cannot remember explicitly. The learning of the very skills, which permit explicit remembrance, will itself be lost in infant amnesia. There is no need to assume that repression is responsible for this loss. On the other hand, there is good reason to suspect that the acquisition of the language skills necessary for remembrance paves the way for the possibility of repression.

[65] Wittgenstein (1975) suggested that personal remembering must be based on public remembering: 'I give myself an exhibition of something only *in the same way* as I give one to other people.' He posed the question how do I give myself an 'exhibition of remembering' (remark no. 665, emphasis in original). Significantly, his answer was posed in terms of an internal question-and-answer sequence: 'Well, I ask myself "How did I spend this morning?" and I give myself an answer' (remark no. 667).

[66] Nelson (1993), p. 363. But see Howe et al. (1994) for an alternative account, which emphasizes the role of the child's conception of the self in the development of autobiographical memory. However, it can be argued that the child's concept of the self depends on acquiring the grammar of 'I' and 'me' (Harré, 1990; Mühlhäusler and Harré, 1990; Shotter, 1993a and 1993b). Gergen (1994) provides an insightful discussion of the way that personal identity is formed through self-narration in social life (see also Michael, 1996).

[67] Fivush et al. (1997).

[68] For studies of the fragmentary nature of infantile memory, see Goodman et al. (1994) and Howe et al. (1994).

Hans learning to remember

In a provocative statement, the developmental psychologists Minda Tessler and Katherine Nelson have claimed that 'all adult–child talk is . . . a form of memory talk or memory instruction'.[69] Perhaps the claim is an exaggeration, but it nevertheless contains an important point. In talking to children, adults are providing models for appropriate talk: they are engaging in implicit instruction, and, thus, each conversation adds to the implicit remembering of the child. As such, the adult is often directing the child's attention, thereby conveying what should be considered important and unimportant in life. In so doing, adults, in talking to children, are offering implicit tutorials in the business of remembering.

This can be seen in the dialogues that Freud reports in the case of Little Hans. Freud, of course, was concerned to interpret these dialogues as signs of childish desire and repression. They can also be read as providing accounts of the way that a child is learning, and being taught, how to remember in culturally appropriate ways. Many of the conversations between Herr Graf and his son are about past events – both the immediate past, such as Hans's dreams of the previous night and a more distant past. In these conversations, the father can be heard to be teaching his son the skills of 'memory-work'.

Such memory-work is rarely neutral, as if speakers are recalling the past for its own sake. Instead, speakers, in talking about the past, are often conducting business in the present. Memory-talk contains what some discursive psychologists have called a 'rhetorical stake'.[70] Points are being made, arguments conducted, as the past is invoked. In Professor Freud's surgery, Papa Graf asks Hans 'Have I ever scolded you or hit you?'[71] The question is not a simple request for information about the past. The father, as was discussed in the previous chapter, in asking the question, is inviting a negative answer, in order to suggest that he is not to blame for the aggressive feelings, which the psychoanalytically informed adults are seeing in the child. The evidence for this interpretation of the father's words is contained in Freud's description of the conversation. He reports that 'Hans *corrected* him: "Oh yes! You have hit me."'[72] The word 'correct' is the give-away. Freud has not heard Papa Graf's question as an innocent request for information about the past. The father is making a point, invoking the past to do so.

[69] Tessler and Nelson (1994), p. 310.
[70] The notion of rhetorical stake is a central concern in the important analyses of remembering provided by Edwards and Potter (1992); Edwards (1997); Potter and Edwards (1990).
[71] 'Analysis of a phobia', *PFL* 8, p. 204. See above chapter 5, p. 119.
[72] Ibid., emphasis added.

The 'question', or at least the point behind the question, is something which can be contested. Thus, Hans corrects his father: the past didn't happen as his father was suggesting by his question.[73]

A few days later, father and son are talking. As is typical of these conversations, the father is asking the questions, cross-examining the son, seeking to discover guilty desires. The issue again is Hans's feelings towards his father. Hans has admitted that 'when you're away, I'm afraid you're not coming home'. And the father asks: 'And have I ever threatened you that I shan't come home?' Again, Hans is being asked to report the past. And, again, the context is not rhetorically neutral. This question, too, has a preferred answer. This time, in response, the young child acquits the father, but accuses the mother: 'Not you, but Mummy. Mummy's told me she won't come back.'[74]

The rhetoric of blame is confirmed by a note which the father adds to his record, presumably for Freud's benefit. He does not challenge Hans's claim, but offers an explanation for the mother's threat: 'He had probably been naughty, and she (the mother) had threatened to go away.'[75] Again, it is Hans's fault. He must have been naughty. The mother must have been justified.

The father is inviting the child to forget the sins of the parents: I've never hit or threatened you, he says. And when challenged, he invites Freud to take his side. If the child has claimed that the father has hit him, or that the mother has threatened him, then these refer to episodes which are not worth remembering. He does not bother to find out the details of the mother's threat. It is unimportant. In this way, the boy's past is reconstructed in front of him, and in front of Freud, as a morality tale, that is based on a mixture of remembering and forgetting. The boy is being provided with an 'official' account of his own history.

Just as the child learns the meanings of words from older speakers, so Hans has to learn what it is meant by 'remembering'. The 'grammar' of remembering does not merely involve telling stories about the past. It generally involves the extra claim that the stories 'really' happened, so that if one claims to 'remember' an event, then one is making some sort of claim to accuracy.[76] Hans has to learn that a claim to remember,

---

[73] See above, chapter 5, for a discussion of Freud's and Graf's dismissal of the young child's claim.

[74] 'Analysis of a phobia', PFL 8, p. 206.

[75] Ibid.

[76] Discursive psychologists have shown how the nature of the claim to accuracy depends on the conversational context. In some situations, the broad 'gist' is considered as adequate; in other cases details are required in order to be said to have 'remembered'. Whether gist or details are required can itself be an object of dispute; see Edwards and Potter (1992); Edwards (1997); Potter and Edwards (1990).

especially when made by a child, is not always taken as sufficient proof. External validation might be required, as memory-stories are checked against other evidence, including the memory-stories of other people.

Hans is asked by his father to recount events, which relate to his fear of horses. The boy tells of seeing a horse fall down in the street. He adds: 'It gave me a fright because it made a row with its feet.' The father asks for some background information about the event: 'Where did you go with Mummy that day?' Hans gives a detailed itinerary: to the Skating Rink, then shopping to buy a waistcoat and some pastries and then home, via the park. Herr Graf adds 'all of this was confirmed by my wife'.[77]

A few days later Herr Graf was asking his son why he had said 'Ugh' with a display of disgust, when his mother had shown him a pair of yellow drawers which she had just purchased for herself. Hans answered that he had given the same reaction to her black drawers as well. The questions, then, focus on the mother's underwear and Hans's past feelings. Some of Hans's statements are confirmed by his mother. Some are not. Hans mentions that Mummy is wearing black drawers today. 'Correct', adds Herr Graf in his text. Hans justifies his claim: 'Because I saw her take them off in the morning.' He claims that she took them off before going out and, when she came back, she put them on again.[78]

Herr Graf checks this. His wife denies the story: 'She said it was entirely untrue. Of course she had not changed her drawers when she went out.' He immediately challenges Hans. You said she took her black drawers off before going out 'but Mummy says it's not true'. Hans replied: 'I think perhaps I may have forgotten she didn't take them off.' Then he added with a show of impatience, 'Oh, do let me alone.'[79] Hans is learning the 'grammar' of 'forgetting'. To claim to forget something is not merely to claim that there is a gap in the memory of the past. Speakers do things in conversation with their claims of 'forgetting'. In this case, the claim is being made in regard to an error of commission, rather than omission. Hans has told a story which fails to be corroborated by the principal actor. He claims that he must have forgotten, thereby deferring to his mother's account of the episode.

Hans's father, by not picking up on the word 'forget', confirms implicitly that it is correct to talk of forgetting in this sort of way. The claim is not merely a report of the speaker's ability to produce a memory-story, but it can be used as a justification. When accused of telling false stories about the past, the claim absolves the speaker from the accusation of lying. I have not deliberately fabricated the story of

[77] 'Analysis of a phobia, *PFL* 8, p. 212.
[78] Ibid., p. 218.   [79] Ibid.

Mummy removing her drawers, Hans is implying: I have forgotten. I cannot be blamed for lying. And if I have forgotten, there is little more that I can say – or you can question me about. Thus, the claim can be used to cut short awkward questioning.[80] Hans is becoming a sophisticated speaker – at least if Max Graf's record of the conversation and of the words used, is to be trusted.

The claim to 'remember' can be used as a justification when a memory-story is being challenged. Hans's father is asking Hans about his feelings towards his younger sister, Hanna. Hans starts talking about the past. He tells of travelling to Gmunden for a summer holiday. Hanna, he says, travelled in a box shortly after she was born. The father was showing signs of disbelief. Hans tries to convince him: 'Really, Daddy. Do believe me . . . Really and truly. I can remember quite well.'[81] 'What can you remember?', asks his father. Hans answers: 'That Hanna travelled in the box: because I haven't forgotten about it.' He emphasizes that his memory is veridical – really and truly, he adds. The proof of the story is his clear memory – that he hasn't forgotten.

The claim, however, is not sufficiently convincing. Hans knows that his father is not persuaded. The extra words of assurance, the 'really' and the 'truly', would not be needed if there were no doubts. Hans is learning that a claim to memory, even if rhetorically emphasized, need not be persuasive, especially if made by a child. His father does not act as if Hans possessed a veridical video-tape of the episode, stored in his brain. Instead, the father argues back, using external arguments to show that Hanna had only been to Gmunden once, and that was when she was old enough to walk: she could not have travelled in a box, as Hans was claiming. Hans disagrees: 'She's been twice. Yes, that's it. I can remember quite well.' It is his turn to seek corroboration: 'Ask Mummy, she'll tell you soon enough'. His father replies: 'It's not true all the same.'[82] The argument continued. Hans's father even gently accuses Hans of lying. Under further questioning, Hans becomes confused and starts backing down.

In effect, but not in intention, Papa Graf is giving Hans a tutorial in memory-work. By his questioning, he is showing how fragmentary accounts of the past can be interrogated, in order to reconstruct a fuller story. He demonstrates how to sort out dates, times and implausibilities. In doing this, he shows the value of constructing the narrative out of

---

[80] Edwards (1997) discusses how the claim to 'not remember' can be used to avoid interrogation (pp. 283f.; see also Edwards and Potter, 1992 and Lynch and Bogen, 1996). Potter (1996) makes an interesting distinction between the uses of 'I don't know' and 'I forget' (pp. 131–2).

[81] 'Analysis of a phobia', *PFL* 8, p. 230.

[82] Ibid., p. 236.

elements that can be corroborated, and also the virtues of citing the corroboration, when telling the story. In this sense, the work of remembering can be collectively accomplished through talk.[83] Most importantly, the father is showing how claims of remembrance can be challenged. Hans's protestations that he remembers events 'really and truly' need not be considered as rhetorically decisive. Hans, of course, has already learnt this lesson. He has challenged, with partial success, his father's claims never to have scolded or hit him. In that case, the father dismissed the challenge by denying that the hitting 'really' was hitting.

By talking of the past – by using the words 'remember' and 'forget' in conversation – the father is demonstrating what conventionally can count as adequate remembering and forgetting. Indeed, what counts as adequate can be contested and worked out in conversation, for there is no *a priori* rule, which can in advance settle whether memory-claims are to be classified as adequate or not.[84] Hans's father also demonstrates that such claims serve rhetorical purposes, being used in the business of blame and justification. Again, he is demonstrating, through practical application, how such blaming and justifying can be persuasively accomplished. In his turn, Hans is learning, and trying out, rhetorical moves. He, too, can invoke the mother as the arbiter of the past. A memory-claim, when challenged forcefully, can be switched to a forgetting-claim. Hans is practising the complex, interrelated rhetoric of explicitly re-membering and forgetting.

None of this could be possible, if Hans had not been able to remember implicitly the skills of dialogue. These skills are displayed and developed implicitly, as the participants explicitly remember the past, and as they argue about this remembrance. In the case of Hans, these conversations are not providing the basic elements of the adult Hans's autobiographical memory. These conversations are doomed to be forgotten, until they are recalled courtesy of Freud's written remembrance of the past.

Hans comes to forget these episodes, but, nevertheless, residues may be retained. Such forgotten conversations provided opportunities for implicit learning. Hans may be incorporating into himself the emotional

---

[83] Discursive psychologists have taken seriously Maurice Halbwach's (1980) notion of 'collective memory'. Because memory can be collectively established, not all the necessary memory-work need be performed by the person who actually claims to have personally experienced the event (see, for instance, Middleton and Edwards, 1990; Billig and Edwards, 1994).

[84] The 'local', or contextual, management of adequacy is an important aspect in the analysis of memory offered by discursive psychologists (Edwards, 1997; Edwards and Potter, 1992).

tone of such conversations, picking up models of challenge and distrust from his parents. Thus, the relationship with his parents may be reproduced in later patterns of communication. More directly, in such early conversations, the adults were providing models for talk and remembrance. Denial, even repression, can be suspected of playing its part in these talks. One might say that the adults are not providing quite the models which they suppose themselves to be providing. Hans may be picking up things of which neither he nor the adults are explicitly aware. Thus, the implicit, or the unconscious, accompanies the explicit, or the conscious, as the unspoken, unrecalled shadow of the past.

Learning to forget

Hans may have been given lessons in remembering, but at the same time he was also being instructed in forgetting, for remembering and forgetting are tightly bound together as social practices. The teaching of forgetting cannot be conducted explicitly. A parallel can be drawn to the rhetoric of shifting topics, that was discussed earlier.[85] Parents use a particular set of rhetorical devices to redirect the child's attention and the child learns from such examples how to shift topics. The parents, as they use such devices, cannot draw attention explicitly to shifting of the topic, even if they are consciously aware of what they have done. To do so would undermine the very practice that they are displaying. The same might be true for the forgetting, which often has to be displayed implicitly in the context of explicit remembering. In pointing out the memorable, one does not necessarily wish to stress the forgettable – the forgettable becomes forgettable because it is unmentioned. To mention it, even as 'forgettable', might contribute to making it memorable.

A general point might be made to the effect that explicit remembering involves implicit forgetting. One cannot remember everything that impinges momentarily upon consciousness. If remembering involved a perfect video-recall of all past experiences, then the act of remembering would take as long as the original experience. Instead, there needs to be coding and abbreviation.[86] As Daniel Schacter has suggested, forgetting may even have an evolutionary advantage: 'We don't need to remember everything that has ever happened to us; engrams that we never use are probably best forgotten.'[87] However, we need to learn what it is we need and do not need. Here the teaching of remembering is crucial.

---

[85] See chapter 4.
[86] This was one of the basic points of the so-called 'New Look' school of perception (Erdelyi, 1974).
[87] Schacter (1995), p. 81.

If adults teach children, either implicitly or explicitly, what is memorable, then, by implication they are teaching what is not worth remembering. Tessler and Nelson recorded mothers taking their three year old children on a trip to a museum.[88] Later, the children were asked to recall the objects that they had seen in the museum. By and large, the children were only able to recall those objects, which their mothers had specifically spoken about. In going round the museum, the mothers had been directing their children's attention. Not only were the mothers, in effect, controlling the memory of the event, while the event was occurring, they were also controlling what should be forgotten. The mothers' words indicated implicitly that the objects, to which they had not drawn attention, were unimportant and forgettable. In this sense, learning to remember explicitly involves learning to forget implicitly.

All this can be seen in the conversations between Hans and his father. Not only is the father guiding the boy in the activity of remembering, but the practice and grammar of forgetting are crucially involved. Hans's father, in his various cross-examinations of the boy, was establishing what were the crucial things which Hans should remember and what was irrelevant for this remembrance. The father's scale of importance was being determined by psychoanalytic theory, as well as by more generally shared cultural assumptions. In the extracts which Freud reproduced, it was clear that Hans should remember matters connected with widdlers, sex and jealousy. Other matters, including the scoldings and threats of the parents, could be forgotten: they were to be dismissed as irrelevant.

After Hans developed his fear of horses, his father spent much effort asking him about horses. Much of the conversations hinged on questions about earlier events, as the father suspected that sexual images lay at the root of the phobia. Herr Graf particularly sought any association which Hans might have made between horses and penises. At one point he asked Hans about playing with the other children on holiday at Gmunden. Did they play horses? Did they go into the stables?

I Did they tell you anything about horses?
HANS Yes.
I What?
HANS I've forgotten.
I Perhaps they told you about their widdlers?
HANS Oh, no.
I Were you frightened of horses already then?
HANS Oh, no. I wasn't frightened at all.

---

[88] Tessler and Nelson (1994).

I Perhaps Berta told you that horses –
HANS (interrupting) – widdle? No.[89]

Through his questions, the father conveys the sorts of memories in which he is interested. He does not want any sort of information about the past. He wants Hans to recall a particular type of information. Previous conversations should have given Hans sufficient inkling that his father wants widdler-related memories. But, he offers sufficient clues in the exchange to remind Hans once more.

Hans indicates that he and his friends had spoken about horses. When his father asks what the other children had told him, Hans replies that he had forgotten. His father tries to prompt him by bringing up the issue of widdlers. Hans denies that the children told him anything about that. The question Hans's father didn't ask is as revealing as the one he asked. He does not challenge Hans's claim to have forgotten, asking words to the effect: if you can remember that you spoke about horses, surely you can remember something that was said? He does not try to encourage Hans to reconstruct those conversations with the friends that may have concerned horses but not horses' widdlers.

The exchange illustrates once again that Hans is understanding, and using, the grammar of 'forgetting'. In guiding Hans to remember explicitly talk about widdlers, his father indicates that not all conversations, which Hans might have had about horses, are equally to be remembered. Conversations, which did not include widdler-themes or fears, can be forgotten. He is patently not interested in all the childish chit-chat. The exchange indicates that Hans had understood this. When the father starts asking what Berta had said about horses, Hans interrupts to complete the question for him. He, not his father, provides the topic of widdling. In so doing, Hans indicates his knowledge that this is the sort of information which his father requires him to remember. His father, by accepting the completed question as his own question, confirms the impression. He does not say 'no, that's not what I wanted to know'. He does not even ask what else Berta might have said. Berta's other words need not be remembered. No memory-work need be expended on them. They, by implication, are being deemed as forgettable.

Freud was at times somewhat critical of Max Graf's mode of questioning, believing him to be asking too many direct questions without letting the boy express his own thoughts.[90] Freud would have preferred Hans to have talked about what he could remember, even if this entailed

---

[89] 'Analysis of a phobia', *PFL* 8, pp. 220–1.
[90] Ibid., p. 225.

the boy rambling on about seeming irrelevancies. In the same vein, Freud used to encourage his adult patients to say the first thing which came into their minds, whether or not it seemed relevant.[91] If patients claimed to be unable to remember those particular points about the past, which Freud has suspected to be psychologically crucial, Freud would encourage them to talk of what they could remember, thereby approaching the forgotten topic obliquely, in the aim of patiently reconstructing fuller memory-stories.[92]

However, there is a difference between Freud, as a therapist, talking to adult patients in a therapeutic situation, and father and child talking in the family home. Freud was not having to teach his patients how to speak appropriately in a general sense, although he might instruct them in the special conventions of psychoanalytic dialogue. Max Graf, on the other hand, would not want Hans to develop conversational habits, which would give him licence to say exactly what he wanted, especially when speaking to adults. He wanted his son to abide by the conversational cues of cultural appropriateness, thereby speaking as a polite young boy. As Graf interrogates Hans about the past, he clearly wants to discover hidden memories. But not everything is to be sacrificed to this aim. He is still the loving, dutiful father, the corrector of his children's misdemeanours, the teacher of politely appropriate ways of talking. He cannot act as a therapist, who is prepared to accept the 'narrative truth' of whatever the patient says. Parents, like the Grafs, want to teach the child to separate truth from falsity and not to tell lies. Thus the role of parent differs from that of analyst.[93]

As Hans was being explicitly instructed to remember his past conversations about horses' widdlers, he was implicitly being shown that the other childish conversations, which he might have been able to remember, are not worth talking about. Hans was being told how to answer adults' questions appropriately. Some types of answer were to be offered, and others were not worth considering. Papa Graf was conducting an implicit tutorial in both remembering and forgetting.

The historian, Michael Kammen, writing about the inaccurate myths in conventional American history, quotes the words of the nineteenth century mystic, Bronson Alcott: 'Can you remember when you did not remember?'[94] As far as infantile amnesia is concerned, the answer is 'no'. We are unable to remember that part of our lives which occurred

---

[91] See, for instance, Freud's comments to Paul Lorenz at the start of treatment ('Notes upon a case of obsessional neurosis', *PFL* 8, p. 40).

[92] Freud described this technique at some length in 'Studies on hysteria', pp. 110f.

[93] On the idea of 'narrative truth' in psychoanalytic practice, see Spence (1994) and Frosh (1997).

[94] Kammen (1995), p. 342.

before we acquired the ability to remember. Hans was later unable to recall those conversations with his father when he was first learning to construct versions of his past. If the skills of explicit remembering include those of forgetting, then there is a paradoxical implication. Hans, like others, could not later recall the period before he could remember. More than this, he was also, in a real sense, unable remember the time before he had learnt to forget.

Remembering as a means of forgetting

The idea that both explicit remembering and forgetting might be acquired skills bears directly on the question how repression could be accomplished. A simple answer might be given. Repression is not to be thought of as some sort of blank – an infantile amnesia writ large. It requires remembering and a knowledge of memory-work, for, often, repressing involves the production of memory-stories and the avoidance of further memory-work. Such an avoidance could not be accomplished, unless the person is aware, in general terms, of what is being avoided.

This notion of repressing depends on the idea that remembrance is not something which has to occur spontaneously and completely. The past frequently has to be carefully reconstructed. Work has to be done. Papa Graf, in directing his son to talk about past events, was imposing memory-work on his son. By doing such work, often jointly with the help of others, memories can be formulated, and what seemed to have been forgotten is recovered. Far from memory fading with time, it can be improved if the time is spent in memory-work.[95] However, there is a downside. One can talk with others about the past, remembering and reconstructing seemingly forgotten details. Similarly, the solitary individual can perform memory-work through internal conversation. However, there is no guarantee that the newly recovered details are accurate. In fact, evidence suggests that not only does the rate of accurate recovery increase with memory-work, but so does the probability of error, as we imagine details, or even whole episodes, which did not occur.[96]

As was discussed in chapter 4, repression demands replacement, as a dangerous topic is replaced by another. Replacement can be seen to occur with the forgetting of memories. If one successfully represses an

[95] Erdelyi (1990 and 1996) has shown that performance on standard memory tasks can improve over time, if subjects are warned that they will be tested at a later date. Similarly memory for the past can be improved by joint recall, as speakers collaborate in conversation to reconstruct past events (Edwards and Middleton, 1986).

[96] For experimental evidence to show that errors of recall can occur along with hypermnesia, see Roediger et al. (1997).

experience the result should not be amnesia – or a gap in the remembered stream of consciousness. A replacement history needs to be found, so one possible memory-story is supplanted by another, which suppresses the former.

No memory-story of an event can include every possible version of that event. Each story, which is told as *the* memory of the event, must contain omissions, as details, interpretations and glosses, that might have been included, are left out. In this respect, remembering involves forgetting.[97] Moreover, once the memories are constructed, the forgettable becomes even more forgotten. It has been shown that the reproduction of particular memory-stories ensures that alternative stories, even if they are more accurate, become less likely to be produced.[98] In short, one works up a standardized memory, which encapsulates some features and consigns others to oblivion. It becomes our own 'official' story of the past event, to be reproduced in well-rehearsed form when we wish to recall the event in question.

The well-remembered anecdote functions to obviate the need for further memory-work. It offers its own proof that the past is being remembered. We have our set stories about what happened at various points in our life: why a marriage failed, an examination was passed, or a parent was distant, and so on. Such stories operate as personal myths in our autobiographical memory.[99] Typically, these stories will contain omissions, not to mention self-serving interpretations. Other witnesses to the past events are likely to formulate their memory-stories, with their own interpretations. Hans's father remembered reacting to his son's aggression, in a way which did not merit the word 'hitting'. Hans remembered the episode differently. Freud's own published short 'Autobiographical study' inevitably contains omissions: he could not present every fact, which he knew about himself, but he had to condense his story into a few pages. In telling this story Freud advanced myths about himself, his work and the origins of psychoanalysis. As will be discussed later in chapter 8, his opening statement about his own family contains a curious and revealing omission.

Omissions in autobiographical accounts can be suspected of tendentiously serving the picture which the writer (or speaker) wishes to present publicly and, by implication, which they want to present to

---

[97] This was demonstrated in the classic memory studies of Sir Frederick Bartlett (1932). Full recall, which might include the reproduction of all themes in a lengthy folk tale, not to mention the original wording, was not possible: selection was inevitable (see also Edwards and Middleton, 1987).

[98] See, for example, Roediger et al. (1997); see also, Schacter (1995, pp. 110f.).

[99] For more on the mythic aspects of autobiographical memory, see Conway (1997); Conway and Rubin (1993).

themselves. The autobiographical accounts of self-made persons, for example, typically tend to overlook help which may have been offered by friends and family.[100] There is no reason to suspect that such persons are behaving in a deliberately deceitful way. Rather, they believe in their own myths. Similar self-serving patterns can be seen to operate at a group level, as cultures and groups celebrate their pasts by creating histories which simultaneously involve collective remembering and forgetting. As Ernest Renan remarked, 'forgetting . . . is a crucial factor in the creation of a nation'.[101] The nation forgets, according to Renan, that it was created in bloodshed and barbarity. The forgetting is accomplished, not by a general amnesia, but by the formulation of historic myths which only recount a gloriously unshadowed past.[102]

Such memory-stories – whether personal, professional or cultural – can be suspected for being partial in their patterns of inclusion and omission. It is not so much that the past is censored, but that the past is being recruited, indeed created, to serve present purposes.[103] What is inconvenient or painful to remember is overlooked in this remembering. In this way, we can hide aspects of the past from ourselves, whether on a personal or group level. In these circumstances, the more we claim to remember the past – or the more the group claims to know its history – the more that the self-serving account is preserved.[104] The end result is that personal or collective forgetting is accomplished by means of a remembering, which becomes solidified into a rehearsed story.

Repression does not rest alone on the construction of self-serving stories, which succeed in omitting disturbing details. As Freud recognized, repression is not a once-and-for-all process: it needs to be constantly practised, in order to prevent the repressed thoughts from re-surfacing into conscious awareness. At its simplest, this involves the avoidance of further memory-work, which might disturb the sovereignty

---

[100] See the analyses of Peneff (1990).

[101] Renan (1990), p. 11.

[102] The notion of history as collective remembering implies that the history is also a forgetting; it has been suggested that nationalist histories are particularly prone to forgetting (Ben-Yehuda, 1998; Schwartz, 1990; Schwartz et al., 1986; Schudson, 1990). Hobsbawm and Ranger's (1983) notion of an 'invented tradition' suggests a shared collective forgetting: as nationalist historians formulate historic myth, so they overlook in their accounts the modern aspects of supposed traditions (see also Pearson, 1998, who discusses whether nationalist historians can be said to repress aspects of the past).

[103] Ross et al. (1981) reports an experimental study to show how, on a personal level, present attitudes can determine accounts of past history (see also Snyder and Uranowitz, 1978).

[104] On self-serving biases and the 'totalitarian ego', see Greenwald (1980); for general reviews of self-serving biases, see Eiser (1986) and Fiske and Taylor (1984).

of the accepted account of the past. One might say that such work must be actively avoided.

The idea of *active avoidance* appears to present yet an other variant of the 'paradoxes of the ego'.[105] How on earth can one avoid what one ostensibly does not know? The very notion seems to indicate what Freud, in 'The studies on hysteria' referred to as 'the strange state of mind in which one knows and does not know a thing at the same time'.[106] Freud went on to suggest that the strange state of mind is neither unusual nor so strange. It can be observed in the avoidance of memory-work.

Psychoanalytic theory gives much importance to the concept of 'resistance'. An analyst, in seeking to uncover repressed desires, must overcome the patient's resistance. Time and again, in discussing cases, Freud described the initial resistances of his patients. Typically, the patient would avoid trying to remember apparently forgotten episodes. If patients declared that 'nothing has occurred to me', Freud would tell them that this was an 'impossibility'. He would assure his patients that 'they had rejected the memory that had come up' and, as such, 'they had certainly become aware of what was wanted'.[107]

In 'Studies on hysteria', Freud reports in a footnote how he overcame the resistances of a thirty-eight year old woman, whom he was treating for agoraphobia and attacks of dizziness. Initially, she claimed to have only a hazy recollection of her first attack. Freud questioned her, trying to fill in the background. She provided a few details, but claimed that she could remember no more, after all the episode occurred twenty-one years ago. 'That makes no difference', countered Freud, 'you will remember all the same'. He continued: 'I shall press your head, and when I relax the pressure, you will think of something or see something, and you must tell me what that is.'[108] And slowly, more details of a personal nature began to emerge.

Initially, the patient was resisting engaging in memory-work. Like Hans, she was claiming to forget, and she used the claim as a reason not to engage in further cross-examination about the past: I forget, oh do let me alone, said Hans. But the psychoanalyst does not take such claims at face value. Both Freud and Hans's father continued to ask their questions. The thirty-eight-year old woman, too, gives way. The pressure of Freud's hands, his imposing presence, and the much remarked upon power of his eyes – all these possibly overcame her

---

[105] See above chapter 3.
[106] 'Studies on hysteria', *PFL* 3, p. 181n.
[107] Ibid., p. 174   [108] Ibid., p. 176n.

resistance as he persuaded her to engage in the conversation, which she was avoiding.[109]

One might suspect the woman of being in that 'strange state of mind', in which one simultaneously knows and not knows. What is 'known' is not articulated: it cannot be articulated, for once it is spoken about, it becomes known. Therefore, the person avoids the sort of conversation in which the unspoken becomes spoken. Without articulating the reasons for the avoidance, the sort of conversation, in which memory-work is being done, is resisted. Repression, then, is maintained by an avoidance of such conversations – an avoidance, whose basis cannot be articulated but which must be practised habitually.

Routine practice without the articulation of the basis of that practice is not something remarkable. As has been argued, it is a part of language practice itself. We speak without saying exactly what we are doing as we speak. And we act without articulating the grounds for our actions. Moreover, in speaking we monitor the conversations, having a feel for their future course, as we orientate our words to the future reactions of our listeners. Topics can be smoothly changed, and new conversational directions started. All this is regularly practised as a habit without conscious articulation.

Something along these lines may be occurring in cases where adults claim to have forgotten, or repressed, memories of childhood sexual abuse. There is no need to posit a special mechanism of repression, as an internal process of mind. Instead, the forgetting may be maintained by unarticulated, but habitually practised, patterns of avoidance. Surveys report that a significant minority of adults, who claim to have experienced childhood sexual abuse, say that for long periods, they were unable to remember the abuse.[110] The surveys differ from each other in the proportions of survivors who report such forgetting.[111] Part of the problem, it has been argued, lies in the meaning of the questions which the surveys ask. For example, the question 'was there a time you *could not* remember the abuse?' is ambiguous. The 'could not' can be interpreted in different ways. If a person says that they 'could not remember' the trauma, does it mean that they were unable to recollect merely because they did not think of it in the intervening years? Or that they did not wish to recollect it, feeling unable to confront the past? Or

---

[109] Hans's father described Freud in his mid-forties: 'The most striking thing about the man was his expression. His beautiful eyes were serious and seemed to look at man from the depths' (Graf, 1942, p. 467).

[110] See, for instance, Herman (1981 and 1992).

[111] See Ceci et al., (1994); Christianson and Engelberg (1997); Schooler (1994) and Schooler et al. (1997); Williams (1995).

that when they tried to recollect such an experience, they were unable to?[112]

In such questions the notion of motive is linked closely with that of ability. There is nothing surprising in this. The classic concept of repression implies that, try as one might, the memory cannot be recovered, except under particular therapeutic conditions. James Schooler has looked at a number of cases where sufferers have claimed to have forgotten childhood abuse, whose occurrence has been independently confirmed. Often survivors of abuse report having used strategies of avoidance, even explicitly talking about 'repression' as such a strategy. One woman, who had been raped years previously, claimed that she managed to 'repress the *meaning* of what happened'; she 'pushed it away, minimized it . . . It wasn't a real rape.'[113] The recovery of the memory involved, of course, a reinterpretation.

The point is not whether such sufferers could have recovered the memory if they had *really* wanted to, any more than whether Freud's agoraphobic patient could have remembered her first dizzy spell had she wished to. The notion of 'wanting' (or 'really wanting') should not be considered unproblematic, as if the processes of repression stand separate from those of 'wanting'. The evidence is that such persons, during the period of forgetting, avoid memory-work. In the case of the rape victim, she has another account of the episode – a minimizing account. The minimizing account helps to dismiss the matter from thought: the original event becomes something trivial, not worth discussing or thinking about, not even to be considered when serious subjects, such as rape, are being discussed. One might say that such persons do not 'want' to do what is necessary to reconstruct their memories. But the notion of 'wanting' can be misleading. The 'want' cannot be articulated. It, too, must be denied.

In this way, repression can be constituted and maintained in a pattern of avoidance. The claim to forget – or alternatively the claim to remember the event as unimportant – can be part of avoiding engagement with memory-work. But, as Freud suspected in the case of the agoraphobic, and in many other instances, denials are not to be taken at face value. The patient is fearing memory-work. The fear indicates a dim awareness of what is to be avoided. But the object of the avoidance cannot be specified in words without breaking the hold of the fear. This is not the fear of the unknown, but the unutterable fear of the knowable.

---

[112] See, for example, Ceci et al. (1994), pp. 401f., for a discussion of the differing interpretations of questions about forgetting childhood sexual abuse.

[113] Quoted in Schooler et al. (1997), p. 268, emphasis in original.

Suggesting the forgotten past

Freud, in persuading his agoraphobic patient to engage in memory-work, was then able to reconstruct an apparently forgotten recollection of the past. This would imply that memory-work can unroll the effects of forgetting. However there is a difficulty. If remembering involves reconstructing, rather than re-running a preserved recording, then there is the serious problem: are the reconstructions accurate accounts of the past or might they be untrustworthy fabrications. As Freud wrote, 'the untrustworthiness of our memory' constitutes 'the weak spot in the security of our mental life'.[114]

This problem of the untrustworthiness of memory lies at the heart of the controversy over recovered/false memories of childhood sexual abuse. Therapists are claiming that, with sympathetic, supportive guidance, the repressed past can be accurately recovered. Critics, by contrast, are claiming that the supportive therapists are implanting false 'memories' in the minds of their clients. Sincerity is not sufficient to resolve the debate. As Hans's father was conveying to his son, claims to remember 'really' and 'truly' need not be persuasive: sometimes listeners require independent confirmation of the memory.

Even if a fragmented experience from the past is recalled – a partial scene, the Proustian taste of a biscuit, the memory of being touched – it has still to be interpreted and put into some sort of narrative ordering, in order to be worked into a meaningful memory. Misattributions can easily be made. What was originally heard as a second-hand story, may have been imagined in detail and, then may later return as a remembered fragment, which is interpreted as if it had originally been a first-hand experience.[115] By no means all our thoughts are direct reactions to personally witnessed experiences. We dream, imagine, fear and listen to the tales of others. If fragments of these return later, they may be difficult to disentangle from fragments of direct experiences. This is why external evidence for memory-claims is so crucial.[116]

It is too simple to think of remembering as the process which ends repression, or, by contrast, to conceive of repression as the process which inhibits remembering. When a victim remembers past abuse, after a long intervening period of non-remembrance, they will typically

---

[114] 'Notes on a case of obsessional neurosis', *SE* 10, p. 243.
[115] On misattributions of memories, especially in relation to the recovered/false memory, debate, see, inter alia, Ceci et al. (1997), Bruck and Ceci (1997) and Ceci (1995). Zaragoza et al. (1997) suggest that the source of a message can be more readily forgotten and misattributed than its content (see, also, Pratkanis et al., 1988, for a review of attitude research investigating this phenomenon).
[116] See Loftus (1993) for an extended discussion of this issue.

tell a story of their remembering: how the memory came flooding back; how it was suggested by a particular sight or sound and so on.[117] These accounts, which remember the remembering, can contain their own forgettings. In a fascinating account, James Schooler has analysed several such accounts. The victims may claim never to have spoken about their experiences to anyone before. However, sometimes their spouses, or others close to them, may claim that they can remember past conversations about the abusive episodes.[118] These past conversations become obliterated in the present narrative of a sudden remembering and a lifting of repression. In this sort of instance, the remembering has itself become a forgetting.

The idea that therapists may have suggested 'memories' to clients is controversial and troubling, as therapists and professional organizations well recognize.[119] Both sides of the debate about recovered/false memories make claims for which there is supporting evidence. There are grounds for believing that some victims have found themselves able to speak about childhood abuse for the first time in therapeutic situations. Similarly, there are grounds for supposing that some therapists have been overstepping the mark, by encouraging vulnerable patients to imagine past abuse and, then, accepting these imaginings as if they were accurate memories of past occurrences.

Critics of Freud, sometimes themselves lining up on the 'false memory' side of the debate, have argued that he suggested past 'memories' to his patients, in ways which conformed to his theories but not their circumstances.[120] Suspicions can be raised particularly when Freud suggested memories of events which would have occurred during the period of infantile amnesia and, therefore, beyond the reach of standard remembering. Had the patient in the case of the Wolf Man accepted Freud's reconstruction of his experiences in the cot and had he begun to add his own details about the suddenly remembered 'primal scene', then it would be reasonable to claim that suggestion and imagination, rather than remembering, were at work. One might have similar suspicions had the nineteen-year-old Hans, having read Freud's

---

[117] Derek Edwards (personal communication) points out that stories, which claim that the memory 'suddenly' came back, express an important rhetorical point. The theme of suddenness suggests that the memory has not been worked up and, thus, is genuine. Consequently, the way that the memory is depicted as returning is rhetorically designed to act as a warrant for the memory's veracity.

[118] For details, see Schooler et al. (1997).

[119] E.g., Yapko (1997); British Psychological Society (1995); Lindsay (1994). See Burman (1998) for an extended discussion of the way that therapists have drawn upon standard developmental psychology in this debate, often attributing more than is warranted to this research and ignoring its ideological elements.

[120] Most notably, see Crews (1995) and also Borch-Jacobsen (1996).

report, begun to recall extra details of all those conversations in which his childish self had participated.

Without full records of what a therapist might have said to particular patients, it is not possible to pinpoint how, in particular cases, suggestions might be transformed into claims of memory. In the case of Freud's analytic sessions, of course no such transcripts exist. On the other hand, there are records from Freud's writings to indicate how, in the course of his own self-analysis, he was able to persuade himself. Changes to the little words in an account, as it is repeated in the retelling, suffice to show how conjecture, when imagined in detail, can pass into a convinced memory-story.[121]

In a letter to Wilhelm Fliess, dated 15 October 1897, Freud wrote that 'my self-analysis is in fact the most essential thing I have at present and promises to become of the greatest value to me if it reaches its end'.[122] In that letter, Freud wrote about a scene 'which in the course of twenty-five years has occasionally emerged in my conscious memory without my understanding it'. In the scene, Freud, as a child, was crying. His older brother, Philipp, unlocked a wardrobe (*Kasten*). Freud continued crying until his mother, 'slender and beautiful' came into the room.[123] This is a typical fragmentary memory, which is not worked up into a meaningful story.[124] Freud wrote to Fliess that he 'suddenly' understood the story. His mother had gone away, presumably to give birth. He must have heard that a previous nurse had been taken away by the police, having been caught stealing from the Freuds: 'So I must have heard that the old woman had been locked up and therefore must have believed that my mother had been locked up too – or rather, had been 'boxed up' (*eingekastelt*) – for my brother Philipp, who is now sixty-three years old, to this very day is still fond of using such puns.'[125]

In this way, Freud wove the fragmented images into a coherent story, adding his own interpretations and observations.[126] The adult Freud, in constructing this story, makes the association between wardrobe (*Kasten*) and being 'boxed up'. He justifies this addition by citing the character of his brother. Philipp has always liked puns, so it is reasonable to expect that he would make such a pun. The letter presents this as

[121] Ceci et al. (1994) show how easily children, having been asked to imagine events, can be persuaded that such events had actually occurred.
[122] Freud (1985), p. 270.
[123] Ibid., p. 271.
[124] If memories do survive from between three and five years old, they are likely to be fragmentary images, rather than coherent memory narratives (Nelson, 1993; Goodman et al., 1994; Howe et al., 1994; Schacter, 1995, pp. 240f.).
[125] Freud (1985), p. 272.
[126] See Schur (1972), pp. 122f for a criticism of Freud's reconstruction.

inference rather than recall: 'I must have heard . . .' writes Freud. He does not say 'I now remember hearing . . .'

'Psychopathology of everyday life' was published in 1901, almost four years after the letter to Fliess. In chapter 4, Freud discusses his memory of the wardrobe. He recounts the scene of crying, the locked wardrobe and his mother's return. He also comments that 'analytic effort led me to take a quite unexpected view of the picture'.[127] Now Freud tells the reconstructed story with a certainty which was lacking in the letter to Fliess. He does not say that 'he must have heard' his brother making a pun. He now writes confidently of conversations with his older half-brother about the disappearance of the nurse. He writes that 'I had turned in particular to this brother and had asked him where she was'; then he had answered 'in the elusive and punning fashion that was characteristic of him: "She's boxed up"'.[128]

In telling his story Freud appears to become more convinced of its details.[129] The status of the story has changed in its telling. Conjecture becomes memory, as possibility is translated into actuality. Small words are crucial in this shift. By these means Freud convinces himself, and, in retelling his story publicly, seeks to convince his readers. No dishonesty need be suspected, merely self persuasion in the accomplishment of memory-work.

Screen memories and the seduction theory

Throughout this discussion of repression and remembering, the controversy about childhood sexual abuse has not been far away. The controversy does not merely touch directly upon the Freudian concept of repression. It encompasses the memory of Freud himself, as argument and counter-argument are made about the relations between his early Seduction Theory and his mature Oedipal Theory of infant sexuality. Critics blame the Oedipal Theory for contributing to the historic dismissal of childhood sexual abuse. In outlining this critique, a new story about Freud is being formulated. Freud, so it is said, initially listened to his young women patients, who came to him with tales of

---

[127] 'Psychopathology of everyday life', *PFL* 5, p. 91.

[128] Ibid., p. 92. The original German text also conveys the sense that the brother actually answered in the way indicated (*GW*, 4, p. 59). The word 'probably' (*wahrscheinlich*) appears in the sentence (as it does in the English translation of the Standard Edition), but it refers to the probable reasons why Freud had asked his brother the question in the first place, not to the brother's answer, which consequently is presented as something that actually occurred.

[129] As Schacter (1995) argues, the telling of a memory-story contributes to its being remembered as a 'genuine' memory' (pp. 110f).

childhood abuse. So convinced was he by these accounts that, in his paper to the Viennese Society for Psychiatry and Neurology, he argued that childhood abuse was the root cause of all adult hysteria. Then for reasons, which are unclear, he abandoned his theory. Perhaps he realized that the theory would always make him an outcast in medical circles. Perhaps Freud was frightened by the implication that his own sisters may have been assaulted by their father. Whatever the reasons, by 1897 he replaced the Seduction Theory with the Oedipal account.[130]

It is now being said that Freud, having abandoned his early ideas, stopped listening to his female patients' accounts of childhood molestation. Instead, he sought to persuade them that their 'memories' were merely projections of infant fantasies. Judith Herman gives such an account of Freud's early work. She writes that 'time after time, Freud's patients, women from prosperous, conventional families, unburdened painful memories of childhood sexual encounters with men they had trusted: family friends, relatives, and fathers'.[131] In a similar vein, Jeffrey Masson claims that 'Freud's female patients had the courage to face what had happened to them in childhood – often this included violent scenes of rape by a father – and to communicate their traumas to Freud.' For his part, 'Freud listened and understood and gave permission to remember and speak of these terrible events.'[132]

This sort of account is now becoming common-place, especially in feminist writings. For example, Carol Gilligan writes of Freud's early patients that 'when these intelligent, sensitive, stubborn, and mute young women began speaking of incestuous relationships with their fathers, Freud wrote to Fliess that he had arrived at *Caput Nili* – the head of the Nile; he had traced the origins of hysteria to childhood sexual trauma'.[133] The official guide-book to the Freud museum speaks in this way about the early work. It says that 'when Freud first embarked on the talking cure, his patients repeatedly presented him with memories of sexual traumas in childhood that he initially believed to be the source of their neuroses'.[134] The picture of the young Freud, sympathetically listening to stories of early abuse, can be supported by references to the older Freud's memories of his early work. In the 'New introductory lectures' of 1933, Freud recounted how 'almost all my women patients told me that they had been seduced by their father'.[135] However, this interpretation, whether given by critics, admirers or Freud himself,

---

[130] See the analyses of Israëls and Schatzman (1993).
[131] Herman (1981), p. 9.　　[132] Masson (1984), p. 9.
[133] Gilligan (1997), p. 153.
[134] The Freud Museum (1998), p. 114.　　[135] *PFL* 2, p. 154.

conflicts with the accounts that Freud himself gave at the time. His letters to Fliess and his 1896 paper tell a very different story.[136]

In the 'Aetiology of Hysteria', Freud mentions that his theory was based on eighteen patients, six of whom were men. Freud not only implicated fathers and close male relatives as perpetrators, but he also identified women, such as nursery maids or governesses, as seducers of little boys.[137] Herman dismisses the mention of female culprits by claiming that Freud deliberately 'falsified' the record of paternal incest, in order to avoid offending public sensibilities.[138] She cites the fact that Freud in 'Studies on Hysteria' mentions two cases of childhood abuse (those of Katherina and Rosalia), but in both he changed the perpetrator from the girl's father to uncle, only admitting this change in later editions.

The problem of Freud's male victims and female perpetrators is not so easily dismissed. Freud mentions instances of females abusing male infants in the letters to Fliess.[139] The two cases in the 'Studies of hysteria' present a problem, which Herman does not specifically discuss. These cases had already been published when Freud gave his public talk. One might have supposed that, in introducing his controversial theme, he would have drawn upon, or at least mentioned, those case histories, in which there existed good *prima facie* evidence for adult abuse (whether by father or by uncle). Yet, surprisingly, the 'Aetiology of hysteria' does not discuss either case.

The simple explanation is that neither case offered an example of what Freud was talking about in his paper. He was not talking about abuse, which was remembered by the victim and which could be reconstructed with the help of a sympathetic listener. He was talking of abuse which was deeply forgotten and which lay behind all childhood memories. This abuse supposedly occurred during the period covered by infantile amnesia. In the 'Aetiology', Freud outlined an early version of the notion of screen memories. The stories, which the patients told him about the origins of their symptoms, were to be treated as signs of earlier, totally repressed memories. Sometimes the young women patients told him about abusive experiences 'which must be regarded as severe traumas – an attempted rape, perhaps, which reveals to the immature girl at a blow all the brutality of sexual desire'.[140] Yet these

---

[136] This point has been made by Schimek (1987) and Israëls and Schatzman (1993) in their careful analyses of the evidence.

[137] 'Aetiology of hysteria', *SE* 3, pp. 207–8.

[138] Herman (1981), p. 9.

[139] Freud, as he makes plain in his correspondence with Fliess, for a while, believed that he had been seduced by his nurse (Freud, 1985, pp. 268f.).

[140] 'Aetiology of hysteria', *SE* 3, p. 200.

remembered experiences, no matter how brutal, were not the cause of the hysteria. Usually they depicted events which took place at puberty or late childhood. Freud was searching for something earlier. As he wrote, it was necessary to search for the causes of hysteria 'in experiences that went still further back' and, thus, 'we arrive at the period of earliest childhood, a period before the development of sexual life'. As a result, Freud arrived at 'infantile experiences with a sexual content', which exerted their psychical effect through the later memories.[141]

Freud was, in effect, outlining a theory of forgotten infantile abuse, rather than remembered childhood abuse. He specifically mentioned that many of his patients with hysteria did not tell stories of abuse in late childhood or early puberty. Their relevant memories, which seemed to be linked to the onset of their symptoms, were of a wholly innocent kind, which, he suggested, could not have been the *real* cause of their hysterical symptoms. Freud did not suspect that such patients had forgotten their *childhood* experiences of abuse. Instead, he proposed that their 'innocent' stories were acting as screen memories of a forgotten abuse, which occurred much earlier during infancy.

In the light of this, it is easy to see why Freud did not mention the cases of either Katherina or Rosalia. In neither case was there any evidence of infantile abuse, as compared with childhood abuse. Katherina was said to be fourteen when the abusive incidents occurred.[142] As for Rosalia, the text of 'Studies of hysteria' makes clear that her memories of abuse did not refer to the earliest parts of her childhood. Freud recounts that she started telling scenes from childhood in 'chronological order', starting with ordinary scenes and working up to the occasion when her 'uncle' asked her to massage him.[143] This episode, which Rosalia 'was clearly loth to remember', appears to have taken place in late childhood, if not early puberty. It was not the sort of, infantile experience, which Freud was claiming in 'Aetiology' to be the cause of hysteria.

It appears that most of the eighteen patients, mentioned in 'Aetiology' were not telling Freud about childhood abuse. And if they were, he was listening for signs of even earlier incidents. He stated in the paper that the patients, when they came for treatment, 'know nothing about these scenes'. Moreover, they become 'indignant as a rule if we warn them that such scenes are going to emerge'.[144] Even when Freud has claimed that such scenes must have occurred, the patients 'still attempt to

---

[141] Ibid., p. 202.
[142] 'Studies on hysteria', *PFL* 3, p. 195.
[143] Ibid., p. 244.
[144] 'Aetiology of hysteria' *SE* 3, p. 204.

withhold belief from them, by emphasizing the fact that, unlike what
happens in the case of other forgotten material, they have no feeling of
remembering the scenes'.[145] Thus, the patients appear not to have
claimed that they eventually 'remembered' the abusive scenes.

All this suggests a different pattern of talk than that conveyed by the
image of young women hesitantly telling their stories of abuse and
Freud listening with sympathy. The letters to Fliess support this. Freud
confided to Fliess a number of details about patients, which, in his view,
offered further confirmation of the Seduction Theory. In only one case
do the details match the picture of a young woman reluctantly remembering a fraught story of sexual abuse. Other cases are very different.
Freud describes a woman patient surmising that her brother, not
herself, must have been seduced by their father.[146] The inference is not
based on a memory of the seduction, but on the brother's memory of
the father being found in a compromising position with the child's
nurse. Another man is reported as receiving external confirmation from
his nurse that she had seduced him.[147] Then there was a female patient,
who initially accepted Freud's suggestion that her father seduced her
during infancy. She then confronted her father with the story. He denied
it, and the patient accepted his denial. She was now, reported Freud,
showing the 'most vehement resistance' against the story of infant
seduction.[148]

There is one letter, in which Freud writes of a female patient actually
recounting her experiences of abuse. The letter is worth examining
closely. Freud told Fliess that the young woman was initially reluctant to
talk. He coaxed her, in similar ways to those he described in 'Studies on
hysteria'. He said to her 'here it surely will not be possible to conceal
anything'.[149] She started to open up, telling Freud that her father
abused her and her sister. Freud's reaction, which he conveys to Fliess,
is significant: 'I told her that similar and worse things must have
happened in her earliest childhood.'[150] He reports that 'she could not
find it incredible'.[151]

Superficially this case resembles the descriptions given by Masson,
Herman, Gilligan and others. The sympathetic Freud is eliciting and
listening to a memory of parental abuse, which a young woman can only
tell with the utmost difficulty. There can be little doubt about Freud's
therapeutic skills, in encouraging such memory-work. On the other

---

[145] Ibid.   [146] Freud (1985), p. 213.
[147] Ibid., p. 219. Another male patient's hysteria was traced back to his relations with his
nurse (pp. 223–4).
[148] Ibid., p. 220.   [149] Ibid., p. 238.
[150] Ibid.   [151] Ibid.

hand, these are not quite the stories which Freud was seeking. The remembered abuse for Freud was always a sign for something which must have occurred earlier. In this instance, the woman is prepared to entertain Freud's hypothesis. If her father had abused her and her sister as girls, then possibly he might have abused them as infants. The idea was not incredible. But the experience, if it ever happened, was not remembered. It remained an inference.

A charge can be made against Freud – and a serious charge it is too. It is not that he once listened to horrific memories of abuse and, then, out of cowardice or self-interest, he stopped listening to his patients. The idea that Freud suddenly developed different habits of listening is not persuasive.[152] On the other hand, Freud can be blamed for not changing his habits of listening and interpreting. Whether convinced of the Seduction or Oedipal theory, he was constantly on the lookout for signs which would take him back to the earliest stages of his patients' lives. It was as if all that happened to them subsequently was of less psychological consequence than the moments lost in infantile amnesia. When young women spoke of childhood abuse, he still pursued his quest for the infantile events. This can be seen in the case of Dora, which will be fully discussed in chapter 8 but which has already been mentioned previously. Dora told Freud that her father's friend had been propositioning her since she was fourteen. Freud believed that the root of Dora's adolescent problems lay elsewhere. He was more interested in the possibility that she had masturbated as an infant than in the reality of the adult, who was harassing her.

Freud's habit of interpretation was based on a theoretical weakness. He believed that childhood memories were merely screens for earlier repressed experiences and that infantile amnesia was caused by repression. However, if repression is a skill which is acquired in the course of learning language, then there is no need to accept that everything must be causally dragged back to the earliest periods, when the infant could neither remember nor forget wilfully. Of course, the earliest period, in which the child is learning implicitly, might be crucial in setting the emotional tone for the child's subsequent development: patterns of trust and distrust, not to mention the bases for communication, are established. But that does not mean that all later difficulties necessarily are symptoms of the earliest traumas.

Besides the theoretical weakness, Freud showed an uncharacteristic lack of sensitivity, which was to become solidified into a routine of psychoanalytic practice. Whatever the patients' earliest memories, there

---

[152] This point is well made by Webster (1995), who is hardly sympathetic to Freud.

was always a hidden story to be recovered. Overt memories were to be distrusted as screens for the *real* memory of a lost infancy, whether it was an infancy of desire or one of abuse. This interpretative habit is particularly misplaced in cases where patients remember their own abuse as children or as adolescents. Freud is most open to criticism here. When his patients told him stories about abuse, he seemed to be acting as if such stories were not the case in point. There had to be something more important that his patients had forgotten – as if the abuse and rape of children were not important enough.

7   Words of unconscious love

According to Freudian theory, the objects of repression tend to be emotional impulses. Inappropriate and shameful feelings of love and aggression have to be driven from the mind, to prevent these impulses from seriously disturbing the person's sense of their moral worth. The Oedipal story exemplifies this. The Oedipal child resolves its complex by acquiring a moral sense that demands the repression of earlier erotic and aggressive desires. This moral sense is, according to Freudian theory, represented by the superego, located within the ego and constituting 'an agency which unceasingly observes, criticizes and compares, and in this way sets itself over against the other part of the ego'.[1] Henceforward, this unceasing observation, criticism and comparison will result in the constant repression of shameful emotions. What is repressed does not disappear, but is relegated to the realm of the unconscious. We are said to continue desiring in shameful ways, feeling shameful things, but we cease to be aware of these feelings. Thus, Freudian theory assumes the reality of repressed emotions.

The idea of an unconscious emotion seems to be troubling, much more so than the idea of an unconscious memory. Forgetting the past is familiar in ordinary life. So is remembering something, which we thought we had forgotten. When we do so, it is easy to suppose that the 'memory' must have been there all along, even though we were not aware of it. In this respect, the idea of an unconscious memory does not contradict common-sense. But the notion of an unconscious emotion seems to be a contradiction in terms. Freud himself acknowledged the problem: 'It is surely of the essence of an emotion that we should be aware of it', he wrote. Yet, as Freud went on to say, 'in psychoanalytic practice, we are accustomed to speak of unconscious love, hate, anger'.[2] So, how is it possible to speak of an unconscious emotion?

Any project to reinterpret Freudian ideas in terms of language must fall to the ground if it cannot deal with the issue of unconscious

---

[1] 'Introductory lectures', *PFL* 1, p. 479.
[2] 'The unconscious', *PFL* 11, p. 179.

emotions. It will be suggested that the root of the problem does not lie in the notion of the unconscious, but in the common-sense notion of emotions. It is easy to think of emotions as entities, which are somehow lodged within the body. For instance anger or love might be thought to be 'things', situated inside the person. Roy Schafer, in his argument to re-write the language of psychoanalytic theory in terms of actions, cautioned strongly against understanding conscious emotions in these terms. We should replace, he argues, the idea of 'anger' by concepts such as 'acting angrily' and, then, we should investigate how people act angrily.[3] Similarly, if we want to understand love, we should investigate 'those actions a person must perform in order to love'.[4]

This chapter will attempt to follow Schafer's advice. It will be suggested that the notion of an unconscious emotion is a reasonable one. It helps to make sense of a variety of behaviour. Freud was right in pointing out that the very idea seems counter-intuitive. However, he did not recognize the extent to which the difficulty rests with the ordinary common-sense idea of emotions, rather than with the idea of the unconscious. Just as Freud's theory of conscious thought provided problems for his theories of unconscious thinking, so it is the same for his theories of emotions. If the discursive and social aspects of emotions are recognized – and emotions are not treated as internal bodily states – then many of the difficulties evaporate. Then, the idea of unconscious love, which is so central to many of Freud's cases, may seem no more strange than the notion of 'ordinary' conscious love.

The problem of unconscious emotions

Common-sense tells us that emotions such as love, hate and anger refer to strong, inner states, which cannot be ignored.[5] Our bodies, surely, give unmistakable signs, which speak louder than words. William James expressed this common-sense view in his *Principles of Psychology*. He argued that strong emotions are accompanied by intense bodily sensations: 'Can one fancy the state of rage and picture no ebullition in the chest, no flushing of the face, no dilation of the nostrils, no clenching of the teeth, no impulse to vigorous action, but in their stead limp muscles, calm breathing, and a placid face?'[6]

If rage comprises such a strong bodily reaction, then it is hard to see

---

[3] Schafer (1976), especially chapter 13.
[4] Ibid., p. 271.
[5] See Lutz (1990b and 1996) for analyses of contemporary, Western common-sense of emotions.
[6] James (1890), volume 2, p. 452.

how it could possibly be unconscious. It would seem to suggest that the ebullition, dilation and clenching can occur, while the person is sublimely unaware of what their body is doing. Or we might imagine that the state of love involves a warm inner glow, with, perhaps, hints of sexual tingling. Yet again, the idea of unconscious emotion suggests something implausible: the glowing and the tingling taking place in the body, without the awareness of the person. Freud's theory of unconscious desire posited something along these lines. The desires are confined to the psychic regions of the id, where they are bodily constituted beyond the sight of the ego. Freud assumed that the common-sense difficulty arose because people were simply unfamiliar with the idea of the unconscious.

There is, however, another way of approaching the problem. The difficulty might lie with the common-sense notion of emotions, which Freud himself took for granted.[7] William James seems to have provided a wonderfully vivid description of anger's internal state. Nevertheless, one can ask whether the state, which James describes, is peculiar to anger. Perhaps it is a state which can occur in other situations, when it is not labelled as 'anger'. One might change a single phrase in James's description. Suppose one read his description, not as an account of the 'state of rage' but of 'the state of sexual arousal'. It all seems to fit. But, the ebullition, flushing and absence of limp muscles now tell a very different story.

Social psychologists have realized that the bodily states, which supposedly underwrite very different emotions, are not easily distinguished one from another: the same state of arousal, with increased blood pressure and heart beat, can be attributed to anger or happiness.[8] Yet ordinarily, we have little difficulty in distinguishing between emotions, often using a very subtle vocabulary of emotional terms. As Wittgenstein argued, the public language of psychological words must be grounded in outward criteria. His point can be applied to the grammar of emotions. Because we have a public vocabulary of emotions, there must be outward, public criteria for distinguishing one emotional term from another. Inner bodily states cannot serve as the criteria for a public vocabulary of emotions.[9]

This would imply that emotions such as 'love' are not primarily inner bodily sensations. Instead, the concept of love, like that of other

---

[7] For an intriguing account of the development of Freud's theories of emotions, see Carveth (1996).

[8] This was the rationale behind the classic social psychological experiments of Schachter and Singer (1962).

[9] This was a major theme of Wittgenstein's *Philosophical Investigations*; see above, chapter 4, and also Edwards (1997); Shotter (1993a and 1993b); Schafer (1976).

emotions, is bound up with social relations, expectancies and a sense of moral order. If it were not, we would not be able to use the term so readily. Repression, it will be suggested, comes into play when we cannot admit to ourselves that we hold particular loves. What is pushed from consciousness, or avoided, is not a bodily feeling, but a means of interpretation.

These general points will be illustrated by examples from some of Freud's cases. Elisabeth's unconscious love for her brother-in-law will be considered. And so, more briefly, will Freud's belief that Dora unconsciously loved Herr K, her father's friend. Unconscious love is not confined to neurotic patients. It was, and possibly continues to be, much more widespread. It can be detected in Freud's own reactions, when still a young man engaged to Martha Bernays. In all this, there will be a general principle: unconscious love can only be understood in relation to declared love. So-called 'normal', conscious love is not unproblematic: it has its own evasions, ambiguities and denied demands. Freud's secret, denied desires have to be considered alongside his outward love for Martha.

If emotions are social products, rather than being the unproblematic reflection of inner bodily states, then more is involved than the feelings of Freud as an individual. Sigmund's professed love for Martha, as well as his denied desires, belong to a particular cultural milieu. He loves – and denies – according to his times, just as Little Hans was learning to love, and behave, in culturally appropriate ways. One might say that Freud's emotions, like those of his patients, were ideological: they belonged to a particular epoch but were experienced as if they were biologically universal.[10]

In Freud's case, there is always an extra dimension. We do not merely see a bourgeois male struggling with his society's demands of masculinity and respectability. We also see the founder of psychoanalysis. He was living the assumptions of psychoanalysis, in an even more direct fashion than were Little Hans's parents. Psychoanalysis, as a theory of emotions, was part of its own emotional climate. It became a cultural pattern, which encouraged certain emotional explanations, while denying others.[11] With Freud, the personal and the theoretical are never completely separate. This is why examples from Freud's own personal life, even from the time before he was a psychoanalyst, are so interesting.

[10] Some theorists have suggested that ideology is the social process by which historically contingent phenomena come to be experienced as if they are necessary, 'natural' and universal (Eagleton, 1991; Billig, 1991).

[11] This point is stressed in feminist critiques of psychoanalysis. On the vast amount of material written on this point, see, for instance, Millet (1971); Mitchell (1974); Gallop (1982); Jacobus (1987); Sayers (1991).

Words of emotion

Of the emotional forces which need to be repressed, according to Freud, the impulses of Eros are most prominent. The boy has to repress love for his mother. Little Hans must learn he cannot sleep in Mummy's bed. Not only does he face the stark reality of being forbidden to sleep there, but he must internalize the prohibition. He must learn not to *want* to slip in beside Mummy in the morning. Freud's women patients were typically troubled by forbidden Eros. Elisabeth von R, in Freud's diagnosis, was secretly in love with her brother-in-law. Dora, despite her protestations, desired Herr K, and perhaps even Frau K. In the 'Introductory lectures', Freud discusses the case of a middle-aged woman, who was behaving obsessively towards her husband. Freud suspected her of being 'really' in love her brother-in-law.[12] In all such cases, shameful love, which transgresses the moral order, must be pushed from consciousness.

One needs to ask exactly what is pushed from consciousness, in order for love to be denied in this way. If emotions are bodily forces, as Freud took them to be, then repressing emotions involves deflecting forces which are primal beyond words. In James's terms, the ebullition and the flushing, together with the energy which has given rise to these bodily reactions, need to be diverted. Yet, if morality, or the image of the ideal, is the conditioning factor of repression, as Freud stated, then it is not the emotional impulse, or inner feeling itself, which contains the danger to the sense of self. The danger lies in the belief that one has an impulse that is shamefully immoral.

Elisabeth, as a moral young lady, would know how wrong it was to love her sister's husband – and, even worse, to fantasize her sister's death so that the husband would be free to marry again. Any flushing or quickening of the heart, which she might experience when her brother-in-law entered the room, would not of itself contain danger. Such feelings could always be ignored or attributed to causes other than forbidden love: perhaps it was the heat or the eggs consumed at breakfast. The danger – the guilt – lies in the label 'love'. Without words there can be no guilt.

Without words there could, in a literal sense, be no love. Wittgenstein's point about psychological words requiring public criteria is directly relevant. The vocabulary of emotions cannot merely refer to inner events, which are unobservable by outsiders. We could not learn to use words such as 'love', 'hate', 'angry' and so on, if the criteria for their

---

[12] 'Introductory lectures', *PFL* 1, pp. 290–1.

use were merely private feelings. As J. L. Austin wrote, 'it seems fair to say that "being angry" is in many respects like "having mumps" because it describes 'a whole pattern of events'.[13]

Rom Harré, in developing Wittgenstein's point, has criticized the 'common-sense' theory that emotions are individual, internal states. According to him, the idea is as wrong as phlogiston theory. If we can talk about emotions, then they must be publicly observable. The language of emotion depends on emotional display: 'An emotional feeling, and the correlated display, is to be understood as a discursive phenomenon, an expression of judgement and the performance of a social act.'[14] Children learn to use the vocabulary of emotions by being told how their displays and reactions are to be called. As was discussed in chapter 5, Little Hans learns the meaning of 'jealous', when his father, with all the confidence in the world, calls him jealous, telling him that his pattern of reactions should be so labelled.

There must be social conventions for the ascription of various emotions. Of course there will be important cultural differences in the vocabulary of emotions.[15] The notion of 'in love' is a case in point. There are conventional signs of 'love', although these signs may differ from culture to culture; and what counts as love may change within one culture over the course of time.[16] The criteria are not strictly personal. We do not need to have personally experienced love in order to recognize what counts as the stereotyped behaviour of the lover. And Hans's father might deny that he himself has any jealousy, but he still can claim with confidence to recognize that his son was being jealous.

Talk of emotions generally concerns more than a description of an internal subjective state. It is essentially talk about social relations.[17] Hans's father, in calling Hans 'jealous', was not telling his son to pay attention to the exact concatenation of bodily sensations, so that he would have the correct label should such states recur in the future. Instead, he was describing how Hans was relating to the members of the family. Evaluation was integrally bound up in the description. Hans is to

---

[13] Austin (1979), p. 109.

[14] Harré and Gillett (1994), p. 147. See also Harré (1987). Similarly, Austin wrote that more is involved in feeling angry than showing symptoms and feeling the feeling: 'there is also the display or manifestation' (p. 108).

[15] For critical discussions of the assumption that emotions must be universal, see Edwards (1997); Harré (1987) and Wierzbicka (1995).

[16] See Zeldin (1993) for a subtle, erudite and playful account of the ways that sentiments and feelings have historically changed.

[17] Cavell (1993), who uses Wittgensteinian notions to understand Freudian ideas of the unconscious, puts the matter well: anger, pride and guilt, she suggests, are not names of private inner states, 'but concepts referring to complex mental states that are essentially relational in nature and complexly related to each other' (p. 149).

learn that the term 'jealous' in such a context carries a moral criticism.[18] To be called jealous is to be accused of falling short of the ideal. In this regard, talk about emotions is frequently talk about moral expectancies and, thus, about the morality of relations.[19]

The integral connections between talk about emotions, morality and relations is illustrated by studies, which examine in detail how couples talk in therapy.[20] As speakers describe their anger, they are not typically just reporting an inner state. They can be heard to be criticizing their partner for making them angry. In so doing, they appeal to moral standards about how partners should behave and how their own partner is falling well short of the required standard. For example, speakers might refer to their feelings of love as a justification to counter the criticisms of the partner ('I love him/her but look how he/she treats me'). As Richard Buttny comments, 'affect display is commonly found in the production of repeated blames, criticisms and accounts'.[21]

This link between talking of emotions and the morality of relationships is not peculiar to contemporary Western culture. Catherine Lutz has shown how the Ifaluk, who live on a small atoll in the Western Pacific, use their word *song* to indicate a feeling of 'justifiable anger'.[22] An Ifaluk, who says 'I am *song* at you', is accusing the other, who has made them justifiably angry, of acting without moral propriety. In English, 'jealous' is often used in an analogous way. When Papa Graf tells Hans that he is jealous, he was implicitly making a moral point and criticizing the boy. The young boy is not yet familiar enough with the word, and its rhetoric, to shift the blame: 'But it's you who are making me jealous.' Or even: 'Come off it, papa, it's you're the jealous one.'[23]

Talk about feelings can often involve discussion, not to mention argument. Speakers have scope for using different value-laden concepts to depict their emotions. As the anthropologist Geoffrey White has written, 'emotions are susceptible to multiple moral readings'.[24] One

---

[18] See Forrester (1996) for an interesting argument that, for Freud, envy was a fundamental feature of social life, without which justice would be impossible.

[19] White (1990) analyses talk about anger in these terms (see also Rosenberg, 1990). Some observers have commented that talk about emotions and relationships is heavily gendered, with women being inscribed as particularly 'emotional' (Lutz, 1996; Crawford et al., 1992). See also Carbaugh (1996) for an analysis of the ways that emotion-talk has assumed a particular importance in contemporary American culture.

[20] See, for instance, Buttny (1993); Edwards (1997 and in press).

[21] Buttny (1993), p. 99.

[22] Lutz (1990). See also White's (1990) analysis of anger and sadness on Santa Isabel in the Solomon Islands.

[23] Woodward (1996) distinguishes between Freudian anger, which is directed inwards, and feminized anger which is directed outwards in politicized justifications. In this regard, feminized anger resembles the Ifaluks' *song*.

[24] White (1990), p. 51.

person's justifiable anger will be another person's 'bad temper' or 'jealousy'.[25] 'You make me angry', says one partner: 'No , I don't', says the other, 'you're always ready to criticize'. Or: 'But I do love you'; 'If you really loved me, you wouldn't get so jealous.' So they criticize and justify, arguing how to depict their relations and emotions, as they argue about how each should behave. Such arguments admit of no objective resolution.[26] The participants cannot settle their argument about the labelling of emotions by opening up their skulls, or taking EEG tests. There is no agreed physiological nucleus of 'true love' to which they could appeal, as seers, in ancient times, could justify their prophecies on the basis of the entrails of animals. No physiological proof can be found to determine whether one partner should be called 'jealous', 'loving' or 'unreasonably angry'. In any case, that is not what the partners are talking about. That is not how speakers use the words of emotion.

Sigmund as a young lover

Wittgenstein, in describing the emotion of love, made a point, whose importance should not be underestimated. He made a distinction between 'love' and 'pain', suggesting that 'love is not a feeling' because love, unlike pain, 'is put to the test'.[27] Wittgenstein's insight has implications for understanding the nature of unconscious love. But as always, such understanding must await an understanding of the more normal, conscious modes. Wittgenstein's point was that love is not to be conceived as merely an inner state. We could not have the idea of love (including self-conscious love, guilty love, innocent love and so on) without there being appropriate, and inappropriate, displays of love. Hans, like other children, has to learn to act appropriately, if he is to be a good loving boy. He is not to go off with older girls, merely to return the next morning so that his mother can provide breakfast and lavatorial facilities. More is expected of him.

The discourse of love is by no means simple.[28] To utter 'I love you' is rarely, if ever, a simple declaration. The utterance can act as a demand, a plea, a commitment, an excuse, and so on. One character in Jane Smiley's novel, *Duplicate Keys*, on hearing her boy friend declare that he loves her, replies that such words usually mean 'you owe it to me to do what I say' or 'thanks for doing what I said'.[29] The character was

[25] As Edwards has commented on emotional talk, there is 'an indeterminate relation between events and how they are described' (1997, p. 187).
[26] Billig (1996).
[27] Wittgenstein (1975), remark 504, p. 88.
[28] Shotter (1993a), pp. 2–3.
[29] Smiley (1996), p. 248.

indicating that the words of love are insufficient, for they can mean much less than they appear to. Something extra is required as a sign of love. The extra is not a hidden bodily state, but a way of relating.

Lovers, if they wish to be accepted as lovers, must demonstrate their love, especially to each other. They must set and pass tests. Uttering the words of love can be part of the test, for, as Wittgenstein noted in relation to the difficulty of making confessions, words are deeds.[30] The lover, to demonstrate appropriate love, must talk in the appropriate way. And since love is supposedly unique, at least for those concerned, the lovers have to negotiate their own relationship, constantly testing themselves against conventional standards and against the standards which they claim for themselves. Because love is also a public shared concept, my love, if declared and recognized, cannot merely be my love. It can only be declared to the extent that it is recognized in others too and belongs to a wider moral order. Thus, my unique love can only be so personally unique to the extent to which it is recognizably other than just mine.[31]

The young Freud provides a case in point. In 1882 he and Martha Bernays announced their engagement after a brief courtship. A four-year engagement followed, during which time, for the most part, the couple were separated. They wrote regular letters to each other. Sigmund's, but not Martha's have been published. Roland Barthes commented that the founder of psychoanalysis in his love letters showed himself to be a 'paragon of normality'.[32]

Sigmund wrote often about his feelings of love. Far from being reports of inner states, Sigmund's letters are themselves ways of performing love. The young couple had not known each other well before their sudden engagement. For his part, Sigmund was quite explicit about the need for them to express their love often, if he and Martha were to remain in love: 'Of course we will have to go on telling each other everyday that we still love each other.'[33] Contemporary readers might be struck by the lack of sexual reference in Freud's continual declarations of love. There is a chaste innocence, which belongs well to the time, place and class of the writers. Sigmund hoped that they would become 'honest friends and good pals'.[34] When he wrote of their future life together, he did not depict a passionate intimacy. What they were 'striving for', he wrote, was for 'a little home in which sorrow might find

---

[30] Wittgenstein (1953), remark 546.

[31] Lacan (1986) may be alluding to this when he asserts in relation to love that 'the subject is uncertain because he is divided by the effects of language' and that the subject 'through the effects of speech realizes himself more in the Other' (p. 188).

[32] Barthes (1990), p. 145.

[33] Freud (1960), p. 27.   [34] Ibid., p. 25.

its way, but never privation, a being-together throughout all the vicissitudes of life, a quiet contentment that will prevent us from ever having to ask what is the point of living'.[35] There are signs that the young Sigmund may have been beset by a sexual frustration, which he could not mention to Martha. He complained of over-work, telling her that his tiredness was 'a sort of minor illness, neurasthenia it is called'.[36] A few years later, he would write knowingly to his friend Wilhelm Fliess that youthful neurasthenia was caused by masturbation and that in most cases it 'terminates at marriage'. In putting these thoughts on paper to Fliess, Freud urged his friend to 'keep the manuscript away from your young wife'.[37]

The description, which the mature Freud used to describe the way that the ego-ideal 'unceasingly observes, criticizes and compares' the ego, matches the reactions of his insecure younger self towards Martha. Continually the young Sigmund observes her responses, critically comparing her replies to the ideal love-letters, which he imagines he should be receiving. Again and again, he finds Martha's words lacking in suitable emotional warmth. Having declared that the two of them will have to go on declaring their mutual love, he continued in the same letter: 'One must not be mean with affection; what is spent of the funds is renewed by the spending itself'.[38] Here, and on other occasions, he reproves Martha for her lack of affection. 'Your latest letters are so tame', he was to write somewhat desperately. Replying to one letter, which he felt to be extra cold, he complained that Martha seemed to 'freeze up in winter'; and 'love me a little bit', he pleaded.[39]

Sigmund's own declarations of love carry the force of both demand and reprimand. He is writing words to the effect: 'If I, who am so busy with the burdens of building a scientific career, still have time to write my words of love, then you should respond with a warm onrush of emotion.' And if you do not, then I suspect you to love me less than I love you. Poor Sigmund really did believe that a young man's letters, mixing details of professional ambitions with conventional declarations of affection, deserved to be met with words of warm love from a faithful girl.

Above all, Sigmund wanted Martha to display the appropriate, outward signs of loving devotion. After one of their rare meetings during the period of engagement, Sigmund complains of Martha's outward

[35] Ibid., p. 71.   [36] Ibid., p. 200.

[37] Freud (1985), pp. 40–1. Freud published his views on the sexual causes of neurasthenia, claiming that the condition was always caused by 'excessive masturbation or arises spontaneously from frequent emissions'. He added that there were 'no negative cases' against this rule ('Sexuality in the aetiology of the neuroses', SE 3, p. 268).

[38] Freud (1960), p. 28.   [39] Ibid., p. 89 and p. 136.

demeanour. Whenever they had been in company and he had disagreed with others, especially with the members of Martha's family, she had taken his side so seldom that 'no one would have realised from your behaviour that you were preparing to share my life'.[40] Sigmund suspects that the onlookers might have grounds for doubting the force of her love. He is pleading with Martha to act differently in the eyes of the world and, thus, in his eyes too.

Freud's complaint rests on the assumption that inner feeling is not enough. Tests must be passed. Martha, if she is really in love, has to display love outwardly. She must not economize with her words of affection; she should publicly assent to his opinions, and privately she should concur with his opinions about the appropriate ways a fiancée should love. He will be her teacher. He will guide her to close the gap between her present conduct and that of the ideal lover. Or so he demands and pleads, exposing his insecurities all the while with his conventional words of love.

Displays of unconscious love

The idea that love depends upon displays and tests has an important bearing on the nature of unconscious love. Freud held the type of Cartesian philosophy of conscious mind, that Wittgenstein was criticizing and that Harré claims is as out-dated as phlogiston theory. As has been seen, Freud supposed that an emotion, such as love, was an internal, bodily based feeling, just as he supposed that thinking was an internal, unobservable process. He also supposed that we *know* our own feelings and thoughts, but can only *guess* those of other people. In fact, he was of the opinion that we can only infer, but never fully know, that other people have mental states at all. In his essay on 'The unconscious', Freud suggested that 'consciousness makes each of us aware only of his mental states of mind; that other people, too, possess a consciousness is an inference which we draw by analogy from their observable utterances and actions in order to make this behaviour of theirs intelligible to us'.[41]

It was precisely such an assumption that Wittgenstein was concerned to lay to rest. Of course, we know that people have minds. We would not be able to describe our own thoughts and feelings, unless we had a public language with a psychological vocabulary, whose concepts apply equally to others and to ourselves. This is just as true, Wittgenstein argued, for the grammar of feelings: we do not have problems with other people's emotions as a general rule. As Wittgenstein wrote, 'every day

---

[40] Ibid.,, p. 117.
[41] Freud, 'The unconscious', *PFL* 11, p. 170.

we hear one man saying of another that he is in pain, is sad, is merry etc. without a trace of doubt'.[42] Wittgenstein's position fits the empirical work on the development of children's speech. Children do not learn to label their own internal states and then, by inference, learn to apply the concepts to others. Instead, like Little Hans, they hear their parents constantly using psychological words to tell them what they are feeling.[43] Children learn the conventional public criteria and value implications of psychological words. Consequently, we can acquire a rich emotional vocabulary which distinguishes between 'angry', 'furious', 'annoyed, 'pissed off', 'jealous' and so on. At root, we learn how to ascribe emotions to ourselves in the same way as we learn to ascribe them to others.[44]

Although there must be outward criteria for the use of emotion words, these criteria cannot be definitively applied in each instance in ways which admit of no disagreement. Because emotional descriptions typically have implications for relational issues, and can refer implicitly to the moral order itself, descriptions can be contestable. How can one decide whether to call oneself, or another, 'furious' or 'annoyed'? And what is at stake with the choice of description? One person might claim to be 'furious', only to be met with the response, 'Oh come off it, you're just a bit annoyed.' There is no objective physiological way of deciding such an argument, but claim and counter-claim, justification and criticism, might continue.

What this means is that we do not have a privileged access to the *vocabulary* for describing our own feelings. It is not merely that everyday we can describe others as being angry or merry without a trace of doubt. Sometimes our descriptions of others' emotions might differ from the way that they might describe themselves.[45] In cases of such disagreement, we do not necessarily have to defer to the judgements of the person concerned, as if they *must* be the best judges of their own feelings. We might feel more confident in our descriptions of their emotional state, than in their own claims. After all, we can observe their emotional displays – the expressions on their face, the speed of their gestures, the tone of their voice. Generally actors lack this crucial information about their own conduct.[46] Thus, we may suspect that someone 'really' is jealous, or angry regardless of what they say. We may think that they are

---

[42] Wittgenstein (1980), remark 138.
[43] See Sylvester-Bradley and Trevarthen (1978).
[44] Harré (1987); Fletcher (1995).
[45] See Austin (1979), pp. 103ff.
[46] A classic social psychological experiment revealed the extent to which people will explain their own actions differently if they can see themselves behave, just as they see others behave (Storms, 1973).

unaware of their feelings: 'if they could only see themselves now, then they'd realize the jealousy written all over their face'.

The case of love is particularly revealing. An outsider might recognize the signs of love, which the person themself is unaware. The outsider might notice the quickening of voice, the ready laugh, the sparkle in the eye, each time a special other walks in the room. The person, whose eyes so sparkle, may dismiss the thought: 'Of course, I don't love him/her – what a ridiculous thought.' But outsiders may smile knowingly – just wait, they say.

It can work in the opposite direction, as young Sigmund well knew. The outsiders might doubt that the lover truly loves the loved one. Look, she so readily disagrees with him; look, she takes the side of her mother; look, her eyes show irritation. But, of course I love you, she continues to write. If I didn't love you, would I still be wearing your ring? Does she not know her own feelings?

All this suggests that the idea of unconscious, or unacknowledged, love is not so absurd. The idea becomes relevant in situations where there is a difference between the ways a person describes their emotions and ways outsiders do. We might want to use the notion of 'unconscious emotion' when we are doubting the person. Consequently, unconscious love might be suspected in situations where three conditions are present: (a) someone is showing some of the conventional displays of love towards an other; (b) the person in question would consider it wrong, or shameful, to love that other; (c) the person strongly denies that they love the other and there is no reason to suspect that they are deliberately lying. In these circumstances, we the outside observer might trust our own judgements of the person's feelings better than we trust their own protestations. It is not that we merely suspect that they are unaware of their feelings, but we also suspect that they are avoiding, or repressing, such awareness.

This suggests something crucial about the idea of unconscious emotion. In terms of its constitution, unconscious emotion is not so much an impulse as a judgement. Moreover, it is a judgement which is rhetorically contested: the person denies that they have the emotion which is being ascribed to them. If they did not so deny, the emotion would be conscious. As will be seen, this denial, or 'resistance', is basic to the psychoanalytic diagnosis of unconscious, or repressed, feeling.

Freud's examples of unconscious love

All three conditions, outlined above, are present in Freud's most famous case of repressed love: the case of Elisabeth. What is easily overlooked is that Elisabeth was displaying the outward signs of love. Freud did not need to interpret the symbolism of her dreams to pick up clues. The evidence was before his very eyes, as it was before those of other observers. At one point in the treatment, the brother-in-law arrived unexpectedly at Freud's house. Elisabeth heard his voice in the next room. She immediately asked to break off the treatment for the day. And just as suddenly her facial pains returned. Freud, unable to compete with the interest that she was showing in the young man, reports that he started suspecting that Elisabeth had stronger feelings than she cared to admit to herself.[47]

Before her sister's death, Elisabeth would probably have been acting in ways which might have led suspicious onlookers to suppose that she is in love. Clearly, she delighted in her brother-in-law's company, enjoying long woodland walks with him; she even admitted to herself feelings of tenderness, hoping that she might one day have a husband like him.[48] She showed complete agreement with him, taking his side during arguments. On one occasion, a lady criticized Elisabeth's future brother-in-law's figure; Elisabeth 'flared up' and defended the young man 'with a zeal which she herself could not understand'.[49] In short, Elisabeth was displaying the very behaviour which Sigmund had wished Martha would demonstrate to the world as a token of her love.

One should not suppose that all outside observers would come to the same conclusion as Freud did. There are outsiders who are simultaneously insiders. If Elisabeth had reason not to interpret her own behaviour as that of a lover, then so also did members of her own family. One might suppose that, while Elisabeth's sister was still alive, the family would collude in not noticing the signs, or, at least, in not categorizing them as indications of a forbidden love. The signs of affection, which Elisabeth was displaying, could easily be interpreted as innocent family feeling. Before the marriage, Elisabeth's sister had joked about the friendship between Elisabeth and the young man, saying that 'the truth is, you two would have suited each other perfectly'.[50] The joke expressed a half formulated thought (or fear). Because the joke is but a joke, the dangerous thought, which was too serious to be expressed seriously, was neutralized. After the sister's death, Elisabeth's mother entertained suspicions. As Freud reports, 'she had long ago guessed Elisabeth's fondness for the young man'. Significantly, the mother justified her guess by citing the hypothetical perspective of 'the onlooker': 'No one seeing the two of them together – though in fact this

---

[47] 'Studies on Hysteria', *PFL* 3, p. 224.   [48] Ibid., p. 225.
[49] Ibid., p. 228.   [50] Ibid., p. 228.

had now become a rare event – could doubt the girl's anxiety to please him.'[51]

Freud's case of the middle-aged woman, whom he suspected of being in love with her son-in-law, is analogous. He writes that the woman herself 'knew nothing, or perhaps only a very little, of this love'. The concealment was not hers alone, but 'in the family relationship that existed between them it was easy for this passionate liking to disguise itself as innocent affection'.[52] All colluded to avoid the sort of talk in which embarrassing issues would be raised. As such, the family turns its eyes, and more importantly its words, away from the ambivalent displays of affection.

In other cases, where Freud suspected unconscious love, there are also outward signs and family collusion to avoid the label of love. The case of Dora provides another instance. Freud suggested that Dora unconsciously loved Herr K, a friend of her father. As will be seen, the family, and especially her father, had good cause not to notice any signs of love, especially the signs which K was showing as he pursued the young woman. Yet, Freud was not alone in having suspicions that Dora might also feel love for Herr K. He put the idea to Dora and she denied it vigorously. She then mentioned that he was not the first person who had said this to her. One of her cousins had told her 'Why you're simply wild about the man!' Freud added that Dora herself 'could not be got to recollect any feelings of the kind'.[53] Unfortunately, Freud does not seem to have asked why the cousin was so confident about Dora's love. What was the cousin claiming to have noticed to give her grounds for telling Dora that she was in love with Herr K?

Apropos of Dora's unconscious love, Freud commented that the task of bringing to light hidden feelings proved to be simpler than he thought it would be. It was not difficult because 'he that has eyes to see and ears to hear may convince himself that no mortal can keep a secret'.[54] Like Elisabeth's mother, Freud is citing the universal onlooker as his witness. Freud, in claiming his patients to have feelings of unconscious love, is not searching for special signs, which only those with specialized psychoanalytic training can detect. He is observing what others, such as Dora's cousin and Elisabeth's mother, also observe and interpret. They, armed with the explanations of commonsense, rather than psychoanalytic theory, also suspect a love, which cannot consciously be admitted by the lover.

---

[51] Ibid., p. 229.
[52] 'Introductory lectures', *PFL* 1, p. 291.
[53] 'Fragment of an analysis of a case of hysteria', *PFL* 8, p. 69.
[54] Ibid., p. 114.

Denial and desire

Unconscious love is not merely unnoticed love. Something else is required over and above not recognizing the outward signs of one's behavioural display. The person in question will avoid interpreting their own behaviour as being that of a person in love. They will dismiss vehemently any suggestion that they might 'really' be in love. Or they might change the subject should the topic arise: that is not something that they wish to consider. In short, the person will display signs of what psychoanalysts call 'resistance'.

Freud claimed in the 'Introductory lectures' that resistance operates 'against our effort to transform what is unconscious into what is conscious'.[55] In Freud's cases, his diagnosis of unconscious love is received as an accusation, which is rejected with disproportionate feeling. The three women patients, whose cases have been mentioned, all showed resistance when Freud suggested that they loved the forbidden man. Freud started questioning closely the middle-aged woman, whom he suspected of loving her son-in-law, about events in the past. She said that nothing occurred to her; and after two sessions, she broke off the treatment pronouncing herself to be well.[56] When Freud told Elisabeth that she was in love with her brother-in-law, she denied it emotionally: 'It was not true, I had talked her into it, it *could* not be true, she was incapable of such wickedness, she could never forgive herself for it'.[57] Her pains returned. Dora did not merely reject Freud's suggestion that she unconsciously loved Herr K, but she did so in a way, which Freud interpreted as further evidence of the hidden desire. Dora's 'emphatic' denial, should not be taken at face value, he wrote, because 'the "No" uttered by a patient after a repressed thought has been presented to his conscious perception for the first time does no more than register the existence of a repression and its severity'. In consequence, '"No" signifies the desired "Yes"'.[58]

The very idea of 'no' signifying 'yes' is a troubling one. In the context of today's climate it smacks of the male claiming that the woman, who says 'no', really means 'yes'. Of course, Freud intended all analysts, whether male or female, to apply the principle to their patients, regardless of gender. Yet, if one accepts John Forrester's insights about the nature of psychoanalytic dialogue, the matter is not lightly dismissed. Forrester argues that the psychoanalytic situation is one of unequal

---

[55] 'Introductory lectures', *PFL* 1, p. 335.
[56] Ibid., pp. 290–1.
[57] 'Studies on hysteria', *PFL* 3, p. 227.
[58] 'Fragment of an analysis of a case of hysteria', *PFL* 8, p. 93.

power, as the analyst metaphorically seduces the analysand, refusing to accept the latter's accounts of themselves. Moreover, as Forrester points out, the majority of Freud's earliest patients were women and all subsequent analyses by Freudian analysts are, in some form or another, repetitions of Freud's original cases. Thus, analysis is founded on the image of the male seducer, taking the woman's 'no' for 'yes'.[59]

There is a further difficulty. The notion of 'resistance' can easily appear like a theoretical sleight-of-hand. Whatever the patient says can be taken to confirm the analyst's theory. If the patient accepts the analyst's explanation of a hidden desire, this is evidence for the correctness of the diagnosis. But if the patient rejects the explanation, then this too is proof. The critics claim that this puts psychoanalysis beyond refutation, as a self-fulfilling prophecy rather than scientific theory.[60] Freud recognized the problem in one of his last works. The critic, he wrote, might accuse psychoanalysts of operating by the principle 'Heads I win, tails you lose', because 'if the patient agrees with us, the interpretation is right; but if he contradicts us, that is only a sign of his resistance, which again shows that we are right'.[61]

Freud rejected this type of criticism and, in one limited respect, he was correct in doing so. As conversation analysts have shown, not all denials are equivalent. The claim not to remember, as was discussed in the previous chapter, can in certain contexts perform the action of not remembering. When Little Hans told his father that he forgot and said 'let me alone', he was using the claim to forget as a way of avoiding the memory work. He was behaving analogously to the middle-aged patient, who told Freud that she could remember nothing more, and broke off treatment. She precluded discussion of the signs of love and unacknowledged desire. Freud, well aware from experience that more memories always can be found if a patient so turned their mind, suspected that a brusque claim to have no memories indicated a refusal to remember.

In discussing resistance, Freud suggested that the emphatic 'no' is more than a simple 'no'.[62] It protests too much, for it is a way of dismissing the question, rather than answering it. Dora dismisses the matter out of hand, as if trying to close the issue. Elisabeth did not

---

[59] Forrester (1990).

[60] For such criticisms, see principally, Popper (1972) and Gellner (1985). Gellner called the idea of resistance, 'one of the neatest and best known' falsification-devices, recognizing that it is a necessary concept for psychoanalytic theory (p. 153). Gellner considered this as an indication that psychoanalytic theory is inherently untestable. For a judicious discussion of the issue, see Frosh (1997).

[61] 'Constructions in analysis', SE vol. 23, p. 257.

[62] See Potter (1996) for a discussion of the conversational and rhetorical uses of 'I don't know'.

merely say 'no' but she started to accuse Freud of shameful lies and to develop pains. She was saying, in effect, 'Look what your questioning has done to me now.' She changes the locus of the conversation ensuring that the question, raised by Freud, cannot be discussed.

Elisabeth's reactions can be compared with those of another character, who appears in 'Studies on hysteria'. Lucy R was a thirty-year-old English governess, who was treated by Freud and who worked in the family home of a rich widower.[63] She was suffering from fatigue, depression and loss of smell. Freud hypothesized that her olfactory problems had a psychological, rather than organic, basis. She was expecting to return to care for her elderly mother in Scotland. She reported that the imminent return was causing her some distress, because she did not want to leave the widower's young children of whom she had grown fond. Freud suspected that the real problem lay elsewhere – with the children's father. He formed the strong impression that Lucy had fallen in love with her employer.

Freud put the idea to Lucy. She did not respond with the sort of emotional denials, which Elisabeth displayed. Lucy's reaction was calm, as she considered the reasonableness of Freud's claim. 'Yes, I think that's true' she replied. Freud asked why she had not mentioned this. She answered: 'I wanted to drive it out of my head and not think of it again; and I believe latterly I have succeeded.'[64] Freud asked why she had been unwilling to admit her feelings: was she ashamed? Her answer, as reported by Freud, was revealing:

Oh no, I'm not unreasonably prudish. We're not responsible for our feelings, anyhow. It was distressing to me only because he is my employer and I am in his service and live in his house . . . And then I am only a poor girl and he is such a rich man of good family. People would laugh at me if they had any idea of it.[65]

Several points can be noted about Lucy R's reaction. In the first place, she readily admits to the suggestion, even though she had tried to put the notion from her mind. But she firmly rejects the idea that she had been ashamed of the feeling. She denies that she is prudish. After all, there is nothing to be ashamed of; she cannot be held accountable for her feelings. The problem is that her love is hopeless. It cannot lead to anything but disappointment or maybe mockery. In consequence, she makes an effort to repress it, or put it out from her mind.

Her willingness to admit the feeling, and to deny any shame, distinguishes her reaction from that of Elisabeth. Elisabeth's responses would

---

[63] There are indications in the text that she was probably Scottish, rather than 'English', as Freud described her.
[64] 'Studies on hysteria', *PFL* 3, p. 181.
[65] Ibid., p. 182.

lead the outsider to suspect that something is being hidden. Her denials are implausible: their vehemence seems to go beyond the strength of the accusation.[66] Lucy, by contrast, shows no resistance: she is willing to talk about the matter. Her 'yes' constitutes no repression while Elisabeth's 'no' frantically seeks to avoid the shameful accusation.

This suggests that not all putting out of mind is repression in the classically Freudian sense. Lucy puts the feeling out of her mind because she calculates that the net result will be discomfort or unpleasure. In this respect, she operates like the calculating ego, which Freud describes in 'Beyond the pleasure principle'. Motivated by the desire to avoid unpleasure, the organism's ego calculates the future result of desires. If a likely imbalance in favour of pain, at the cost of pleasure, is estimated then the desire will be kept from conscious awareness. No moral sense is involved in such a cost-benefit computation. Lucy similarly does her calculation and shows her mental discipline in withdrawing her mind from a topic which, she estimates, will cause pain. Thus, she embodies the principle that 'the motive and purpose of repression' is 'nothing else than the avoidance of unpleasure'.[67]

The comparison between Elisabeth and Lucy shows the difficulty of translating repression into calculations of pleasure and unpleasure, as Freud was trying to do in some of his metapsychological writings. No powerful inhibition keeps Lucy from acknowledging her own secret love. She is prepared to admit its existence and even to discuss calmly its possibilities. 'Morality' is not the condition for her repression, but reason is. Where shamefulness enters the picture, all is transformed with tension. Indeed, as theorists such as Helen Lewis and Thomas Scheff have maintained, shame is the spur for repression proper, and, indeed, underlies the less rational features of human social life.[68] Elisabeth's desire is too shameful for her to consider, let alone compute in terms of cost and benefit. Forcefully all discussion must be stopped. This resistance, manifested in agitated avoidance, is the sign of repression in its full force.

Inevitably, an analyst's diagnosis of repressed emotion must be controversial, as indeed must any such judgement by an outside observer.

---

[66] See Potter (1996) for a discussion of the pragmatics of 'plausible denial'. See also Lynch and Bogen (1996).

[67] 'On repression', *PFL* 11, p. 153.

[68] See Lewis (1983) for an extended interpretation of Freudian theory in terms of guilt and shame. Helen Lewis's ideas have been most notably incorporated into contemporary social science by Thomas Scheff (i.e., Scheff, 1990; 1993 and 1997; Scheff and Retzinger, 1991). Significantly, it has been argued that victims of childhood sexual abuse can feel shame and that it is this reaction which leads them to repress the memory (Schooler et al., 1997). The notion of 'repression proper' is taken from Freud's essay 'Repression'.

The analyst is consciously discounting patients' own account of themselves. Not only do patients stand accused of having shameful desires, but also of hiding the evidence from themselves. In this way, the analyst proposes a counter explanation to that offered by the patient, who may continue to reject the analyst's interpretation. Many years later, Elisabeth was still denying the charge but, perhaps, with less force, telling her own daughter of the 'young bearded nerve specialist' who tried 'to persuade me that I was in love with my brother-in-law, but that wasn't really so'.[69]

There is no conclusive proof that Freud could offer in order to demonstrate that Elisabeth 'really' was in love with her brother-in-law. No bodily state nor chemical reaction could be decisive. Her mother might be called as a witness, but her testimony, too, need not be conclusive. Freud, like any analyst, can only interpret the evidence. His most persuasive evidence is that which is available to other observers, such as Elisabeth's mother. But ultimately it comes down to one interpretation against another – one set of justifications and supporting evidence against a counter set. In this respect, Freud was right in calling psychoanalysis 'an interpretative art'.[70]

When Sigmund's 'no' means 'yes'

Elisabeth was denying an interpretation of her conduct suggested by another person, namely Freud. Similarly, in the case of Dora and the middle-aged patient, the overt suggestions, to be denied, were coming from Freud. But there are occasions when the accusation to be denied does not come from another person. In such cases, the person rejects an accusation, which they themself might be making. This may not be a simple matter, if repression is suspected and the self defence is a means of simultaneously answering the accusation while preventing the accusation from being voiced directly. To make an accusation, the shameful thought must be articulated, as Freud articulated his interpretations to Elisabeth and Dora. The defence, however, might be uttered, in order to prevent the accusation from being articulated in the first place. Where there is denial without accusation, the outsider might take this, too, as a sign of an unconscious wish.

Freud gave several instances in the case of the lawyer, Paul Lorenz. They relate to incidents in which Paul had been thinking about the

---

[69] Quoted in Gay (1995), p. 72.

[70] Freud *PFL* 15, 'Two encyclopaedia articles', p. 135. Later psychoanalysts follow Freud in this regard when they too stress that psychoanalysis cannot produce final explanations, only further interpretations; see, for instance, Frosh (1997) and Schafer (1997).

possibility of his father dying. In one instance, Paul was recounting when he had been in love with a woman, but had lacked the financial means to effect a marriage. If Paul's father had died, he might become rich enough to marry the woman. Instead of thinking the thought directly, he started wishing that his father would leave him no money at all. Freud offered an explanation. The wish that his father would leave no money was a way of countering the wish for his father's death. It was, thus, a sign that Paul had desired his father's death. Freud drew the analogy with forms of *lèse-majesté* which were punishable by law: 'It was well known, of course, that it was equally punishable to say "The Emperor is an ass" or to disguise the forbidden words by saying "If one says, etc., . . . then he will have me to reckon with"'.[71]

The law against *lèse-majesté*, according to Freud, was based upon psychological understanding. An overt denial indicates a wish, if no one else is making the accusation. The person, who denies that the Emperor is an ass, is the only one who is making the suggestion. When the young lawyer argued with Freud that the thought of his father's death was not a wish, Freud merely asked him 'why, if it had not been a wish, he had repudiated it'.[72] When the young man objected to this, Freud had offered the analogy of insulting the Emperor with indirect speech. Freud thought this was convincing enough, but the patient persisted in resisting the interpretation. Freud then broke off the argument and tried another tack to persuade Paul.

Had Elisabeth, in talking of her brother-in-law, kept saying unbidden to Freud, 'I'm not in love with him, you know', then Freud would have suspected something. Why should one defend oneself against an unmade accusation, unless one is seeking to prevent or counter a self-accusation? The self-accusation would be impossible without the imagination of the shameful wish. Elisabeth could not have said 'I'm not in love with him', unless she had imagined, in some form or another, the possibility. The denial then stifles the wish, turning it psychologically into something unwished for.

Of course, Elisabeth did not volunteer the defence. By contrast, there is a defence against an unmade accusation in two examples that will be considered. In both, the manner of denial can be taken as evidence for a temptation or feeling which is being denied. Both instances are taken from the life of the young Freud, during the period of his engagement with Martha.

At the time, Sigmund was loving insecurely and without the passionate response he desired. As a moral young man with a desire to follow

[71] 'Notes upon a case of obsessional neurosis', *PFL* 9, p. 59.
[72] Ibid.

the conventional duties of courtship and to be rewarded in return by devoted love, he wanted to believe that he only had eyes for his beloved Martha, whom he had chosen from among all the women in the world. To keep his piece of mind, Sigmund must convince himself that he has no shameful desires or dissatisfactions. All must be argued down, even before they appear. But the arguing down indicates the very opposite. As Sigmund tells himself 'no', the presence of 'yes' is indicated.

(a) Charcot's Daughter. In October 1885, Sigmund left Vienna for Paris, having obtained a grant to work with Jean-Martin Charcot, universally recognized to be the most distinguished neurologist and psychiatrist of the age. Large crowds packed into Charcot's lectures on hysteria at the Salpêtrière Hospital. The doctor brought his patients onto stage, making them display their dramatic symptoms on cue, and demonstrating his own powers of hypnosis.[73] Freud was obviously eager to impress the great man. Soon after his first meeting, he was reporting back to Martha that 'as long as he is present I try to keep near to him'.[74]

After Freud had been working at Charcot's laboratory for three months, he was invited to his hero's house for dinner. He wrote to Martha: 'I accepted with a bow, feeling delighted.'[75] Freud could scarcely afford the new items of clothing, which he bought specially for the occasion. To calm his nerves before setting off in the hired carriage, he took a small dose of cocaine.[76] Afterwards, he wrote excitedly to Martha about the dinner, the other guests, the richly furnished house and, above all, the Charcot family. He recounted his own clever contributions to the evening's conversation, adding that Martha would 'probably be as interested in the personalities of Madame and Mlle Charcot as in my achievements'.

In describing Madame Charcot to Martha, Sigmund mentioned that she was the source of Charcot's wealth. He then depicted the daughter – 'small, rather buxom, of an almost ridiculous resemblance to her great father'.[77] The resemblance was so striking that 'one doesn't ask oneself whether she is pretty or not'. Sigmund went on: 'Now just suppose I were not in love already and were something of an adventurer: it would

[73] See Ferris (1997), pp. 62f.
[74] Freud (1960), p. 176. Gay (1990), following Jones (1953), attributes Charcot with moving Freud's intellectual interests from laboratory work towards psychology. Sand (1992) points to the importance of Charcot's interest in dreams and their interpretation. Freud expressed his respect for Charcot in the obituary he wrote in 1893 ('Charcot', *SE* 3). That Freud never lost this respect is evident from the fact that a lithograph of Brouillet's painting of Charcot at Salpêtrière hung in Freud's consulting-room above the famous couch (see The Freud Museum, 1998, pp. 55f).
[75] Freud (1960), p. 194.   [76] Ibid., p. 196   [77] Ibid.

be a strong temptation to court her for nothing is more dangerous than a young girl bearing the features of a man whom one admires.'[78]

The temptation is denied in its expression. He would be tempted, or so he says, if he were someone else; if he were not engaged; if he were an 'adventurer' – the very term which, a few years later, Freud would use to describe himself in a letter to Fliess.[79] Calculations are made to dismiss the imagined pleasures, converting them into unpleasure. Courting the daughter, who bears the hero's face above a buxom body, is fraught with danger. Sigmund imagines the disaster: 'I would become a laughing-stock, be thrown out.' And he concludes to Martha: 'It is better as it is, after all.'[80]

The desire is apparent. Quite apart from the psychological attractions of being intimate with a woman who looked just like one's male hero, there would be financial and professional advantages. If he married Charcot's daughter, he would immediately be admitted to the family. He would meet the great man regularly: none of his rival physicians could get nearer. Charcot would undoubtedly put his son-in-law on the path to scientific fame. The great man would treat him as a son.[81] Financial worries would be a thing of the past. Mlle Charcot, like her mother before her, would come with the sort of dowry, which Martha could only envy and which Sigmund might have dreamt of.[82] And Freud would be following in the footsteps of his hero.

The shameful desires are projected onto the image of a hypothetical other, the 'adventurer', who Freud implies to Martha is not himself, but who, at least on other levels and later to Fliess, he dreams of being. As if this is not safe enough, the desires are immediately neutralized by the calculation of unpleasure. All would be lost if he were to become a laughing-stock, to be expelled forever from the world of Charcot. Only an adventurer would chance his arm in this way. Sigmund does not mention that the young Charcot might have been somewhat of an adventurer, marrying into money. That thought is left undeveloped.

By committing himself on paper to Martha, Sigmund pushes tempta-

---

[78] Freud (1960), pp. 196–7.

[79] 'I am by temperament nothing but a conquistador – an adventurer, if you want it translated – with all the curiosity, daring, and tenacity characteristic of a man of this sort' (letter to Fliess, 1.2. 1900; in Freud, 1985, p. 398).

[80] Ibid., p. 197.

[81] As Gelfand (1992) points out, Freud hardly ever mentions Charcot's actual son and, when he does, he gives him the wrong first name. All this, suggests Gelfand, squares with Freud's wish to have Charcot as a father figure. In his obituary to Charcot, Freud mentions the daughter but not the son ('Charcot', *SE* 3, p. 16).

[82] In an early letter, Sigmund had written to Martha: 'Oh my darling Marty how poor we are! . . . What is your dowry? Nothing but our love for each other' (Freud, 1960, p. 27).

tion away. The mere fact of writing is his witness that he has nothing shameful to hide. Now, Martha is enrolled in the repression. She is the audience to the public calculation, as Sigmund commits himself to the denial of temptation. If he can speak outwardly to Martha, then he cannot have had the troubling, shameful desires. He, thus, affirms his love for Martha as he denies desire for Mlle Charcot. We do not know, of course, Martha's reaction to this display.

Sigmund's descriptions of Charcot's daughter express the ambivalence. He claims that he does not even ask himself whether she is pretty: all he sees in her face is her father's countenance. Perhaps it is all he wants to see. But he has noticed that she is rather buxom. When he is invited the next time, he will sit next to Mlle Charcot during the meal. He will then describe her to Martha as 'very pretty'.[83] By then, he has discharged the thought of temptation. He has no need to feel guilt. He can now feel secure enough to mention her attractiveness to Martha.

Sigmund ended the letter, which detailed his first visit, by saying that everything is better as it is, 'after all'. The final words on the subject – 'after all' – are a give-away. They are simultaneously a sigh of resignation, a reassurance to Martha and to himself, and a dismissal of the thought that he denies thinking. 'After all' makes do with the present, and narrows dreams for the future. There is also a reversal of meaning. 'After all' is after nothing – and before nothing – except denied desire.[84]

(b) Sigmund's Sister-in-Law. Recent biographers have been fascinated by a topic, which, even during Freud's lifetime, was a matter of speculation: whether Freud had an affair with his sister-in-law Minna. Some onlookers, most notably Jung, had their suspicions. The signs were there. Freud was close to Minna. In a letter to Fliess, written in 1894, Freud described Minna as his 'closest confidante'.[85] She showed a deep interest in psychoanalytic matters, in a way that Martha never did. Like Elisabeth and her brother-in-law, Freud enjoyed lengthy walks with his sister-in-law. The two went on holidays unaccompanied.[86] In addition, the unmarried Minna lived for many years with Martha, Sigmund and their children.

Ernest Jones, in his uncritical, official biography, gave a most

---

[83] Ibid., p. 207.
[84] Freud was certainly aware of the Yiddish version of 'after all' – *tomer doch*. The phrase overtly signifies resignation and a coming to terms with disappointment. Freud used it thus in his correspondence with Fliess. He had hoped that the Fliess's would have been able to visit him and Martha. But, as he wrote, 'once again it was not meant to be'. He added: "Tomer doch?" the Jew asks in such cases' (1985, p. 367). In this case, the wish was expressed openly; it did not have to be disguised as conjecture.
[85] Freud (1985), p. 73.
[86] Ferris (1997), pp. 146–7.

emphatic 'no' to the rumour of an affair, dismissing it as unworthy of discussion. His emphatic 'no', like Dora's, is designed to answer a charge which has been made. Jones in his defence conjures up the image of Minna as an intellectual, not sexual, companion: as a girl she had gone about her housework with a duster in one hand and book in another.[87] Peter Gay, in his careful analysis of the evidence, says that the matter cannot now be settled one way or another, and probably never will be.[88] What matters here is not whether the mature Freud actually slept with his sister-in-law. As Freudian theory often stresses, the later deed is less significant than the earlier desire.

It is to the young, tense pre-Freudian Freud, that one can turn. He is courting Martha while getting to know her younger sister, who, unlike his fiancée, was already displaying an interest in his intellectual life. From the early years there were signs that he could discuss matters with Minna that he could not, or dare not, raise with Martha. From Paris, Sigmund wrote to Minna, but not to Martha, about Parisian crowds knowing no shame: 'the women no less than the men crowd round nudities'.[89] His letters to Martha mention neither naked statues nor the women who stare at them.

Was there a parallel with Elisabeth, whose situation he was to understand sympathetically a few years later? Minna was at that time engaged to a young scholar of Sanskrit, Ignaz Schönberg, who was to die of tuberculosis before the marriage could take place.[90] Sigmund and Ignaz were close friends, seeing each other regularly, while separated from their respective fiancées. Onlookers, Sigmund complained to Martha, might not have suspected her love for him, because of the coolness of her behaviour. He doesn't ask whether the same onlookers might have detected an over-fondness for Minna in him?

Like Elisabeth's own sister, Sigmund raised the question whether brother-in-law and sister-in-law might have better suited each other. And similarly, his answer is a denial of the question. Ernest Jones reports a letter to Martha in which Freud discusses the two Bernays sisters and their respective fiancés. Martha and Ignaz were similar in

---

[87] Jones (1953), p. 168.

[88] Gay (1990 and 1995). As Gay points out, crucial material seems to be missing from the Freud archive (on the complex politics of the Freud archive, see Malcolm, 1986). Critics of Freud sometimes mention the possibility of an affair with Minna as another indication of Freud's lack of trustworthiness (Webster, 1995). Roazen (1996), however, claims that an affair would not diminish Freud's reputation, but Freud and Minna's 'ability to function in the case of such unconventionality would be a tribute to their largeness of spirit' (pp. 16–7).

[89] Freud (1960), p. 187.

[90] In fact, Schönberg, as his condition deteriorated, broke off the engagement with Minna.

that both were 'thoroughly good people'. Minna and himself were the passionate ones. That is why 'we get on better in a criss-cross arrangement; why two similar people like Minna and myself don't suit each other specially'.[91]

Here is another 'after all', arguing against troublesome desire, answering a question which only the self has raised. The voice of reasonableness, or the ego of bourgeois respectability, is coming to terms with itself, resigned to its steady avoidance of unpleasure, rather than pursuing passionate desire. Yet, the wish shines through, despite, or rather *because of*, the rhetorical conclusion. Sigmund is constantly telling Martha that he wants her to be more like himself, to be more passionate in her responses. But now, after all, he does not specially suit the passionate sister. The wording is careful. 'Specially' carries the dangerous implications of 'really'. It permits the reversal to be expressed. If he and Minna don't suit each other *specially*, then, in some unspecified, non-special ways, they do suit each other.

One might imagine what the mature Freud would have made of such a letter had Elisabeth written those words about her brother-in-law; or if the middle-aged woman had spoken thus about her son-in-law. He, and other onlookers, would have been hard put not to acknowledge the surfacing and negating of desires. They might have taken the denial ('we don't specially suit each other') as another negation which is taming subversive desire. It is a means of both raising and dismissing the topic. All the while Sigmund proclaims his own innocence to an accusation which no one had made. 'After all', if he had something to hide, he would not have discussed the issue with Martha herself, would he? But the hiding is accomplished by the open discussion. The denial signifies its opposite. The protestation of innocence assumes the charge. As Freud was to tell his patients again and again, 'no' indicates 'yes'. One cannot deny what has never been thought.

Counter-denial and counter-transference

A further point can be made about Freud, desire and the analytic situation. The analyst claims to have discovered the real, but shameful, desires of the patient. In response, the patient resists, denying the analyst's claim. In the analyst's mind, the relationship with the patient is likely to have become difficult already. According to Freudian theory, 'transference' occurs in successful analysis. The patient supposedly transfers onto the analyst part of the feelings which are basic to their

[91] Jones (1953), p. 180.

condition and whose 'real' object lies elsewhere. The most common form of transference, according to Freud, was for the woman patient to fall in love with the male doctor. In such a case 'the patient has transferred on to the doctor intense feelings of affection which are justified neither by the doctor's behaviour nor by the situation that has developed during the treatment'.[92] According to orthodox psychoanalytic theory, transference offers vital diagnostic clues, because it reveals the crucial desires which were hitherto repressed. In 'Studies on hysteria', Freud described the case of a woman whose current hysterical symptom owed its psychological origin to a repressed urge that a particular man would suddenly kiss her. The origin lay concealed until, as Freud recounted, at the end of one analytic session, 'a similar wish came up in her about me'.[93] Only after this wish had surfaced and been interpreted, could Freud uncover the crucial, earlier wish.

Later critics, especially feminist critics, have rightly pointed to troubling aspects of transference. So many of Freud's patients were young women.[94] The middle-aged man sits in a pose of professional dignity. The young, troubled woman, stretched out before his gaze, has to keep talking, telling the man her most intimate secrets. The man will ultimately inform her of her 'real' shameful desires. She will find this distressing. She will probably repudiate his claims. In addition, she supposedly will fall in love with the middle-aged man. She might even need to, if he is to cure her. It is part of the treatment.

But where in this picture, ask the critics, are the analyst's desires? He sits there, impassive and wise, as if he is above desire. Yet, as John Forrester has argued, psychoanalysis 'is constituted around the desire to analyse women', with later analysts repeating the desires of their founder.[95] It is no wonder, then, that feminists, in looking at Freud's treatment of a young woman such as Dora, do not accept the image of the impervious, detached Freud. If the patient can have unconscious feelings for the doctor, then so can the doctor have denied desires for the patient.[96] Psychoanalysts have called the analyst's 'unconscious reaction' for the patient 'counter-transference'.[97] The point, here, is not to sort out who 'really', or unconsciously, loves whom. It is to link the possibilities of transference and counter-transference with those of

[92] 'Introductory lectures', *PFL* 1, p. 492.
[93] 'Studies on hysteria', *PFL* 3, p. 390.
[94] See Appignanesi and Forrester (1993).
[95] Forrester (1990) p. 240.
[96] For feminist analyses of the Dora case, see, inter alia, Ramas (1983), Rose (1986), Gallop (1986) and Gearhart (1986). The case of Dora will be discussed in detail in the following chapter.
[97] Laplanche and Pontalis (1983), p. 82.

denial and counter-denial. Here we are dealing with the possibility of emotion, or, to be more exact, the possibility of claiming that the other has unadmitted emotions.

The analytic relationship is not an equal one, for it is based on a lop-sided dialogue. The doctor sets the rules for the conversation. The patients divulge their secrets. In return, analysts give little away about themselves. It is predicted that the patient will resist, or argue against, the doctor's diagnosis of hidden desire. The patient, however, cannot conduct this argument on an equal footing. Analysts can accuse patients of shameful desires, but patients will find it difficult to return the accusation convincingly, for they will have not been talking of the analyst's secrets. Come the decisive moment, the patient lacks the evidence to make a counter-accusation of counter-transference. When Elisabeth rejected Freud's suggestion that she loved her brother-in-law, she did not know about Minna. Paul would similarly have been ignorant of Freud and Mlle Charcot. If either had known, they would have had the capacity to embarrass the doctor in their own moments of intense embarrassment.

Freud told Elisabeth what her feelings were and she tried to accuse him: he had talked her into it, she countered. But why should he have done so? She would not have anything plausible to add; her accusation lacked the grounds of motive. Had she known more, she might have hurled back at her doctor during that emotional moment: 'You're only saying that, because you loved your sister-in-law – you still do – she gives you the support which your wife won't – it's yourself you're talking about, not me – you're jealous.' No turning of the tables was possible. She had no grounds for making the accusation of counter-transference: she hadn't read Sigmund's private letters, nor seen him walking with Minna.

It was the same for Paul, during what Freud called 'an obscure and difficult part of the treatment'.[98] Freud clearly liked the young man.[99] In the course of the treatment, Freud taught the young lawyer about psychoanalytic theory, lecturing him at length. If the patient, in the process of transference, supposedly identifies with Freud as a father-figure, then so, it may just as easily be suspected, Freud identifies with the young lawyer. Perhaps the doctor sees his younger self in the young man, sitting there in the consulting room, anxious, unsure of women and learning psychology from a great teacher. The young man also is chastely and conservatively in love with a young lady, whose affections

---

[98] 'Notes upon a case of obsessional neurosis' *PFL* 9, p. 80.
[99] Mahony (1986).

he is unsure of. Freud reproduces his own relations with Charcot when he asks Paul to dine.

The relationship between Freud and his patient has its tense moments, especially when the dialogue touches matters concerning Paul and the Freud family. Freud, at one point, suggests that the young man desires to marry Anna, Freud's daughter, in order to inherit his money. In fact, it is slightly more complicated. Paul imagines that Freud wants him as his son-in-law. Freud described the position: 'he pictured to himself that the only reason I was so kind and incredibly patient with him was that I wanted to have him for a son-in-law'.[100] Freud interprets a dream, which the young man has of Anna. Freud's interpretation suggests that Paul wishes to marry Anna, but 'not for her *beaux yeux* but for her money'. The patient resists the very idea with 'the severest and bitterest vituperations'.[101] Freud does not tell us what the young man said so vituperatively.

Perhaps Paul, in that moment of tension, accused Freud of the most shameful wishes. However, Paul would not have been able to turn his doctor's accusation around completely. He might have been able to say 'It's you who want me as your son-in-law, not me wanting you as a father-in-law.' But he could not have completed the accusation: 'You accuse me of the very crime, which, years ago, you wanted to commit, but were too cowardly to do so. Go on, deny it, Doctor, just as you denied it years ago to Martha. Deny it. After all, you're the one who's taught me that a denial is a wish.'

The speech could neither be delivered, nor thought. The patient has not been permitted the necessary knowledge. If he is the fantasized son in the consulting-room, then he resembles Little Hans. The parents will tell the child what he is feeling – what he is 'really' and shamefully feeling. They, as accusers, present themselves as having no motives in identifying the hidden, possibly unfelt, feelings of the other. This dialogue of emotions is not equal. The child is to be found guilty, while the parent, or the analyst, is the innocent accuser. But how can accusers be innocent of all desire? If they were, how could they possibly recognize the hidden desires of others?

Projection and denial as an ideological reflex

Emotions and temptations belong to more than the individual concerned. As has been said, talk about emotions typically involves talk about morality and social expectations. As Sigmund tells Martha how

---

[100] 'Notes upon a case of obsessional neurosis', *PFL* 9, p. 80.
[101] Ibid.

she should react to his letters, he is citing as his justification a whole moral order of gender relations. He is acting out, and displaying, the social conventions of love. In denying temptation towards Mlle Charcot and claiming not to suit Minna, he is not merely struggling with himself; he is struggling to uphold the particular social values, which permit him and Martha to plan for a small house and quiet life. As such, patterns of culture and ideology determine what is to be desired and what is to be an object of shame.

If emotions are socially and culturally constructed, then the particular patterns of arguing down shameful desires might also be socially available as cultural habits. In Freud's bourgeois Vienna, the voice of desire is to be answered by the voice of duty. The latter should follow the former as a rhetorical habit of thought, like a policeman whose mere presence quells a disturbance on the streets. The calculations and the 'after alls' should become what Marx and Engels, in *The German Ideology*, called 'ideological reflexes'.[102]

Freud's own curtailment of desire, to be observed in his letters with Martha, echoes wider patterns. Most remarkably his words prefigure his own brilliant psychological theories, in ways which show how difficult it is to draw distinctions between the personal, the ideological and the theoretical.

In late August 1883, almost two years before Sigmund's stay in France, Martha had written about a trip to Wandsbek Fair. She appears to have commented on the fair's vulgarity. Sigmund, in his reply, was pleased: 'Beloved, you are quite right, it is neither pleasant nor edifying to watch the masses amuse themselves.' He then distinguished between the mob and refined people like themselves: 'the mob gives vent to its appetites, and we deprive ourselves'. He continued: 'we save ourselves for something, not knowing what', depriving ourselves in order 'to maintain our integrity'. We make calculations. We don't get drunk because 'the discomfort and disgrace of the after-effects gives us more "unpleasure" than the pleasure which we derived from getting drunk'. Similarly, we don't fall in love with a different person each month. In consequence 'we strive more toward avoiding pain than seeking pleasure'. If this means 'the habit of constant suppression of natural instincts', then this suppression 'gives us the quality of refinement'.[103]

The letter is remarkable. The young Freud is speaking as a Freudian, before he had become one. The later psychological ideas, even the terminology, are there. Sigmund writes of the suppression of natural instincts and the avoidance of 'unpleasure'. It is the avoidance of

[102] Marx and Engels (1970), p. 47.
[103] Freud (1960), p. 50.

unpleasure, rather than the pursuit of pleasure, which necessitates the suppression.[104] In one crucial respect, the letter differs from later metapsychological speculations about the ego and the pleasure/ unpleasure principle. In the later writings, Freud assumed that the principle is rooted in a universal biology, affecting all humans. The letter, by contrast, argues sociologically rather than biologically. People 'like us', but not the whole of humanity, make such calculations. 'Our' moderation is compared with the immoderation of the poor, whose way of life offers them no reason to 'scorn the pleasures of the moment'. In consequence, 'the poor are too helpless too exposed, to behave like us', and, as Sigmund continued to Martha, 'there is a psychology of the common man which differs considerably from ours'.[105]

Freud is speaking for his class, the sober *petit bourgeois*, who works hard to avoid poverty, but who does not expect the rewards of the *haute bourgeoisie* (unless, like Professor Charcot, a fortunate marriage is contracted). This is the class of people, who settle for the dream of a small home, dutiful spouse and quiet contentment. Noisy, unrefined happiness is for others, to be decried as unrefined. Self-discipline, or rather class-discipline, depends on a denial of desires. Not only do we not get drunk, but we do not *want* to (cigars and brandy *chez* Charcot, not to mention an earlier aperitif of cocaine, are altogether different from common drinking). Nor do we want to fall in love promiscuously.

Martha has seen and written about the pleasures of the fair, the sensual pleasures of the moment. Sigmund responds by saying that these are not our pleasures. We prefer the delights of opera; our gratifications 'are so different that it would be affectation to pretend that one really enjoys the kind of spectacle you describe'.[106] His letter carries the tone of obligation: we *should* not enjoy these pleasures – and, in particular, you shouldn't, Martha. We're saving ourselves: 'we economize in our health, our capacity for enjoyment, our emotions'.[107] We should remain awkward at the fair, distancing ourselves from the mass.

Freud, in his metapsychological essay 'Negation', wrote that 'the content of a repressed image or idea can make its way into consciousness, on condition that it is *negated*'.[108] The repressed idea remains unaccepted, but negation lifts the total ban on its expression: 'a negative judgement is the intellectual substitute for repression; its "no"; is the hall-mark of repression, a certificate of origin'.[109] The negation,

---

[104] See Sackheim (1983) for an argument that Freud's theory of repression is based on the motivating factor of avoidance of unpleasure, rather than the seeking of pleasure.
[105] Freud (1960), p. 51.
[106] Ibid., p. 50.   [107] Ibid.
[108] 'Negation', *PFL* 11, pp. 437–8, emphasis in original.
[109] Ibid., p. 438.

however, need not be accomplished merely by the attachment of a simple "no", but a counter-argument may be used. Because the speaker, or letter-writer, is expressing the counter-argument, the desires can be described in some detail, whether they be the pleasures of the fair or Mlle Charcot's figure. If not *lèse majesté*, it is a *lèse bourgeoisie*.

A wider ideological habit can be detected in this mixture of expression and denial. Freud was using stereotypes to reinforce social duty and family propriety. In Freud's case, there is, nevertheless, something extra alongside the familiar priggish voice of class rectitude and masculine condescension. There is brilliant, original insight, which does not oppose the stereotypes but which is woven within them. The insights were both a product and transcendence of the conventional moral order. In the letters to Martha, we cannot distinguish Freud's own personal voice, the spirit of the times and the voice of the founder of psychoanalysis. Denial and desire can be heard simultaneously in all three. The letters of the pre-Freudian Sigmund not only illustrate how psychoanalysis belonged to its own time. That much can be expected. They show also that Freud's genius itself needed to be part of the very self-deceptions and denials which he courageously exposed.

Habits of language are habits of life. Young Sigmund and Martha, in denying themselves the fun of the fair, were setting their lives on a course of bourgeois respectability. Like all couples, they would develop their domestic routines and their habits of talk. Habitually, speakers find their words moving in particular directions, which are not random. What is said habitually ensures that there are unspoken matters. In this sense, habits of language are repressive. As parts of wider cultural patterns, they are ideological, for ideology embraces the unsaid.

But what of psychoanalytic thinking itself? It is a habit of language, which has affected Western culture generally.[1] Its explanations of human conduct claim to reveal what has been concealed. But maybe the habits of revelation themselves can hide. And what of the ideological background from which these habits of revelation arose? Perhaps, because Freud was leaving some matters unsaid, he was able to formulate new ways of analysing, which were also repressing as they were expressing their new forms of understanding.

This chapter explores the ideological background of Freudian psychoanalysis. It does so in relation to Freud's social position as a Jew in Austria. He had the misfortune to live at a time and in a place least favourable for Jews. In Freud's case, as with others, the insecurities of the outsider were translated into an extraordinary, unrepeatable creativity. However, the social catastrophe, which was building up throughout Freud's lifetime, was surprisingly absent in his writings. As Freud himself taught, absence is not to be equated with insignificance. Quite the reverse, some matters are conspicuous by their lack of presence. So it is with anti-semitism and Freud's writings.

The absences in Freud will be examined and it will be suggested that some of these absences are being reproduced in the writings of today's critics. As always, it is insufficient to remain at the level of grand theory, or to talk in general terms about the shape of discourses. Repression lies

---

[1] Moscovici (1961); Parker (1998b); Kirschner (1996).

in the details of language. Similarly, the details of Freud's writings must be examined for themes which may be absent, but whose traces are significantly present. Therefore, this chapter will turn to the famous case of Dora. There, it will be possible to see how both doctor and patient managed to avoid painful Jewish issues; and how critics today, claiming to re-examine the case, have taken both Freud and Dora at their word. In this way, the dialogic repressions of almost a century ago are being reproduced today as a continuing habit.

Background: Dora and Freud

In October 1900, Philip Bauer, a Jewish industrialist living in Vienna, took his eighteen-year-old daughter to see Freud. A few years earlier, Freud had discreetly and successfully treated him for venereal symptoms. Now, Bauer's daughter was acting peculiarly, saying strange things; she had even threatened suicide; could Dr Freud restore her to reason? From Freud's point of view, the case did not seem to be particularly promising, at least in terms of offering new features for the theories which he was developing. The young woman was displaying the typical signs of 'hysteria', which he had encountered many times previously. However, Freud took her on. His finances at the time were none too secure. A few days later, writing to his friend Wilhelm Fliess, Freud mentioned that the 'case has smoothly opened to the existing collection of picklocks'.[2] The young patient was to terminate the treatment abruptly at the end of that December. Freud wrote up his case-notes in the January of the new year. It was not until 1905 that the cautiously entitled 'Fragment of an analysis of a case of hysteria' was published in a specialist journal.

This was the inauspicious background of a report which has become recognized as 'the first of Freud's great case histories' and which has taken its place as 'one of the classic reports in the psychiatric literature'.[3] As Anthony Storr has commented, the case 'served for years as a model for students of psychoanalysis'.[4] 'Dora', the pseudonym, which Freud gave to the patient, Ida Bauer, has become a familiar name in psychoanalytic circles.[5] In recent years, there has been a revival of interest in

---

[2] Freud (1985) p. 427.
[3] Loewenberg (1985), p. 188; see also Marcus (1986), who claims that the case history 'is a great work of literature' (p. 57).
[4] Storr (1989), p. 101.
[5] For background studies of 'Dora' and her family, see Appignanesi and Forrester (1993); Deutsch (1986); Rogow (1978 and 1979); and, above all, Hannah Decker (1991 and 1992).

Dora and in Freud's treatment of her. Psychoanalysts have been reinter-preting the case in the light of developments in psychoanalytic theory.[6] Nevertheless, much of the recent interest has come from feminist critics, often approaching the case from a background in literary studies.[7] The feminist re-examination of Dora's case is part of the wider questioning of psychoanalysis, as scholars have debated whether psychoanalytic ideas should be rejected outright for their masculine assumptions or whether a reformulation is possible.[8]

These debates have led feminist scholars to look at the famous case-studies in new ways, questioning exactly what went on in the Bauer household and in Dr Freud's cramped consulting-room. For some feminists, Dora has become a heroine, who disrupts the deceits of the patriarchal family. Others have seen Dora as a tragic victim of masculine power.[9] Freud's role in the saga is being reassessed. He no longer appears as a passive listener and detached scientist. He is part of patriarchal power. He thinks like a man; acts like one, and his new theories, it is said, expressed masculine assumptions in the guise of science.

Without doubt feminist re-analyses have succeeded in revealing aspects of the case which previously lay unnoticed. Now, it is hard not to see the behaviour of the males in the story as the problem, with Dora's symptoms as the effect. Dora tells Freud of the complex web of deception which has drawn her family close to the life of the K's. The two families often go on holiday together. Dora looks after the K's young children. She is particularly friendly with Frau K. The connec-tions are not innocent. Her father is having a protracted affair with Frau K, who is somewhat younger than himself. He has encouraged the closeness of the two families, in order to manipulate more occasions to conduct the affair. Herr K, rejected by his wife, has been pursuing Dora since she was fourteen. On a couple of occasions, he grabs hold of her, trying to kiss her. One holiday he even tries to enter her bedroom while

---

[6] See, for instance, Blum (1994); Erikson (1986); Glenn (1980); Kanzer (1980); Lacan (1986b); Langs (1980); Masson (1990); Ornstein (1993b); Scharfman (1980). See Macmillan (1997, pp. 249ff) for a critical review of Freud's and other psychoanalytic interpretations of the case.

[7] See, inter alia, Cixous and Clément (1986); Gallop (1982 and 1986); Gearhart (1986); Jacobus (1987); Kahane (1996); Moi (1986); Ragland (1996); Ramas (1983); Rose (1986).

[8] See, for example, Brennan (1989); Frosh (1994); Gallop (1982); Hollway (1989); Mitchell (1974); Sayers (1990).

[9] Cixous and Clément's *The Newly Born Woman* provides a fascinating example of this debate. Cixous takes the side of Dora, presenting her as both victim and heroine, 'who resists the system' (1986, p. 154), while Clément takes issue with Cixous for romanticizing Dora: 'You love Dora, but to me she never seemed a revolutionary character' (p. 157).

she sleeps. After an incident by a lake, when again he propositions her, Dora tells her father. However, her father accuses Dora of inventing the whole tale, suggesting that she is engaging in unhealthy sexual fantasies.

Freud, for his part, accepts Dora's story. Yet he wonders why Dora claims to feel disgust, rather than sexual desire, when Herr K grabs her, pressing his erect penis against her body. As was discussed in the previous chapter, Freud is of the opinion that Dora unconsciously desires Herr K – something that Dora denies. But that is not all. Freud is perplexed by Dora's close relationship with Frau K. He cannot understand how Dora can remain friendly with her father's mistress. He comes to the conclusion that Dora also unconsciously loves Frau K. The insight struck him too late to be discussed fully with the patient, for Dora has had enough of the treatment. As Freud adds in a footnote to the postscript of the case-report: 'I failed to discover in time and to inform the patient that her homosexual (gynaecophilic) love for Frau K. was the strongest unconscious current in her mental life.'[10]

Today, the problem is no longer seen to be Dora's resistance to the male penis. It has become Freud's assumptions about women's desires. How could he have supposed that a young girl would be automatically aroused by Herr K's crude advances? And how could he have failed to appreciate the bonds between Dora and Frau K? Freud claimed that he was uncovering hidden desires, but critics suggest that his revelations conceal as much as they expose. Freud's unconscious desires have become the problem. As Lacan suggested, Freud was blind to the problem of countertransference.[11]

The issue of countertransference, and with it the problem of Freud's desires, is at the centre of many of the feminist critiques. As Claire Kahane has argued, Freud 'presses Dora to recognize his desire as hers'.[12] In the first place, Freud is using Dora to satisfy his 'theoretical desire to know'.[13] No wonder, he was so annoyed when she broke off the treatment, before he had time to organize the case theoretically.[14] But worse, Freud may himself have had unacknowledged desires for the patient, whom he describes as being 'in the first bloom of youth – a girl of intelligent and engaging looks'.[15] Toril Moi follows Lacan in

---

[10] 'Fragment of an analysis of a case of hysteria', *PFL* 8, p. 162n.
[11] Lacan (1986b).
[12] Kahane (1996), p. 102.
[13] Ibid. See also Scharfman (1980), who from a psychoanalytic, rather than feminist, perspective, claims that for Freud treatment may have taken second place to theoretical discovery, and, thus, Freud was 'using Dora and taking advantage of her' (p. 54).
[14] Roazen (1992), however, suggests that Freud might have been pleased to have seen the back of Dora as a patient.
[15] 'Fragment of an analysis of a case of hysteria', *PFL* 8, p. 53.

suggesting that Freud may have unconsciously identified with Herr K.[16] If that was the case, then his insistence that Dora was really in love with Herr K may have a hidden psychological motive. If Freud can persuade Dora that she loves Herr K. and if Freud imagines himself to be Herr K, then Freud can imagine, albeit unconsciously, that this young, intelligent and attractive woman is in love with him – or, at least, that she might love a middle-aged man like himself. Moi suggests that Freud's unacknowledged desires – his countertransferences – affect his understanding of Dora. He wants to believe that Dora loves Herr K, rather than Frau K. In consequence, Freud's own desires blind him 'to the possibility that Dora's hysteria may be due to the repression of desire, not for Herr K, but for his wife'.[17] More generally, it is argued that Freud all the time interprets Dora's psychology in terms of men. He cannot see that women may be the important figures in her life.[18]

The point, here, is not to sort out who really loved whom – whether Dora really loved Frau K more than she did Herr K; or whether Freud's undoubted irritation with Dora signifies a deeper and denied attraction. Such matters are undecidable. Nevertheless, the basic point of today's critics should be acknowledged. Freud's claims of revelation themselves involved omissions or forgettings. These omissions are not haphazard; nor are they even a reflection of Freud's personal psychology. As feminist critiques emphasize, the omissions are political in the widest sense. They reflect the ideological currents of patriarchy. Yet, as will be seen, the omissions are not all one sided. Some of today's revelations of what Freud forgot to reveal also contain omissions. And, it will be argued, politics is central to these combinations of revelation and forgetting.

Omitting politics

Feminist critics and other radicals have often accused Freudian psychoanalysis of being apolitical. It is said that Freud reduces everything to family dramas, which he then interprets in terms of universal, or biological drives. In consequence, Freud not only fails to discuss politics in general, but he does not notice the specific politics of the family. The

---

[16] Lacan (1986b) suggests that Freud 'feels a sympathy for Herr K' (p. 100). Moi writes of 'Freud's incessant identification with Herr K' (1986, p. 189). Moi claims that Freud's analysis of Dora bears the marks of his fear of losing control (Moi, 1988).

[17] Moi (1986), p. 191. Decker (1991), in her scholarly and judicious analysis of the Dora case, writes that 'Freud's countertransference was broad, including not only unrecognized libidinal involvement, identifications, and discomfort with frank sexuality, but also anger and jealousy' (p. 120).

[18] See, for example, Moi (1986) and Forrester (1990).

Oedipal situation is taken as a universal characteristic, rather than a feature of male-dominated family life. Thus, Jane Gallop, a distinguished feminist critic of Freudian thought, writes of 'the pernicious apoliticism of psychoanalysis'. She claims that 'one of psychoanalysis's consistent errors is to reduce everything to a family paradigm, sociopolitical questions are always brought back to the model father–mother–child'.[19] Toril Moi argues that an understanding of gender politics is vital for any re-analysis of Dora's case, and, for this, one must not 'forget the ideological context of theory'.[20] Freud, Moi suggests, showed himself to be unconcerned about the inequalities of gender. In his treatment of Dora, he was necessarily on the side of oppression, for he was in a 'patriarchal society . . . an educated bourgeois male, incarnating *malgré lui* patriarchal values'.[21]

Freud appears in such critiques as the powerful male, at one with the patriarchal forces of his society. The psychoanalyst is hired by the wealthy industrialist to sort out the girl, not to expose the family relations. Consequently, the doctor conspires with the industrialist, whether knowingly or unknowingly, against the young woman. Freud duly performs the task for which he is being paid. He seeks the origins of Dora's problems in her unconscious fantasies: he wants to know her dreams, whether she masturbated as a young child and so on. Herr K becomes, in Freud's understanding, an object of the girl's desire, not another source of her problems. And Freud, by offering Dora such explanations of her problems, becomes another problem. Thus, critics argue that orthodox psychoanalysis, with its lack of political perspective, cannot understand its own complicity in the operation of social power.

There is much that can be said to support such a general picture. However, something crucial is being omitted. Freud was not a comfortable member of his society. The description 'educated, bourgeois male' neglects a category which was central to Freud's political and social position. He was a member of a much discriminated against minority; and so was Dora. Ultimately both Freud and Dora were to be driven from their society in fear of their lives.

The politics of anti-semitism did not begin in Vienna with the arrival of the Nazis. When Freud and Dora met at the turn of the century, the anti-semitic parties controlled the city. The elected mayor was a notorious demagogue, whose popularity stemmed from his anti-semitic tirades. Neither Toril Moi nor Jane Gallop, in calling for political

---

[19] Gallop (1982), p. 144.
[20] Moi (1986), p. 184.   [21] Ibid., p. 112.

analyses, discuss this political context. Their 'politicizing' of psycho-analysis involves finding the political in the personal, thereby extending the conventional definition of what is political. This concern with the politics of the personal leads them to overlook the more conventional politics of public power. Given the nature of conventional politics in *fin-de-siècle* Vienna, this entails a neglect of the overt politics of race.

It might be thought that there is something curious about a stance that is self-consciously political, but can ignore the party politics of racism. The oddity of this position can be illustrated by a hypothetical parallel, which would be virtually unthinkable in the current intellectual climate. The equivalent would be a radical academic, whose topic is the work of a black male doctor, living under the apartheid regime in South Africa. The academic, being a radical, claims that any discussion of the doctor should be political. Imagine, then, such an academic, in an avowedly political discussion, never once mentioning apartheid – nor, indeed, mentioning the politics of race, nor that the doctor in question was black. Were this to occur, one might suspect something strange was going on. It would be hard to accept that the omissions were haphazard. Nevertheless, this is exactly what is occurring in some current 'politicized' reanalyses of Freud's relations with his patients and his society.

When the political dimension is removed from Dora's life, all that seems to be left is the sad history of her relationships and maladies. Ellie Ragland has recently written that Ida Bauer 'spent the rest of her life going from analyst to analyst, medical doctor to medical doctor, always sick'.[22] She, thereby, repeats 'the image of the old, nagging, whining and complaining Dora', that Moi conveys.[23] This unflattering image of the old Dora is incorrect in its detail: there is little evidence that she was obsessed by ailments, trailing from doctor to doctor.[24] Moreover, the image misses out something so momentous in Dora's life that the omission cannot be attributed merely to a scholarly oversight, as if an index card had been misplaced or a footnote accidentally deleted on a word processor. Dora spent her last years as a refugee. She had fled from the Nazis with her son in late 1938, at almost the last moment when it was possible to do so.[25] The very act, for which no records remain, must have required resourcefulness and spirit, not to mention

[22] Ragland (1996), p. 163.   [23] Moi (1986), p. 192.

[24] As Decker shows, there is scant evidence that Dora spent her adult and elderly years as a continual invalid, seeking medical attention. Deutsch (1986), who is the source of much of the unflattering comments, only saw Dora twice. Dora did not wish to make a further appointment, declaring herself to be cured (Decker, 1991, p. 171).

[25] Decker (1991), chapter 9.

courage.[26] In her final years, the pain of physical maladies must surely have been overshadowed by the pain, not only of exile, but of the knowledge that most of her acquaintances, friends, and relatives had been murdered.

It is necessary to look again at the relations between Freud and Dora with all this in mind. In doing this, the focus is not upon criticizing those feminist reanalyses, which ignore the political context of Freud's life. Indeed, it is to be hoped that following the publication of Hannah Decker's superb *Freud, Dora and Vienna 1900* such neglect will become far less common.[27] There is, however, a wider point. One can ask how the political dimensions can have been so easily overlooked. This question takes us to the heart of psychoanalysis. The issues of forgetting, and the pushing of awkward thoughts from conscious memory, are central to psychoanalytic theory. As feminist critics have argued, psychoanalytic writers themselves, including Freud, often created a forgetfulness: as the personal unconscious is remembered, so politics is forgotten. And, similarly, as the politics of the personal is remembered so the politics of race can be pushed aside.

The dialectic of remembering and forgetting can be examined in relation to language and dialogue. As one matter is spoken (or written) about, so others are kept from immediate dialogic attention. Where topics of conversation become ritual, what is habitually spoken about may be dialogically functioning to prevent, as a matter of routine, other matters from coming to conscious, conversational attention. The dialogues of psychoanalysis need not be excluded. Not only might such dialogues reveal, or express, what is elsewhere repressed, so they might also create their own silences. The 'Fragment' presents an early account of the psychoanalytic dialogue. The text permits us to catch echoes of conversations between Freud and Dora, although the precise words are lost. And so are the notes, which Freud, according to his practice, would have written in the evening after each session and on which he would have based his final, published report. What is reported in the published text can be read for absences. The two speakers can be heard collaborating to avoid the sort of Jewish themes which Freud overtly excludes from his published text.

[26] The sheer difficulties of getting out of Austria are conveyed in horrific detail by Clare (1980).

[27] It may take a while for Decker's historical study to permeate the boundaries of literary criticism. In the same volume as Ragland's (1996) essay, which does not quote Decker, Claire Kahane, one of the editors of the compendium *In Dora's Case*, also ignores Decker's work in her re-examination of Freud and Dora. Kahane concentrates on the relations within the consulting room, where Freud was 'especially empowered' (1996, p. 99).

Background and politics

The 'Fragment' contains no overt signs that the author was Jewish. In this respect, it differs from 'The interpretation of dreams' and 'Jokes and their relation to the unconscious', which were also written during this period. In 'Dreams' Freud analyses a number of his own dreams which have Jewish themes and which he interprets in terms of his Jewish identity. In 'Jokes', he gives numerous examples of Jewish jokes, with enough hints to suggest that he is an 'insider' bearing tales to 'outsiders', although, as will be seen, Freud's presentation of the jokes is not straightforward.

By contrast, the case history of Dora does not even hint that the doctor is Jewish; nor does it indicate that the other main characters – Dora, her family and the K's – were also all Jews. In this regard, the 'Fragment' resembles Freud's other famous case studies of Jewish patients, such as those of Paul Lorenz, the so-called 'Rat Man', and Little Hans. In the case of Lorenz, the process notes contain ample evidence of the patient's Jewishness. There are Yiddish words, which the patient quotes from his relatives, as well as details about his mother's plans for the patient to marry rich, Jewish relatives. In the published case-history, these tell-tale signs have been removed. The case of Little Hans even contains a misleading footnote which might lead the unsuspecting reader to suppose that the young patient was a gentile. Freud draws attention to the link between circumcision and fear of castration. Instead of suggesting that Little Hans's castration fears might be derived from his circumcision, Freud implies that gentiles' awareness of Jewish circumcision might be a cause of anti-semitism.[28] The unstated and misleading implication is that Little Hans might share such a view and, thus, he, too, might be a Christian who fears and despises the circumcision of Jews. The reader of the footnote would not gather that Hans was an already circumcized Jewish boy. Freud does not discuss how Little Hans's circumcision may have contributed to his fear of castration. Certainly, Freud does not mention his own possible role in the circumcision. Freud himself had recommended to Hans's hesitant father that the newly born Hans be brought up as a Jew, with all the implications that such advice had for the issue of circumcision.[29]

Freud's reluctance to indicate the Jewish background of his patients cannot be attributed merely to a desire to preserve the patients' anonymity. In the case of gentile patients, Freud showed little comparative discretion. For example, the case-report of Serge Pankejeff, the so-called

---

[28] 'Analysis of a phobia in a five-year-old boy', *PFL* 8, p. 198n.
[29] Graf (1942).

'Wolf Man', contains ample indicators that the patient was Christian. Freud mentions that the young child, 'was obliged before he went to bed to kiss all the holy pictures in the room, to recite prayers, and to make innumerable signs of the cross upon himself and upon his bed'.[30] No such details are provided about the Lorenz's religious practices, which persisted through adolescence.

Whatever the reasons behind Freud's failure to mention Dora's ethnic background, the omission conveys the rhetorical impression that Jewishness was irrelevant to the themes of the 'Fragment'. It was as if Dora's problems stemmed from her family relations and her own suppressed desires – not from her ethnic background. Similarly, her doctor was offering scientific diagnoses about universal problems and these did not depend upon his particular ethnicity. Thus, the patient's problems and the doctor's analyses are presented in universal terms, as if to a 'universal audience'.[31] Freud's intellectual ambition was to construct psychoanalysis as a universal science, which would apply across culture and history to all humans.

In other political contexts, it might not be particularly significant should a psychoanalyst omit to mention that a patient was, or was not, Jewish. For instance, it might be argued that, for many purposes in anglophone societies today, the Jewish/Christian division does not carry major sociological weight and that in describing psychoanalytic relations the categories can often be omitted without crucial loss of understanding.[32] In this respect, these categories differ from racial categories, such as 'black' and 'white', which continue to have major sociological force, and which, as such, shape personal and interpersonal relations in countless ways.

In turn-of-the-century Vienna, however, the Jewish/Christian division was central, politically, socially and culturally. It fashioned the very conditions of Freud's and Dora's lives, including those moments which they shared in the consulting-room on the Berggasse. In order to illustrate this, a two-step argument is necessary. First, there will be a brief outline of the situation of the Jews in Vienna at that time, and to show how the lives of Freud and Dora fitted this background. It is not enough to say that background factors pushed the two towards each other, at least for a brief period, so that Freud's status as doctor and the patient's choice of physician were shaped by the racial politics of the

---

[30] 'From the history of an infantile neurosis', *PFL* 9, p. 296.
[31] See Perelman and Olbrechts-Tyteca (1971) for a discussion of the concept of the 'universal audience'.
[32] In some circumstances the Jewish identity of patient and doctor might be vital for explaining their interaction. For such an instance in the United States, see Jacobs (1993).

time. A second step in the argument is necessary to show how the background might have come to the foreground as Freud and Dora spoke to one another. The 'Jewish Question' seems to have crept shamefacedly into their conversations, only for them to push it out again in ways which were very much part of the Jewish situation of those times.

To begin with, it is necessary to present a few words about the historical position of the Jews in turn-of-the-century Vienna.[33] For most of the nineteenth century, an ever increasing number of Jews in the Austro-Hungarian empire were leaving the restrictions of ghetto life, and its traditional culture, to join the wider civil society. Emperor Joseph II, in his *Toleranzpatent* of 1782, had at last recognized the Jews as citizens of the empire.[34] Economically successful Jews could reasonably look forward to a progressively assimilated life. This was especially true of the many Jews who had travelled from the outlying areas of the Empire to Vienna. Such was the migration that the Jewish population of Vienna rose from six thousand in the mid-nineteenth century to nearly one hundred and fifty thousand in 1900.[35]

The journey taken by the Freuds was typical of many bourgeois Jews in turn-of-the-century Vienna.[36] Sigmund Freud was born in the mid-nineteenth century in Moravia. His father had been descended from a long line of Chasidic Jews, while his mother came from the ghettos of Galicia.[37] When Sigmund was a young child, the family moved to Vienna, to lead a bourgeois, but not altogether prosperous life. Freud's parents passed down to their children less of their Jewish heritage than they had received from their parents. Sigmund's mother was decidedly anti-religious, while his father ensured that the household at least marked Jewish festivals such as Passover and Purim.[38] In his turn,

---

[33] For more details see, inter alia, Decker (1991), Oxaal et al. (1987), Pulzer (1964), Rozenblit (1983), Schorske (1980) and Wistrich (1989).

[34] Oxaal (1987).

[35] For demographic details, see Pulzer (1964), Rozenblit (1983), Oxaal (1987).

[36] George Clare's family history, wonderfully recounted in *Last Waltz in Vienna*, shows great similarity with the Freuds. Like Freud, Clare came from a bourgeois family which had made its way to Vienna in the mid to late nineteenth century from outlying districts of the Austro-Hungarian empire. Clare's forebears (the Klaars and the Schapiras) like Freud's (the Freuds and the Nathansohns) were moving from ghetto to mainstream European culture.

[37] On the Jewish background of Freud, see Gay (1995); Roith (1987), Yerushalmi (1991). It appears from Freud's letters to his adolescent friend Eduard Silberstein that he was growing up in a family that marked the Jewish festivals with traditional meals (Freud, 1990, pp. 62–3).

[38] See Yerushalmi (1991) and Gay (1995). See Derrida (1996) for a theoretical analysis of, and tribute to, Yerushalmi's analysis of Freud's knowledge of Hebrew, as transmitted from his father.

Sigmund, who had been taught Hebrew as child, was to transmit even less to the next generation.[39] His son, Martin, recounts growing up in a household which celebrated no Jewish festivals and in which the children were not taught to read Hebrew.[40] Nevertheless, as has been pointed out, none of Martha and Sigmund's children converted to Christianity or married Gentiles.[41]

Sigmund belonged to that generation of Viennese Jews, who grew up expecting the old restrictions against Jews to disappear in good time. No position, they believed, would be barred to them in the future. Jews, at least male Jews, might even become political leaders in the new liberal Austria. In a famous phrase, written in the final years of the century, Freud described the hopes of his youth: he wrote that in the 1860s and 1870s 'every industrious Jewish schoolboy carried a Cabinet Minister's portfolio in his satchel'.[42] Many Austrian Jews expressed their optimism by embracing the German culture wholeheartedly, often showing their allegiance by becoming committed pan-German nationalists. Freud, again, was typical. As a first year undergraduate at the University of Vienna in 1878, he joined a pan-German nationalist student society, the Leseverein der deutschen Studenten.[43] Ten years later, he would not have been able to so join. By that time, the nationalist societies were officially excluding Jews.[44]

Hannah Arendt described the Jews of Germany as having an un-requited love affair with German culture.[45] The tragedy for such Jews was that the culture, which they embraced so passionately, was routinely anti-semitic. The same was true for the German-speaking Jews of the Austro-Hungarian Empire. Those, who were enthusiastic to be cultu-rally German, adopted many of that culture's prejudices against things Jewish. The bourgeois, assimilating Jews directed these prejudices against the ghetto Jews from eastern Europe, the *Ostjuden*, who dis-played overt, and shameful, characteristics of Jewishness.[46] Traces of this attitude can be found in Freud's family. A painful early letter to Martha tells of his embarrassment at the funeral of a colleague who had committed suicide. The family mourners were behaving in

---

[39] Yerushalmi (1991). It appears that Freud did not have his three sons circumcized (Ferris, 1997, p. 379).

[40] Martin Freud (1957). Martha, who had a more Jewish upbringing, was always more sympathetic to religious practices than was Sigmund. During their long engagement, she would never write on the Sabbath (Wistrich, 1990). Moreover, it is said that she would have wished to have observed some Jewish practices in the home, but was overruled by Sigmund (Gay, 1995).

[41] Roazen (1974), pp. 47ff.

[42] 'Interpretation of dreams', *PFL* 4, p. 281.

[43] McGrath (1986), pp. 97f.   [44] Scheichl (1987).

[45] See Arendt (1970), pp. 33ff.   [46] Weitzmann (1987).

unconstrained Jewish ways and 'we were all petrified with horror and shame in the presence of the Christians who were among us'.[47] Freud, like many others of his background, enjoyed telling Jewish jokes, which traded on stereotypes of meanness and unclean habits: 'dirty-Jew' jokes were to find their way into Freud's 'Jokes and their relation to the unconscious'. Although the writer clearly presents himself to his readers as a Jew, he is not telling jokes about educated, assimilated Jews like himself. Freud is careful to point out that the jokes refer to Galician Jews and their 'aversion to baths'.[48] Freud's very language distances himself from the subjects of the jokes and their Yiddish punch-lines. As Sander Gilman perceptively comments, Freud 'framed the telling of such stories in the purest of German academic prose'.[49] In 'Interpretation of dreams', Freud went out of his way to present himself to readers, rather implausibly, as someone who has to consult philologists to understand elementary Yiddish words.[50]

A brittle and painful constellation of feelings was involved: the desire

[47] Freud (1960), p. 65.

[48] 'Jokes and their relation to the unconscious', *PFL* 6, pp. 84ff. Freud did not discuss the possibility that his Jewish jokes, being told by a Jew distancing himself from the ghetto world, might resemble the jokes told by 'foreigners'. Personal themes might have been involved in the telling of such jokes. Ernest Jones recalls the poverty of Freud's parents after they had moved to Vienna. Their flat contained no bathroom. When the young Freud was old enough, his mother used to take him fortnightly to the public baths (Jones, 1953, p. 19).

[49] Gilman (1994), p. 37.

[50] Freud discusses the phrase *auf Geseres* as if he needed philologists to tell him the precise meaning ('Interpretation of dreams', *PFL* 4, p. 573). Yerushalmi (1991) points out that it is inconceivable that Freud would not have been familiar with the word, not least from the speech of his own mother. Yet, Freud's public distancing himself from knowledge of Hebrew and Yiddish does create a scholarly problem, which Yerushalmi recognizes. In a letter to Martha, Freud appears to be uncertain of the Hebrew word *menorah* (candlestick) (Freud, 1960, p. 261). Yerushalmi comments that he finds it 'almost impossible to believe that the term was not part of Freud's vocabulary or that he had not seen a menorah in his father's house' (1991, p. 11). After all, as Yerushalmi points out, Freud, in his letters with Martha, showed a detailed knowledge of minor Jewish festivals such as Tisha B'Av. Yerushalmi demonstrates that Freud himself possessed an antique Chanukah menorah. Freud might have wished to distance himself from Hebrew/Yiddish terms in public texts, such as 'Interpretation of dreams', but he would have no such need to do so in a private letter to his wife. If the latter indicates genuine ignorance, then so might the former. Perhaps there is a simple explanation to the mystery. Freud, in writing to Martha, was describing Roman carvings of the seven branched candlestick in the Temple ('I think it's called Menorah', he wrote). He may well have been familiar with the typical nine-candled Chanukah *menorah* (eight branches plus an extra candle), as well as with the word itself. Perhaps he was uncertain whether *menorah* was a technical term for the candle-sticks used in the Chanukah ritual, or whether it could apply to all candlesticks, including the Great Candelabrum of the Temple. It would be characteristic of Freud to express linguistic caution, rather than risk making a bloomer in front of Martha, whose knowledge of such matters would have been more extensive.

to be German, the separation from Jewishness, the association of Jewishness with despised traits, and a recognition that the true Germans would still see Jewishness in themselves, despite their all efforts. At its extreme, this constellation formed the basis of what has become known as 'self-hatred' (*Selbsthass*).[51] Freud was never to deny his Jewishness. If anything his sense of identity was to grow stronger with the increase of anti-semitism.[52] Yet, at the same time, his distancing from the yiddishkeit of the *Ostjuden* was to continue, even as this entailed a distancing from, or denial of, a part of the self. The ambivalence is captured by the opening paragraphs of Freud's autobiographical sketch, published in 1925. He declared in the second sentence about himself: 'My parents were Jews and I have remained a Jew myself.'[53] The third sentence claims German origins: his father's family had lived in Cologne until the fourteenth or fifteenth century, and in the nineteenth century had 'migrated back . . . into German Austria'.[54] About his mother and her family, of whom there could be no tale of German origins, the text is embarrassingly silent.[55]

Freud's mother was, like the subjects of his Jewish bath-house jokes, a Galician. She too possessed traits to be disparaged by those wishing to be absorbed into high German culture. There is evidence that she was a Yiddish speaker, or at least that she spoke German with a pronounced Jewish accent.[56] The writer George Clare, a second generation Viennese Jew, remembers how he grew up to be embarrassed by his grandmother's eastern tones: 'I resented the Yiddish singsong intonation with which (she) spoke German, a 'Yoich' sigh at the start and end of almost every sentence.'[57] It could have been Martin Freud talking of his paternal grandmother: as he was to write, she was a Polish Jew, uncivilized and without manners.[58] The lack of manners was, of course, attributed to her Galician, Jewish nature.

Freud was to say in 1926 that his culture was German and that he considered himself to be German 'until I noticed the growth of anti-

---

[51] On Jewish self-hatred, see Gay (1978); Lewin (1948), pp. 186–200; but see also Janik (1987) for criticisms of the notion.

[52] Gay (1995) and Yerushalmi (1991).

[53] 'Autobiographical study', *PFL* 15, p. 190.   [54] Ibid.

[55] More general factors, beyond the particular position of German Jews, may also have been at play, for Freud was not the only major male figure of the nineteenth century to omit his mother from his autobiography. As Mazlish (1975) shows with great insight, John Stuart Mill also failed to mention his mother. Mazlish outlines the psychodynamic features which may have lay behind Mill's omission.

[56] See Yerushalmi, 1991, p. 69; Roith (1987), p. 97.

[57] Clare (1980), p. 31. Clare was punished by his father if he used inappropriate Yiddish expressions.

[58] Martin Freud (1957), p. 11.

semitic prejudice in Germany and German Austria'.[59] While Freud was an undergraduate, he encountered vociferous prejudice, from what he called 'the compact majority'.[60] At that time, Freud was able to dismiss the bigotry as representing remnants of the old pre-modern era, rather than as a foretaste of things to come. In the 1890s, however, the liberal left was to collapse in Vienna and political anti-semitism was revealed as a growing, not contracting force, with agitation against the Jews gathering pace across the Empire.

In Vienna, the two principal anti-semitic demagogues, Karl Lueger and Georg von Schoenerer, joined forces in 1889 to establish the United Christians. The new organization was designed to defend Christians against 'Jewish domination'.[61] From this union, Lueger developed the Christian Socials, which attracted support principally from Catholics. In 1895 the Christian Socials became the leading party in Vienna. Although the Emperor initially refused to ratify Lueger as mayor, he was forced to do so in 1897, following Lueger's repeated electoral victories. The Christian Socials strengthened their hold on power in the local elections of 1902, when liberals and rival nationalists were comprehensively defeated.[62] Thus, while Dora was being treated by Freud, the city of Vienna was firmly and popularly in the hands of the political anti-semites.[63]

The background of Freud and Dora

Freud's choice of career, and his prospects within that career, were directly affected by anti-semitic discrimination. Freud had originally wished to be a lawyer.[64] Because of discrimination in the legal profession, disproportionately less Jewish graduates entered the law than would be expected.[65] Freud, in common with many other young male Jews, felt there to be more opportunities within medicine. The popularity of medicine for Jews, in its turn, brought a reaction. Senior medical figures were calling for quotas for Jews entering medicine. Lectures by Jewish teachers were boycotted in the university. Promotion was difficult for those Jews, who had managed to enter the profession.

---

[59] Quoted in Gay (1995), p. 448.
[60] 'Autobiographical sketch', *PFL* 15, p. 4.
[61] Pulzer (1964), pp. 177f.   [62] Beller (1987).
[63] When in power, Lueger showed himself to be pragmatic on the issue of anti-semitism, not putting into practice many of his party's anti-semitic policy aims, which might have brought chaos to Vienna. His notorious declaration 'I decide who is a Jew' was said as a counter to those of his supporters who criticized him for associating with wealthy Jews (see, Wistrich, 1990 chapter 4; Pulzer, 1964).
[64] McGrath (1986).   [65] Beller (1987).

In addition, there was the threat of political action. The United Christians had specifically included in its founding programme the policy of excluding Jews from the practice of medicine, as well as other professions.[66]

Freud was under no illusions that his progress in the medical profession was being impeded because he was a Jew. The prestigious fields were dominated by Christians. Psychiatry was, of course, not the most prestigious branch – certainly, senior Christian doctors would not expect to rise to the height of their profession by talking to Jewish girls about sex.[67] If Freud's chosen career, and his speciality within that career, were influenced by discrimination, then so were his prospects for academic advancement. Shortly after Lueger was confirmed as mayor, Freud himself was proposed for promotion to a professorship, which he felt his scientific achievements had long merited. He had little hope of success. As he recounted in 'Interpretation of dreams', he had evidence that others had been refused for 'denominational considerations'.[68] He had no doubt that 'denominational considerations' were being applied in his case too. When he treated Dora, he had already been turned down several times, the last time just a month previously.[69]

Freud's reaction is notable. A growing number of Viennese Jews at that time were responding to discrimination by rejecting their background and seeking conversion to Christianity. One historian has noted that the level of conversion in Vienna at that time was 'an exceptionally high percentage', certainly higher than in other parts of the Austro-Hungarian Empire.[70] Conversion was particularly prevalent among bourgeois assimilating Jews, among whom the Bauers and the Freuds would have counted themselves, especially as parents hoped to provide better prospects for their sons.[71] Freud's philosophy teacher at university, the eminent Franz Brentano, advised his Jewish students to convert to Christianity if they hoped to pursue successful academic careers.[72]

Freud rejected the path of conversion, as one of cowardice: he was not going to share the prejudices of the 'compact majority'.[73] In bitterness, he turned inwards, rejecting the society which was rejecting him. In the

---

[66] Pulzer (1964).

[67] But see Shorter (1992) for an argument that Viennese psychiatry was not over-represented by Jews in comparison with dermatology.

[68] 'Interpretation of dreams', *PFL* 4, p. 218.

[69] Decker (1991), p. 90.

[70] Pulzer (1964), p. 6; Endelman (1989).

[71] See Oxaal (1987), p. 32, for details.

[72] Endelman (1989). For a discussion of Brentano's influence on Freud, see McGrath (1986).

[73] Gilman (1994), p. 93. Freud, in his quarrel with Alfred Adler, added the betrayal of baptism to his psychoanalytic betrayals (Wistrich, 1989, pp. 572–3).

year in which Lueger became Mayor, he joined the Jewish defence and cultural organization, the B'nai B'rith.[74] At the same, he withdrew from membership of academic and medical organizations. He ceased delivering lectures at the University. His only audience, at this time, was the B'nai B'rith, to whom he delivered early drafts of his important theoretical papers and whose sympathetic contact he greatly valued. Years later, he was to write that at that time he felt 'shunned by all', except that 'circle of excellent men' in the Vienna Lodge of the B'nai B'rith.[75] To a large extent, Freud blamed his situation upon the growing forces of anti-semitism. In late 1901 Freud was finally to visit Rome. He wrote to Fliess about his reaction to the sights of the Catholic Rome, as distinct from those of ancient and Italian Rome: 'I could not cast off the thought of my own misery and all the misery I know about.'[76]

Although assimilating Jews, such as the Freuds and the Bauers, might have hoped to have joined mainstream Austrian society, their lives were spent almost entirely amongst other Jews. Gentile Viennese society was unwelcoming and few Jews mixed socially with non-Jews.[77] Freud's daughter, Anna, was to recall that she mixed with non-Jewish girls at school, but was never invited to their homes.[78] One might presume that Dora, who was sent to a convent school, faced similar exclusion.[79] Martin Freud said that he could hardly recall a non-Jewish guest in his parents' home.[80] Freud's own professional relationships followed the pattern of his social ones. His patients and close colleagues were Jewish. In 1902 Freud formed the Wednesday Group, which met at his house to discuss psychoanalytic issues. The early participants of this society, which was later to become the Vienna Psychoanalytic Society, were entirely Jewish. Not until 1906 were there any non-Jewish members.[81]

In short, Dora met Freud at the gloomiest, most isolated point in his life, when he was experiencing a bitter sense of rejection from mainstream, or Christian, Austrian society. If Freud was rediscovering his identity as a Jew, in the face of growing anti-semitism, then this did not entail a rediscovery of traditional Jewish culture. He continued to reject

[74] Klein (1981); Meghnagi (1993).
[75] Freud (1960), p. 367.   [76] Freud (1985), p. 449.
[77] Oxaal (1987); Rozenblit (1983).
[78] Young-Bruehl (1988), p. 47.
[79] Decker (1991).   [80] Martin Freud (1957).
[81] Shorter (1992); Klein (1981) is almost certainly incorrect in stating that, until Jung and Binswinger started attending in 1907, every member of the circle was Jewish. As Shorter shows, Edwin Hollerung and Rudolf Urbantschitsch were participating in 1906 (see also Nunberg and Federn, 1967). By 1910, according to Shorter, the group had six non-Jewish medical members.

religious traditions. His dreams suggest he was experiencing difficulty in divesting himself of the desire to be a genuine German. This can be seen in Freud's famous 'yellow beard dream', dreamt in 1897 in anticipation of being rejected for the professorship. In the dream, one of Freud's friends appears as his uncle with his face surrounded by a yellow beard. Freud's complex interpretation suggested that he wished to put himself in the place of a government minister who had refused promotion to Jewish candidates, including two of Freud's own colleagues.[82] Freud suggests that the underlying theme is his own personal ambition, which dates from childhood, to be a government minister. Freud's explanation omits a crucial implication. If, as his theory was proposing, all dreams express hidden wishes, which are too shameful to admit consciously, then so should this dream be powered by unconscious motives. Consequently, the dream would seem to express more than the desire to be a powerful government minister, which is not exactly a shameful wish and to which the text openly confesses. The dream-logic also suggests the less admissible desire to be German, not Jewish, and, moreover, to be a persecutor of Jews. Freud's published interpretation does not probe these themes.

To put the matter briefly, Freud, like so many of his background was marooned in the worsening climate. There was no going back to the ghetto, or the traditions of Jewish religion; on this issue, he shared many of the prejudices of the compact majority. His culture was German, but, as he realized, this culture was rejecting him. His way forward was the attempt to construct a universal perspective through the science of psychoanalysis. He realized that this universal outlook, which would reject all religions, needed to be created by Jews, but could not be seen to be exclusively Jewish. Hence, it would be unwise to stress the Jewish background of the patients. Certainly, it was common-place among psychiatrists of the time to suppose that Jews were particularly prone to mental illness.[83] The Wednesday group shared this view.[84] Yet, this was not to become a theme in the published writings, as Freud sought to relate the origins of neurosis to universal factors.[85] Above all, Freud was conscious of the need for psychoanalysis to avoid being seen as a 'Jewish science'. He was to write to Karl Abraham in 1908 that 'our Aryan

[82] 'Interpretation of dreams', *PFL* 4, p. 282; for political interpretations of this dream, see Schorske (1980) and McGrath (1986).

[83] See Gilman (1994), pp. 83f and McGrath (1986), p. 151f.

[84] At one meeting in 1907. Max Eitingon asked the question whether the frequency of neurosis was greater among Jews. The minutes record that 'most participants answer "yes" to this question' (Nunberg and Federn, 1967, p. 94).

[85] Gelfand (1992) writes that 'for Freud what was true for the Jew became true for everyone'. (p. 51).

comrades are really completely indispensable to us, otherwise psycho-analysis would succumb to anti-semitism'.[86]

Dora was twenty-six years younger than her doctor, but she was living through similar dilemmas, although born too late to have experienced at first hand the optimism of the seventies. Her parents had come from Bohemia, to which the family periodically returned. Her father retained business interests there, but these were being affected by the growing anti-semitism, which was taking disturbingly dramatic forms.[87] Two years before Dora came to Freud, Leopold Hilsner, a Bohemian Jew living not far from where Dora's mother had grown up, was accused of the ritual murder of a Christian child. The accusation was becoming common. Between 1898 and 1905, the year in which Freud published the 'Fragment', there were thirty different cases of blood libels against Jews in the Austro-Hungarian empire.[88]

Like the Freuds, the Bauers looked towards an assimilated future. Socially they avoided unassimilated *Ostjuden*.[89] Dora's parents observed no religious practices; nevertheless, they made sure that their son, Otto, was circumcised.[90] Dora's older brother, like Freud, sought a way to 'universalize' German culture. Otto's path was socialism, which he combined with a sense of German nationalism. He became one of the leading theoreticians of Austro-Marxism and, later, briefly Foreign Minister of Austria, only to resign when his policy of *Anschluss* with Germany was rejected. His great work *Die Nationalitätenfrage und die Socialdemokratie* (published in 1907) claimed that nations were based upon a psychological sense of 'common-fate'. In his book, Otto expressed sympathy for the nationalist aspirations of the peoples of the Empire. *Die Nationalitätenfrage* has become recognized as the classic work of Marxist theory to take seriously the problem of nationalism, and, as such, it has influenced later works on nationalism.[91] If, according to Otto, the peoples of the old Austro-Hungarian empire could legitimately aspire to nationhood, there was one significant excep-tion. The Jews, he argued, were a 'historyless' people, whose fate lay with the nations in which they lived. For Otto, this meant allegiance to the ideals of Pan-Germanism, interpreted through a socialist frame-work.[92]

---

[86] Abraham and Freud (1965), p. 64.
[87] See Decker (1991) for details of Dora's background.
[88] Wistrich (1989).
[89] Decker (1991), p. 29.   [90] Ibid., p. 28.
[91] For example, Benedict Anderson's (1983) notion of the nation as an 'imagined community' has been much influenced by Bauer's ideas.
[92] See, for example, the extracts in Bauer (1978); and more generally Wistrich (1982) and Loewenberg (1985).

Dora was always to admire her brother, keeping a picture of him in her room.[93] She was to attempt to put into practice what Otto preached in theory: the dissolving of Jewish identity. When Freud published the 'Fragment', he noted that Dora had recently married. The following year Dora gave birth to a son. Almost immediately after the birth, she had her child baptized as a Protestant, while she and her husband also converted.[94] The turn to Protestantism, rather than Catholicism, tended to be the course taken by those Jews who converted for career reasons, rather than factors of faith.[95] In Dora's case, the timing suggests that it was her infant son's future career that concerned her. Perhaps there would have been no conversion had the child been a daughter for whom the parents, following the discriminatory conventions of the time, would have entertained few hopes of a successful career.

Ostensibly, Karl Lueger's party claimed to accept Jewish converts as Christians. Indeed, Hitler, who lived in Vienna between 1907 and 1913, absorbing the anti-semitic atmosphere of the city, was later in *Mein Kampf* to compare Lueger unfavourably with Schoenerer: the latter did not accept Jewish converts to Christianity as Christian.[96] In practice, however, the converts were socially ostracized. One of Lueger's close associates, Ernst Schneider, had publicly recommended in 1901 an improved technique for baptizing Jews: they should be immersed in the baptismal water for a period of five minutes.[97] It was the sort of joke to gain a laugh at that time.

Baptism would not ensure Dora or her family received better treatment in Vienna than did the unbaptized Freud. If Otto believed that the Jews as a non-national people shared no common fate, then the fate of his sister and her famous doctor was to prove him wrong. Years later, Hitler was to be welcomed into Austria, ostensibly to realize the ideal of *Anschluss*, which the young Freud and Otto Bauer had supported in theory. No distinctions, then, were made between male and female, baptized and unbaptized Jew. Freud and Dora, despite differences in fame, achievements, gender and professed identity, were to suffer a common fate. Both were to become refugees, Freud fleeing to Britain and Dora to the States, as their familiar world was violently destroyed.

---

[93] For details, see Decker (1991). Loewenberg (1985) suggests that Otto, in return, kept a large picture of Dora in his room and that Dora always held up Otto as 'the ego ideal' to her own son (p. 193).
[94] Decker (1991), p. 127.
[95] Endelman (1989).
[96] Hitler (1974 edn), p. 110. It has been said that Hitler learnt his techniques of propaganda from Lueger and took his racist ideology from Schoenerer (Wistrich, 1990).
[97] Wistrich (1989), p. 222.

Christmas for Freud and Dora

The background factors suggest why Freud became a doctor, not a lawyer; why, like his mentor Josef Breuer, he was specializing in nervous ailments; why Philip Bauer might have chosen Freud, rather than any gentile specialist; why Dora might have been isolated with few friends of her own age. The background details may help to understand how Dora and Freud happened to meet when they did. Similarly, the background might also explain, as Hannah Decker suggests, why young Jewish women, suffering from double discrimination, might be particularly vulnerable to mental illness in general, and the diagnosis of hysteria in particular. However, 'background', if it is to be socially important, cannot remain as background all the time: it must intrude upon foreground. As far as the conversations between Freud and Dora are concerned, one would need to know whether 'Jewish themes' were discussed or whether, just as importantly, they were avoided; and if they were avoided, then how was this managed. No substantiated record of the conversations exists, for all that survive are Freud's reconstructed fragments, which are employed to tell their own particular stories.

These fragments indicate that Freud directed the conversation to the personal, not the political – that is, of course, to Dora's personal world, not to his own intimate life. As feminist scholars have been pointing out, Freud made no effort to make the personal political. Nor does he seem to have made the political personal. Decker remarks that there is no evidence that Freud and Dora talked about the Hilsner case nor about the boycotts of Jewish shops that were taking place in Vienna; nor even about Dora's feelings about being Jewish.[98] This is not altogether surprising. There is evidence that educated Jews of the time often avoided talking about such matters. The leading liberal newspaper of Vienna, which Freud, and no doubt, the Bauers read, tended not to comment on anti-semitic outrages, despite (or perhaps, because of) having Jewish editors.[99]

Just because speakers happened not to speak of a particular topic does not of itself indicate that they were unconsciously avoiding that topic. Extra signs would be required and to obtain these one would generally need to examine just the sort of details, which Freud omits as irrelevant to his story about the discovery of Dora's hidden (personal) desires. Freud's 'Fragment', like his other case-histories, leaves out the routine,

---

[98] Decker (1991), pp. 126f.

[99] For *Neue Freie Presse* and its avoidance of reporting anti-semitism, see Wolff (1988). In 'Psychopathology of everyday life', Freud quotes from an article published in the paper in August 1900 (*PFL* 5, pp. 100–1).

banal elements of his conversations with patients. The greetings, the small talk, the ways of saying goodbye – all these are gone. Instead, the case-histories aim to preserve the psycho-dynamically dramatic features – the reports of dreams, the slips of the tongue, the vehement denials and so on. In so doing, the reports suggest that the conversationally banal has little to do with the business of repression and its exposure. Yet, the conversationally banal, even in psychoanalytic dialogues, can fulfil repressive functions.

Freud, in reporting his conversations with Dora's case, presents himself and his patient as bourgeois figures, with nothing marking them as members of a discriminated against minority. We do not know whether they spoke 'formally', as if respectable Austrians, repressing the 'ethnic' intonations, expressions and other give-away signs of the Jewish *Mauscheln*.[100] There is evidence that Freud switched his talk, when addressing specifically Jewish audiences as compared with more general ones. His published version of 'Death and Us' omits the Jewish asides and jokes to be found in the earlier version, which he used as a lecture to the B'nai B'rith.[101] In his correspondence with Jewish friends, Freud would include occasional Yiddishisms, such as, for example, the word *meschugge* in the letter to Fliess of 12 December 1897.[102] If there were moments when Freud and Dora spoke in ways, which well attuned eavesdroppers might have characterized as Jewish, then no hint reaches the 'Fragment'. On the other hand, if they did not so speak, then this too says something of the formality in which the doctor and patient conversed about matters of sexual delicacy. Particularly, it would indicate how Jews of their time and class would assume that 'proper', 'polite' speech, even between Jews, should adopt the tones of gentiles.

Freud's fragmentary record can be searched for clues. Small dialogic scraps, to which Freud attached little psychoanalytic significance, may indicate conversational presences and absences. For the present, one tiny phrase in the 'Fragment' will be noted. It is a phrase which easily escapes attention and which is used in relation to the second of Dora's two dreams, analysed by Freud in detail. If the phrase is examined closely, other considerations, which the text glosses over, come to the

---

[100] See Cuddihy (1987) for a discussion of Jewishness and psychoanalytic discussion; see also Gilman (1994), chapter 1.

[101] Freud (1993).

[102] Freud (1985), p. 286. Yerushalmi (1991) counts thirteen different Yiddish words in his published letters (p. 69). There are a couple more in the process-notes of the 'Rat Man' case, although these are used in reporting the words of the patient, who was, in his turn, reporting the words of relatives. Significantly, the 'Death and Us' talk, given to the B'nai B'rith contains no Yiddish, but three Latin quotations.

surface, opening up a pattern of avoidance in relation to this second dream.

The dream starts with Dora, wandering in a strange town. Freud, in conformity with his approach outlined in 'Interpretation of dreams', makes a connection with the dream-location and events of the previous days. He states that 'at Christmas she had been sent an album from a German healthy-resort, containing views of the town'. In the context of the report, 'at Christmas' is an unimportant phrase. The German ('*zu den Weihnachtsfeiertagen*') suggests that the gift was given for 'the Christmas celebration', and, thereby, that it was a Christmas present.[103] The phrase appears to set the scene, but not have any intrinsic significance. The Christmas gift was to trigger off psychoanalytically interesting connections, but these relate to the gift rather than to Christmas. Readers, on their way to meatier aspects of the report, need not pause. The very unimportance of the phrase rhetorically conveys a message to the reader about the characters in the text. These are people – doctor and patient – for whom the giving of presents for the Christmas holiday is entirely 'natural'. Readers, too, are expected to share this sense of Christmas being a 'natural' festival to celebrate.

By its unobtrusiveness, the phrase blurs the position of the protagonists, positioning them firmly within the German, or rather Christian, culture, whose calendar 'naturally', or secularly, commemorates the birth of Jesus. Freud himself and Dora's parents would have almost certainly belonged to the first generation of Freuds and Bauers to celebrate the festival. Although today we know that Sigmund and his family used to celebrate Christmas – and so apparently did the Bauers – neither Dora nor Sigmund may have known for certain that the other did.[104] After all, Dora was talking to a respected member of the B'nai B'rith. Perhaps, there were subtle conversational manoeuvres to establish exactly where on the trajectory between ghetto and assimilation their respective households stood regarding the matter of Christmas. Of course, the crucial banal moments of the dialogue are irredeemably lost.

We do not know how the last session before Christmas ended – whether they wished each other a 'happy Christmas' or offered the more ambiguous 'happy holiday'; and what negotiated steps might have led to a mutual greeting, which could be uttered without the risk of embarrassment. Perhaps the matter was left in polite silence, as Freud and Dora

---

[103] 'Fragment of an analysis of a case of hysteria', *PFL* 8, p. 135; *GW* 5, p. 258.

[104] Martin Freud (1957) records that the family, including his paternal grandmother, celebrated Christmas as a family event (p. 11). For evidence that the Bauers likewise celebrated Christmas, see Decker (1991), p. 28. Ernest Jones records that the Wednesday Society in its earliest years, used to arrange a social evening just before Christmas (1955), p. 10.

arranged the next appointment without alluding to the reasons for the gap in their sessions. If the matter had been left unspoken, then was Dora embarrassed later to mention her Christmas present? Did Freud, by nods and smiles, reassure her as she spoke. We cannot know.

We can, however, see that the matter of the Christmas greeting was not simple for assimilated Jews like Freud. In his correspondence with Jewish friends, the letters of late December preserve the subtleties of manoeuvre surrounding the assimilating Jew's Christmas celebrations. Some letters mention Christmas; some offer explicit Christmas greetings; and some cover the festival in silence. In the case of Freud's correspondence with Wilhelm Fliess, it is the latter who, apparently, takes the first move towards the Christmas greeting. Fliess, the more established man, early in the correspondence, gives Freud a present in late December. Freud, in his thanks, specifically accepts the present as a Christmas gift.[105] Thereafter they are at ease with Christmas greetings and occasional Yiddishisms.

With Karl Abraham, a younger colleague, just a few years older than Dora, it is different. Freud in 1907, early in their relationship, acts as Fliess had to him: he gives Abraham a late December gift, after Abraham had visited him in Vienna. Freud arranges for the present to be left in Abraham's hotel, rather than giving it to him directly. Presumably, the present is not presented unambiguously as a Christmas gift and the recipient has a choice of interpretation. Abraham replies to Freud differently than had Freud to Fliess. In his letter of 21 December, Abraham thanks Freud, but does not describe the present as a Christmas gift.[106] So the pattern of subsequent December letters is set. Freud edges politely towards the possibility of offering Christmas greetings, but Abraham, just as politely, ignores the advances, offering only wishes for the New Year. Once, and only once – in 1916 – Freud actually offers 'my best wishes for Christmas'.[107] The wish is unacknowledged and unreturned. As if admitting his solecism, Freud two years later writes to Abraham on 25 December without even mentioning the public holiday.[108] Finally, after Abraham has tragically and prematurely died on 25 December 1925, Freud, writing in sympathy to his widow, makes no mention of the particular date of death.

Dora and Freud only used the spoken word, and so their Christmas talk is unpreserved. All we know is that Dora mentions to Freud that she has received a particular Christmas present and Freud reproduces this in the 'Fragment', as if no significance should be attached to the fact.

---

[105] See Freud's letter of 28 December 1887 (Freud, 1985, p. 16).
[106] Abraham and Freud (1965), p. 14.
[107] Ibid., p. 244.　　[108] Ibid., pp. 282–3.

Thus, Freud conveys the pattern of the conversations: they talk openly of sex and he draws attention to their modern daring. They mention Christmas presents, but he draws no attention to this bit of modern emancipation.

Madonna and the nodal moment

Freud presents the conversations between himself and Dora as revelatory dialogues, which uncover what has been hidden in relation to the patient's repression. The question must be asked whether the talk, which ostensibly recovers what has been buried by repression, may itself have been accomplishing other forms of repression. If that happened, then the record of the talk should contain evidence of social taboos which are keeping some topics from the conversational agenda. It is necessary to show how speakers collaborated discursively to create an avoidance. For this purpose, what can be called 'nodal moments' are crucial. These are moments in the dialogue, when the conversation could move – indeed, it seems to be moving – towards a topic under taboo. If there is avoidance, then one would expect to see how the conversationalists combined to push away the threatening topic, perhaps displaying signs of embarrassment as the conversation is saved from advancing towards uncomfortable matters.

From Freud's account of the conversations, Dora appears ready to talk and to argue. She is not fazed by the sexual topics. The doctor offers his diagnoses of hidden desires, and the young girl, far from outwardly acquiescing, or lapsing into embarrassed silence, readily disagrees. The more Dora protested, the more confident Freud was, for, as he wrote, 'repression is often achieved by means of excessive reinforcement of the thought contrary to the one which is to be repressed'.[109] Dora is prepared to be ironic. When Freud interprets the jewel-case, which appears in her first dream, in terms of female genitalia, she comments 'I knew *you* would say that.'[110] She has understood the conversational game; and she goes along with it, partially.

The 'Fragment' describes one moment when the conversation seems to be in difficulty. Significantly the nodal moment does not concern sex. Freud asks a question, which threatens to raise sensitive Jewish issues and Dora appears stuck for an answer. There was a pause – a moment of embarrassment. The nodal moment passed. The talk safely returned to sexual matters.

---

[109] 'Fragment of an analysis of a case of hysteria', *PFL* 8, p. 89. See the previous chapter for an extended discussion of Freud's notion of resistance.
[110] Ibid., p. 105, emphasis in original.

This key moment occurred just after Christmas during Freud's interpretation of the second dream. As has been mentioned, the dream-story begins with Dora walking in a strange town. She wishes to return home because she had heard that her father is ill. She meets a young man, who offers to accompany her to the railway station. She cannot reach the station. The dream ends with Dora back home; her father is dead and the maid tells her that her mother is out with 'the others' at the cemetery. There is a coda, which Dora apparently forgot when she first told Freud of the dream, but which she added subsequently. Dora climbs the stairs to her bedroom and reads 'not the least sadly' from a big book.[111]

Freud describes his analysis of the dream, but admits that he is unsure of 'the order in which my conclusions were reached'.[112] As he stressed in 'Interpretation of dreams', events of the preceding day or days can trigger off the content of dream-stories. The interpretation, presented in 'Fragment', begins with the theme of wandering in the strange town. The theme, as Freud claimed was 'overdetermined', in that it combined very recent events, more distant ones and, of course, repressed desires and memories.[113] The recent events included Dora's Christmas present, the photograph album, which a young man had sent her. The town square, which Dora dreamt about, was in one of the photos. Freud, in his interpretation, attaches no significance to the Christmas aspect. His 'picklocks' are designed to open the closed doors of sexual taboo.

Freud claimed that there was another trigger for the dream. He connects her dream of being in a strange town with an event the day before, when Dora had offered to show a visiting young cousin around Vienna. This reminded her of a previous visit to Dresden, when another cousin had wished to show her around the art gallery. She declined the offer, and went alone. As Dora told Freud, she stood for two hours in front of Raphael's picture of the Madonna.

At this point, Freud asks an apparently innocent, indeed obvious, question. And Dora cannot answer:

When I asked her what had pleased her so much about the picture she could find no clear answer to make. At last she said: 'The Madonna.[114]

This is the nodal moment. Dora is in dialogic difficulty. It cannot be known exactly how she conveys her lack of clear answer. Does she offer unclear, mumbled ones, which Freud interrogates? Does she look down in silence? Does Freud repeat the question, when no answer is forth-coming? None of this can be known. What we do know is that Dora, in

---

[111] Ibid., pp. 133–4.   [112] Ibid., p. 134.
[113] Ibid., p. 135.   [114] Ibid., p. 136.

reacting to the question, gives the sort of response which, as conversation analysts suggest, indicates that the speaker has difficulty in providing a ready (or 'preferred') answer to the question.[115]

From a psychoanalytic perspective, one might have thought that the reluctance to reply indicated a resistance, signifying a conflict between social convention and a desire which cannot be openly admitted. What is extraordinary is that Freud draws no attention to Dora's difficulty. Nor, it appears, did he probe the matter with Dora. As Freud writes, the association with Dresden was 'a nodal point in the network of her dream-thoughts'.[116] The nodal point in Freud's analysis leads back to sexual issues. Freud makes the connection with station (*Bahnhof*), box, and woman: 'the notions begin to agree better', he comments at the end of the paragraph.[117] The nodal connection helps the nodal moment to pass. The conversation, and the interpretations, move back towards sex. Things begin to agree better. But something has remained unexpressed.

Freud does not leave the issue of Madonna totally without interpretation. He offers a footnote. In confining the matter to a footnote, he textually downgrades the significance of the theme. Moreover, his interpretation is implausible as an explanation of Dora's reluctance, or inability, to explain what she liked about the picture. But, then, it is not offered as an explanation: Dora's failure to answer readily is not presented as a problem in need of explanation. Nor is the two hours in front of a single picture.

The footnote concentrates upon the sexual aspect. Here, Freud suggests that Dora identified with the 'Madonna', who 'was obviously Dora herself'.[118] He adds that the Madonna is 'a favourite counter-idea in the minds of girls who feel themselves oppressed by imputations of sexual guilt – which was the case with Dora'.[119] The term counter-idea (*Gegenvorstellung*) suggests that a socially acceptable image takes the place of another less admissible one. An identification with the virgin mother enables young girls to fantasize motherhood without appearing to fantasize sexual relations. The resulting identification is chaste and socially acceptable. Freud added in his footnote that, had his analysis with Dora continued, her 'maternal longing for a child would have probably been revealed as an obscure though powerful motive in her behaviour'.[120]

These remarks are curious. Superficially they seem to explain why the symbol of the Madonna appeals to young girls. However, as an explana-

---

[115] On the notion of conversational preference, see Pomerantz (1984), Bilmes (1987) and Nofsinger (1991).

[116] 'Fragment of an analysis of a case of hysteria' ', *PFL* 8, p. 136.   [117] Ibid.

[118] Ibid., p. 145n.   [119] Ibid.   [120] Ibid.

tion of Dora's behaviour, and particularly of her reluctance to admit the identification, they are completely unconvincing. Freud is suggesting that the Madonna provides a cultural symbol into which socially unacceptable sexual desires can be channelled in an acceptable manner. Accordingly, Freud's question about what attracted Dora to the picture was inviting a socially 'preferred' response: she needed only voice a 'favourite counter-idea', which functions to dispel guilt and which was presented in a famous gallery as a respectable icon of high culture. Educated young women need not be ashamed to visit galleries and to admire the image of the chaste Madonna. Why should a young woman, who regularly looked after the Ks' young children, be ashamed to admit her attraction to the image of a young mother and baby? Why, indeed, should she be ashamed of her own wishes for a baby, for such wishes carry the full force of cultural conservatism behind them?

The simple fact is that Freud's account omits something obvious and unspoken. Dora is a Jewish girl, staring for two hours at the image of Madonna and Jesus. If she identifies with the Madonna, then she is identifying with the mother of Jesus and with the Christians, who, in the context of Lueger and his Christian Socials, were oppressing in the name of Christianity both doctor and patient, and practically everyone they both knew. The logic of Dora's alleged identification with the Madonna, which is contained in that two hour stare, is that she dreams of being a Christian mother – as, indeed, she was to become in the year following the publication of the 'Fragment'. Thus, Dora, like Freud in his dream of the yellow-beard, was edging towards admitting an identification with the oppressor.

It makes little sense to imagine that Freud would have been incapable of making such connections. As his letter to Fliess nine months later indicated, Freud associated the symbols of Catholicism with his own miseries. In addition, Freud knew the picture in question. Seventeen years earlier, also in late December, he had visited the same art gallery in Dresden. He had written to Martha, who was then his fiancée, about the visit. He had spent an hour in the whole gallery, and, amongst other pictures, he had looked at, was Raphael's Madonna. The religious themes did not escape him then. He was acutely aware that he was looking as a Jew at Christian art. He compared the depictions of divinity in the various paintings, including Raphael's. Commenting on Titian's 'Maundy Money', he wrote that 'this head of Christ, my darling, is the only one that enables even people like ourselves to imagine that such a person did exist'.[121]

---

[121] Freud (1960), p. 82, letter dated 20 December 1883.

Dora sees Raphael's Madonna and is captured by it, in a way which the young Freud had not been, but the doctor, who pursues so many other desires, lets this one pass. Textually, his footnote brushes aside the matter. Identification with the religion of the oppressor was a topical, even poignant issue. Practically every well-to-do Viennese family at that time had one member, who had converted or was contemplating conversion.[122] The issue could split families. Martha's uncle, Michael, had converted and then been shunned by the rest of the family.[123] The Zionists were publishing 'lists of shame', giving the names of Jews who had betrayed their people by converting.[124] So many painful themes, touching on guilt, betrayal and cowardice, beckoned, should the topic have been pursued. Neither Freud nor Dora seem to have pushed the matter in the original conversation; and certainly Freud does not do so in his published text.

Freud had asked his question what she liked about the picture. An answer was demanded. At last (*endlich*), the brief, unelaborated answer comes. Freud does not want to follow up the matter. For once, he attaches no significance to a failure to answer a simple question. Instead, he directs the readers of the 'Fragment' back to sexual themes. Thus, the nodal moment is circumvented both conversationally and then later textually.

Still not noticing

Readers of the 'Fragment' have often allowed their critical attention to be guided by the author's own stage-management of the scenes which he is depicting. They might remember Dora's two-hour gaze, but overlook her hesitation in answering Freud's simple question. Even feminist thinkers, who have criticized Freud's attempts to control the conversations with Dora, have themselves followed Freud's directions in this matter. There is, however, an obvious difference. Whereas Freud claimed to see in the stare a repressed sexual fantasy for the male phallus, some feminists celebrate an absence of phallus. For them, Dora's stare represents a woman enjoying the company of women, as well as the image of motherhood without fathers. Dora is identifying with the woman, who did not need a phallus to become a mother. If this

---

[122] Endelman (1989).

[123] Jones (1953), p. 112. Martha herself had been forbidden by her family from attending a lecture given by her Christian uncle, who was a distinguished scholar. Grinstein (1990) suggests that Freud's yellow beard dream may have been stimulated by thoughts about how much easier life would have been had he converted to Christianity like Martha's uncle (pp. 65ff).

[124] Decker (1991), p. 249n.

is all that is seen in the scene with the Madonna, then critics fail to see in Dora a Jew staring at the mother of Jesus.

Mary Jacobus, in her book *Reading Woman*, suggests that Dora was attracted by the figure of Madonna as 'the only consecrated version of femininity available to her'.[125] Jacobus does not add the consecration was not available in her own tradition: it was only available, if she forsook her people and joined a dominating majority, which, in any case, would never truly accept her. Jacobus comments that 'if Dora identified with the Madonna, it was in order to represent herself as the sexual innocent'.[126] Thus, the politics of race are omitted. Maria Ramas claims that she is looking at the case of Dora 'with feminist eyes'.[127] She does not mention the Jewish identity of the protagonists. When she mentions Dora looking at the Madonna, she sees the denial of the phallus.[128] The religious theme and its political aspects are not mentioned. Similarly, Ellie Ragland suggests that Dora, by identifying with the Madonna, sees herself as 'blameless, a victim, a martyr, a *belle âme*, a sufferer who believes herself morally superior to others'.[129] She does not consider the ethnic theme, which would hardly characterize the identification as blameless, morally superior and siding with victims.

These interpretations assume that the main feature of the two-hour stare is that a young girl is identifying with a woman, thereby excluding in her imagination the influence of males. John Forrester takes this line. He claims that the key to understanding the stare is 'communication between women' and that in the Fragment 'the Madonna is the pivot around which the shift from the masculine to the feminine takes place'.[130] According to Forrester, Dora 'experiences complete gratification contemplating the image of the Madonna'.[131] Freud, owing to his countertransferences and his insistence on the importance of the male, cannot understand this; and, indeed, he does not wish to, for it threatens his authority. This type of explanation, like Freud's own explanation, overlooks Dora's difficulty in answering the seemingly simple question. If she has obtained such complete gratification – if she sees the image as so blameless and morally superior – why cannot she say so?

Mary Jacobus bases her analysis on Julia Kristeva's discussion of the image of the Madonna. For Kristeva, the Madonna represents motherhood and, in this respect, Christianity comes closer to pagan beliefs with its 'pre-conscious acknowledgement of a maternal feminine', as contrasted with 'Judaic rigour'.[132] Freud, according to Kristeva, offers 'only

---

[125] Jacobus (1987), p. 138.   [126] Ibid., p. 141.
[127] Ramas (1983), p. 74.   [128] Ibid., p. 101.
[129] Ragland (1996), p. 163.   [130] Forrester (1990), p. 56.
[131] Ibid., p. 50.   [132] Kristeva (1986), p. 177.

a massive *nothing'* on the experiences of motherhood.[133] Kristeva makes some comparisons which should be disturbing: maternal, affective Christianity is being contrasted favourably with paternal, rigorous Judaism. According to this logic, it should be no wonder the young girl gazes longingly at the Madonna – and no wonder the Jewish doctor can offer nothing. The resulting analyses of Dora and Madonna, bear uncomfortable, unconscious echoes of Dora's own cultural climate. The symbols of Christianity are presented as desirable. They offer the Jew something better than the Judaic tradition. The analysis seems to celebrate the moment when the Christian images, backed by centuries of cultural and political domination, work their magic over the mind of the young Jewish woman.[134]

The notable French feminist writer Hélène Cixous has written of her own identification with Dora, seeing the latter's hysterical symptoms as a revolt against the constrictions of patriarchy. In a much-quoted passage in *The Newly Born Woman*, Cixous declared that 'the hysterics are my sisters' and that 'I am what Dora would have been if women's history had begun.'[135] Earlier in the book, Cixous discusses her own background and declares 'I am a Jewish woman'.[136] Yet, she does not see Dora specifically as a *Jewish* sister. Cixous thinks 'the famous scene of the Madonna was terrific.' She continues: 'It is the capacity for an adoration that is not empty – it is the belief in the possibility of such a thing.'[137] In one respect, Cixous is right: the adoration is not empty. However, Cixous seems not to notice the obvious content of the adoration, nor its political and historical context. The consequence is that a Jewish author rejoices in the image of a young Jew staring in adoration at the image of Jesus.[138]

Cixous has not invented her own failure of attention. She is following other examples, including the example of that nodal moment, when Freud and Dora rescued themselves by talking of sex and by dialogically repressing other pressing themes. One might think of the original

---

[133] Ibid., p. 179, emphasis in original.

[134] Lacan's explanation of the stare also overlooks the Jewish dimension. He suggests that Dora 'in her long meditation before the Madonna' is being 'driven toward the solution Christianity has given to this subjective impasse, by making the woman the object of divine desire' (1986b, p. 99). He does not comment on the nature of a Christian 'solution' for a Jewish girl in a deeply anti-semitic society.

[135] Cixous and Clément (1986), p. 99.

[136] Ibid, p. 71.   [137] Ibid, p. 155.

[138] Schiach (1989) points to an interesting difference between Cixous's later plays and her two Freudian plays, *Le Nom d'Oedipe* and *Portrait de Dora*. The Freudian plays offer no political context in contrast with the plays set in North Africa or Indo-China, where Cixous represented 'the process of differentiation in more social terms' (p. 165). To have depicted Freud and Dora in relation to 'the process of differentiation' would have entailed portraying the context of anti-semitism.

moment as accomplishing a primary repression. As Freud's report becomes a classic and as commentators criticize this classic, so secondary and tertiary repressions are accomplished. The association between the Madonna and Christianity continues to be left ignored or unexplored. The stress on the personal as the relevant form of politics permits the historical association between Christianity and the politics of the Christian Socials to disappear in this context. Instead, the words of analysis arrange themselves into a matrix of 'Dora', 'mother', 'sexual desire' 'feminine' and 'identification'. With this verbal habit, something is forgotten: the 'Jew' continues to be dialogically repressed.

The dream's missing interpretation

Freud viewed his analysis of Dora's two dreams as central to the case. As he wrote in the preface, he originally intended to call the paper 'Dreams and Hysteria'.[139] He wrote to Fliess, on finishing the early draft of the manuscript, that he considered the analysis to be 'a continuation' of 'The interpretation of dreams'. He explained that 'it is a fragment of an analysis of a case of hysteria in which the explanations are grouped around two dreams'.[140] If Freud himself gave special status to the dreams, then this is reason enough, when looking for gaps in his analysis, to pay close attention to his interpretation of the dreams. In particular, the second dream, whose interpretation begins with Christmas and Madonna, can be re-analysed. In recent years, some analysts have offered alternative interpretations, in order to reconstruct Dora's state of mind.[141] There is another reason for reinterpretation. This is to understand the repressed elements of Freud's thinking, rather than Dora's mentality. Here, the attention should shift from the unconscious motives behind Dora's dream to the assumptions behind Freud's interpretation of that dream – and, most particularly, to the themes which were being repressed by such assumptions.

Two considerations should be borne in mind, when considering whether Freud's unspoken themes are repressed, rather than merely unspoken. First, we know Freud's great sensitivity to allusions and his genius for connecting seemingly disparate themes. In this task, he is theoretically committed to the notion of 'overdetermination': one set of

---

[139] Freud, 'Fragment', *PFL* 8, p. 39.
[140] Freud (1985), p. 433.
[141] See, for instance, Blum (1994); McCaffrey (1984). Blum's interpretation focuses on Jewish themes. His concern, however, is not to examine what Freud omits, but what may have been running through Dora's unconscious, particularly in relation to self-hatred and her wish to leave the Jewish people and convert to Christianity. Blum sees her first dream as a precursor to the Holocaust.

connections does not rule out others. Theoretically, the sexual signifi-
cances, which Freud finds in Dora's dreams, should not preclude other
sets of meanings. There is a second consideration. We also know that, at
the time of seeing Dora, Freud was preoccupied with his position as a
Jew in an inhospitable society. He was turning away from an innocent
identification with German culture. Given this preoccupation, and given
Freud's unsurpassed talent for interpretation, his failure to develop
'Jewish' themes, which lie near the surface of the dream, is surprising.
This is particularly so because the themes of Madonna and Christmas
are evoked at the start, together with his patient's resistance to answering
a simple question connected directly with the Madonna.

In her dream, Dora is wandering in a strange country. She hears that
her father dies and she seeks the railway station in order to return home.
Freud suggests that Dora is fantasizing revenge against her father.
Freud's language at this point is almost biblical in its simplicity: 'she had
left home and gone among strangers, and her father's heart had broken
with grief and with longing for her'.[142] Freud's language echoes wider
stories: the children of Israel dwelling among strangers and, more
germane to Freud's times, daughters breaking their fathers' hearts by
marrying outside the traditional faith. The latter theme connects death
and sex. Freud would have known that orthodox Jews often go into a
formal state of mourning when a close relative marries a non-Jew.[143]
The dream also expresses the fantasy of being free to marry the stranger,
should the father die. Dora is dreaming of meeting a man in the strange
country – in thick woods. Freud concentrates upon the symbolism of
the woods, not whether the stranger symbolizes a Christian, who could
be married if the ancestral restrictions were disposed of.

Dora's dream-story continues with her asking the stranger to direct
her to the station, which she is unable to reach. Freud makes little of the
train symbolism. Sander Gilman has argued that train journeys had
particular significance for Austrian Jewry. They provided one of the few
occasions for social contact with non-Jews; as such, 'confrontations with
anti-Semites took place on trains'.[144] Again, there were thematic connections which Freud could have made. Freud himself had suffered a
particularly nasty experience some years earlier, to which he alludes
briefly in 'Interpretation of dreams'.[145] The incident has a further
connection with Raphael's picture of the Madonna. It happened when

---

[142] 'Fragment of an analysis of a case of hysteria', *PFL* 8, p. 137.
[143] If for no other reason, Freud would have been aware of this from the reaction of the
Bernays family to the apostasy of Martha's uncle, Michael (Grinstein, 1990, p. 66).
[144] Gilman (1993), p. 126.
[145] 'Interpretation of dreams', *PFL* 4, p. 304.

he was travelling to Dresden, the time he visited the art gallery and wrote to Martha about his reactions to Raphael's picture.[146] Even if Freud made such connections mentally, he kept them from the report and, presumably, from the analysis itself.

Dora, in her dream, does not take the train, but she is suddenly home. Her father is dead; the family is at the cemetery. Freud does not offer the wish to assimilate as an interpretation: to run away with a non-Jewish man, to kill her father, but not be responsible for his death. Instead, with typical brilliance, he pursues the allusions inwards. He connects station, cemetery and sexuality. The words *Bahnhof* (station) and *Friedhof* (cemetery), as Freud wrote, directed 'my awakened curiosity to the similarly formed *Vorhof* ["vestibulum"; literally, "forecourt"] – an anatomical term for a particular region of the female genitalia'.[147] Freud adds, in a footnote, that a station is used for *Verkehr* (traffic or sexual intercourse).

Freud does not pick up on Dora's phrase that the mother and the others had gone to the cemetery (*auf dem Friedhofe*).[148] As significant as the word *Friedhof* is the use of the definite article. It is *the* cemetery. Then, as now, Jews and Christians were buried separately; even an irreligious Jew, like Dora's father, would be expected to be buried in the Jewish cemetery. For a Jew, talking of the funeral of another Jew, *the* cemetery would be assumed to be the Jewish cemetery. Any other cemetery would need to be linguistically marked: e.g. 'the Catholic cemetery' or 'the Protestant cemetery'.[149] The dream story, by its routine language, implies that Dora's father is being given a Jewish burial. None of this outwardly appears in Freud's text. Nor does Freud do anything to recover the implicit meaning. He does not appear to have asked Dora to specify in which cemetery was her father being buried. Nor, in the 'Fragment', are readers invited to notice the insignificant definite article.[150]

As has been mentioned, Dora added a coda about reading a big book in her bedroom, 'not the least sadly'. Freud's interpretation seeks sexual

---

[146] Freud (1960), pp. 92–3.
[147] 'Fragment of an analysis of a case of hysteria', *PFL* 8, p. 139.
[148] *GW* 5, p. 137.
[149] For a discussion of the routine use of the definite article, see Billig (1995) chapter 5.
[150] It might be objected that this interpretation places too much on the definite article. In Vienna, middle class Jews would be buried in the Jewish section of Vienna's Central Cemetery (Clare, 1980, p. 101). '*The* cemetery' could be understood to refer to the Central Cemetery, which includes Jewish and Christian graves. However, the speakers would understand that Dora's father would be buried in the Jewish section: for Jewish speaker's *the* cemetery would refer to the specially sectioned Jewish part of the general burial ground.

significance. He asks Dora whether the big book may have been printed in 'encyclopedia format'.[151] She said it was. According to Freud, children read encyclopedias to find sexual knowledge. Freud adds a further footnote to suggest that Dora 'on another occasion' substituted the word 'calmly' for 'not the least sadly'.[152] He offers a sexual interpretation: children never read 'calmly' about sex from encyclopedias, because they fear being interrupted by their parents. In the dream, Dora can read calmly 'thanks to the dream's powers of fulfilling wishes', for the dream has already disposed of her father, and the rest of the family are out of the way at the cemetery.[153]

Another line of questioning and interpretation would have been possible. Freud could have asked whether the big book was a Bible – a Christian Bible – of the sort Dora would have been familiar with from her years at the convent school. Could the Christian Bible be a book, which Dora might have unconsciously fantasized about reading? Its typographical format would differ from the typical Hebrew/German bible, such as the Philippson Bible, with which Freud was familiar from childhood.[154] If Dora's father were buried in the (Jewish) cemetery, and if the rest of family and friends ('the others') were there too, would she not be able to read the Christian Bible, even bear Christian children, free from guilt? And, perhaps, she might even be free to desire the strange man.

The point is not to uncover the structures of Dora's unconscious mind, but the interpretations, which Freud might readily have made, but did not do so. These unmade interpretations depend upon avoidances, both textual and dialogic. Such avoidances would indicate areas of deep pain and dilemma. When Freud wrote to Fliess about the sight of Christian Rome reminding him of all his miseries, he did not specify these miseries. There is a reticence. The Viennese Psychoanalytic Society, for all its interest in human irrationality, never specifically took the topic of anti-semitism for one of its weekly evening meetings.[155]

Years later, when finally Freud was to leave Vienna, he was obsessed with finishing a book in which he discussed Jewish themes more openly than in any of his previous works. Strangely, this was not a book to analyse hatred against Jews, whose worst persecution in a long history of persecution was underway. *Moses and Monotheism* was devoted to showing that Moses was an Egyptian, not a Jew, and, thus, that Jewish identity was based upon an illusion. The issue of anti-semitism was not

[151] 'Fragment of an analysis of a case of hysteria', *PFL* 8 p. 140.
[152] Ibid., p. 140n.   [153] Ibid., p. 140.
[154] McGrath, 1986; Yerushalmi, (1991).
[155] Decker (1991), p. 127.

completely ignored. At one point the book suggests that the common Christian complaint against the Jews – 'you killed our God!' – may be true, although Freud quickly adds that not all the other reproaches of anti-semitism might have similar justification.[156]

Having fled to England in 1938, Freud was asked by the editor of the magazine, *Time and Tide*, to comment on the rising tide of anti-semitism. He declined the invitation, quoting the French proverb 'A fuss becomes the fop, complaining fits the fool; an honest man deceived will turn his back in silence.'[157] To the end, Freud was reproducing the signs of avoidance, which could be observed, many years earlier, in the surviving fragments of his talk with Dora.

Final words

Such avoidances were not the personal foibles of Freud or Dora, but they reflect the times and precarious place of the speakers. Hannah Arendt discussed how bourgeois Jews of Germany showed self-deception, in refusing to accept the signs that things were really as bad as they feared.[158] Freud, it appears, shared that state of mind. Max Schur, Freud's doctor in his final years, has written of Freud's refusal to anticipate the full dangers of Nazism.[159] According to Schur, Freud maintained an unwarranted optimism, believing both that the situation in Germany was improving and that Austrians were incapable of the anti-semitic brutalities of the German Nazis. Freud did not leave Vienna until it was nearly too late. In this, he was at one with Dora.

The time and place of Freud's work – arguably the greatest analysis of self-deception in Western culture – is no coincidence. The shared pattern of self-deception was deep-seated, lasting over years and built into the routines of family life. Freud read a newspaper, which did not report anti-semitic incidents. He did not discuss anti-semitism in front of his children. His son Martin recalls that he and his siblings 'were never conscious of anything approaching discrimination against us because of our race'.[160] It is not surprising that traces of self-deception should cling to Freud's work, as he avoids considering how the tensions

---

[156] 'Moses and Monotheism', *PFL* 13, p. 334.
[157] Freud (1960), p. 456.
[158] Arendt (1970)
[159] Schur (1972), pp. 442f. See also Roazen (1985), who quotes Freud as saying that 'a nation that produced Goethe could not possibly go to the bad'. Roazen comments that Freud, in common with many others, indulged in 'wishful thinking', convincing himself that he need not leave Vienna (p. 172).
[160] Martin Freud (1957), p. 101.

of persecution could be reproduced within the psyche of his patients.[161] The unbending search for the roots of universal, personal irrationality involved, at least in a small way, turning aside from looking too closely at a particular, public irrationality.

From the perspective of those times, too clear a gaze at the public irrationality could itself seem irrational. This attitude touched Freud and his family, as can be glimpsed in comments about Adolphine, the youngest of Sigmund's five sisters. In a letter to Martha, Sigmund described 'Dolfi' as 'the sweetest and best of my sisters'; she had, he continued, 'such a great capacity for deep feeling and alas an all-too-fine sensitiveness'.[162] Sigmund's son Martin, in his delicate tribute to his family, indicates that 'Dolfi' was considered slightly dotty. She had a tendency to imagine insults – a tendency which the other members of the family attributed to a mixture of silliness and almost pathological phobia. When walking on the streets of Vienna, she would grip Martin's arm and whisper 'Did you hear what that man said? He called me a dirty stinking Jewess and said it was time we were all killed.'[163] It was a family joke. She was talking absurdly.

In the family of psychoanalysis's founder, the one member, who heard clearly what was too painful to understand, was affectionately, but condescendingly, dismissed. Today, Adolphine's perception – her understanding – cannot be so lightly brushed aside. On one matter, the youngest sister had heard more acutely than her famous brother who listened fearlessly to the words of personal desire. In the most awful way, Adolphine was to be proved correct. She and three of her sisters were taken by the Nazis to the camps, from which none of them returned.

---

[161] One should not exaggerate the role of possible self-deception; there were genuine fears. Freud himself may not have wished to make matters worse by drawing attention to faults which could be publicly labelled by anti-semites as 'Jewish faults'. One might speculate about Freud's reluctance to confront sexual misconduct, like that of Herr K, in the families of his patients. Freud's abandonment of the 'seduction theory', in favour of the theory of infantile fantasy, took place between 1895 and 1897, at precisely the point when Lueger was advancing towards being mayor of Vienna. Freud would be aware that anti-semites would welcome a theory (or admission), proposed by a Jewish doctor, based upon analyses of predominantly Jewish patients, that fathers (Jewish fathers) regularly seduced their daughters (Wolff, 1988).

[162] Freud (1960), p. 58.

[163] Martin Freud (1957), p. 16.

9 Ideological implications

Psychology should always be more than psychology – that is one of the lessons to be learnt from Freud. Technical matters, in Freud's hands, do not stay technical but become comments on the human condition. Repression, thus, is not merely a description of a particular mental process, on a par with the majority of today's psychological concepts, which remain restricted to the vocabulary of a few specialists. Freudian repression is an idea that has become public property, as Freud always intended it to be. The concept of repression is more than the cornerstone of a psychological theory. Freud's psychology spreads over history, society, politics and much more besides.

Any attempt to reformulate Freudian repression must acknowledge these wider implications. This does not mean that the person attempting the reformulation should try to follow Freud's example, by making reformulated pronouncements on each of the topics that Freud covered. That would inevitably look like a small child skipping on tiny legs along a trail of giant's footprints. Any resulting indentations could only look comically puny in comparison with the original depths. It is more advisable to offer a brief comparison between the social implications of the original theory and its reformulation.

Biological versus social repression

Probably the biggest difference between the present notion of dialogic repression and Freud's original concept concerns the relations between psychology and biology. Freud envisaged the relationship to be close, for he argued that repression had, above all, a biological function. Repression was an inevitable means of dealing with the inborn drives of sex and aggression. The Oedipus complex was established by heredity and its resolution demanded that humans repress their infantile urges. Freudian psychology assumes that the skill to repress comes as part of this biological package. The desires to be repressed stand outside of culture and language. Unless these biologically based desires are curtailed, social life is impossible.

The present reformulation, by contrast, sees repression as dialogical rather than biological. Of course, language itself has a biological component – only the human species is equipped to talk and to construct languages in the way we do. But repression itself need not be understood in biological terms, if one assumes that socially inappropriate responses or thoughts, rather than biological urges, constitute the objects of repression. Conversation demands constraints and what is forbidden becomes an object of desire. Language creates these forbidden desires, but also provides the means for pushing them from conscious attention. In this way, the habitual business of conversation – and, thus, of social life itself – can continue. The desires which must be repressed will reflect whatever is socially forbidden and whatever may not be uttered. As such, other topics, besides sex and aggression, may be repressed. This difference from classic Freudian psychology carries implications for the task of understanding what might be being repressed in the cultural climate of today.

Freud, in taking the biological position, believed that he had largely completed the task of exposure. Psychoanalysis, in his view, had revealed aggressive and sexual impulses to be the major sources of human conduct. These two forces might be combined in novel ways to form fresh patterns of human behaviour. Yet, essentially, underneath it all, would lurk the same two biological drives. The details might always require updating; constant vigilance would be needed to ensure that biology be kept in check. But there were no other great impulsive forces awaiting discovery.

The present position does not share such optimism. No complete set of basic drives is being claimed. On the contrary, the task of uncovering the repressed must be continued, for as long as humans continue to speak. Just as we formulate new utterances, so will we be formulating new realms of the unsaid. There is no guarantee that what is repressed in one historical epoch will be repressed in another, as if the underlying forces always remain constant. Each moment of human history will produce its own restrictions. Consequently, the task of exploring the unsaid is endless. Ideological analysis, to adapt a Freudian phrase, should be an interminable analysis.[1]

---

[1] See, especially, 'Analysis terminable and interminable', *SE* 23.

Sex, pleasure and repression

In the wake of Freud, there is a temptation to equate repression with sexual repression. Freud encouraged such an equation, for it matched his clinical experience. So often, it seemed that unadmitted sexual desires lay behind the neuroses of his patients. However, one should not generalize from these cases to the whole of humanity. Many of Freud's Oedipal patients were being raised by Oedipal parents. The case of Little Hans shows this. Hans was not the universal boy, as Freud imagined him to be. Nor were his parents acting in biologically pre-ordained ways. They were enacting the fears and insecurities of their times. To modern eyes, they appear ill at ease with sexuality, being obsessed by a desire to prevent childish masturbation. Constantly Hans is harried, threatened and punished should his behaviour, or even his dreams, show signs of the dreaded vice.

Today's parents are unlikely to behave in such a way. Thanks to many factors, including the efforts of Hans's doctor, we have been largely cured of that neurosis. Sexuality is no longer a banned topic. In our times, a young British or American woman of the same age as Dora will, as likely as not, have read hundreds of magazines, which are targeted at her age group and which, issue after issue, take sexuality as their main topic. Dora's equivalent is likely today to be better informed than a middle-aged male doctor. She might enjoying saying things about the sexual practices of her generation to discomfort such a doctor. For young women – and, indeed, for young men – sexual discourse, far from being taboo, is *de rigeur*. The new codes of politeness demand an ability to converse on matters, which would have shocked Martha and Sigmund had their children, especially their daughters, spoken with the freedom that is expected today.

It is easy to interpret this freedom as a sign that nowadays we have cast off the bounds of repression.. The equation between sex and repression encourages us to believe that, because we are free from the sexual inhibitions of the tightly corseted Victorians, we live unrepressed lives. From current perspectives, it becomes easy to mock the prudery of previous, apparently repressed generations. We can smile knowingly at Martha, who did not want psychoanalytic ideas about sex discussed in front of her children. How things have improved . . . how much more open we are today . . . how great our knowledge of ourselves . . . we have no need of repression . . .

This type of self-congratulation can be dangerously soothing. Each age finds it easy to take its own presuppositions as 'natural', as if it has no secrets to hide. Hans's parents, as well as Freud, could see nothing strange about the way that Hans was cajoled if he so much as touched his little penis. Freud seemed to believe that all mothers would threaten castration in such circumstances. Today, it seems so bizarre, so 'unnatural'. But the question to ask ourselves is not whether we today have any hidden sexual secrets: as if there is further shameful baggage to be fetched from that lumber room, which, by now, must be almost empty. The question is whether other forms of repression are being concealed by our easy equation of repression with sexuality and by our ready boasts to be unrepressed.

Zygmunt Bauman, one of the most perceptive sociological observers of today's times, has commented that Freud's theory of the mind belongs to its own times. No longer do most people possess a stern, punitive superego to keep the temptations of pleasure from conscious awareness. Instead, there is now an 'insatiable drive to enjoyment'.[2] The values which the young Sigmund celebrated in his letters to Martha – values of thrift, sobriety and a strong sense of duty – seem hopelessly old-fashioned. In their place, we follow the imperative to consume, purchase and enjoy. If Sigmund and Martha hoped for a future which would bring an absence of pain, today's lovers demand pleasure and demand it now. As Bauman suggests, late capitalism is marked by a different psychological dynamic than was current in Freud's time: 'in its present consumer phase, the capitalist system deploys the pleasure principle for its own perpetuation'.[3] Seduction rather than repression, according to Bauman, is demanded: the consumer must be constantly seduced in the pursuit and expectation of gratification.

One might query whether repression is totally passé, or whether we are simply failing to notice those aspects which conventionally have us in their thrall. Our customary ways of talking may be pointing our attention towards matters that we take for granted, and, in so doing, hiding elements which would disturb the pleasure-seeking consciousness that Bauman describes. The very notion of the 'consumer society' offers a clue. This is a phrase that easily slips off the tongue. Academic sociologists, journalists and laypersons alike will use the phrase without second thought. It is a truism that we live in such a society. Yet, a moment's thought should be sufficient to convince ourselves that one cannot have consumption without production. A capitalism based on consumption rather than production is not possible. What is to be bought and enjoyed must have been produced. Yet, the phrase seems to forget this. Perhaps the images of production, and the feelings of guilt, that such images

---

[2] Bauman (1992), p. 50.   [3] Ibid., p. 49.

might provoke, must be pushed from conscious awareness, lest they spoil the all-consuming party.

This is not the place to develop this argument, whose details have been published elsewhere.[4] However, the outlines might be briefly sketched. Consumers today often define themselves through their purchases, constructing their identity in terms of possessions.[5] The pleasurable business of buying and consuming – together with one's own sense of self – would be threatened by thoughts about the origins of the products which are regularly purchased. The miseries of production must be kept from the consuming consciousness, lest sparks of guilt threaten commercially driven habits. Not many details of production today are commercially provided on products. We rarely know who has made the things that we buy, let alone where the raw materials may have come from. In this way, the miseries of production can be routinely pushed aside in the busy-ness of shopping.

If my clothes and other possessions are to be *mine*, then my imagination needs to be habitually curtailed. I can imagine the relationship between my commodities and their commercial labels. Indeed, the label might provide a deal of the pleasure. I might assume that the label signifies the producer of the commodity. But, beyond that, there is territory, forbidden to the consuming imagination. I should not imagine those strange hands, which once touched my possessions. Indeed, my possessions would cease to feel mine – and I would cease to be my good consuming self – if I took seriously the dark, busy fingers, working in conditions of oppression far removed from my life-world. Those anonymous fingers, no matter how many hours they labour, will never be able to own the sorts of possessions that I take for granted. This is not a pleasurable line of thinking. It is more comfortable to act habitually as if there can be consumption without production.

Sigmund, Martha, Little Hans's parents, Paul Lorenz, Dora – indeed the whole cast list of Freud's books – may today seem naive in their misgivings about sex. How fearful Sigmund now appears when he contemplated female sexuality. At other times, how pompously certain he sounded. And how formal those daily lunches seem, when he pointed silently with his fork. But Sigmund, like the actors in his dramas, knew something that few of us today know. He would have known where the solid table, on which his family was eating, was made and what sort of people made it. They all would know who sewed the clothes that they were wearing. The basis of their material world would not be an

---

[4] For an expanded treatment, see Billig (1999).
[5] See, for instance, McRobbie (1997); Miles (1996).

unknown mystery. They would scarcely understand the ignorance that we take for granted.

Repression desirable and undesirable

If repression is equated with sexual repression, then we may easily assume that repression is a 'bad' thing, which must always be reversed. Today, we have undone the sexual repressions of former times, or so we proudly proclaim. We are unrepressed, without Victorian 'hang-ups'. The corsets have been unbuttoned – and a good thing, too, we tell ourselves. If repression rears its head again, then, thanks to Freud, televised chat-shows and interminable magazines, we will know how to beat it down.

Yet, this is a distortion of Freud, for whom repression was to be understood, rather than undone. Freud did not champion free sexuality. Indeed, the logic of his theory suggested that the social order depended on the repression and sublimation of sexual energy. Even the radical Freudian, Herbert Marcuse, who depicted a utopia of liberated eros, recognized this. Hence Marcuse, in his rewriting of Freudian theory, distinguished theoretically between necessary and surplus repression. An erotic utopia would require a certain level of repression, so that food can be produced, clothes stitched and shelters built.[6]

If repression is seen to be linked to language, rather than to sexual impulses, then there is less temptation to overlook its ideologically changing forms. Moreover, some repressions are to be defended rather than dismantled. With regard to sexuality, there is no doubt that we are shameless in our discourse, as compared with the speakers of Freud's times. But that is not true of all topics. Today, there are taboos firmly in place that did not exist then. Most notably this can be seen in relation to race. Freud's Vienna was dominated by a politics of race, that could be outwardly expressed. Victims, such as Freud and Dora, might be ashamed, often silent in their shame. But the perpetrators were unashamedly confident and incessantly vocal in their confidence.

Today, it is all different. What was a common currency of talk over half a century ago has been withdrawn from circulation: only the morally suspect would try to pass its counterfeit coinage. Otto Weininger's *Sex and Character* could not now become a best-seller, as it was during the period when Freud was treating Dora. The book outwardly championed Aryan and masculine superiority over Jewish and feminine inferiority. Its young author and his suicide were the talk of bourgeois

---

[6] Marcuse (1969). See also Reich (1975) and Robinson (1972) for a sympathetic discussion of Freudian radicalism.

Vienna. Today, *Sex and Character* not only appears empirically wrong but morally repugnant.[7] Such a work cannot be enjoyed guiltlessly, as it was in the early years of the twentieth century. It now must gather dust in library vaults. Similarly, some of the Jewish jokes, that Freud told in 'Jokes and their relation to the unconscious', are embarrassing. No academic today could repeat them with such obvious enjoyment. In the shadow of Auschwitz, a whole way of talking – of laughing even – has become socially impermissible.

One might say that the topic of race today has slid into the seat vacated by sexuality. There are taboos, which restrict what can be uttered. Overt, uninhibited anti-semitism and racism are not to be spoken in polite company. Those, who wish to criticize non-whites or Jews from the outside, must find complex, indirect and apologetic ways of doing so. Sometimes the criticism is projected onto others, as if speakers deny their own guilt.[8] The projection allows the socially shameful desires to be indirectly expressed, just as in previous generations sexual desire had to be denied and projected if it were to be mentioned politely.

It is too simple merely to say that one way of talking – one system of discourse – has replaced another, as if there were no psychological dynamics in play. More than outward expression is at stake. What is not to be uttered must not even be thought. Inner and outward taboos should coincide: we should blame ourselves for the shameful thought, just as much as Hans's parents wanted their boy to be ashamed of his private desires. Only when the previous way of talking is firmly repressed in this way – only when it has been exposed as an object of public and private shame – can the new ways of talking routinely trip off the tongue without second thought.

The topic of racism illustrates why repression is not necessarily something to be mocked. As Freud realized, and as was mentioned in chapter 2, one of the aims of psychoanalysis is to strengthen the ego, or rationality, in its battle against disruptive temptation. In Freudian terms, repression can be rational. Even if one puts aside the notion of 'rationality', it is still possible to argue that on an ideological level, psychological repression can be justified as progressive, moral and

---

[7] Weininger (1906). On Weininger, his fame and influence, see Harrowitz and Hyams (1995). Weininger, whom Freud cites without approval in a footnote in the little Hans case (*PFL* 8, p. 198), played a part in the falling out between Freud and Fliess (for details, see Gay, 1995, chapter 4).

[8] For examples and analyses of such projections in contemporary discourses about race, see Billig (1991 and 1998); Wetherell and Potter (1992). The denials permit the prejudices to be expressed while apparently distancing the speakers from the expression.

socially beneficial. It can be a means of replacing ways of talking that belong to discriminatory times.

The case of South Africa can serve as an example. During the apartheid era, the population of whites would use an outward discourse of race in order to maintain a racist political system, just as the Christian Socials did in the Vienna of Freud. Without the outwardly racist ways of talking, the institutions of apartheid could not have functioned. With the collapse of apartheid those old ways of talking have become unacceptable. White speakers cannot be seen to be racist. They must not blithely talk of 'inferior' races, just as post-1945 Austrian politicians needed to find a different way of talking about Jews. Laws can prohibit the public utterance of racist remarks that previously were commonplace. However, to ensure that the previous way of talking is tipped into the garbage can of history, it is not sufficient merely to prohibit certain forms of public utterances. Internal controls also have to be set in place, so that the thought, as much as the outwardly spoken act, becomes shameful.

The task for white South Africans, in the creation of the new South Africa, is not merely to keep their mouths shut, but to ensure that they and their children do not think the previously utterable. As has been mentioned, Freud wrote that morality conditions the need for repression. And so it is with political morality. Once racism is accepted as immoral, so the temptations of racism – including the racist joke, the racist bit of fun – must be resisted. The desire itself must be accepted as shameful. The forbidden words must not even make their appearance in the privacy of thought.

The lesson of Freud is that a certain amount of repression is necessary for the moral order. As has been suggested, we could not have conversation without repression. But this does not mean that all forms of repression are equal. The task of analysing ways of talking is endless. Some forms of repression are to be exposed and found wanting. Their routine practice then becomes an obstacle to be overcome. Other forms of repression will be deemed beneficial. Not only does morality condition repression, but it also should condition the analysis of repression. A danger always stalks such analysis. As we talk about repression, so we are using language. We will be looking in a particular direction, unaware of what we are overlooking, unaware of our own silences. Always there is more analysis to be done. As the case of Dora shows, even the sexually open talk of the psychoanalytic dialogue has its own unwitting silences.

We should avoid being seduced by the tempting ideal of a perfect repression-free social order. Conversation, kindness and morality would not be possible if the infantile situation were writ large. Nor could there be humour. Only with language and its demands come both the pleasures and the dangers of subversion. In conversing, we must also create silences. Constantly, we must engage in repression. Similarly, as Freud well recognized, we must seek to understand the repression that we practice. This double requirement is neither easy nor terminable. But there is a comforting thought. So long as there is a need to analyse repression, the works of Freud should retain their value. Future generations, too, should enjoy reading and reinterpreting the greatest of all psychologists.

References

In citing works by Freud taken from collected editions, the following abbreviations are used:

GW Gesammelte Werke (18 vols.), ed. A. Freud, E. Bibring, W. Hoffer, E. Kris and O. Isakower, with the collaboration of M. Bonaparte. Frankfurt am Main: S. Fischer Verlag.
PFL Penguin Freud Library (15 vols.). Harmondsworth: Penguin.
SE Standard Edition of the Complete Psychological Works of Sigmund Freud, (24 vols.), ed. by J. Strachey, with A. Freud, A. Strachey and A. Tyson. London: Hogarth Press.

Other references to Freud's work are to be found in the following reference list and are referenced in the standard way.

Abraham, H. C. and Freud, E. L. (eds.) (1965). *A Psycho-Analytic Dialogue: The Letters of Sigmund Freud and Karl Abraham*. London: Hogarth Press.
Aitchinson, J. (1996). *The Seeds of Speech: Language Origin and Evolution*. Cambridge: Cambridge University Press.
Anderson, B. (1983). *Imagined Communities*. London: Verso.
Antaki, C. (1994). *Explaining and Arguing*. London: Sage.
Appignanesi, L. and Forrester, J. (1993). *Freud's Women*. London: Virago.
Arendt, H. (1970). Walter Benjamin. In W. Benjamin, *Illuminations*. London: Fontana.
Aronsson, K. (1991). Facework and control in multi-party talk: a pediatric case study. In I. Marková and K. Foppa (eds.), *Asymmetries in Dialogue*. Hemel Hempstead: Harvester\Wheatsheaf.
Atkinson, J. M. and Heritage, J. (1984) (eds.). *Structures of Social Interaction*. Cambridge: Cambridge University Press.
Austin, J. L. (1979). *Philosophical Papers*. Oxford: Oxford University Press.
Bakhtin, M. M. (1986). *Speech Genres and Other Late Essays*. Austin: University of Texas Press.
Barthes, R. (1982). *Image Music Text*. London: Flamingo.
(1990). *A Lover's Discourse*. Harmondsworth: Penguin.
Bartlett, F. C. (1932). *Remembering*. Cambridge: Cambridge University Press.
Bass, E. and Davis, L. (1994). *The Courage to Heal: A Guide for Women Survivors of Child Sexual Abuse*. New York: Harper and Row.

Bauer, O. (1978). The concept of the 'nation'. In T. Bottomore and P. Goode (eds.), *Austro-Marxism*. Oxford: Clarendon Press.

Bauman, Z. (1992). *Intimations of Postmodernity*. London: Routledge.

Beller, S. (1987). Class, culture and the Jews of Vienna, 1900. In I. Oxaal, M. Pollak and G. Botz (eds.), *Jews, Antisemitism and Culture in Vienna*. London: Routledge and Kegan Paul.

Ben Yahuda, N. (1998). Archaeology and national identity. Talk given at Annual Conference of Association for the Study of Ethnicity and Nationalism, London.

Bergmann, J. R. (1990). Of the local sensitivity of conversation. In I. Markovà and K. Foppa (eds.). *The Dynamics of Discourse*. Hemel Hempstead: Harvester\Wheatsheaf.

Bettelheim, B. (1986). *Freud and Man's Soul*. London: Flamingo.

Billig, M. (1985). Prejudice, categorization and particularization: from a perceptual to a rhetorical approach. *European Journal of Social Psychology*, 15, 79–103.

(1990). Collective memory, ideology and the British Royal Family. In D. Middleton and D. Edwards (eds.). *Collective Remembering*. London: Sage.

(1991). *Ideology and Opinions*. London: Sage.

(1995). *Banal Nationalism*. London: Sage.

(1996). *Arguing and Thinking: A Rhetorical View of Social Psychology*, second edition. Cambridge: Cambridge University Press.

(1997a). The dialogic unconscious: psychoanalysis, discursive psychology and the nature of repression. *British Journal of Social Psychology*, 36, 139–59.

(1997b). Keeping the white queen in play. In M. Fine, L. Weis, L. C. Powell and L. M. Wong (eds.). *Off White*. London: Routledge.

(1997c). From codes to utterances: cultural studies, discourse and psychology. In M. Ferguson and P. Golding (eds.), *Cultural Studies in Question*. London: Sage.

(1998). Dialogic repression and the Oedipus complex: reinterpreting the Little Hans case. *Culture and Psychology*, 4, 11–47.

(1999). Commodity fetishism and repression: reflections on Marx, Freud and the psychology of consumer capitalism. *Theory and Psychology*.

Billig, M. and Edwards, D. (1994). La construction sociale de la mémoire. *La Recherche*, 25, 742–745.

Bilmes, J. (1987). The concept of preference in conversation analysis. *Language in Society*, 17, 161–87.

Blades, M. W. (1989). Identity theme and *mythe personnel*: two views of the Rat Man. *American Imago*, 46, 85–103.

Blum, H. P. (1994). Dora's conversion syndrome: a contribution to the prehistory of the Holocaust. *Psychoanalytic Quarterly*, 63, 518–35.

Boden, D. (1994). *The Business of Talk*. Cambridge: Polity Press.

Bonaiuto, M. and Stirponi, L. (1996). Attribuzione di intenzionalità retorica nell'interazione adulti-bambini. Talk given at conference, La Mente Argomentativa, University of Rome, 'La Sapienza', July 1996.

Borch-Jacobsen, M. (1996). *Remembering Anna O.* London: Routledge.

(1997). Basta Così!: Mikkel Borch-Jacobsen on psychoanalysis and philosophy – interview by Chris Oakley. In T. Dufresne (ed.), *Returns of the 'French Freud': Freud, Lacan and Beyond*. New York: Routledge.

Bos, J. (1997). *Authorized Knowledge: A Study of the History of Psychoanalysis from a Discourse Point of View*. Utrecht: University of Utrecht.

Bougnoux, D. (1997). Lacan, sure – and then what? In T. Dufresne (ed.), *Returns of the 'French Freud': Freud, Lacan and Beyond*. New York: Routledge.

Bower, G. H. (1990). Awareness, the unconscious and repression. In J. L. Singer (ed.), *Repression and Dissociation*, Chicago: University of Chicago Press.

Bourdieu, P. (1990). *The Logic of Practice*. Cambridge: Polity Press.

Bouveresse, J. (1993). *Wittgenstein Reads Freud: The Myth of the Unconscious*. Princeton, N. J.: Princeton University Press.

Brearley, M. (1991). Psychoanalysis: a form of life. In A. P. Griffiths (ed.), *Wittgenstein's Centenary Essays*. Cambridge: Cambridge University Press.

Brennan, T. (1992). *The Interpretation of the Flesh: Freud's Theory of Femininity*. London: Routledge.

Brennan, T. (ed.) (1989). *Between Feminism and Psychoanalysis*. London: Routledge.

British Psychological Society (1995*). Report of the Working Party on Recovered Memories*. Leicester: BPS.

Brown, R. H. (1994). Rhetoric, textuality and the post-modern turn in socio-logical theory. In S. Seidman (ed.), *The Postmodern Turn*. Cambridge: Cambridge University Press.

Brown, P. and Levinson, S. C. (1987). *Politeness: Some Universals in Language Use*. Cambridge: Cambridge University Press.

Bruck, M. and Ceci, S. J. (1997). The description of children's susceptibility. In N. L. Stein, P. A. Ornstein, B. Tversky and C. Brainerd (eds.), *Memory for Everyday and Emotional Events*. Mahwah, N. J.: Lawrence Erlbaum.

Bruner, J. (1992). Another look at New Look 1. *American Psychologist*, 47, 780–3.

Burman, E. (1996/7). False memories, true hopes and the angelic: revenge of the postmodern in therapy. *New Formations*, Winter, 122–34.

 (1998). Children, false memories, and disciplinary alliances: tensions between developmental psychology and psychoanalysis. *Psychoanalysis and Contemporary Thought*, 21, 307–33.

Buttny, R. (1993). *Social Accountability in Communication*. London: Sage.

Carbaugh, D. (1996). Mediating cultural selves: Soviet and American cultures in a televised 'spacebridge'. In D. Grodin and T. R. Lindlof (eds.), *Constructing the Self in a Mediated World*. London: Sage.

Carveth, D. L. (1996). Psychoanalytic conceptions of the passions. In J. O'Neill (ed.), *Freud and the Passions*. University Park, Penn.: Pennsylvania State University Press.

Cavell, M. (1993). *The Psychoanalytic Mind: From Freud to Philosophy*. Cambridge, Mass.: Harvard University Press.

Ceci, S. J. (1995). False beliefs: some developmental and clinical considerations. In D. L. Schacter (ed.), *Memory Distortion: How Minds, Brains and Societies Reconstruct the Past*. Cambridge, Mass.: Harvard University Press.

Ceci, S. J., Huffman, M. L. C., Smith, E. and Loftus, E. F. (1994). Repeatedly thinking about a non-event: source misattribution among preschoolers. *Consciousness and Cognition*, 3, 388–407.

Chilton, P. (1990). Politeness, politics and diplomacy. *Discourse and Society*, 1, 201–24.

Christianson, S.-A. and Engelberg, E. (1997). Remembering and forgetting traumatic experiences. In A. F. Collins, S. E. Gathercole, M. A. Conway and P. E. Morris (eds.), *Theories of Memory*. Hove: Lawrence Erlbaum.

Cioffi, F. (1991). Wittgenstein on Freud's 'abominable mess'. In A. P. Griffiths (ed.), *Wittgenstein's Centenary Essays*. Cambridge: Cambridge University Press.

Cixous, H. and Clément, C. (1986). *The Newly Born Woman*. Manchester: Manchester University Press.

Clare, G. (1980). *Last Waltz in Vienna: The Destruction of a Family, 1842–1942*. London: Pan Books.

Conway, M. A. (1997). Past and present: recovered memories and false memories. In M. A. Conway (ed.), *Recovered Memories and False Memories*. Oxford: Oxford University Press.

Conway, M. A. and Rubin, D. C. (1993). The structure of autobiographical memory. In A. F. Collins, S. E. Gathercole, M. A. Conway and P. E. Morris (eds.), *Theories of Memory*. Hove: Lawrence Erlbaum.

Courtois, C. A. (1997). Delayed memories of child sexual abuse: critique of the controversy and clinical guidelines. In M. A. Conway (ed.), *Recovered Memories and False Memories*. Oxford: Oxford University Press.

Crawford, J., Kippax, S., Onyx, J., Gault, U. and Benton, P. (1992). *Emotion and Gender: constructing meaning from memory*. London: Routledge.

Crews, F. (1995). *The Memory Wars: Freud's Legacy in Dispute*. New York: New York Review.

Cuddihy, J. M. (1987). *The Ordeal of Civility: Freud, Marx, Lévi-Strauss and the Jewish Struggle with Modernity*. Boston: Beacon Press.

Czyzewski, M. (1995). 'Mm hm' tokens as interactional devices in the psychotherapeutic in-take interview. In T. ten Have and G. Psathas (eds.), *Situated Order*. Washington, D. C.: University Press of America.

Davidson, D. (1983). Paradoxes of irrationality. In R. Wolheim and J. Hopkins (eds.), *Philosophical Essays on Freud*. Cambridge: Cambridge University Press.

Decker, H. S. (1991). *Freud, Dora, and Vienna 1900*. New York: Free Press.
    (1992). Freud's 'Dora' case in perspective: the medical treatment of hysteria in Austria at the turn of the century. In T. Gelfand and J. Kerr (eds.), *Freud and the History of Psychoanalysis*. Hillsdale, N. J.: Analytic Press.

Dennett, D. C. (1991). *Consciousness Explained*. Harmondsworth: Penguin.

Derrida, J. (1996). *Archive Fever: A Freudian Impression*. Chicago: University of Chicago Press.

Deutsch, F. (1986). A footnote to Freud's 'Fragment of an analysis of a case of hysteria'. In C. Bernheimer and C. Kahane (eds.), *In Dora's Case*. London: Virago.

Diener, E. (1980). De-individuation: the absence of self-awareness and self-regulation in group members. In P. Paulus (ed.), *The Psychology of Group Influence*. Hillsdale, N. J.: Erlbaum.

Drew, P. (1995). Conversation analysis. In J. A. Smith, R. Harré and L. Van Langenhove (eds.), *Rethinking Methods in Psychology*. Oxford: Blackwell.

Dufresne, T. (1997). Introduction: beyond the French Freud. In T. Dufresne (ed.), *Returns of the 'French Freud': Freud, Lacan and Beyond*. New York: Routledge.

Dunn, J. (1988). *The Beginnings of Social Understanding*. Oxford: Blackwell.

  (1991). Understanding others: evidence from naturalistic studies of children. In A. Whiten (ed.), *Natural Theories of Mind*. Oxford: Blackwell.

  (1994). Changing minds and changing relationships. In C. Lewis and P. Mitchell (eds.), *Children's Early Understanding of Mind: Origins and Development*. Hillsdale, N. J.:Lawrence Erlbaum.

Dunn, J. and Munn, P. (1987). Development of justification in disputes with mother and sibling. *Developmental Psychology*, 23, 791–798.

Dunn, J. and Slomkowski, C. (1995). Conflict and the development of social understanding. In C. U. Shantz and W. W. Hartup (eds.), *Conflict in Child and Adolescent Development*. Cambridge: Cambridge University Press.

Eagleton, T. (1991). *Ideology*. London: Verso.

Eder, C. R. (1994). *The Grammar of the Unconscious*. University Park, Penn.: Pennsylvania State University Press.

Edwards, D. (1978). Social relations and early language. In A. Lock (ed.), *Action, Gesture and Symbol*. London: Academic Press.

  (1997). *Discourse and Cognition*. London: Sage.

  (in press). The discourse of emotions. *Culture and Psychology*.

Edwards, D. and Middleton, D. (1986). Joint remembering: constructing an account of shared experience through conversational discourse. *Discourse Processes*, 9, 423–59.

  (1987). Conversation and remembering: Bartlett revisited. *Applied Cognitive Psychology*, 1, 77–92.

  (1988). Conversational remembering and family relationships: how children learn to remember. *Journal of Social and Personal Relationships*, 5, 3–25.

Edwards, D. and Potter, J. (1992). *Discursive Psychology*. London: Sage.

Edwards, D., Middleton, D. and Potter, J. (1992). Towards a discursive psychology of remembering. *The Psychologist*, 15, 441–6.

Eiser, J. R. (1986). *Social Psychology*. Cambridge: Cambridge University Press.

Elias, N. (1982). *The Civilizing Process: State Formation and Civilization*. Oxford: Blackwell.

Ellenberger, H. F. (1970). *The Discovery of the Unconscious*. London: Allen Lane.

  (1972). The story of 'Ann O. ': a critical review with new data. *Journal of the History of the Behavioral Sciences*, 8, 267–279.

Endelman, T. M. (1989). Conversion as a response to antisemitism in modern Jewish history. In J. Reinharz (ed.), *Living with Antisemitism: Modern Jewish Responses*. Hanover: University of New England.

Erdelyi, M. H. (1974). A new look at the New Look: perceptual defense and vigilance. *Psychological Review*, 81, 1–25.

  (1990). Repression, reconstruction and defense: history and integration of the psychoanalytic and experimental frameworks. In J. L. Singer (ed.), *Repression and Dissociation*. Chicago: University of Chicago Press.

  (1996). *The Recovery of Unconscious Memories: Hypermnesia and Reminiscence*. Chicago: University of Chicago Press.

Erikson, E. H. (1986). Reality and actuality: an address. In C. Bernheimer and C. Kahane (eds.), *In Dora's Case*. London: Virago.

Erwin, E. (1996). *A Final Accounting: Philosophical and Empirical Issues in Freudian Psychology*. Cambridge, Mass.: MIT Press.

Eysenck, H. J. (1986). *Decline and Fall of the Freudian Empire*. Harmondsworth: Penguin.

Fairclough, N. (1992). *Discourse and Social Change*. Cambridge: Polity Press.

(1995). *Critical Discourse Analysis*. London: Sage.

Farr, R. M. (1996). *The Roots of Modern Social Psychology*. Oxford: Blackwell.

Ferris, P. (1997). *Dr Freud: A Life*. London: Sinclair-Stevenson.

Festinger, L., Pepitone, A., and Newcomb, T. (1952). Some consequences of de-individuation in a group. *Journal of Abnormal and Social Psychology*, 47, 382–89.

Fingarette, H. (1983). Self-deception and the 'splitting of the ego'. In R. Wolheim and J. Hopkins (eds.), *Philosophical Essays on Freud*. Cambridge: Cambridge University Press.

Firth, A. (1995). Multiple mode, single activity: 'telenegotiating' as a social accomplishment. In T. ten Have and G. Psathas (eds.), *Situated Order*. Washington, D. C.: University Press of America.

Fisher, S. and Greenberg, R. P. (1996). *Freud Scientifically Appraised: Testing the Theories and Therapy*. New York: John Wiley.

Fisher, S. and Greenberg, R. P. (eds.) (1976). *The Scientific Evaluation of Freud's Theories and Therapy: A Book of Readings*. Hassocks, Sussex: Harvester Press.

Fiske, S. T. and Taylor, S. E. (1984). *Social Cognition*. New York: Random House.

Fivush, R. and Kuebli, J. (1997). Making everyday events emotional: the construal of emotion in parent–child conversations about the past. In N. L. Stein, P. A. Ornstein, B. Tversky and C. Brainerd (eds.), *Memory for Everyday and Emotional Events*. Mahwah, N. J.: Lawrence Erlbaum.

Fivush, R., Pipe, M. -E., Murachver, T. and Reese, E. (1997). Events spoken and unspoken: implications for the recovered memory debate. In M. A. Conway (ed.), *Recovered Memories and False Memories*. Oxford: Oxford University Press.

Fletcher, G. (1995). *The Scientific Credibility of Folk Psychology*. Mahwah, N. J.: Lawrence Erlbaum.

Foppa, K. (1990). Topic progression and intention. In I. Markovà and K. Foppa (eds.), *The Dynamics of Discourse*. Hemel Hempstead: Harvester\ Wheatsheaf.

Forrester, J. (1990). *The Seductions of Psychoanalysis*. Cambridge: Cambridge University Press.

(1996). Psychoanalysis and the history of the passions: the strange destiny of envy. In J. O'Neill (ed.), *Freud and the Passions*. University Park, Penn.: Pennsylvania State University Press.

Fowler, R., Hodge, B., Kress, G. and Trew, T. (1979). *Language and Control*. London: Routledge.

Freud, A. (1968). *The Ego and Mechanisms of Defence*. New York: International Universities Press.

Freud, M. (1957). *Glory Reflected: Sigmund Freud – Man and Father*. London: Angus and Robertson.

Freud, S. (1960). *Letters of Sigmund Freud, 1873–1939*, ed. E. L. Freud. London: Hogarth Press.

(1963). *Two Short Accounts of Psycho-Analysis*. Harmondsworth: Penguin.

(1985). *The Complete Letters of Sigmund Freud to Wilhelm Fliess, 1887–1904*, ed. by J. M. Masson. Cambridge, Mass.: Harvard University Press.

(1990). *The Letters of Sigmund Freud to Eduard Silberstein, 1871–1881*, ed. W. Boehlich. Cambridge, Mass: Harvard University Press.

(1993). 'Wir und der Tod': a previously unpublished version of a paper given by Sigmund Freud on the attitude towards death. In D. Meghnagi (ed.). *Freud and Judaism*. London: Karnac Books.

Freud, S. and Jung, C. G. (1991). *The Freud/Jung Letters*. Harmondsworth: Penguin.

Fromm, E. (1970). *The Crisis of Psychoanalysis*. New York: Holt, Rinehart and Winston.

Frosh, S. (1994). *Sexual Difference: Masculinity and Psychoanalysis*. London: Routledge.

(1997). *For and Against Psychoanalysis*. London: Routledge.

Galasinski, D. and Jaworski, A. (1997). The linguistic construction of reality in the 'Black Book of Polish Censorship'. *Discourse and Society*, 8, 314–57.

Gallop, J. (1982). *Feminism and Psychoanalysis: The Daughter's Seduction*. London: Macmillan.

(1986). Keys to Dora. In C. Bernheimer and C. Kahane (eds.), *In Dora's Case*. London: Virago.

Gardiner, J. M. and Java, R. I. (1993). Recognising and remembering. In A. F. Collins, S. E. Gathercole, M. A. Conway and P. E. Morris (eds.), *Theories of Memory*. Hove: Lawrence Erlbaum.

Garfinkel, H. (1967). *Studies in Ethnomethodology*. Englewood Cliffs, N. J.: Prentice Hall.

Garry, M., Loftus, E. F. and Brown, S. W. (1994). Memory: a river runs through it. *Consciousness and Cognition*, 3, 438–51.

Gay, P. (1978). *Freud, Jews and Other Germans*. New York: Oxford University Press.

(1990). *Reading Freud: Explorations and Entertainments*. New Haven: Yale University Press.

(1995). *Freud: A Life for our Time*. London: Papermac.

Gearhart, S. (1986). The scene of psychoanalysis: the unanswered questions of Dora. In C. Bernheimer and C. Kahane (eds.), *In Dora's Case*. London: Virago.

Gelfand, T. (1992). Sigmund-sur-Seine: fathers and brothers in Charcot's Paris. In T. Gelfand and J. Kerr (eds.), *Freud and the History of Psychoanalysis*. Hillsdale, N. J.: Analytic Press.

Gellner, E. (1985). *The Psychoanalytic Movement*. London: Paladin.

Gergen, K. J. (1994a). *Realities and Relationships*. Cambridge, Mass.: Harvard University Press.

(1994b). *Toward the Transformation in Social Knowledge*, 2nd edn. London: Sage.

Gilligan, C. (1997). Remembering Iphigenia: voice resonance and the talking cure. In E. R. Shapiro (ed.), *The Inner World in the Outer World: psychoanalytic perspectives*. New Haven: Yale University Press.

Gilman, S. L. (1993). *Freud, Race and Gender*. Princeton: Princeton University Press.

(1994). *The Case of Sigmund Freud: Medicine and Identity at the fin de siècle*. Baltimore: John Hopkins University Press.

Glenn, J. (1980). Freud's adolescent patients: Katharina, Dora and the 'Homosexual Woman'. In M. Kanzer and J. Glenn (eds.), *Freud and his Patients*. New York: Jason Aronson.

Glover, E. (1956). Journeys in the unconscious. *The Times*, May 2.

Goffman, E. (1959). *The Presentation of Self in Everyday Life*. Harmondsworth: Allen Lane.

(1976). *Interaction Ritual: Essays on Face to Face Behaviour*. New York: Doubleday.

(1981). *Forms of Talk*. Oxford: Basil Blackwell.

Goodman, G. S. and Quas, J. A. (1997). Trauma and memory: individual differences in children's recounting of stressful experiences. In N. L. Stein, P. A. Ornstein, B. Tversky and C. Brainerd (eds.), *Memory for Everyday and Emotional Events*. Mahwah, N. J.: Lawrence Erlbaum.

Goodman, G. S., Quas, J. A., Batterman-Faunce, J. M., Riddlesberger, M. M. and Kuhn, J. (1994). Predictors of accurate and inaccurate memories of traumatic events experienced in childhood. *Consciousness and Cognition*, 3, 269–94.

Graf, M. (1942). Reminiscences of Professor Sigmund Freud. *Psychoanalytic Quarterly*, 11, 465–76.

Greenwald, A. G. (1980). The totalitarian ego: fabrication and revision of personal history. *American Psychologist*, 35, 603–18.

(1992). New Look 3: unconscious cognition reclaimed. *American Psychologist*, 47, 766–79.

Grice, H. P. (1975). Logic and conversation. In P. Cole (ed.), *Syntax and Semantics: Volume 9 Pragmatics*. New York: Academic Press.

Grinstein, A. (1990). *Freud at the Crossroads*. Madison, Conn.: International Universities Press.

Grubrich-Simitis, I. (1997). *Early Freud and Late Freud: Reading Anew 'Studies on Hysteria' and 'Moses and Monotheism'*. London: Routledge.

Grünbaum, A. (1989). *The Foundations of Psychoanalysis: A Philosophical Critique*. Berkeley, Calif.: University of California Press.

(1993). *Validation in the Clinical Theory of Psychoanalysis: A Study in the Philosophy of Psychoanalysis*. Madison, Conn.: International Universities Press.

Grundy, P. (1995). *Doing Pragmatics*. London: Edward Arnold.

Halbwachs, M. (1980). *The Collective Memory*. New York: Harper Row.

Harré, R. (1990). Language games and texts of identity. In J. Shotter and K. Gergen (eds.), *Texts of Identity*. London: Sage.

Harré, R. (ed.) (1987). *The Social Construction of Emotions*. Oxford: Blackwell.

Harré, R. and Gillett, G. (1994). *The Discursive Mind*. London: Sage.

Harrowitz, N. A. and Hyams, B. (1995). *Jews and Gender: Response of Otto Weininger*. Philadelphia: Temple University Press.

Harvey, M. R. and Herman, J. L. (1994). Amnesia, partial amnesia and delayed recall among adult survivors of childhood trauma. *Consciousness and Cognition*, 3, 295–306.

Hawelka, E. R. (ed.) (1974). *L'Homme aux Rats: Journal d'une analyse*. Paris: Presses Universitaires de France.

Hayashi, R. (1997). Hierarchical interdependence expressed through conversational styles in Japanese women's magazines. *Discourse and Society*, 8, 359–89.

Heritage, J. (1984). *Garfinkel and Ethnomethodology*. Cambridge: Polity Press.

(1988). Explanations as accounts: a conversation analytic perspective. In C. Antaki (ed.), *Analysing Everyday Explanation*. London: Sage.

Herman, J. L. (1981). *Father-Daughter Incest*. Cambridge, Mass: Harvard University Press.

(1992). *Trauma and Recovery*. New York: Basic Books.

Hitler, A. (1974). *Mein Kampf*. London: Hutchinson.

Hobsbawm, E. J. and Ranger, T. (eds.) (1983). *The Invention of Tradition*. Cambridge: Cambridge University Press.

Holmes, D. (1990). The evidence for repression: an examination of sixty years of research. In J. Singer (ed), *Repression and Dissociation: Implications for Personality Theory, Psychopathology and Health*. Chicago: University of Chicago Press.

Holquist, M. (1990). *Dialogism: Bakhtin and his World*. London: Routledge.

Hollway, W. (1989). *Subjectivity and Method in Psychology*. London: Sage.

Horowitz, A. D. (1996). 'A good old argument': the discursive construction of family and research through argumentation. Unpub. Ph.D. thesis, Loughborough University.

Howe, M. L., Courage, M. L. and Peterson, C. (1994). How can I remember when 'I' wasn't there: long-term retention of traumatic experiences and emergence of the cognitive self. *Consciousness and Cognition*, 3, 327–55.

Hunt, E. and Love, T. (1982). The second mnemonist. In U. Neisser (ed.), *Memory Observed*. San Francisco: W. H. Freeman.

Isbister, J. N. (1985). *Freud: An Introduction to his Life and Work*. Cambridge: Polity Press.

Israëls, H. and Schatzman, M. (1993). The seduction theory. *History of Psychiatry*, 4, 23–59.

Jacobs, T. J. (1993). The inner experiences of the analyst: their contribution to the analytic process. *International Journal of Psycho-Analysis*, 74, 7–14.

Jacobus, M. (1987). *Reading Woman: Essays in Feminist Criticism*. London: Methuen.

(1996). Russian tactics: Freud's 'Case of Homosexuality in a Woman'. In J. O'Neill (ed.), *Freud and the Passions*. University Park, Penn.: Pennsylvania State University Press.

James, W. (1890). *The Principles of Psychology*. London: Macmillan.

Janik, A. (1987). Viennese culture and the Jewish self-hatred hypothesis: a critique. In I. Oxaal, M. Pollak and G. Botz (eds.), *Jews, Antisemitism and Culture in Vienna*. London: Routledge and Kegan Paul.

Jefferson, G. (1985). An exercise in the transcription and analysis of laughter. In T. A. Van Dijk (ed.), *Handbook of Discourse Analysis*, volume 3. London: Academic Press.

Jones, B. P. (1993). Repression: the evolution of a psychoanalytic concept from the 1890's to the 1990's. *Journal of the American Psychoanalytic Association*, 41, 69–93.

Jones, E. (1953). *Sigmund Freud: Life and Works. Volume I, The Young Freud, 1865–1900*. London: Tavistock.

(1955). *Sigmund Freud: Life and Works, Volume II, Years of Maturity, 1901–1919*. London: Tavistock.

(1957). *Sigmund Freud: Life and Works. Volume III, The Last Phase, 1919–1939*. London: Tavistock.

Kahane, C. (1996). Freud and the passions of the voice. In J. O'Neill (ed.), *Freud and the Passions*. University Park, Penn.: Pennsylvania State University Press.

Kammen, M. (1995). Some patterns and meanings of memory distortion in American history. In D. L. Schacter (ed.), *Memory Distortion: How Minds, Brains and Societies Reconstruct the Past*. Cambridge, Mass.: Harvard University Press.

Kanzer, M. (1980). Dora's imagery: the flight from a burning house. In M. Kanzer and J. Glenn (eds.). *Freud and his Patients*. New York: Jason Aronson.

Katriel, T. (1986). *Talking Straight*. Cambridge: Cambridge University Press.

Kiersky, S. and Fosshage, J. L. (1990): The Two Analyses of Dr L: a self-psychological perspective on Freud's treatment of the Rat Man. In B. Magid (ed.), *Freud's Case Studies: Self Psychological Perspectives*. Hillsdale, N. J.: Analytic Press.

Kihlstrom, J. F. (1996). The trauma-memory argument and recovered memory therapy. In K. Pezdek and W. P. Banks (eds.). *The Recovered Memory/False memory Debate*. San Diego: Academic Press.

(1997). Suffering from reminiscences: exhumed memory, implicit memory, and the return of the repressed. In M. A. Conway (ed.), *Recovered Memories and False Memories*. Oxford: Oxford University Press.

Kirschner, S. R. (1996). *The Religious and Romantic Origins of Psychoanalysis*. New York: Cambridge University Press.

Klein, D. B. (1981). *Jewish Origins of the Psychoanalytic Movement*. New York: Praeger.

Kline, P. (1972). *Fact and Fantasy in Freudian theory*. London: Methuen.

Kline, P. (1981). *Fact and Fantasy in Freudian theory, second edition*. London: Methuen.

Kohut, H. (1984). *How Does Analysis Cure?* Chicago: University of Chicago Press.

Kress, G. (1988). *Linguistic Processes in Sociocultural Practice*. Oxford: Oxford University Press.

Kristeva, J. (1986). Stabat Mater. In *The Kristeva Reader*, ed. T. Moi. Oxford: Blackwell.

Kuebli, J., Butler, S. and Fivush, R. (1995). Mother–child talk about past emotions: relations of maternal language and child gender over time. In J. Dunn (ed.), *Connections Between Emotion and Understanding in Development*. Hove, Sussex: Lawrence Erlbaum.

Lacan, J. (1977). *Écrits*. London: Tavistock.

(1986). *The Four Fundamental Concepts of Psycho-Analysis*. Harmondsworth: Penguin.

(1986b). Intervention on transference. In C. Bernheimer and C. Kahane (eds.), *In Dora's Case*. London: Virago.

Langs, R. J. (1980). The misalliance dimension in the case of Dora. In M. Kanzer and J. Glenn (eds.). *Freud and his Patients*. New York: Jason Aronson.

Laplanche, J. and Pontalis, J.-B. (1983). *The Language of Psycho-analysis*. London: Hogarth Press.

Levine, R. A. (1990). Infant environments in psychoanalysis: a cross-cultural view. In J. W. Stigler, R. A. Shweder and G. Herdt (eds.), *Cultural Psychology*. Cambridge: Cambridge University Press.

Levinson, S. C. (1983). *Pragmatics*. Cambridge: Cambridge University Press.

Lewin, K. (1948). *Resolving Social Conflicts*. New York: Harper.

Lewis, H. B. (1983). *Freud and Modern Psychology*. New York: Plenum Press.

Lindsay, D. S. (1994). Contextualizing and clarifying criticisms of memory work in psychotherapy. *Consciousness and Cognition*, 3, 426–37.

Lipton, S. D. (1992). Les avantages de la technique de Freud d'après l'analyse de l'Homme aux rats. *Revue Française de Psychanalyse*, 56, 1181–212.

Loewenberg, P. (1985). *Decoding the Past: The Psychohistorical Approach*. Berkeley: University of California Press.

Loftus, E. F. (1993). The reality of repressed memories. *American Psychologist*, 1993, 48, 518–37.

Loftus, E. F. and Ketcham, K. (1994). *The Myth of Repressed Memory*. New York: St Martin's Press.

Loftus, E. F., Feldman, J., and Dashiell, R. (1995). The reality of illusory memories. In D. L. Schacter (ed.), *Memory Distortion: How Minds, Brains and Societies Reconstruct the Past*. Cambridge, Mass.: Harvard University Press.

Lutz, C. (1990a). Morality, domination, and understandings of 'justifiable anger' among the Ifaluk. In G. R. Semin and K. J. Gergen (eds.), *Everyday Understandings*. London: Sage.

(1990b). Engendered emotion: gender, power, and the rhetoric of emotional control in American discourse. In C. A. Lutz and L. Abu-Lughod, *Language and the Politics of Emotion*. Cambridge: Cambridge University Press.

(1996). Cultural politics by other means: gender and politics in some American psychologies of emotions. In C. F. Graumann and K. J. Gergen (eds.), *Historical Dimensions of Psychological Discourse*. Cambridge: Cambridge University Press.

Lynch, M. and Bogen, D. (1996). *The Spectacle of History: Speech, Text and Memory at the Iran-Contra Hearings*. Durham, NC: Duke University Press.

Macmillan, M. (1997). *Freud Evaluated: The Completed Arc*. Cambridge, Mass.: MIT Press.

Mahony, P. J. (1984). *The Cries of the Wolf Man*. Madison: International Universities Press.

(1986). *Freud and the Rat Man*. New Haven: Yale University Press.

(1987). *Psychoanalysis and Discourse*. London: Tavistock.

Malcolm, J. (1986). *In the Freud Archives*. London: Flamingo.

Marcus, S. (1984). *Freud and the Culture of Psychoanalysis*. London: George Allen and Unwin.

(1986). Freud and Dora: story, history, case-history. In C. Bernheimer and C. Kahane (eds.), *In Dora's Case*. London: Virago.

Marcuse, H. (1969). *Eros and Civilization*. London: Sphere Books.

Marx, K. and Engels, F. (1970). *The German Ideology*. London: Lawrence and Wishart.

Masson, J. M. (1984). *The Assault on Truth*. London: Fontana.

(1990). *Against Therapy*. London: Fontana.

Mazlish, B. (1975). *James and John Stuart Mill: Father and Son in the Nineteenth Century*. London: Hutchinson.

McCaffrey, P. (1984). *Freud and Dora: The Artful Dream*. New Brunswick: Rutgers University Press.

McGrath, W. J. (1986). *Freud's Discovery of Psychoanalysis*. Ithaca: Cornell University Press.

McNamee, S. (1996). Therapy and identity construction in a postmodern world. In D. Grodin and T. S. Linlof (eds.), *Constructing the Self in a Mediated World*. London: Sage.

McRobbie, A. (1997). Bridging the gap: feminism, fashion and consumption. *Feminist Review*, 55, 73–89.

McTear, M. (1985). *Children's Conversation*. Oxford: Blackwell.

Meghnagi, D. (ed.) (1993). *Freud and Judaism*. London: Karnac Books.

Michael, M. (1996). *Constructing Identities*. London: Sage.

Middleton, D. and Edwards, D. (1990). Conversational remembering: a social psychological approach. In D. Middleton and D. Edwards (eds.), *Collective Remembering*. London: Sage.

Miles, S. (1996). The cultural capital of consumption: understanding 'postmodern' identities in a cultural context. *Culture and Psychology*, 2, 139–58.

Millett, K. (1971). *Sexual Politics*. London: Rupert Hart-Davis.

Mitchell, J (1974). *Psychoanalysis and Feminism*. London: Allen Lane.

Moi, T. (1986). Representation of patriarchy: sexuality and patriarchy in Freud's Dora. In C. Bernheimer and C. Kahane (eds.), *In Dora's Case*. London: Virago.

(1988). *Sexual/Textual Politics*. London: Routledge.

Moscovici, S. (1961). *La Psychanalyse: son image et son public*. Paris: Presses Universitaires de France.

(1985). *The Age of the Crowd*. Cambridge: Cambridge University Press.

Much, N. and Shweder, R. A. (1978). Speaking of rules: the analysis of culture in breach. In W. Damon (ed), *New Directions in Child Development*, volume 2. San Francisco: Jossey-Bass.

Mühlhäusler, P. and Harré, R. (1990). *Pronouns and People*. Oxford: Basil Blackwell.

Mulkay, M. (1988). *On Humour*. Cambridge: Cambridge University Press.

Neisser, U. (1976). *Cognition and Reality*. San Francisco: W. H. Freeman.

(1981). John Dean's memory: a case study. *Cognition*, 9, 1–22.

(1982). Snapshots or benchmarks. In U. Neisser (ed.), *Memory Observed: Remembering in Natural Contexts*. San Francisco: W. H. Freeman.

Neisser, U. and Harsch, N. (1992). Phantom flashbulbs: false recollection of hearing the news about *Challenger*. In E. Winograd and U. Neisser (eds.), *Affect and Accuracy in Memory*. Cambridge: Cambridge University Press.

Nelson, K. (1993). Explaining the emergence of autobiographical memory in early childhood. In A. F. Collins, S. E. Gathercole, M. A. Conway and P. E. Morris (eds.), *Theories of Memory*. Hove: Lawrence Erlbaum.

Nofsinger, R. E. (1991). *Everyday Conversation*. Newbury Park: Sage.

Nunberg, H. and Federn, E. (eds.). (1967). *Minutes of the Vienna Psychoanalytic Society, Volume 1: 1906–1908*. New York: International Universities Press.

Obeng, S. G. (1997). Language and politics: indirectness in political discourse. *Discourse and Society*, 8, 49–83.

Ochs, E. and Schieffelin, B. (1984). Language acquisition and socialization: three developmental stories and their implications. In R. A. Shweder and R. A. Levine (eds.), *Culture Theory*. New York: Cambridge University Press.

(1995). The impact of language socialization on grammatical development. In P. Fletcher and B. McWhinney (eds.), *Handbook of Child Language*. Oxford: Blackwell.

Ochs, E. and Taylor, C. (1992). Family narrative as political activity. *Discourse and Society*, 3, 301–40.

Ofshe, R. and Watters, E. (1994). *Making Monsters: False Memories, Psychotherapy and Sexual Hysteria*. New York: Scribner.

Ornstein, A. (1993a). Little Hans: his phobia and his Oedipus complex. In B. Magid (ed.). *Freud's Case Studies: Self-Psychological Perspectives*. Hillsdale, N. J.: The Analytic Press.

Ornstein, P. H. (1993b). Did Freud understand Dora? In B. Magid (ed.). *Freud's Case Studies: Self-Psychological Perspectives*. Hillsdale, N. J.: Analytic Press.

Oxaal, I. (1987). The Jews of young Hitler's Vienna: historical and sociological aspects. In I. Oxaal, M. Pollak and G. Botz (eds.), *Jews, Antisemitism and Culture in Vienna*. London: Routledge and Kegan Paul.

Oxaal, I., Pollak, M. and Botz , G. (eds.) (1987). *Jews, Antisemitism and Culture in Vienna*. London: Routledge and Kegan Paul.

Parker, I. (1992). *Discourse Dynamics*. London: Sage.

(1998a). Discourse analysis and psycho-analysis. *British Journal of Social Psychology*, 36, 479–95.

(1998b). *Psychoanalytic Culture: Psychoanalytic Discourse in Western Society*. London: Routledge.

Parks, T. E. (1997). False memories of having said the unsaid: some new demonstrations. *Applied Cognitive Psychology*, 11, 485–94.

Pearson, R. (1998). Imagining, imaging and imagineering the nation. Talk given at Annual Conference of Association for the Study of Ethnicity and Nationalism, London.

Pendergrast, M. (1995). *Victims of Memory: Incest, Accusations and Shattered Lives*. Hinesberg: Upper Access.

Peneff, J. (1990). Myths in life stories. In R. Samuel and P. Thompson (eds.), *The Myths We Live By*. London: Routledge.

Perelman, C. and Olbrechts-Tyteca, L. (1971). *The New Rhetoric*. Indiana: University of Notre Dame Press.

Pinker, S. (1994). *The Language Instinct*. Harmondsworth: Penguin.

Plato. (1942). *Sophist*. London: Loeb Classical Library.

Pomerantz, A. (1984). Agreeing and disagreeing with assessments: some features of preferred/dispreferred turn shapes. In J. M. Atkinson and

J. Heritage (eds.), *Structures of Social Action*. Cambridge: Cambridge University Press.

Pontecorvo, C. and Fasulo, A. (1995). Learning to argue in family shared discourse. In L. Resnick, C. Pontecorvo and R. Saljo (eds.), *Discourse, Tools and Reasoning*. Berlin: Springer Verlag.

Popper, K. (1972). *Conjectures and Refutations*. London: Routledge and Kegan Paul.

Potter, J. (1996). *Representing Reality*. London: Sage.

Potter, J. and Edwards, D. (1990). Nigel Lawson's tent: discourse analysis, attribution theory and the social psychology of fact. *European Journal of Social Psychology*, 20, 405–24.

Potter, J. and Wetherell, M. (1987). *Discourse and Social Psychology*. London: Sage.

(1995). Discourse analysis. In J. A. Smith, R. Harré and L. van Langenhove (eds.), *Rethinking Methods in Psychology*. London: Sage.

Pratkanis, A. R., Greenwald, A. G., Leippe, M. R. and Baumgardner, M. H. (1988). In search of reliable persuasion effects: III. The sleeper effect is dead. Long live the sleeper effect. *Journal of Personality and Social Psychology*, 54, 203–18.

Pulzer, P. G. J. (1964). *The Rise of Political Anti-Semitism in Germany and Austria*. New York: John Wiley.

Ragland, E. (1996). The passion of ignorance in the transference. In J. O'Neill (ed.), *Freud and the Passions*. University Park, Penn.: Pennsylvania State University Press.

Ramas, M. (1983). Freud's Dora, Dora's hysteria. In J. L. Newton, M. P. Ryan and J. R. Walkowitz (eds.), *Sex and Class in Women's History*. London: Routledge and Kegan Paul.

Reich, W. (1975). *The Mass Psychology of Fascism*. Harmondsworth: Penguin.

Reicher, S. (1982). The determination of collective behaviour. In H. Tajfel (ed.). *Social Identity and Intergroup Relations*. Cambridge: Cambridge University Press.

Renan, E. (1990). What is a nation? In H. K. Bhabha (ed.), *Nation and Narration*. London: Routledge.

Riikonen, E. and Smith, G. M. (1997). *Re-imagining Therapy*. London: Sage.

Roazen, P. (1973). *Brother Animal: The Story of Freud and Tausk*. Harmondsworth: Penguin.

(1974). *Freud and his Followers*. London: Allen Lane.

(1985). Freud and Woodrow Wilson. In P. Roazen (ed.), *Sigmund Freud*. New York: Da Capo.

(1992). Freud's patients: first person accounts. In T. Gelfand and J. Kerr (eds.), *Freud and the History of Psychoanalysis*. Hillsdale, N. J.: Analytic Press.

(1996). Nietzsche, Freud and the history of psychoanalysis. In T. Dufresne (ed.), *Returns of the 'French Freud': Freud, Lacan, and Beyond*. New York: Routledge.

Robinson, E. J. (1994). What people say, what they think and what is really the case: children's understanding of utterances as sources of knowledge. In C. Lewis and P. Mitchell (eds.), *Children's Early Understanding of Mind: Origins and Development*. Hillsdale, N. J.:Lawrence Erlbaum.

Robinson, P. A. (1972). *The Sexual Radicals: Reich, Roheim and Marcuse.* London: Paladin.

Roediger, H. L., McDermott, K. B. and Goff, L. M. (1997). Recovery of true and false memories: paradoxical effects of repeated testing. In M. A. Conway (ed.), *Recovered Memories and False Memories.* Oxford: Oxford University Press.

Rogoff, B. (1990). *Apprenticeship in Thinking: Cognitive Development in Social Context.* New York: Oxford University Press.

Rogow, A. A. (1978). A further footnote to Freud's 'Fragment of an analysis of a case of hysteria'. *Journal of the American Psychoanalytic Association,* 26, 331–56.

(1979). Dora's brother. *International Review of Psychoanalysis,* 6, 239–59.

Roith, E. (1987). *The Riddle of Freud: Jewish Influences on his Theory of Female Sexuality.* London: Tavistock.

Roland, A. (1996). *Cultural Pluralism and Psychoanalysis: The Asian and North American Experience.* New York: Routledge.

Rose, J. (1986). Dora: fragment of an analysis. In C. Bernheimer and C. Kahane (eds.), *In Dora's Case.* London: Virago.

Rosenbaum, M. and Muroff, M. (eds.) (1984). *Anna O.: Fourteen Contemporary Reinterpretations.* New York: Free Press.

Rosenberg, D. V. (1990). Language in the discourse of the emotions. In C. A. Lutz and L. Abu-Lughod (eds.), *Language and the Politics of Emotion.* Cambridge: Cambridge University Press.

Ross, M., McFarland, C. and Fletcher, G. J. O. (1981). The effect of attitude on the recall of personal histories. *Journal of Personality and Social Psychology,* 40, 627–34.

Roudinesco, E. (1997). *Jacques Lacan.* Cambridge: Polity Press.

Roustang, F. (1990). *The Lacanian Delusion.* New York: Oxford University Press.

(1997). Sublimation: necessity and impossibility. In T. Dufresne (ed.), *Returns of the 'French Freud': Freud, Lacan, and beyond.* London: Routledge.

Rozenblit, M. L. (1983). *The Jews of Vienna, 1867–1914.* Albany: State University of New York Press.

Sachs, D. (1992). In fairness to Freud: a critical notice of *The Foundations of Psychoanalysis.* In J. Neu (ed.), *The Cambridge Companion to Freud.* Cambridge: Cambridge University Press.

Sackheim, H. A. (1983). Self-deception, self-esteem and depression: the adaptive value of lying to oneself. In J. Masling (ed.), *Empirical Studies of Psychoanalytical Theories,* vol. 1. Hillsdale, N. J: Lawrence Erlbaum.

Sacks, H., Schegloff, E. A. and Jefferson, G. (1978). A simplest systematics for the organization of turn-taking for conversation. In J. Schenkein (ed.), *Studies in the Organization of Conversational Interaction.* New York: Academic Press.

Sampson, E. E. (1993). *Celebrating the Other.* Hemel Hempstead: Harvester/ Wheatsheaf.

Sand, R. (1992). Pre-Freudian discovery of dream meaning: the achievements of Charcot, Janet and Krafft-Ebing. In T. Gelfand and J. Kerr (eds.), *Freud and the History of Psychoanalysis.* Hillsdale, N. J.: Analytic Press.

Sayers, J. (1990). Psychoanalytic feminism: deconstructing power in theory and therapy. In I. Parker and J. Shotter (eds.), *Deconstructing Social Psychology*. London: Routledge.

(1991). *Mothering Psychoanalysis*. London: Hamish Hamilton.

Saywitz, K. J. and Moan-Hardie, S. (1994). Reducing the potential for distortion of childhood memories. *Consciousness and Cognition*, 3, 408–25.

Schachter, S. and Singer, J. E. (1962). Cognitive, social and physiological determinants of emotional state. *Psychological Review*, 69, 379–99.

Schacter, D. L. (1993). Understanding implicit memory: a cognitive neuroscience approach. In A. F. Collins, S. E. Gathercole, M. A. Conway and P. E. Morris (eds.), *Theories of Memory*. Hove: Lawrence Erlbaum.

(1995). Memory distortion: history and current status. In D. L. Schacter (ed.), *Memory Distortion: How Minds, Brains and Societies Reconstruct the Past*. Cambridge, Mass.: Harvard University Press.

(1996). *Searching for Memory: The Brain, the Mind and the Past*. New York: Basic Books.

Schacter, D. L., Norman, K. A. and Koustaal, W. (1997). The recovered memory debate: a cognitive neuroscience perspective. In M. A. Conway (ed.), *Recovered Memories and False Memories*. Oxford: Oxford University Press.

Schafer, R. (1976). *A New Language for Psychoanalysis*. New Haven: Yale University Press.

(1997). Conformity and individualism. In E. R. Shapiro (ed.). *The Inner World in the Outer World: Psychoanalytic Perspectives*. New Haven: Yale University Press.

Scharfman, M. A. (1980). Further reflections on Dora. In M. Kanzer and J. Glenn (eds.). *Freud and his Patients*. New York: Jason Aronson.

Scheff, T. J. (1990). *Microsociology: Discourse, Emotion and Social Structure*. Chicago: Chicago University Press.

(1993). Toward a social psychological theory of mind and consciousness. *Social Research*, 60, 171–95.

(1997). *Emotions, The Social Bond, and Human Reality*. Cambridge: Cambridge University Press.

Scheff, T. J. and Retzinger, S. (1991). *Emotions and Violence*. Lexington: Lexington Books.

Schegloff, E. (1995). Parties and talking together: two ways in which numbers are significant for talk-in-interaction. In T. ten Have and G. Psathas (eds.), *Situated Order*. Washington, D. C.: University Press of America.

Schegloff, E. and Sacks, H. (1974). Opening up closings. In R. Turner (ed.), *Ethnomethodology*. Harmondsworth: Penguin.

Schegloff, E. A., Jefferson, G. and Sacks, H. (1977). The preference for self-correction in the organization of repair in conversation. *Language*, 53, 361–82.

Scheichl, S. P. (1987). The contexts and nuances of anti-Jewish language: were all the 'antisemites' antisemites? In I. Oxaal, M. Pollak and G. Botz (eds.), *Jews, Antisemitism and Culture in Vienna*. London: Routledge and Kegan Paul.

Schenkein, J. (ed.) (1978). *Studies in the Organization of Conversational Interaction*. New York: Academic Press.

Schiach, M. (1989). Their 'symbolic' exists, it holds power – we, the sowers of disorder, know it only too well. In T. Brennan (ed), *Between Feminism and Psychoanalysis*. London: Routledge.

Schiffrin, D. (1984). Jewish argument as sociability. *Language in Society*, 13, 311–35.

(1987). *Discourse Markers*. Cambridge: Cambridge University Press.

Schimek, J. G. (1987). Fact and fantasy in the seduction theory: a historical review. *Journal of the American Psychoanalytic Association*, 35, 937–65.

Schneiderman, S. (1993). *Rat Man*. New York: New York University Press.

Schooler, J. W. (1994). Seeking the core: the issues and evidence surrounding recovered accounts of sexual trauma. *Consciousness and Cognition*, 3, 452–69.

Schooler, J. W., Bendiksen, M. and Ambadar, Z. (1997). Taking the middle line: can we accommodate both fabricated and recovered memories of sexual abuse? In M. A. Conway (ed.), *Recovered Memories and False Memories*. Oxford: Oxford University Press.

Schorske, C. E. (1980). *Fin-de-siècle Vienna*. London: Weidenfeld and Nicolson.

Schudson, M. (1990). Ronald Reagan misremembered. In D. Middleton and D. Edwards (eds.), *Collective Remembering*. London: Sage.

Schur, M. (1972). *Freud: Living and Dying*. New York: International Universities Press.

Schwartz, B. (1990). The reconstruction of Abraham Lincoln. In D. Middleton and D. Edwards (eds.), *Collective Remembering*. London: Sage.

Schwartz, B., Zerubavel, Y., and Barnett, B. (1986). The recovery of Masada: a study in collective memory. *Sociological Quarterly*, 2, 147–64.

Searle, J. (1992). *The Rediscovery of the Mind*. Cambridge, Mass.: MIT Press.

Shantz, C. U. and Hartup, W. W. (1995). Conflict and development: an introduction. In C. U. Shantz and W. W. Hartup (eds.) *Conflict in Child and Adolescent Development*. Cambridge: Cambridge University Press.

Shengold, L. (1980). More on rats and rat people. In M. Kanzer and J. Glenn (eds.), *Freud and his Patients*. New York: Jason Aronson.

Shorter, E. (1992). The two medical worlds of Sigmund Freud. In T. Gelfand and J. Kerr (eds.), *Freud and the History of Psychoanalysis*. Hillsdale, N. J.: Analytic Press.

Shotter, J. (1990). The social construction of remembering and forgetting. In D. Middleton and D. Edwards, *Collective Remembering*. London: Sage.

(1993a). *Conversational Realities*. London: Sage.

(1993b). *Cultural Politics of Everyday Life*. Buckingham: Open University Press.

(1993c). Becoming someone: identity and belonging. In N. K. Coupland and J. F. Nussbaum (eds.), *Discourse and Lifespan Identity*. London: Sage.

Shotter, J. and Billig, M. (1998). A Bakhtinian psychology: from out of the heads of individuals and into the dialogues between them. In M. M. Bell and M. Gardiner (eds.), *Bakhtin and the Human Sciences*. London: Sage.

Shweder, R. A. (1991). *Thinking Through Cultures*. Cambridge, Mass.: Harvard University Press.

Shweder, R. A. and Much, N. C. (1987). Determination of meaning: discourse and moral socialization. In W. M. Kurtines and J. L. Gewirtz (eds.), *Moral Development Through Social Interaction*. New York: John Wiley.

Shweder, R. A., Mahapatra, M. and Miller, J. G. (1990). Culture and moral development. In J. W. Stigler, R. A. Shweder and G. Herdt (eds.), *Cultural Psychology*. Cambridge: Cambridge University Press.

Silverman, M. A. (1980). A fresh look at the case of Little Hans. In M. Kanzer and J. Glenn (eds.), *Freud and his Patients*. New York: Jason Aronson.

Smiley, J. (1996). *Duplicate Keys*. London: Flamingo.

Snyder, M and Uranowitz, S. W. (1978). Reconstructing the past: some cognitive consequences of person perception. *Journal of Personality and Social Psychology*, 36, 941–50.

Soyland, A. J. (1994). *Psychology as Metaphor*. London: Sage.

Spence, D. P. (1982). *Narrative Truth and Historical Truth*. London: W. W. Norton.

(1994). *The Rhetorical Voice of Psychoanalysis*. Cambridge, Mass.: Harvard University Press.

Sperber, D. and Wilson, D. (1986). *Relevance: Communication and Cognition*. Oxford: Blackwell.

Squire, L. R. (1995). Biological foundations of accuracy and inaccuracy in memory. In D. L. Schacter (ed.), *Memory Distortion: How Minds, Brains and Societies Reconstruct the Past*. Cambridge, Mass.: Harvard University Press.

Stevenson, R. J. (1993). *Language, Thought and Representation*. Chichester: John Wiley.

Stirponi, L. and Pontecorvo, C. (in press). Discourse at family dinner: how children are socialized throughn arguing. *Interaction et Cognition*.

Storms, M. D. (1973). Videotape and the attribution process: reversing actors' and observers' points of view. *Journal of Personality and Social Psychology*, 27, 165–75.

Storr, A. (1989). *Freud*. Oxford: Oxford University Press.

Strachey, J. (1955). Editor's note. In *Standard Edition of the Complete Psychological Works of Sigmund Freud*, Volume X. London: Hogarth Press.

Sulloway, F. J. (1980). *Freud: Biologist of the Mind*. London: Fontana.

(1992). Reassessing Freud's case histories: the social construction of psychoanalysis. In T. Gelfand and J. Kerr (eds.), *Freud and the History of Psychoanalysis*. Hillsdale, N. J.: Analytic Press.

Sylvester-Bradley, B. and Trevarthen, C. (1978). Baby talk as an adaptation to the infant's communication. In N. Waterson and C. Snow (eds.), *The Development of Communication*. Chichester: John Wiley.

Tannen, D. (1984). *Conversational Style: Analyzing Talk among Friends*. Norwood, N. J.: Ablex.

Terr, L. C. (1994). *Unchained Memories*. New York: Basic Books.

Tessler, M. and Nelson, K. (1994). Making memories: the influence of joint encoding on later recall by young children. *Consciousness and Cognition*, 3, 307–26.

Thalberg, I. (1983). Freud's anatomies of the self. In R. Wolhiem and J. Hopkins (eds.), *Philosophical Essays on Freud*. Cambridge: Cambridge University Press.

The Freud Museum (1998). *20 Maresfield Gardens: Guide to the Freud Museum*. London: Serpent's Tale.

Thomas, J. (1995). *Meaning in Interaction*. London: Longman.

Thompson, C. P., Skrowronski, J. J., Larsen, S. F. and Betz, A. L. (1996). *Autobiographical Memory: Remembering What and Remembering When*. Mahwah, NJ: Lawrence Erlbaum.

Trabasso, T. (1997). Whose memory is it? The social context of remembering. In N. L. Stein, P. A. Ornstein, B. Tversky and C. Brainerd (eds.), *Memory for Everyday and Emotional Events*. Mahwah, N. J.: Lawrence Erlbaum.

Tracy, K. (1990). The many faces of facework. In H. Giles and W. P. Robinson (eds.), *Handbook of Language and Social Psychology*. Chichester: John Wiley.

Valsiner, J. and Cairns, R. B. (1995). Theoretical perspectives on conflict and development. In C. U. Shantz and W. W. Hartup (eds.) *Conflict in Child and Adolescent Development*. Cambridge: Cambridge University Press.

van der Kolk, B. A. and Fisler, R. (1995). Dissociation and the fragmentary nature of traumatic memories: overview and exploratory study. *Journal of Traumatic Stress*, 8, 505–25.

Vološinov, V. N. (1973). *Marxism and the Philosophy of Language*. Cambridge, MA: Harvard University Press.

(1976). *Freudianism: a Marxist critique*. New York: Academic Press.

(1994). Critique of Freudianism. In P. Morris (ed.), *The Bakhtin Reader*. London: Edward Arnold.

Vygotsky, L. S. (1978). *Mind in Society*. Cambridge, Mass.: Harvard University Press.

(1988). *Thinking and Speech*. New York: Plenum.

Webster, R. (1995). *Why Freud was Wrong*. Harmondsworth: Penguin.

Weininger, O. (1906). *Sex and Character*. London: William Heinemann.

Weiss, S. S. (1980). Reflections and speculations on the psychoanalysis of the Rat Man. In M. Kanzer and J. Glenn (eds.), *Freud and his Patients*. New York: Jason Aronson.

Weitzmann, W. R. (1987). The politics of the Viennese Jewish community, 1890–1914. In I. Oxaal, M. Pollak and G. Botz (eds.), *Jews, Antisemitism and Culture in Vienna*. London: Routledge and Kegan Paul.

Wellman, H. M. and Bartsch, K. (1994). Before belief: children's early psychological theory. In C. Lewis and P. Mitchell (eds.), *Children's Early Understanding of Mind: Origins and Development*. Hillsdale, N.J.: Lawrence Erlbaum.

Wertsch, J. (1991). *Voices of the Mind*. London: Harvester/Wheatsheaf.

West, C. (1995). Women's competence in conversation. *Discourse and Society*, 6, 107–31.

Wetherell, M. and Edley, N. (in press). Gender practices: steps in the analysis of men and masculinities. In K. Henwood, C. Griffin and A. Phoenix (eds.), *Standpoints and Differences: essays in the practice of feminist psychology*. London: Sage.

Wetherell, M. and Potter, J. (1992). *Mapping the Language of Racism*. Hemel Hempstead: Harvester/Wheatsheaf.

White, G. M. (1990). Moral discourse and the rhetoric of emotions. In C. A. Lutz and L. Abu-Lughod (eds.), *Language and the Politics of Emotion*. Cambridge: Cambridge University Press.

Wieder, L. (1972). Telling the code. In R. Turner (ed.), *Ethnomethodology*. Harmondsworth: Penguin.

Wierzbicka, A. (1995). Emotion and facial expression: a semantic perspective. *Culture and Psychology*, 1, 227–58.

Williams, L. M. (1995). Recovered memories of abuse in women with documented child sexual victimization. *Journal of Traumatic Stress*, 8, 649–73.

Wistrich, R. S. (1982). *Socialism and the Jews*. London: Associated University Presses.

(1989). *The Jews of Vienna in the Age of Franz Joseph*. Oxford: Oxford University Press.

(1990). *Between Redemption and Perdition: Modern Antisemitism and Jewish Identity*. London: Routledge.

Wittgenstein, L. (1953). *Philosophical Investigations*. Oxford: Blackwell.

(1975). *Zettel*, second edition. Oxford: Blackwell.

(1980). *Remarks on the Philosophy of Psychology*. Oxford: Blackwell.

(1992). *Culture and Value*. Oxford: Blackwell.

Wodak, R. (1996). *Disorders of Discourse*. London: Longman.

Wolff, L. (1988). *Postcards from the End of the World: An Investigation into the Mind of fin-de-siècle Vienna*. London: Collins.

Woodward, K. (1996). Anger . . . and anger: from Freud to feminism. In J. O'Neill (ed.), *Freud and the Passions*. University Park, Penn.: Pennsylvania State University Press.

Yapko, M. (1997). The troublesome unknowns about trauma and recovered memories. In M. A. Conway (ed.), *Recovered Memories and False Memories*. Oxford: Oxford University Press.

Yerushalmi, Y. H. (1991). *Freud's Moses: Judaism Terminable and Interminable*. New Haven: Yale University Press.

Young-Bruehl, E. (1988). *Anna Freud: A Biography*. London: Macmillan.

Zaragoza, M. S., Lane, S. M., Ackil, J. K. and Chambers, K. L. (1997). Confusing real and suggested memories: source monitoring and eyewitness suggestibility. In N. L. Stein, P. A. Ornstein, B. Tversky and C. Brainerd (eds.), *Memory for Everyday and Emotional Events*. Mahwah, N. J.: Lawrence Erlbaum.

Zeldin, T. (1993). *An Intimate History of Humanity*. London: Minerva.

Zimbardo, P. G. (1969). The human choice: individuation, reason and order versus de-individuation, impulse and chaos. *Nebraska Symposium on Motivation*, 17, 237–307.

Subject index

Name index